CULTURAL POLITICS IN A GLOBAL AGE

CULTURAL POLITICS IN A GLOBAL AGE

Uncertainty, Solidarity and Innovation

Edited by
David Held and Henrietta L. Moore
with Kevin Young

ONEWORLD

OXFORD

A Zamyn-Oneworld book

First Published by Oneworld Publications 2008

Oneworld Publications
185 Banbury Road
Oxford
OX2 7AR
England
www.oneworld-publications.com

Zamyn was established in 2001 to analyse the dynamics of the relationship between corporate globalisation and cultural practice. These effects are communicated addressing, in particular, the role of corporations as agents of socio-cultural change.

Zamyn proposes new ways of exploring and understanding the cultural transformations and effects of globalisation through collaborative arts-based productions, cultural research, and analysis. Its activities bring together cultural theorists, corporations, artists, writers, psychoanalysts, anthropologists, cultural institutions, visionary business leaders and socio-political figures, to create a space in which heterogeneous voices from periphery to centre can be heard.

Cultural Politics in a Global Age marks the first of Zamyn's publications, based on two seminars held at The London School of Economics, which were initiated and produced as part of Zamyn's research and development period. For further information visit www.zamyn.org.

ISBN 978–1–85168–540–0 (Hbk)
ISBN 978–1–85168–550–9 (Pbk)

Typeset by Jayvee, Trivandrum, India
Cover design by Mungo Designs
Printed and bound in Great Britain by TJ International, Padstow, Cornwall

Contents

Acknowledgements

The essays collected here are based on two seminars held at the London School of Economics under the title 'Thinking Aloud' in June and July 2005. The seminars were researched and produced by Zamyn and sponsored by Shell International. We are very grateful to Zamyn, Shell and the London School of Economics for their support and assistance. Our particular thanks go to Michael Aminian, the founder of Zamyn, and as well to the wonderful research team at Zamyn who made the intellectual and logistical work of running the seminars possible: most especially, Dionne Ibikunle, Annu Jalais, Eva-Maria Nag, Isabella Lepri, Anoucka Grose, Philipa Mladovsky, Gregor Murbach, and Petica Watson.

The hard work of preparing the manuscript, providing research assistance, and negotiating with authors and editors was done by Kevin Young. We cannot thank him enough for his intellectual support, patience, practical good sense and enduring humour.

David Held
Henrietta L. Moore

Introduction
Cultural Futures

David Held and Henrietta L. Moore

The essays collected here provide an account of culture as a major force in social, economic and political transformations. They examine how culture is contesting, amplifying, and altering the nature, direction and understandings of globalisation processes, and they discuss these processes from the perspective of diverse audiences, including the academy, business, policy makers, cultural institutions and community activists. The aim of this collection is to change the terms of debate, and to suggest new ways of conceptualising and theorising the links between culture and economic and social well-being by combining critical thinking from a broad range of philosophical and geo-political perspectives.

In the context of contemporary globalisation, culture – in its broadest senses, from the anthropological notion of culture as a system of meanings, values and symbols through to popular views of culture as religion, ethnicity, nationality and politics, and narrower senses, as business practices, elite cultures and art – is a cause of concern. There are those who talk of irremediable differences of world view, even a 'clash of civilisations', whilst others fear the erosion of values and life ways, an overall homogenisation of cultural understandings and products. Many contemporary analysts of globalisation characterise it as a process folded over on itself, simultaneously producing difference and homogenisation. The character, scale and scope of globalisation and its historical antecedents are the subject of much debate. What seems more evident is that an interconnected set of institutions, technologies and products are affecting lives everywhere in the world. People's values, aspirations and expectations are changing; their symbols, life ways and ideals are altering; and their identities, self-understandings and perspectives are being transformed. Cultures have never been static, but the scale of change, its interconnected and media mediated nature are new (see Tomlinson, this volume). Culture has become a focal point both for consumerism and for conflict. However, most contemporary critiques are based on an analysis of the impact of globalisation on culture, there is very little theoretical or empirical work that examines how culture is shaping social, economic and political transformations now or how it will propel them over the coming decades.[1] This project takes an innovative approach in that it explores culture not as the 'victim' of globalisation, but as one of its major drivers: culture as a major force for change in the world. It identifies and analyses case studies that show how culture is driving globalisation, how cultural innovations and developments are related to processes of inclusion and exclusion, new forms of identity and their interpretation, and new forms of network, cohesion and co-operation.

FORMS OF THOUGHT

The larger question of culture – arguments about definition notwithstanding – is bound up with how we think about society, with what we believe to be the nature of the social and the character of the good life. Views of society clearly differ, and they provide not just models for the functioning of the economy, the analysis of geopolitical systems and the governance of nations, but also, and perhaps more importantly, they provide the concepts that structure the ways individuals think about and act in the world (see Appadurai, Bhabha, this volume). Without a notion of society, for example, there would be little point in devising policies for the betterment of society and the international arena, and the conduct of nations would be very different if there was no concept of human rights. Historical transformations cannot be driven by ideas – concepts, forms of thought, ways of speaking – alone, but there is an increasing urgency to understand the conditions of their production, transformation and durability. The social sciences are the source of many ideas about the character and functioning of society, but they do not just arise *de nouveau* out of the feverish imaginations of social scientists. They are always the product of a complex interplay between the professional social science imagination and the everyday experiences and practices of ordinary individuals, as well as the management, development and transformation of institutions and markets by governments, business, elites, policy makers and others.

Individuals and groups are motivated by complex interrelations between their ideas and the ideas of others, between their experiences, emotions and practices and the ethos of the day, the reigning ideas of any particular historical moment. Governments, multinationals, corporations and civil society organisations as well as academics are involved both in collecting empirical data on which to base policies, interventions and strategies, and in devising theories to explain how and why the world works the way it does. Research is now a definitive part of the world it describes. In the globalised world we live in if we do not acknowledge, criticise and analyse the way social, economic and political theories are tied up in processes of globalisation, in global networks of ideas, images, markets and capital transfers we will simply find that we do not have the tools to analyse globalisation at all. This is what makes new ways of conceptualising and theorising the role of culture in driving social, economic and political transformation an urgent one.

Human beings are motivated in complex ways by ideas, and by all that ideas entail in terms of interests, emotions, habits and aspirations. Ideas, however, rest on the interplay between the public and the private. Ideas that arise in the public domain influence personal understandings, relationships and self-conceptualisations. Research activities – whether conducted by academics, governments, corporations, civil society institutions and cultural think tanks – produce the categories through which individuals, groups and institutions think and act. For example, the concept of gender has had a definitive impact on the work of international, national and civil society institutions in the arena of social development, and has redefined social policy objectives within welfare states. Such ideas and the conceptualisations and categories to which they give rise do not act alone; they are part of circuits of knowledge and asset transfer that are bound up with the changing nature of the family, work and leisure, the work of civil society institutions and international bodies to mention only the most obvious. And yet they influence individual ideas, aspirations, emotions and practices which in turn shape issues of governance, policy making, markets and the development of civil society. One could point to the way corporations concern themselves with preferences, desires and consumer choice, or to the interface of ideologies and religious belief with questions of security and governance. Our private pleasures are very often matters of public concern, and the other way around.

Two concepts that have had a very major impact on the way individuals, governments, civil society organisations and business have thought about the world and acted upon it are 'the West' and 'globalisation'. Both of these are of particular concern when we think about our futures because how we understand them will have a defining impact on how we shape the future. In 2020, the world will look different, not only because it will be different, but because we will look at it differently. What will the world look like in 2020? One possibility is that the concept of the West with all that it has entailed through the twentieth century will be of minimal philosophical or practical value. The West that we have known is largely the product of the post World War II era. At the beginning of the twentieth century there was no coherent category to which those who later became part of the NATO alliance clung and in terms of which they defined their relation to the rest of the world. The West that emerged through NATO took on a particular cast in relation to the Cold War and what was then seen as the socialist menace. Since the end of the Cold War there has been much that is threatening to dissolve the entity known as the West. There are cultural, economic, political and even religious factors pushing the USA and Europe apart. There are many who argue that the USA deserves gratitude for safeguarding the freedom of Europe, but many Europeans of a younger generation simply resent the culture and the influence of the superpower. The French voted no to the EU constitution and when asked why a good number said because they are against free trade and American capitalism, as well as the fact that they wanted to send a message to M. Chirac. The divisions of the world into blocks: the West versus Asia, the north versus the south are increasingly meaningless in a world where the US and Western Europe are divided over sovereignty and multilateralism, and where dominant patterns of influence on the world scene are altering rapidly. The expected rise of India and China is the potential engine for further decisive change. In 2020, the entrenched inequalities between north and south of trade and resources will persist, but India and China will no longer be part of the south, nor will they be developing or emerging nations. They will be winners.

New alignments among nations are emerging. Inequalities between many countries are sharpening, and with economic growth comes exclusion from the global economy for some. The result could be an increased number of failed states from Africa to the Middle East, to Central Asia and South East Asia. Economics is not the only thing dividing us. We know full well that inequalities sharpen conflicts of values. Among the sharpest of these are the divisions of faith. There was a moment in the twentieth century when modernity and secularism seemed indissoluble, and yet in the twenty-first century faith is of increasing importance to people around the world. Exposure to the successes of consumerism, and its perceived assault on values, have heightened the perceived need for spiritualism. The relationship between religion and identity is once again taking on a geo-political character (see Ahmed, Rose, this volume). For many societies, divisions between and within religious groups may become boundaries that are as significant or even more significant than national borders. Splits within the Muslim world between Shia and Sunni communities, Christian-Muslim divides in Southeast Asia and Europe, conflicts between Hindus and Muslims in South Asia, schisms in the Anglican community world wide, and Jewish-Muslim disputes in the Middle East all have the potential to ferment potential religious and/or ethnic disaffection which could threaten economic and political stability. Under these circumstances, new alignments will arise and they are likely to be between those countries, regions and cities that are integrating into the global future and those that are not. The question then of how we think about and map that global future in the academy, business, government, civil society and cultural institutions will be of paramount importance.

Weber argued that human beings are motivated both by ideal and material interests: 'Not ideas, but material and ideal interests, directly govern men's conduct. Yet very frequently the "world images" that have been created by "ideas" have, like switchmen, determined the tracks along which action has been pushed by the dynamic of interest' (Weber, 1946: 280). Interests are the engine of action, but it is ideas that define the courses of action. Ideas in this context are not, of course, abstract constructions, but the product of direct historical engagement with the world. Weber's famous treatise on the importance of culture and human action sought to explain rational, capitalist economic behaviour with reference to the Protestant ethic, and the question of how ideas and values influence actions is an old one (Weber, 2002 [1905]). From an anthropological point of view, people do not build up lines of action from scratch, choosing each one as the most efficient means to an end. Instead, people build up broad-based strategies for action, and cultural values influence the form and content of those strategies. Culture does not just influence action through end values, so that people will hold fast in changing circumstances to their preferred ends, but simply alter their strategies for attaining them. Rather, culture also provides the means through which people construct lines of action, and thus the styles or strategies of action that people deploy can be much more long running than the ends they seek to attain (Bourdieu, 1977).

However, cultures change. Far from maintaining continuity, changing ideas and values have driven the transformations that societies have sought especially in the modern period. Explicitly formulated and articulated cultural models play a powerful role in organising and transforming social life. Thus, cultures are involved both in sustaining strategies of action and in developing new ones. While this is true, analysts have frequently drawn a distinction between ideologies and cultural traditions, between explicit life projects and tacit or taken for granted beliefs and practices. Ideologies battle to take over the world views, assumptions and habits of people, and to a significant extent the success of ideological transformation depends on the balance between transforming habits and values, and appropriating, absorbing and building on them.

Ideas, however, and most particularly those that are involved in conceiving and managing social transformation are about imagining what is possible and desirable. Much of the literature in the social sciences has historically focused on nation states and their role in imagining and guiding social transformation. Much political thought is centred on the same entity; in one way or another, political thinkers posit that 'the good' inheres in the state. From such a perspective, modernity is pre-eminently a state project. This gives a particular role to political elites and sometimes also to intellectual elites, and it effectively ties the project of modernity to nation building and nationalism. However, the distinction between ideologies and cultures is in many ways eroding in the contemporary moment. Important projects of transformation have taken effective shape through such things as the emergence of neoliberalism and its impact on markets, corporate governance and financial institutions, and through the ideologies of human rights, feminism and environmentalism and their links to governmental and intergovernmental agencies, civil society institutions, popular movements, foundations and academic networks. These projects of transformation and the ideas that underpin them cannot be clearly labelled cultures – in the sense of the beliefs, values and lifeways of distinct and identifiable groupings – nor ideologies – in the determinate sense of communism or anarchism for example. However, they do represent beliefs and values that structure and shape the practices and lifestyles of ordinary individuals in their everyday existence. Such individuals will have a multifaceted and complex relationship to different sets of values, beliefs and identities, being perhaps an Indian, Hindu, graduate of Yale, software technician, working for an international environmental NGO. Here circuits of knowledge and asset transfer link many individuals into networks of shared and yet differentiated value systems. Consumer protection, environmental sustainability and feminism are all global movements whose members retain strong and differentiated relationships to cultural identities, values and beliefs connected to definitive social and national groupings.

From this perspective, it seems possible to speak of international, perhaps global cultures, that are neither cultures in the traditional sense nor ideologies, but coherent and widely shared values and beliefs that govern practices and actions. They would include such diverse things as market neoliberalism and its social entailments, corporate management culture, New Age ideas and the Moonies. Cultural affiliations are no longer geographically localised, and neither are they based on single sets of affiliations, or on forms of identification, communication and interaction that operate on a single analytical level (see Casely-Hayford, Rose, this volume). In other words, our affiliations may be multiple, but they are not all multiple in the same way. In certain times, places and contexts, some affiliations are more important than others.

This vision of cultural identity is regularly criticised for being elitist and Western, a form of individualism of choice that only applies to a small minority of the world's population. It is also a vision of culture and of the global that is viscerally contested by those who see culture as increasingly connected to local areas, to a politics of anti-Americanism and anti-globalisation, to popular movements for self-determination and to specific understandings of cultural identity. What is evident is that something is happening to the contours of people's sense of belonging and that culture is the terrain on which this contestation is being played out. This is true not just of elites in certain parts of the world, but of workers, entrepreneurs, consumers and ordinary people of different ages and backgrounds across the globe. This cultural transformation in the sense of belonging is the major form assumed by contemporary modernity. State projects of modernity, wherever they occur in the world, are concerned with the production of national subjects, but alternative projects of modernity are seeking to constitute and celebrate subjects of a different kind. Major points of tension can thus arise between nations and their subjects, as well as between national cultures. We may characterise these ideas as definitive of the ethos of the day, as providing the switches which channel action along certain courses, but each has its origins in different ways of imagining the nation state and affiliation to it, and of imagining transnational communities and cultures and traditional values. What is clear is that both those who see cultures and identities as multiple, and those who view them as intrinsically constructed and unchanging are speaking of modern cultures, contemporary values, modern modes of belonging.

TECHNOLOGIES OF REPRESENTATION

Mass media and digital technologies increasingly frame our understanding of the world we live in. Religious progressives, indigenous organisations, governments, corporations and many others are determined to take advantage of new technologies. Their actions are often framed by a world audience of news agencies, newspapers, media outlets, websites, weblogs and so on. Image and information management are the new arbiters of truth and authenticity, and the media plays a powerful political role in setting the terms of the debate (see Schecter, this volume). There are many who see new information technologies and the media – and in particular film and television – as responsible for the death of culture, as eroding distinctiveness and leading to homogenisation, if not Americanisation by the back door. There is little evidence for such a view, and the presumption that 'media', 'modernity', or 'Western culture' as unspecified and monolithic entities are dissolving 'cultures' and 'traditions' around the world is clearly based on a reified notion of cultures as static traditions that cannot respond with innovation and creativity to new challenges, new economic and political circumstances, changed aspirations (see Appiah, Slater, this volume).

What media technologies do offer is an expanded domain of symbolic production, new forms and powers of representation and transmission that have an impact on how we envision ourselves, our connections and our communities. New technologies of representation create new structures, institutions and subjects (see Castells, 2001; Orbach, this volume). The process is not itself new. Habermas, Anderson and others have discussed transformations in self-understandings from the eighteenth century onwards with regard to print media which offered both new narratives of the self and self development, and also new ways of reflecting on and constructing those narratives from an individual point of view (see Habermas, 1992 [1962]; Anderson, 1991). One consequence was the emergence of a distinction between the public and the private which was to have a profound effect on political cultures and institutions, and on the development of the nation as a form of imagined community. The internet is clearly having an impact of a comparable scale, allowing diverse individuals to bind together around shared and specific interests, linking diasporic communities, re-forging the bonds of allegiance and faith in established religions and newly established communities of observance, recentring communities around cities and regions, and connecting the members of popular movements and civil society organisations (see Casley-Hayford, this volume). It is arguable that the old distinction between public and private is shifting its ground, if not dissolving under the influence of new technologies of representation and communication. Our private pleasures are still matters of public concern, but in new ways. The kinds of communities we make are linked to the manner in which we imagine them, and in the world of mediated connection the imagination expands to generate new forms of connection, solidarity and dependency: new forms of belonging that are made possible by and through the material mechanisms we use to forge and imagine them.

A number of authors in this volume discuss the new forms of representation and of symbolic production that are emerging through new ways of imagining the world, many of them explicitly mediated by various technological, media, scientific and market structures (see Kapila, Ahmed, Yang, Hutnyk, this volume). One issue is the degree to which the nature of symbolic production – the means through which we achieve it and the contexts of its social production – has an impact on how we imagine ourselves and others. This is a question

John Tomlinson (this volume) struggles with directly in trying to determine whether the speed and proximity of symbolic production is changing the way we perceive not only the boundary between work and leisure, but between ourselves and others. Is the nature of labour and the experience of embodiment beginning to be refigured in forms that fundamentally alter the way we think of time and place? And yet, to pose the question in this way is to already underplay the scale of cultural transformation digital mediation makes possible. As Augustus Casely-Hayford points out, the internet is a medium for selective social interaction and symbolic belonging. It is the very selectivity and symbolic malleability of the internet, and of other digitally mediated cultural forms, that makes them a potentially unstable basis for political action where intention and irony are difficult to disentangle and where the nature of participation and of community activism as politics works at a tangent to the main political and economic determinants of political power (see also Hutnyk, this volume). The critical edge of politics is thus potentially displaced into networking, critique, art, even play without altering the enframing representational, economic and political structures (see Schecter and Hutnyk, this volume). Political participation may be possible on a much greater scale than ever before and no longer confined to the structures of the nation state, but it is equally and simultaneously much more effectively deflected, absorbed by the ecology of the representational and symbolic systems.

With changes in the imagined nature of belonging, in forms of participation, and in forms of symbolic production come corresponding shifts in the nature of political power, and its relationship to nations, regions and markets. It is evident that not all these changes – not even perhaps the preponderance of them – can be laid at the door of new technologies of mediation, information and communication. Such important determinants as increasing social inequality within states, environmental degradation, asset transfers, armed conflict, failed states, poverty and immiseration have their origins elsewhere in proximate and long-running structural relations. However, the changing nature of modes of belonging, the discourses and ideas of the local and the global, the indigenous and the transnational are all the product of a re-imagining of connections, identities and locations that owe much to the cultural forms and structures within which they are possible. The current phase of globalisation – contrary to the views of many critics – does much to promote nationalism because of the manner in which neoliberal discourses underpinning strategies for economic growth figure the nation as a competitive player in a world market, seeking to establish the best possible climate for doing business. Cultural nationalism is an important part of a global struggle for position (Harvey, 2005: 84–86;

see Gilroy, this volume). In this context, economic strategies and the management of market mechanisms are fully inflected by the forms of representation
which shape the ideas, the practices and the course of nationalisms. It is in this
context that we must perhaps situate those groups, networks, forms of political
and social association and devotion that transcend the state, and push to hollow
it out from within. The number of non-state actors grows consistently and all are
dependent on the forms and the means of symbolic production that can be
brought to bear on and indeed constitute their identities. Modern digital and
information technologies play a major role here in reworking and redistributing
patterns of information flow and the means for identity and group formation in
a manner that is quite beyond the reach of any national state (see Gilroy, this volume). It is a remarkable fact of the twenty-first century that religions are once
again not just political, economic and social forces in the world, but also productive of forms of belonging that are global in scope and scale, and yet not
dependent on the forms of the nation state. The supporters of Hizbullah claim
that they are a non-state within a non-state, a form of belonging that presupposes both a notion of the state and its transcendence through other modes of
imagining the social and the political. A view of the relation to the global not
only produces global phenomena such as the major faiths of the world, but also
a set of specific locations and local identities whose specificity is the product of
the global optic they defy. It is in these contexts that the results of new ways of
imagining identities in a globalised world are often particular versions of cultural authenticity. These 'local' cultural responses will have a defining impact on
the shape of globalisation to come (see Moore, Sen, Njongonkulu Ndungane,
this volume).

CONSUMING CULTURE

Habermas argued that states and markets together created and then colonised
the public sphere in Europe, but that over time the political dimension of the
public sphere has evolved from being a culture-debating one to a culture-
consuming one (see Habermas, 1992 [1962]). The rise of consumer culture and
its role in the production of new desires and subjectivities has been seen by many
as destructive of traditional cultures and as embodying a drive towards
homogenisation and forms of Western individualism. This process of the
remaking of the self, and its consequences for group identification and political
action are discussed by a number of authors in this volume (see Bauman, Leader,
Salecl, Orbach, Baingana). What is notable is the language of self-making, and

the dominant framing of politics both as a right and as a mode of self expression (see Bauman, Baingana, this volume). Consumption and the rhetoric of choice augment these forms of representation and give them material referents in ways that produce an illusion of self-fashioning which occludes the determinations of social, economic and political structures. One consequence is a social and political fragmentation of the public sphere which is increasingly figured in terms of private desires and their perceived connection to choice and liberty.

Corporations and media technologies play a major role in this process. Consumerism is predominantly driven by the young and the middle classes, but their desires are significantly fuelled and shaped by the media and the market. In this context, transnational corporations are actually major drivers of social change, acting as innovative cultural institutions in their own right. The assumption, however, that modern consumer society simply kills off traditional cultures fails to examine the ways in which consumption drives cultural innovation through the provision of new contexts, new media and new technologies for the expression of values and identities. For example, the market in world music combined with access to new digital technologies is driving recording, distribution and innovation in Sufi music. It is true that such developments are not uncomplicated and are always inflected by inequalities of power and resource, but they do suggest that simple antagonistic binary between consumer culture and traditional culture does not provide an adequate framework for analysis. Such binaries are reinforced by their over-determination by related binaries such as Western versus non-Western, culture versus capitalism. In China and India for example, where once one might have been able to distinguish the foreign from the domestic, culture from capitalism, Western from Asian is no longer possible in any straightforward way (see Yang, this volume).

One reason for this is that the issue of culture has become part of corporate market and risk management strategies, and the 'localisation' strategies they employ in different markets – both for labour and consumption – around the world means that the literal 'incorporation' of culture has become part of their drive for innovation, market share and profit seeking. MTV (music television) for example, employs a policy of 70 per cent local content in all international markets. The relationship between state and corporations are often instructive in this regard. In China, for example, it is the international media and internet suppliers who dictate the content and shape of programmes, and the scope and pace of service development to ensure that they retain access to this important emerging market. Corporations take both the viewers and government into account. They are aware that both need to resolve or find accommodation between collectivist values (Confucian morals and socialist ethics) and individual values, aspirations and desires (see Cheah, Yang, this volume). The public good has to be meshed with private pleasures. Corporations not only recognise this, but they study it and work at it (see Sturchio, this volume; Trompenaars and Hampden-Turner 1998, Parhizgar 2001). Profits depend on it. Culture is no longer separable from globalisation; it is no longer something that exists outside the economy or outside of capital, but is rather part of the self-definition of both capital and globalisation, and a major driving force in corporate institutional innovation and in market strategisation (see Watts 2003, Hardt and Negri 2000, Sturchio, Hamied, Davies, Hutton, this volume). Corporations as cultural institutions actively seek to enter into new forms of relationship with diverse cultures, and to enhance cultural diversity and innovation (see Born, Sturchio, this volume).

FRAMING CULTURAL DIVERSITY

The question of cultural diversity, value pluralism and the pluralisation of identities is also at the heart of liberalism and the liberal polity – and the increasing global contest between liberal principles and identity or faith-based politics (see Held, Kelly, Tan, this volume). One of the leading institutional clusters of modernity is the modern state itself – with its distinctive claim to offer security, the rule of law, impartial authority and limited power (see Skinner, 1978: 352 f). The modern democratic state became the mechanism by which 'governors' could be held accountable to the 'governed' through political participation, either directly or indirectly through the ballot box. Moreover, modern democracy offers the promise of linking together the notion of 'the people', sovereignty, territory and political outcomes into a coherent and legitimate whole.

The core claim of liberalism and its democratic child, liberal democracy, is that citizenship is the medium to ensure the necessary political conditions for equal membership in a polity, and within that framework the possibility of people living together peacefully despite plural values, cultural diversity and different faiths. Liberalism defends an institutional order that seeks, in principle, to enable citizens as individuals to go about their business and pursue their chosen beliefs and ends. Only polities, the argument goes, that acknowledge the equal status of all persons, that seek neutrality with respect to personal ends, hopes and aspirations, and that pursue the public justification of social, economic and political arrangements can ensure a basic or common structure of political action which allows individuals to pursue their projects – both individual and collective – as free and equal agents.

Liberal principles have a universal component, often referred to as cosmopolitanism (see Held, this volume). Cosmopolitanism defends, and is at the root of, attempts at the global level since 1945 to check and place limits on sovereignty while creating spaces for humans to flourish independently of state control, tradition or particular faiths. Many global governance institutions were founded on these concerns, including the UN Charter system, the Human Rights regime and the International Criminal Court. The embrace of universal principles by such institutions was always partial and one-sided and, from the beginning, in tension with the countervailing values of the primacy of statehood, also embedded in these same structures. Yet today, the challenge to them goes much deeper than the charge of hypocrisy or double-standards, for they are often criticised and condemned for simply pursuing Western agendas and being at the mercy of the big powers, or for doing nothing. The dominance of the USA after the end of the Cold War, intensified this sense. 9/11 and the US-led reaction magnified it further. The start of the twenty-first century has witnessed an intensification of conflicts, violence, territorial struggle and the clash of identities in many parts of the world. As a result, the foundations of the liberal order are being questioned, internally as a result of the failures of assimilationist and multicultural policies in many countries (and not just in the West), and externally as a result of the 'war on terror' and the backlashes it has provoked (see Held 2004).

Tensions between national identity and cosmopolitan identity are marked (see Guibernau, this volume), and the debate about the nature and legitimate role of the 'great powers', and in particular that of the US, is worldwide (see Nye, Slaughter and Hale, Cox and Quinn, this volume). The USA remains simultaneously a much criticised and sometimes reviled country while remaining the most attractive destination for migrants the world over. At the global level politics is now an arena in which liberalism, secularism and Westernism are being challenged by a diverse array of political projects, some of which aim to defeat them. There are grave dangers here, as well as political and cultural opportunities, for instance, to reconstitute democratic life itself (see Tully, this volume).

The rise of fundamentalism in recent years – Muslim, Christian, Jewish and Hindu, among other forms – is one response to the complex and sometimes unwelcome and bewildering impacts of globalisation, and the way they have been mediated by great power politics. Fundamentalism is, on the one side, a call for a return to the codes and principles of basic scriptures and texts and, on the other side, an expression of 'beleaguered tradition' – tradition under pressure from modernity, given greater force and shape by contemporary globalisation (Giddens 1999: 48–50). Fundamentalism is less about what people believe and more about why they believe it and how they justify it, refusing a world that asks for reasons and public justification (see Habermas, Beck, this volume; Habermas 2001: 126–129). It has no time for multiple identities, complex allegiances and cultural ambiguity. In the contemporary world, fundamentalism can be uncovered not just among religious groupings but also among many different kinds of community – political, economic, ethnic and environmental, among others. The fault line running through contemporary society divides those who call for the guardians of tradition to reassert themselves and those who accept and welcome cultural diversity and seek dialogue and the minimum rules of co-existence so that all can live peacefully without resort to violence and coercion. It is a deep fault line. The essays that follow explore this fault line reflecting on people's remarkable capacities, under changing conditions, to hold tight to traditional values and practices, to forge new ones and to be able, sometimes, to reason from the point of view of others.

BIBLIOGRAPHY

Anderson, Benedict. 1991. *Imagined Communities: reflections on the Origin and Spread of Nationalism* (London: Verso)

Berger, Peter and Huntingdon, Samuel (eds). 2002. *Many Globalizations: Cultural Diversity in the Contemporary World* (Oxford: Oxford University Press)

Bourdieu, Pierre. 1977. *Outline of a Theory of Practice*. (Cambridge: Cambridge University Press)

Castells, Manuel. 2001. 'The Culture of the Internet' in *The Internet Galaxy: Reflections on the Internet, Business, and Society* (Oxford: Oxford University Press), pp. 36–63

Giddens, Anthony. 1999. *Runaway World: How Globalization is Reshaping Our Lives* (London: Profile)

Habermas, Jürgen (trans. Thomas Burger with the assistance of Frederick Lawrence). 1992 [1962]. *The Structural Transformation of the Public Sphere: An Inquiry into a Category of Bourgeois Society* (Cambridge: Polity)

Habermas, Jürgen (trans. Max Pensky). 2001. *The Postnational Constellation: Political Essays* (Cambridge: MIT Press)

Hardt, Michael, and Negri, Antonio. 2000. *Empire* (Cambridge MA: Harvard University Press)

Harvey, David. 2005. *A Brief History of Neoliberalism* (Oxford: Oxford University Press).

Held, David. 2004. *Global Covenant* (Cambridge: Polity)

Parhizgar, Kamal Dean. 2001. *Multicultural Behaviour and Global Business Environment* (New York: Haworth)

Skinner, Quentin. 1978. *The Foundations of Modern Political Thought* – Volume 2: *The Age of Reformation* (Cambridge: Cambridge University Press)

Trompenaars, Alfons and Hampden-Turner, Charles. 1998. *Riding the Waves of Culture: Understanding Diversity in Global Business* (New York: McGraw-Hill)

Watts, Duncan. 2003. *Six Degrees: The Science of a Connected Age.* (New York: W.W. Norton)

Weber, Max. 1946. 'The social psychology of the world religions' in H. H. Gerth and C. Wright Mills (eds) *From Max Weber* (Oxford: Oxford University Press), pp. 267–301

Weber, Max (trans. Stephen Kalberg). 2002 [1905]. *The Protestant Ethic and the Spirit of Capitalism* (Oxford: Blackwell)

PART I

Culture and the Public Domain

INTRODUCTION

This section of the book examines how culture has developed in the last twenty years as a specific form of the political and the impact this has had on our understandings of the political and the public domain. It also explores how we might identify new theoretical frameworks for understanding the links between cultural policy and economic and social well-being. The first two contributions explore the question of why culture matters.

Henrietta L. Moore begins this section by considering the current debates surrounding the commodification of culture and the claims to authenticity, right and location that are embedded within these discussions. Moore notes that while there is nothing new about the commodification of culture, the heated debate it is fuelling today regarding the ownership and protection of culture has reached a new, global tenor. Issues of culture and its transmission have 'become part of a complex discourse about the relationship between property, human rights and self-determination over the last century.' At the same time, we have to acknowledge the paradoxes in commodification, such as the fact that markets both erode and create distinctiveness. The striking thing about these debates, Moore argues, is that indigenous communities, governments, civil society organisations, international organisations and corporations have all begun to conceive of culture as a form of property, over which it is possible and desirable to exercise monopoly rights. Moore asks us to consider how the increasingly narrow definition of property we are all refiguring culture within essentially pre-fabricates a condition ripe for conflict.

Noting that in terms of economic development culture is often seen, as opposed to development, as tradition, as 'a drag on the forward momentum of planned economic change,' **Arjun Appadurai** provides a framework for understanding the importance of cultural orientations towards the future. Appadurai contends that it is in culture that ideas of the future are embedded and nurtured, and that it is by developing what he calls the 'capacity to aspire' that individuals and groups may find the resources to address questions of poverty and development. Appadurai suggests three useful building blocks for such an understanding, each of which are derived from key anthropological insights over the last few decades. First, cultural coherence should be understood in terms of systemic and generative relationships, not simply individual cultural character-istics. Second, contestation of 'shared' norms and practices within a culture must be acknowledged as part of that culture. Finally, there is the recognition of the dynamic nature of culture, the fact: 'that the boundaries of cultural systems are leaky, and that traffic and osmosis are the norm, not the exception.' Cultures are the product of long-run historical trajectories and interconnections. Appadurai concludes by suggesting that it is through developing the idea of aspiration – the ability to envision a future – as a cultural capacity that we can bring the politics of dignity and the politics of well-being into a single framework.

How do we come to terms with the barbarism of the past, a barbarism which is a meaningful part of our cultural heritage? **Homi Bhabha** engages with this question by reflecting on a visit to the *Zeppelinfeld* in Nuremberg, Germany – the infamous site of Nazi rallies. The visit dramatised the impor-tance and complexities of thinking about cultural heritage, responsibility and cultural transmission. Bhabha asks how one might 'dis-possess' cultural spaces that have developed such an appalling global resonance, while simultaneously preserving and protecting the traumatic heritage of their memory which serve a significant purpose. Bhabha considers how brutality of the past can become the starting point for conceiving of an ethically sound global political commu-nity. Considering such possibilities means, he argues, facing unresolved con-tradictions. The key to Bhabha's approach is a notion of ambivalence – a way of confronting the contentious and sometimes traumatic processes of life. He suggests that ambivalence uniquely registers what is contradictory and unre-solved, and that a global ethics based upon it allows us to take responsibility 'for a world that is caught between a past that refuses to die, and a future that refuses to wait to be born.'

Amartya Sen discusses the relationship between cultural bigotry and polit-ical tyranny, arguing that the two can be closely and dangerously associated with one another in all too many instances. He examines how famines in both Ireland and India were not seen as calamitous failures of government and pub-lic policy but as the inevitable product of cultural tendencies and practices. He goes on to critique the impoverished reasoning that explains divergence in economic performance in terms of 'cultural' factors, pointing out that it is often not 'culture' in the common sense of the term that necessarily shapes outcomes but institutions. Yet these institutions are, he argues, themselves often the result of cultural-historical factors and strategic cultural adaptation. Sen also advocates paying attention to cultural interrelations as a useful way of understanding development and change – we should recognise the importance of culture but at the same time take care not to privilege it as an independent and stationary force. For Sen, acknowledging the influence of culture must always go hand-in-hand with a recognition that other factors, 'such as class, race, gender, profession, politics, also matter, and can matter profoundly,' as it should with a sense that culture is in fact highly heterogeneous, always in flux.

Ulrich Beck and Jürgen Habermas both discuss how cultural differences have to be incorporated into public discourses and institutions to minimise conflict and create the grounds for tolerance and a workable cosmopolitanism. **Ulrich Beck** distinguishes a number of ways in which societies handle otherness, through the guise of universalism, ethnicism, nationalism, multiculturalism and cosmopolitanism. Beck unpacks the differences between what he calls the universalism of difference and the universalism of sameness. Beck notes that while the universalism of difference is inherently hierarchical and is associated with domination, the universalism of sameness presupposes a universalising gaze which can be equally hegemonic, in the sense that the Other's voice is included only on the basis that it may emphasise sameness and discount particularity, 'with the result that cultural differences are either transcended or excluded'. In other words, the universalism of sameness has the drawback that it imposes its standpoint on others. Yet attempts to contest the universalism of sameness are often seen to be arguments in favour of relativism – but relativism in its different variants 'categorically rejects what universalism affirms: the very possibility of developing and recognising general norms.' On the other hand, Beck notes, 'a certain dose of relativism may serve as an antidote to the hubris of universalism.' Recognising that relativism can in some cases 'serve as an antidote to the hubris of universalism', Beck tries to draw a middle path, arguing that relativism is most dangerous only when absolutised, when it is 'disoriented', and when 'navel-gazing becomes a gaze upon the world.' We are thus led to Beck's defence of cosmopolitanism, which entails both a recognition of otherness and the non-dissolution of difference into universality. Differences are accepted. For Beck, the univeralism/relativism sameness/diversity debate strikes of a false dichotomy – an intellectual affliction that can be best overcome with a proper understanding of realistic cosmopolitanism and a more sophisticated social handling of difference.

Considering the issues surrounding the notion, practice and institutional-isation of religious tolerance, **Jürgen Habermas** argues that only through a process of reciprocal recognition and reciprocal delineation of the borderline of what is tolerable and what is not can a legitimate and acceptable sense of toleration be delineated. Habermas offers the means to think through the link between the universalistic justification for religious tolerance and democracy as the basis for legitimation for a secular state. For Habermas, the oft-purported tension between religious and cultural diversity and secularism is a misrepresentation, in the sense that the practice of religious tolerance occurs 'precisely under those conditions which the citizens of a democratic community mutually accord one another'.

However, Habermas emphasises that the norm of complete inclusion of all citizens as members with equal rights must be accepted before members of a democratic community can mutually expect one another to be tolerant. Drawing on a number of examples of contentious legal–cultural issues in Germany, Habermas argues that legal conflicts show why the spread of religious tolerance has now become a stimulus for developing further cultural rights, since the active inclusion of religious minority cultures in the polity fosters sensitivity to the claims of other discriminated groups. Thus the recognition of religious pluralism fulfils the role of a 'pace-maker' in legal development, as it encourages awareness of the claims of minorities to civic inclusion. The point of cultural rights, Habermas reminds us, is to guarantee all citizens equal access to the environments, relations and traditions that may be deemed essential to them in order to form and secure their personal identity. At the same time, however, members of discriminated groups can only legitimately benefit from a morality of equal inclusion by making this morality their own: cultures must adapt their internal ethos to the egalitarian standards of the community at large.

Chapter 1

The Problem of Culture

*Henrietta L. Moore**

On a recent trip to Nairobi, my attention was taken by an advertisement – presumably intended for the discerning, rather than the undiscerning traveller – which described the Masai blanket it depicted as 'The fabric with a culture'. We are used, of course, to the idea that blankets have culture, that material items are the products/expressions of authentic difference. We accept nonchalantly, for the most part, that culture is a commodity to be bought and sold like any other. The consumption patterns of the 'middle classes' around the world are based on the appreciation and ingestion of difference. Their only residual anxiety is whether the differences consumed are authentic ones. Is the Thai food, Kashmiri textile, Aboriginal art, Guatemalan pottery authentically representative of the culture it exemplifies? Discernment and judgement are at issue, those in the know are able to tell what is authentic from what is not.

The commodification of culture finds evident expression in the development of a raft of intermediaries – cultural entrepreneurs, brokers, curators and consultants – who make their living through selling discernment, forming markets and creating new objects for aesthetic appreciation. National governments around the world concern themselves with the contribution of culture to GDP whether through tourism, social regeneration or the contributions of the culture industries, and compete with each other to invest in cultural monuments and projects. International corporations invest in understanding, maintaining and exploiting cultural distinctiveness, focusing on how to make their products and labour regimes more culturally appropriate, appease local populations affected by their activities, and assert monopoly rights (patents, licences) to off-set competition and create new forms of value. These

* **Henrietta L. Moore** is Professor of Social Anthropology at the London School of Economics and Political Science, and the Director of the Cultural Globalisation Programme at the Centre for the Study of Global Governance.

developments are not entirely new, but they are fuelling an increasingly heated debate about who owns culture and who has rights to trade in it.

In these debates a good deal is laid at the door of capitalism, globalisation and digital technology. Their critics claim that what they share is the ability to strip distinctiveness from its context and make a profit from it. This is of particular concern with regard to the question of culture because once value is removed from its context it is no longer embedded within social institutions and norms. Walter Benjamin writing about the mechanical reproduction of art and its intersection with forms of modern knowledge made a critical link between authenticity and context: 'the unique value of the "authentic" work of art has its basis in ritual, the location of its original use value'.[1] His claim was that once the authenticity of art ceases to be based on ritual, on its relevant use in context, then it necessarily becomes based on quite another practice, that of politics.[2] Benjamin's insight helps us to understand something of the politicisation of culture in contemporary public life, why it has become such a political battlefield.

A disembedded, deracinated value is one which must always be morally questionable; to what institutions, contexts, communities does it refer, who can claim it for their own? But, there are many commentators and communities who see in this process of debate the potential for participation, for enhanced choice, for sharing, perhaps even democracy and freedom. Digital technology provides the means for many individuals to be connected, for new communities to arise, for improved accessibility, and for the means to undermine the proprietary claims of others. Digital technology, like the market itself, both creates and destroys distinctiveness. Music is one of those domains where technology has enhanced the number of potential creators, and the boundaries between producers, distributors and consumers have become porous. Free file sharing makes music available without paying for the costs of production or distribution, and without regard for profit. What is at issue ultimately here is the question of property, who owns the music so produced? It's not just a matter of using material without permission and distributing it for free, but it is also a question of who owns hybrid compositions made up of many elements from different cultural contexts and backgrounds. Is this an enhancement of cultural creativity or the theft of authentic material?

This question is a familiar one and posing it in this stark way does little to resolve it, but it does demonstrate why nations, corporations, communities and individuals are concerned not just with culture in the broadest sense, but with what one might term the elements of culture, melodies, motifs, designs, images and the like. Every bit of culture can be made to have a value, and most particularly in recombinant forms. Changes in form make for new regimes of commodification. Bronwyn Parry has discussed, for example, how the translation of biological materials from a corporeal to an information state, has made them more mobile, more amenable to circulation, made of them, in effect, new forms of tradeable items.[3] The idea that there are things that should not be traded, that there should be limits to commodification is an insistent theme in contemporary discussions about culture. Recent discussions on cultural property have focused on the interrelated questions of who owns culture, whether it should be traded, and whether or not it can be copyrighted.[4] Key questions here involve how indigenous communities can have their traditional knowledge and creative capacities recognised and compensated for under existing intellectual property laws, and how instruments might be developed to protect their cultures from appropriation, commodification and subsequent incorporation into the forms of intellectual property asserted by outsiders. The difficulties are many, but they are rarely subject to robust scrutiny when they are reduced to the antinomies of the market versus tradition, globalisation versus the local, or corporations versus indigenous communities.

The commodification of culture is not per se new, and is not necessarily the product of capitalism or the inequalities of power, resource and opportunity that are characteristic of recent globalisation processes. Writing about pre-colonial Melanesia, Simon Harrison, discusses how the societies of the region shared a 'deep preoccupation' with differences in language, ritual, art, architecture etc. The differences might have seemed minor to outsiders, but to community members they were crucial identity markers. Ambitious men might import new cultural practices in order to establish new groups under their leadership and over time the result was a pattern of small, fragmented, interdependent social groups. The primary concern was not just the maintenance of difference, but the prevention of unauthorised copying and adoption by outsiders of key cultural traits symbolic of group identity. But, this was not a matter of the preservation of fixed traditions or the defence of cultural repertoires as wholistic entities, for there existed well established mechanisms for the sale, licensing and franchising of cultural practices and other symbols of identities to outsiders.[5] Such transactions might involve such things as songs, spells, dances, ceremonies and the rights to make certain art forms.

The exact nature of these exchanges and the degree of commodification varied from group to group, but what was characteristic was a view of culture used less to commemorate history than to create social and political relationships. Thus social groups were entities that produced culture, held proprietary rights in their cultural products and conducted authorised sales and purchases of these rights, and in so doing created a sense of themselves – that is of community identity – in relation to others. These were also societies in which information and knowledge played a key role in determining regimes of commodification. Knowledge was regarded as a thing, a commodity, and a person could possess, exchange and consume that knowledge in the form of magical spells, medical compounds, dance steps, ritual sequences and artistic elements. The ritual knowledge of the Europeans when it first came in was often treated in the same way and mission Christianity was exchanged between groups. Exchanges of objects and knowledge could involve much more than the transaction of the item, since what was also implied was an entitlement to replicate what was transmitted and use it to create further social, economic and political relationships.[6]

In such contexts, culture is both distinctive and shared across cultural boundaries, expressing both identity and relationships with others, and in consequence individuals might have affiliations with several cultural identities. Harrison argues that while the objectification and commodification of culture are not new what has changed over time is the notion of property that underpins Melanesian concepts of culture. His central thesis is that contemporary views of culture, largely because of political mobilisation against colonial powers and the development of nationalist and inter-ethnic politics, are now based on the notion of culture as a reified possession, one that is holistically conceived as belonging to a unique and bounded group. From this perspective, cultural groups are depicted as discrete entities to which people have fixed and exclusive affiliations, and culture is something that belongs not only to its creators, but more crucially to their heirs.[7] There is considerable debate about the changing nature of ethnic and cultural identities in Melanesia, and the historical shift Harrison describes – where what was once thought of as involving transaction is now conceived as a form of inheritance – is by no means unidirectional, complete or monolithic. However, his claim that what is at issue is a change in the manner in which culture is objectified, a transformation in the concept of ownership that underpins the conceptualisation of culture, speaks to an emerging thread of consensus within academic debates and policy formulation.

If the contemporary problem we seem to be having with culture cannot simply be glossed as one arising from its commodification, then where does the trouble reside? A frequent response is to point to the interconnections between culture and identity, and to the emergence of the idioms of heritage and inheritance in determining the ownership of cultural property. The origins of this idiomatic way of speaking about culture are not singular and have evolved in fits and starts over the course of the twentieth century. To see this process as over determined by cultural nationalism and the reifications involved in projects of nation-building would be to underestimate the formative role played by international bodies, indigenous movements and NGOs. The 1948 Universal Declaration of Human Rights guarantees fundamental rights relating to, inter alia, labour, culture, privacy and property, including the right to own collective property and not to be deprived of it. It also provides for the safeguarding of moral and material interests in scientific, literary and artistic productions. The International Labour Organisation's Convention 169, concerning indigenous and tribal peoples in independent countries, requires states to adopt special measures to safeguard the institutions, property, culture and environment of indigenous peoples, and to respect 'the special importance of the cultures and spiritual values of the peoples concerned, of their relationship with their lands or territories ... which they occupy or otherwise use, and in particular the collective aspects of this relationship'.[8] The force of these international provisions may be very limited for many practical purposes, but they do encapsulate the way in which issues of culture and its transmission, have become part of a complex discourse about the relationship between property, human rights and self-determination over the last century.

The reigning assumption is that the preservation of culture and community go together, if culture is lost then distinctive lifeways and people are lost. This perception underpins the very widespread anxiety felt by many, and incorporated in the anti-globalisation movement and in the political claims of indigenous groups, that globalisation is driving a process of homogenisation, that it necessarily leads to a loss of cultural diversity. The paradox is that markets both erode and create distinctiveness, and in consequence the processes of globalisation alongside the interconnectedness and speed of digital technology produce sameness and difference in long-run circuits of non-linear interactions. It is therefore rather misleading simply to claim that globalisation and/or new technologies are destroying culture. Many protagonists have argued that Third World and indigenous arts have blossomed in the global economy, that music, painting, textiles and the performing arts are more vibrant and more diverse than ever before, reaching far wider audiences. New technologies, including digital technologies, give artists and other cultural producers new ways of turning creative visions into marketable products. Tyler Cowen is one who supports this thesis, and he discusses how the flowering of African music in the twentieth century was contingent on new technologies (phonograph, radio, cassette players, electricity), social mobility, urbanisation and industrialisation. Change is essential for cultural development. He makes the well-established argument that historically most cultures are multicultural products, the result of exchange, borrowing and imitation, and that this is particularly true of what is termed 'Western' culture.[9] However, he acknowledges the problem of loss, highlighting that exchange necessarily undermines the moral and institutional matrices of cultural production, eroding what he refers to as 'ethos'. The irony he identifies is that in the realm of culture more knowledge does not necessarily expand our opportunities because cultural production is dependent upon background assumptions (values) that are subject to change and potential decay. He suggests that we might be facing a choice about whether we want diversity within societies or diversity across societies.[10] Cowen's conclusion is that we cannot cast trade as the villain in this process of inevitable cultural mingling and reshuffling – this is the fate of culture – but that we should accept that globalisation will tend to encourage large, internally diverse and culturally complex polities.[11]

Both Cowen and Harrison support the view that trade in culture is not new, that cultures have always been hybrids, and that individuals within social groupings often have affiliations with several cultural identities now and in the past. So what makes the contemporary moment seem so startlingly new? Why do the spectres of threat and loss seem to haunt all discussions of culture? Perhaps the problem is just one of scale, the size of global diasporas, the degree of cultural mingling and sharing, the breadth of cultural possibilities. The fact that cultures have historically been made and remade through travel and trade, and complex processes of political subordination and incorporation means that there are now many societies within societies. Most members of nation states have multiple cultural affiliations, and the families, communities, landscapes and sacred spaces through which they constitute their sense of cultural selves are physically, digitally and imaginatively located in various 'societies'. In this sense, a group's or an individual's heritage can never be naturally or evidently 'authentic'. This model of diversity, of difference within, is one where culture is remade – physically, digitally and imaginatively – in the idiom of free trade, a life world created in the image of contemporary capitalism and globalisation.[12]

Perhaps then it is not that globalisation, capitalism and new technologies are destroying culture and distinctive lifeways, but more that large sections of the world are increasingly modelling their sense of distinctiveness, community and sacredness on these types of exchanges, interconnections and communications. Where once culture was the means for social, political and economic relations, now it is the other way around. It is instructive in this regard that many communities around the world are responding by insisting on quite a different conceptualisation of culture, one based on an explicit refusal not just of commodification, but of transaction and exchange of information. Indigenous groups have been mobilising to protect their cultural resources, including landscapes and flora and fauna (these biological and material resources embodying accumulated and managed knowledge) from exploitation by outsiders, from incorporation into conventional intellectual property regimes, and from degrading and misleading forms of use and display. It is not only that in many cases the communities gain no economic benefit from the exploitation of their resources, assets and knowledge, but that active harm is done to the stewardship of values and beliefs, and to relationships between living communities, spirits, ancestors and environments. The current debate on cultural property and how it might best be protected is a contentious one with a wide variety of actors and institutions involved. International bodies play a significant role – often with the impetus coming from key nation states – in defining what is culture and what is property. UNESCO has developed a series of conventions on intangible cultural heritage and cultural diversity, taking the task of 'defending the cultural heritage of humankind' as a priority. The World Intellectual Property Organisation sponsors an online database and registry of traditional knowledge and genetic resources which publishes traditional pharmacopoeias, preventing patent applications which draw on forms of traditional knowledge from claiming that they have discovered something novel. The actual utility of these various international instruments and resources for indigenous groups is very variable, but both nation states and the communities within them find a purpose in trying to redefine the forms of ownership applicable to culture and exclude culture or aspects of cultural knowledge from certain forms of trade and transactions. It is notable in this regard that culture is specifically excluded from TRIPs (Trade Related Aspects of Intellectual Property). With very different goals in mind, nation states and indigenous communities, just like corporations, are seeking to extend the scope and reach of intellectual property rights in space and time.[13]

The power differences between small-scale societies and the world's nation states and massive corporations is obvious, and the necessity for regimes within which the future, viability and prosperity of indigenous communities and cultures can be safeguarded is indisputable. However, what the exigencies of politics should not blind us to are the similarities in the way in which these very different actors conceive of culture as a form of property. It is easy enough to deny these similarities by saying that corporations are only in it for profit and that indigenous communities are safeguarding their heritage, while nation states are involved in something of both. But, all three players are engaged in seeking to reassert claims to monopoly rights. The collective cultural property of communities cannot be modelled along the lines of individual private property and it is true that not all forms of intellectual property in law provide for absolute rights of exclusion,[14] but what is crucial is an emerging idiom of culture as a form of property over which it is possible and desirable to exercise monopoly rights. As David Harvey points out, monopoly rights confer monopoly rents, and the latter depend on seeking out criteria of speciality, uniqueness, originality and authenticity.[15] The irony is that culture has become the idiom through which capitalists and anti-globalisation supporters, nation states and the communities who seek self-determination within them, corporations and the guardians of traditional lifeways all make their claims to uniqueness and authenticity. Whether or not the market is destroying cultural distinctiveness, we are increasingly refiguring our notion of culture within an increasingly narrow definition of property over which we seek to assert monopoly rights. The inevitable result is competition, and as Benjamin warned, 'All efforts to render politics aesthetic culminate in one thing: war.'[16]

Chapter 2

The Capacity to Aspire:
Culture and the Terms of Recognition*

*Arjun Appadurai***

This essay seeks to provide a new approach to the question: why does culture matter? Let us lengthen the question and ask why it matters for development and for the reduction of poverty. This both narrows and deepens the question. The answer is that it is in culture that ideas of the future, as much as of those about the past, are embedded and nurtured. Thus, in strengthening the capacity to aspire, conceived as a cultural capacity, especially among the poor, the future-oriented logic of development could find a natural ally, and the poor could find the resources required to contest and alter the conditions of their own poverty. This argument runs against the grain of many deep-seated images of the opposition of culture to economy. But it offers a new foundation on which policy makers can base answers to two basic questions: why is culture a capacity (worth building and strengthening), and what are the concrete ways in which it can be strengthened?

GETTING PAST DEFINITIONS

We do not need one more omnibus definition of culture any more than we need one of the market. In both cases, the textbooks have rung the changes over

* This piece is a partial extract from a larger chapter: Arjun Appadurai, 'The Capacity to Aspire: Culture and the Terms of Recognition', in *Culture and Public Action*, Rao, Vijayendra and Michael Walton (eds). Stanford University Press. 2004.
** **Arjun Appadurai** is John Dewey Distinguished Professor in the Social Sciences at The New School in New York. His current writing projects concern the deep history of religious violence in South Asia; quality of life issues in the study of development; and the anthropology of the future. He is the author, most recently, of *Fear of Small Numbers: An Essay on the Geography of Anger* (Duke University Press, 2006).

the long century in which anthropology and economics have taken formal shape as academic disciplines. And not only have the definition mongers had ample say, there has been real refinement and academic progress on both sides. Today's definitions are both more modest, and more helpful. Others are better equipped to tell the story of what we really ought to mean when we speak of markets. Here I address the cultural side of the equation.

General definitions of culture rightly cover a lot of ground, ranging from general ideas about human creativity and values, to matters of collective identity and social organization, matters of cultural integrity and property, and matters of heritage, monuments, and expressions. The intuition behind this capacious net is that what it gains in scope, it loses in edge. In this chapter, I do not deny the broad humanistic implications of cultural form, freedom, and expression. But I focus on just one dimension of culture – its orientation to the future – that is almost never discussed explicitly. Making this dimension explicit could have radical implications for poverty and development.

In taking this approach to culture, we run against some deeply held counter-conceptions. For more than a century, culture has been viewed as a matter of one or other kind of pastness – the keywords here are habit, custom, heritage, tradition. On the other hand, development is always seen in terms of the future – plans, hopes, goals, targets. This opposition is an artifact of our definitions and has been crippling. On the anthropological side, in spite of many important technical moves in the understanding of culture, the future remains a stranger to most anthropological models of culture. By default, and also for independent reasons, economics has become the science of the future, and when human beings are seen as having a future, the keywords such as wants, needs, expectations, calculations, have become hardwired into the discourse of economics. In a word, the cultural actor is a person of and from the past, and the economic actor a person of the future. Thus, from the start, culture is opposed to development, as tradition is opposed to newness, and habit to calculation. It is hardly a surprise that nine out of ten treatises on development treat culture as a worry or a drag on the forward momentum of planned economic change.

It is customary for anthropologists to pin the blame for this state of affairs on economists and their unwillingness to broaden their views of economic action and motivation and to take culture into account. And economics is hardly blameless, in its growing preoccupation with models of such abstraction and parsimony that they can hardly take most real world economics on board, much less the matter of culture, which simply becomes the biggest tenant in the black box of aggregate rationality. But anthropologists need to do better by their own core concept. And this is where the question of the future comes in.

In fact, most approaches to culture do not ignore the future. But they smuggle it in indirectly, when they speak of norms, beliefs, and values as being central to cultures, conceived as specific and multiple designs for social life. But by not elaborating the implications of norms for futurity as a cultural capacity, these definitions tend to allow the sense of culture as pastness to dominate. Even the most interesting recent attempts, notably associated with the name of Pierre Bourdieu (1977), to bring practice, strategy, calculation, and a strong agonistic dimension to cultural action have been attacked for being too structuralist (that is, too formal and static) on the one hand, and too economistic on the other (Bourdieu 1977). And what is sometimes called "practice" theory in anthropology does not directly take up the matter of how collective horizons are shaped and of how they constitute the basis for collective aspirations which may be regarded as cultural.

There have been a few key developments in the anthropological debate over culture that are vital building blocks for the central concern of this essay. The first is the insight, incubated in structural linguistics as early as Saussure, that cultural coherence is not a matter of individual items but of their relationships, and the related insight that these relations are systematic and generative. Even those anthropologists who are deeply unsympathetic to Lévi-Strauss and anything that smacks of linguistic analogy in the study of culture, now assume that the elements of a cultural system make sense only in relation to one another, and that these systematic relations are somehow similar to those which make languages miraculously orderly and productive. The second important development in cultural theory is the idea that dissensus of some sort is part and parcel of culture and that a shared culture is no more a guarantee of complete consensus than a shared platform in the democratic convention. Earlier in the history of the discipline, this incomplete sharing was studied as the central issue in studies of children and of socialization (in anthropology, of "enculturation"), and was based on the obvious fact everywhere that children become culture bearers through specific forms of education and discipline. This insight became deepened and extended through work on gender, politics, and resistance in the last three decades, notably through the work of scholars such as John and Jean Comaroff, James Scott, Sherry Ortner, and a host of others, now so numerous as to be invisible (Comaroff and Comaroff 1991, Scott 1990, Ortner 1995). The third important development in anthropological understandings of culture is the recognition that the boundaries of cultural systems are leaky, and that traffic and osmosis are the norm, not the exception. This strand of thought now underwrites the work of some of the key theorists of the cultural dimensions of globalization (Beck 2000, Hannerz 1992, 1996, Mbembe 2001, Sassen 1998,

1999), who foreground mixture, heterogeneity, diversity, and plurality as critical features of culture in the era of globalization. Their work reminds us that no culture, past or present, is a conceptual island unto itself, except in the imagination of the observer. Cultures are and always have been interactive to some degree.

Of course, each of these developments in anthropology is accompanied by a host of footnotes, debates, and ongoing litigations (as must be the case in any serious academic discipline). Still, no serious contemporary understanding of culture can ignore these three key dimensions: relationality (between norms, values, beliefs, etc.); dissensus within some framework of consensus (especially in regard to the marginal, the poor, gender relations, and power relations more generally); and weak boundaries (perenially visible in processes of migration, trade, and warfare now writ large in globalizing cultural traffic).

This chapter builds on and returns to these important developments. They are of direct relevance to the recovery of the future as a cultural capacity. In making this recovery, we will also need to recall some of these wider developments within anthropology. But my main concern here is with the implications of these moves for current debates about development and poverty reduction.

BRINGING THE FUTURE BACK IN

The effort to recover, highlight, and foreground the place of the future in our understandings of culture is not a matter, fortunately, where anthropology has to invent the entire wheel. Allies for this effort can be found in a variety of fields and disciplines, ranging from political theory and moral philosophy to welfare economics and human rights debates. My own thinking on this project builds on and is in dialogue with three important sets of ideas which come from outside anthropology and some from within it.

Outside anthropology, the effort to strengthen the idea of aspiration as a cultural capacity, can build on Charles Taylor's path-breaking concept of "recognition," his key contribution to the debate on the ethical foundations of multiculturalism (Taylor 1992). In this work, Taylor showed that there is such a thing as a "politics of recognition," in virtue of which there was an ethical obligation to extend a sort of moral cognizance to persons who shared world views deeply different from our own. This was an important move, which gives the idea of tolerance some political teeth, makes intercultural understanding an obligation, not an option, and recognizes the independent value of dignity in cross-cultural transactions apart from issues of redistribution. The challenge today, as many scholars have noted, is how to bring the politics of dignity and the politics of poverty into a single framework. Put another way, the issue is whether cultural recognition can be extended so as to enhance redistribution (see especially Fraser and Honneth 2003, Fraser 2001).

I also take inspiration from Albert Hirschman's now classic work (Hirschman 1970) on the relations between different forms of collective identification and satisfaction, which enabled us to see the general applicability of the ideas of "loyalty," "exit," and "voice," terms that Hirschman used to cover a wide range of possible relations that human beings have to decline in firms, organizations, and states. In Hirschman's terms, I would suggest that we have tended to see cultural affiliations almost entirely in terms of loyalty (total attachment) but have paid little attention to exit and voice. Voice is a critical matter for my purposes since it engages the question of dissensus. Even more than the idea of exit it is vital to any engagement with the poor (and thus with poverty), since one of their gravest lacks is the lack of resources with which to give "voice," that is, to express their views and get results skewed to their own welfare in the political debates that surround wealth and welfare in all societies. So, a way to put my central question in Hirschman's terms would be: how can we strengthen the capability of the poor to have and to cultivate "voice," since exit is not a desirable solution for the world's poor and loyalty is clearly no longer generally clear-cut?

My approach also responds to Amartya Sen, who has placed us all in his debt through a series of efforts to argue for the place of values in economic analysis and in the politics of welfare and well-being. Through his earlier work on social values and development (Sen 1984), to his more recent work on social welfare (loosely characterized as the "capabilities" approach) (Sen 1985) and on freedom (Sen 1999), Sen has made major and overlapping arguments for placing matters of freedom, dignity, and moral well-being at the heart of welfare and its economics. This approach has many implications and applications, but for my purposes, it highlights the need for a parallel internal opening up in how to understand culture, so that Sen's radical expansion of the idea of welfare can find its strongest cultural counterpoint. In this chapter, I am partly concerned to bring aspiration in as a strong feature of cultural capacity, as a step in creating a more robust dialogue between "capacity" and "capability," the latter in Sen's terms. In more general terms, Sen's work is a major invitation to anthropology to widen its conceptions of how human beings engage their own futures.

Within anthropology, in addition to the basic developments I addressed already, I regard this chapter as being in a dialogue with two key scholars. The first, Mary Douglas, in her work on cosmology (Douglas 1973/1982), later on commodities and budgets, and later still on risk and nature (Douglas and

Wildavsky 1982), has repeatedly argued for seeing ordinary people as operating through cultural designs for anticipation and risk reduction. This is a line of thought that helps us to investigate the broader problem of aspiration in a systematic way, with due attention to the internal relations of cosmology and calculation among poorer people, such as those members of the English working classes studied by Douglas in some of her best work on consumption (Douglas and Isherwood 1979/1996).

Finally, James Fernandez has had a long-term interest in the problem of how cultural consensus is produced. In this exercise, he has reminded us that even in the most "traditional" looking cultures, such as the Fang of West Africa whom he has written about extensively, we cannot take consensus for granted. His second major contribution is in showing that through the specific operations of various forms of verbal and material ritual, through "performances" and metaphors arranged and enacted in specific ways, real groups actually produce the kinds of consensus on first principles that they may appear to take simply for granted (Fernandez 1965, 1986). This work opens the ground for me, in my own examinations of activism among the poor in India and elsewhere to note that certain uses of words and arrangements of action that we may call cultural, may be especially strategic sites for the production of consensus. This is a critical matter for anyone concerned with helping the poor to help themselves, or in our current jargon, to "empower" the poor. With Fernandez, we can ask how the poor may be helped to produce those forms of cultural consensus that may best advance their own collective long-term interests in matters of wealth, equality, and dignity.

[...]

BIBLIOGRAPHY

Beck, U. 2000. *What is Globalization?* London: Blackwell.

Bourdieu, P. 1977. *Outline of a Theory of Practice.* Trans. R. Nice. Cambridge: Cambridge University Press.

Comaroff, J. and J. Comaroff. 1991. *Of Revelation and Revolution.* Chicago: University of Chicago Press.

Douglas, M. 1973/1982. *Natural Symbols: Explorations in Cosmology.* New York: Pantheon Britain Books.

Douglas, M. and B. Isherwood. 1979/1996. *The World of Goods: Toward an Anthropology of Consumption.* London: Routledge.

Douglas, M. and A. B. Wildavsky. 1982. *Risk and Culture: An Essay on the Selection of Technical and Environmental Dangers.* Berkeley: University of California Press.

Fernandez, J. 1965. 'Symbolic Consensus in a Fang Reformative Cult.' *American Anthropologist* Vol. 67: 902–27.

Fernandez, J. 1986. *Persuasions and Performances: The Play of Tropes in Culture.* Bloomington: Indiana University Press.

Fraser, N. 2001. *Redistribution, Recognition and Participation: Toward an Integrated Conception of Justice* World Culture Report 2. Paris: UNESCO Publications.

Fraser, N. and A. Honeth. 2003. *Redistribution or Recognition: A Philosophical Exchange.* London: Verso.

Hannerz, U. 1992. *Cultural Complexity: Studies in the Social Organization of Meaning.* New York: Columbia University Press.

Hannerz, U. 1996. *Transnational Connections: Culture, People, Places.* London: Routledge.

Hirschman, A. 1970. *Exit, Voice and Loyalty: Responses to Decline in Firms, Organizations, and States.* Cambridge, MA: Harvard University Press.

Mbembe, A. 2001. *On the Postcolony: Studies on the History of Society and Culture.* Berkeley: University of California Press.

Ortner, S. 1995. 'Domination and the Arts of Resistance: Hidden Transcripts.' *Comparative Studies in Society and History* Vol. 37: 173–93.

Sassen, S. 1998. *Globalization and Its Discontents.* New York: New Press.

Sassen, S. 1999. *Guests and Aliens.* New York: New Press.

Scott, J. C. 1990. *Domination and the Arts of Resistance: Hidden Transcripts.* New Haven: Yale University Press.

Sen, A. 1984. *Resources, Values and Development.* Oxford: Blackwell.

Sen, A. 1985. *Commodities and Capabilities.* Amsterdam: Elsevier.

Sen, A. 1999. *Development as Freedom.* New York: Knopf.

Taylor, C. 1992. *Multiculturalism and the Politics of Recognition: An Essay.* Princeton: Princeton University Press.

Chapter 3

Notes on Globalisation and Ambivalence

*Homi K. Bhabha**

I t was an unsettled, wet morning in late May. The rain skidded across the windscreen blinding us for a moment, and then suddenly clearing, giving us no hint of what kind of day we were to expect. My host, a German professor from Munich, suddenly suggested that we make a stop in Nuremberg. 'You must see Nuremberg ... I must take you there.'

'Where?' I stuttered, really meaning 'Why?' and then, of course, I quickly recovered: 'Yes, certainly, what a good idea.' I vaguely remembered a film about the Nuremberg trials with Spencer Tracy and Marlene Dietrich – *Judgement at Nuremberg* – seen as a child in Bombay, much before I knew anything about Albert Speer, or the millions of Nazis who frequently gathered in what Hitler called 'The City of the Rallies'. Just these distant recollections, the heinous echolalia of Hitler's high-pitched ravings, and a tired, overused phrase from Hannah Arendt – 'the banality of evil' – trailed along in my mind as we drove off the *Autobahn*, and after some innocuous suburban manoeuvering, arrived at the *Zeppelinfeld*, Hitler's massive parade-ground.

The vast stadium of soaring stone and empty crumbling terraces was almost soundless. Where hundreds of thousands once stood to rapturous, roaring

* **Homi K. Bhabha** is the Anne F. Rothenberg Professor of the Humanities in the Department of English and American Literature and Language at Harvard University, and the Director of the Humanities Center at Harvard. He is the author of numerous works exploring colonial and post-colonial theory, cultural change and power, and cosmopolitanism, among other themes. Some of his works include *Nation and Narration* (Routledge, 1990), and *The Location of Culture* (second edition includes a new introduction, republished as a Routledge Classic, 1994) is currently translated into seven languages. Harvard University Press will publish his forthcoming book, *A Global Measure*, and his next book, *The Right to Narrate*, will be published by Columbia University Press.

attention, today, in the rain, there were only a few of us – a man scraping the rust off his car, children baiting a dog – a few of us, tourists and visitors, at a loss for words, and what was far worse, without any sense of how to behave, where to look, what truism of history to utter. Nobody wanted to climb onto the pinnacle of the *Zeppelintribune* to stand at the podium and assume Hitler's viewpoint from which he commanded the attention of his followers. Nobody pointed a camera at anything or anybody – there was no photograph to take home, no family-group, no quick shot of the children at play in the *Zeppelinfeld*, now overgrown with weeds and grasses, its serried balconies chipped and bruised, its colonnades long-since demolished. This site was neither background nor foreground; it was strangely *there* and *nowhere.*

How do you 'dis-possess' a cultural space, a heritage site, that has developed a global resonance, a demonic presence? How do you 'dis-possess' a site or subject of the past – that is, at once, tangible and intangible – and yet preserve and protect the traumatic heritage of its memory without which history is silenced, and memory is made mute. Guilt, Reparation, Apology, Truth and Reconciliation – these are important moral dispositions and political strategies that strive to surmount the internecine violence of nations and states 'in transition' by practicing the virtue of public confession, and the balm of collective introspection. But there is nothing in the ethic of ameliorative witnessing, however sincere in its pursuit of human 'fairness' and historic justice, that prepares you for the 'vacuum' that such *dis-possessed* cultural monuments create – 'the half-life of heritage', on the other side of which lies the death of culture and the destruction of humanity. As I stood in this place of *barbaric cultural transmission* (if I may coin a phrase) I was startled to hear a loud triumphant roar, a raucous chorus of celebration that rose from behind a bank of trees. I froze. Was I hallucinating? Alexander Kluge's remarkable film *Brutality in Stone,* that explores the architectural tomb of the half-dead *Zeppelintribune,* flashed before my eyes. It brought back those voices – Hitler, Himmler, anonymous camp commandants – that Kluge had dug up from the Nazi archive to accompany his silent visuals. These 'dis-possesed' moments and monuments, merely mortar and marble, are not free of the morality of human choice.

Why begin this essay on global culture in the twenty-first century by returning to the ruins of the past? By harking back to the charnel house of historical memory? 'An internationalism relevant to our global age', David Held writes in *Global Covenant,* 'must take [the most brutal episodes] as a starting point, and build an ethically sound and politically robust conception of the proper basis of political community, and of the relations among communities.'[1] Held's proposal has a moral urgency at a time in which, post-9/11, internationalism seems to have yielded to unilateralism; and cosmopolitanism is threatened by a new global Empire. But beyond these exigent considerations, Held evokes a humane tradition of civility and peace-making that prevails in the preambles of most international 'rights' conventions. But is there another story to be told about the barbaric cultural transmission of history's brutal, global memories?

Perhaps the most salutary instance in which brutality becomes the starting point for conceiving of an ethically sound political community is to be found in Hannah Arendt's concept of the 'right to have rights'. Arendt traces the origins of this idea to the brutish, teeming lives of the 'stateless' between the wars, and after the Nazi ascendancy. 'We became aware of the existence of the right to have rights', she writes, '... only when millions of people emerged who had lost and could not regain these rights because of the new global political situation.'[2] There is, of course, a difference between Arendt's concept of a global polity organised in terms of an equivalence of nation-states, and contemporary notions of global governance emerging out of the displaced or diminished sovereignty of nations and regions. The relevance of Arendt's argument, for my purposes, lies in her insight into the 'global' as a structure of contradiction and ambivalence. Arendt has been properly acknowledged for insisting on the importance of the political artifice of the public sphere for defining and defending what is 'human' in human rights rather than attaching the moral authority of rights to the 'abstract nakedness of being human'. But what this reveals about the 'global' political situation – crucial to Arendt's argument and to our experience of globalisation – has been barely touched upon.

Initiating a discourse of international polity and political rights that begins with the violence of statelessness leads Arendt to reveal an interesting contradiction between the ethical aspirations of a global polity – 'One World' – and its underlying political culture and social structure. Statelessness, she argues, is not a calamity caused by a lack of civilisation; it is, on the contrary, the perverse consequence of the political and cultural conditions of modernity. In an integrated world-system of nation-states there is no 'free space' – no proper place for the right to action and opinion – for the stateless, for refugees, minorities, displaced persons, *apatrides*. '[T]he people, and not the individual was the image of Man', Arendt brilliantly observes, and those who having been 'thrown out of one of these tightly organised closed communities [finds] himself thrown out of the family of nations altogether.'[3] The brutal post-war experience of being thrown out of the family of nations is Arendt's starting point; and this experience of statelessness yields a fascinating insight into the dialectical structure of an interrelated global internationalism that consists, as David Held puts it, 'of interlocking lives, projects and communities.'[4] If the global (as a cosmopolitan project) is an extensive, totalising condition of equivalent moral and social units, then all forms of social transformation or contradiction – whether their effects are progressive, affiliative, antagonistic, or alienatory – emerge out of the global system itself. There is no 'outside' – ideological, political or ethical – to the global system. Whatever alienates global interdependency, or annihilates cosmopolitan values, must be seen to be an effect of the internal dialectic – a demonic dynamic – of the global condition itself. 'Deadly danger to any [global] civilization is no longer likely to come from without', Arendt writes. 'The danger is that a global universally interrelated civilisation may produce barbarians *from its own midst* by forcing millions of people into conditions which, despite all appearances, are the conditions of savages.'[5] (my emphasis). What kind of monstrous birthplace is this when barbarism emerges from the sack of civility and seeks succour at its teats?

The stateless, whose witness is crucial to the ethics and politics of a new internationalism, stand neither at the centre nor at the margins of society. They emerge from *within the midst of* the ambivalent, *internal* dialectic of the global condition, often spoken of as a 'surplus' population, but in real terms, the motor of unorganized labour and the service industries. As illegals, undocumented, *sans papiers*, they may be hidden from legality, but in their invisibility they become crucial, ubiquitous presences in the everyday material lives of civil society and the public sphere. From a February 2004 policy brief:

> The Pew Hispanic Center estimates that, in 2001, undocumented workers comprised 58 percent of the workforce in agriculture, 23.8 percent in private household services, 16.6 percent in business services, 9.1 percent in restaurants, and 6.4 percent in construction.

The stateless – migrant workers, minorities, asylum seekers, refugees – represent emergent, undocumented lifeworlds that break through the formal legal language of 'protection' and 'status' because, as Balibar writes, they are '*neither insiders or outsiders, or (for many of us) ... insiders officially considered outsiders.*'[6] Their indeterminate presence – legal or illegal – turns cosmopolitan claims of global ethical equivalences and interrelationships into the chains of international alienage. As insider/outsiders they damage the cosmopolitan dream of a 'world without borders' or *l'humanité sans frontières* by opening up, *in the midst of* international polity, a complex and contradictory mode of being or surviving somewhere in between legality and incivility. It is a kind of no-man's land that, in the world of migration, shadows global success; it frequently splits ethical obligations (family and community obligations *behind* the border) from economic interests (foreign labour markets, economic migrancy *across* the border); it substitutes cultural survival in migrant *milieux* for full civic participation.

The shifting dimensions of the inside/outside status of minorities frequently leads to the restriction of rights and representations in the name of the enemy 'within' who is seen as coming across the border from 'without'. As I suggested in my reading of Arendt, the very nature of the border has changed and within and without are no longer territorial limits as much as they constitute complex conceptual and legal zones *in the midst of* the political community. These are zones in which, for instance, the difference between legal and illegal migrants often becomes invisible in the experience of everyday life because society turns a blind eye to the sources of cheap labour that service its needs. But this is precisely the zone that becomes cathectic with social anxiety, or infected with xenophobic racism, as soon as a political party or a community group decides to make political capital out of the issue of migration by pitting the indigenous inheritance of an exclusive and nativist metaphysic of 'belonging' against the formal conditions and legal rights of citizenship. This domain of 'insecure security' signifies the boundary of the nation's alterity, the frontier of democracy's agonistic double. Of course, security is politically necessary; but it is also in danger of becoming a structure of legitimation that replaces the laws of participation with the prerogatives of the 'police', while transforming public opinion into collective neurosis and xenophobic projection. Those who inhabit the space of 'insecure security' live in fear of the danger of encountering the alienation of the democratic promise. Not the extinction of the imagined community of the nation, but its reproduction through the creation of the fear of a culturally alien nation of the 'stateless' emerging *in the midst of* the nation's democratic habitus. This *affect* of alienation constitutes what Foucault describes as the 'right to kill' that stalks modernity's normalising biopolitical power: 'the fact of imposing someone to death, increasing the risk of death for some people, or, quite simply, political death, expulsion, rejection, and so on.'[7] Etienne Balibar echoes E.P. Thompson when he recognises the same phenomenon as 'the growing division of the globalised world into life zones and death-zones ... a decisive and fragile *superborder* which raises fears and concerns about the unity and division of mankind – something like a global and local "enmity line".'[8] In a series of occasional columns in the *New York Times* under the general title of *Insecure Nation*, the editorial writers now refer with some regularity to areas they consider to be inadequately policed or protected from terrorist attacks, as the 'the kill-zone'.

Arendt's condition of statelessness opens up a space of double-articulation (what I earlier called an *unresolved* dialectic) *in the midst of* the discourse of global polity. Here the universally interrelated principles of international integration – civility, cosmopolitanism, rights conventions, global covenants, transnational citizenship, 'overlapping communities of fate'[9] – are confronted in a kind of *double-bind* with the contingent conditions of dis-integration – exclusion, violence, injustice, security, discrimination. The universalist principles of integration are articulated in a discourse of regularity and seriality establishing a synchronic order of similitude – 'To think of people as having equal moral value is to make a general claim about the basic unit of the world as comprising persons as free and equal beings.'[10] The contingency of time and space that I associate with the forces of 'dis-integration' are acutely expressed by W.E.B. Du Bois in his figurative account of what it means to live under the shadow of the colour-line as it darkens daily life in the US. Asked by a sympathetic white friend whether racial discrimination and civic exclusion 'happens to you each day', Du Bois answers: 'Not all each day – surely not. But now and then – now seldom, now sudden: now after a week, now in a chain of awful minutes; not everywhere but anywhere – in Boston, in Atlanta. That's the hell of it. Imagine spending your life looking for insults or for hiding places from them – shrinking ... from blows that are not always but ever ...'[11]

The double-bind of universality and contingency that shackles the life of minority subjects or stateless groups is articulated in a discourse that is contradictory and ambivalent. Integration and disintegration intersect in an unresolved dialectic that expresses the on-going tension within values and beliefs in determining what is legal and what is (un)just, and what may be illegal but ethically and politically fair. The ambivalent relations between 'integration' and 'dis-integration' as they emerge *in the midst of one another* do not create conditions of indecision or passivity. It is by working through, or living through, the process of ambivalence – its tensions and contentions, its incompletions and emergencies, its shuttling between antagonisms and alternatives, between rule and exception – that we derive a more appropriate, if agonising measure of global ethical and political conflicts.

Ambivalence introduces a performative sense of 'being in the midst' of things – *in medias res* – into the activities of reflection and judgement, choice and decision. The ambivalent perspectives of contradictory realities, differential aspects, and oblique relations of knowledge differ substantially from what Richard Rorty once described as the metaphor of epistemological truth 'as being that of having our beliefs determined by being brought face-to-face with the object of the belief.'[12] The 'subject' of ambivalence that moves back and forth, hither and thither, must not be hastened (chastened) even though it seems to be out of time with the accelerative technologies and mentalities of global teleologies. 'Thus a public', Kant writes in *What Is Enlightenment*, 'can only achieve wisdom slowly.'[13]

Ambivalence fosters a vigilant ethics (and epistemology) of process and procedure, of means and mediation, of embodied affective experiences and conceptual visions and revisions. For instance, on the question of transnational citizenship, the legal scholar Linda Bosniak resorts to an analytic of ambivalence as she draws her book to a close: 'Aliens are liminal characters, subjects of contrasting and sometimes competing citizenship worlds. The worlds are ultimately inseverable at the point of alienage because it is alienage's very condition to be at their interface. Alienage, we might say, pits citizenship against itself ... Our condition ... is one of ambivalence and ethical conflict.'[14] On the importance of public reason as part of the ethics of globalisation, Amartya Sen emphasises the importance of speaking *from the midst of* moments of contingency or transition (part of the process of ambivalence) because 'there is a strong case for advancing widespread "public discussion,"[15] even when there would remain many inescapable limitations and weaknesses in the reach of the process.'[16] If public reason is to be effective there has to be an ethic of toleration in the global dialogue that puts you in the position of being in the midst of 'cognitive dissonances that will remain unresolved for the time being', Habermas argues. He proposes a theory of pluralist tolerance based on the 'endur[ance] of a form of on-going non-concurrence at the level of social interaction, while we accept the persistence of mutually exclusive validity claims at the cognitive level of existentially relevant beliefs.' Tolerance represents a form of *endurance* that is a result of a consciously negotiated and contained contradiction between non-concurrence at the level of social interaction and dissonance in the realm of cognitive belief. Tolerance, as a universalist principle of integration, must continually endure the unsettling contingency of 'unresolved contradictions' at the level of dis-integration, and, in my view, it is reasonable to suggest that the ambivalence that marks the practice of tolerance strengthens the ethic of endurance by giving it a pliability that allows it to be effective in the midst of unresolved contradictions; or, in Habermas's words, 'to neutralize or contain specific practical consequences of unresolved contradictions.' It is strange to think that these elements of a global covenant – an ambivalent analytic of citizenship, a transitional sense of public reason, and a contradictory yet effective ethic of tolerance – should emerge from my attempt to explore what it means to take history's most brutal episodes as the starting point for an ethics of global community. This genealogy of global ambivalence leads me back to Nuremburg ...

In the lengthening shadows of the *Zeppelintribune* I felt a gathering sense of being in the midst of many unresolved experiences and narratives. At first I shrunk away from this dispossessed site of shame – *Noli me tangere*; and then I realised that there was no way out of it, the half-life of heritage was also mine to embrace. Only by identifying with this conflictual ambivalence between cultural appropriation and alienation, could I make a moral alignment between what *we* know now and what *we* should have done then. But who is the global 'we'? Why me? I, who was not even there, born in another country, years after the event?

The life of memory exceeds the historic event by keeping alive the traces of images and words. Cultural memory, however, is only partially a mirror, cracked and encrusted, that sheds its light on the dark places of the present, waking a witness here, quickening a hidden fact there, bringing you face-to-face with that anxious and impossible temporality, the past-present. Other than playing on the planes of the past and the present, memory is also a move-ment of the mind that suddenly shifts between the scenes of conscious life, and the *mise-en-scène* of unconscious dreams and desires. Like a Moebius strip, memory does not merely transform the appearance of things but changes the very dimensions of our thinking and feeling, bending time into strange, yet semblant, shapes so that our past experiences take unexpected turns and twists and open up passages that lead to the present and the future ...

A few verses from a poem by Adrienne Rich explore this global *ambivalence* in order to provide a political and ethical map to help us in negotiating our dif-ficult world. The poem is partly written from the kill-zone; partly located in landscapes of freedom. The poet attempts to establish a moral *measure* – a combination of poetic meter and political vision – as she narrates a global his-tory of 'rights and wrongs' from the perspective of global doubt, or what she terms 'Unsatisfaction':

> Memory says: Want to do the right thing? Don't count on me
> I'm a canal in Europe where bodies are floating
> I'm a mass grave I'm the life that returns
> I'm a table set with room for the Stranger
> I'm a field with corners left for the landless
> ....
> I'm an immigrant tailor who says *A coat*
> is not a piece of cloth only
> ....
> I have dreamed of Zion I've dreamed of world revolution
> I'm a corpse dredged from a canal in Berlin
> A river in Mississippi. I am a woman standing
> With other women dressed in black
> with naked face listening
> I am standing here in your poem Unsatisfied.[17]

Adrienne Rich's 'unsatisfied' verses assume an ethical stance that leads us back to the beginning of my essay, where I spoke of the cultural transmission of barbaric memories and traumatic events. I traced a path of ambivalence as I picked my way through the human debris, arguing that ambivalence has emerged as one of the complex ethical and cultural qualities of the global experience. In trying to comprehend what it would mean to make minorities and the stateless the starting point for a new internationalism, we found ourselves in the midst of 'unresolved contradictions' that tempered our ethical endurance and engaged our human solidarity. As I approach the end of this essay I want to suggest that the lessons of ambivalence do not, however, end with endurance. The experience of ambivalence is also a spur to speech, an urge to utterance, a way of working-through what is contradictory and unresolved in order to seek the right to narrate. The most extreme forms of cultural ambivalence – 'There is no document of civilisation, which is not at the same time a document of barbarism'[18] – are also moments that pressurise endurance into claiming the agency of address and interlocution. What story do you tell when you realise that barbarism and civilisation are too often linked only by an open sewer running with blame and blood and tears?

Early in October 2003, in an interrogation chamber in Abu Ghraib prison, 'an interpreter put up his hand, looked away, said that he was not comfortable with the situation, and exited the interrogation booth ... SOLDIER-28 recalled a conversation with SOLDIER-11 concerning an interpreter walking out of an interrogation due to a "cultural difference", but could not remember the incident.'[19] A 'cultural difference' that certainly amounted to abuse, and probably violated the Torture conventions is not something you can easily 'look at'. And yet this gesture of non-compliance – the interpreter's tale – highlights the place of narrative and the ethical response it compels us to adopt. The story of the Iraqi response to Abu Ghraib does not end with the interpreter's silent protest. Riverbend, an eloquent woman blogger from Baghdad, continues the narrative as she demands a moral resolution for victim and witness which teeters between retribution and revenge:

> I want something done about it and I want it done publicly. I want those
> horrible soldiers who were responsible for this to be publicly punished and
> humiliated. I want them to be condemned and identified as the horrible
> people they are. I want their children and their children's children to carry
> on the story of what was done for a long time – as long as those prisoners
> will carry along with them the humiliation and pain of what was done
> and as long as the memory of those pictures remains in Iraqi hearts and
> minds ...[20]

'Carrying on the *story*' does not merely require the repetition or elaboration of the event itself. Riverbend makes an appeal to the power of global memory to fulfil the ethical task of transmitting this barbaric event across the generations, through the mouths of the children of American soldiers so that the shameful story of Abu Ghraib is disseminated in rural Virginia, acknowledged in the urban canyons of Chicago, kept alive in the plains of Kansas. *Carrying on the story* assumes that we embrace the responsibility of the weight of public deliberation. How to connect event and narrative? How to conjugate geo-political events and conditions – war, tyranny, inequality, social division, political discrimination – with the temporal and narrative norms of interlocution: fictionality, judicial inquiry, deliberative dialogue, archival record, truth commissions, journalistic reportage? *I want something done about it and I want it done publicly:* the 'public' that Riverbend seeks as judge and jury is, in part, an international public sphere in which human rights are defended, and through which global information is disseminated – the media, military inquiries, Geneva Conventions, the public acknowledgement of the testimony of the tortured and their torturers.

But beyond this sphere of public opinion as we know it, there is another public site that Riverbend seeks to realise in her appeal to a future in which the barbaric event will circulate through the mouths of babes. The children of the American soldiers involved in the event, must pass on the story from generation to generation because the shame of Abu Ghraib is not simply something that happened to the Iraqis; it must be seen as part of the national history of the US, and its future citizens must tell the story as if it were part of their own striving for an ethical – if not actual – identification with the barbaric event. Narrative, that peculiar intersection of words and actions, is part of a moral universe that floods the conscious experience of the present with the disruptive ghosts of memory, and draws upon the future *that has not yet taken place* to provide a virtual, yet aspirational, location for the activity of ethical judgement: *How will I look back upon the principles which determine my present actions and current choices? What impression will my judgements make on the shape of the future for myself and others?* The role of narrative in ethical thinking is to introduce this dimension of the future into the midst of the present so as to create a temporal disjunction *within* the practice of judgement – a disjunction that allows ethical and political judgements to ponder on the fact that documents of civilisation are *at the same time* documents of barbarism.

The relation between speech and action is at the very heart of the human condition. Human interest, that which lies intangibly in-between (*inter-est*) peoples and yet binds them together, as Hannah Arendt argues, 'is no less real than the world of things we visibly have in common. We call this reality the "web" of human relationships, indicating by the metaphor its somewhat intangible quality ...' These stories may then be recorded in documents and monuments, they may be visible in use-objects or art-works, they may be told and retold and worked into all kinds of materials.[21] In the global age it is the 'human interest' – the virtual mediatic systems that connect the interstices of internationalism – that becomes, at once, electronically *extended* and elastic, while facing the danger of becoming politically and ethically *attenuated*. If, as David Held argues, 'the agent at the heart of modern political discourse, be it a person, group or government, is locked into a variety of overlapping communities and jurisdictions, then the "proper home" of politics and democracy becomes difficult to resolve.'[22] What is it that complicates the agent's political and narrative choice?

The challenge of a mimesis of *mondialisation* (the practice of claim-making upon the 'global' as an aleatory, processual reality) lies in the *ambivalence* generated by the dynamic of global choice as a democratic practice, both deliberative and narrative. It consists in a structure of ambivalence – an ambivalence that I earlier associated with barbaric historic memory – that raises issues about the scale and measure of things that bear a relation to each other that may be epistemologically or ideologically 'assymetrical', while being ethically and affectively analogous. There is, for instance, a strange ambivalence in Riverbend's demand that the American Military Police at Abu Ghraib must be publicly punished – presumably by being brought before some recognised form of the Law – while immediately resorting to the genealogical language of domesticity (a kind of familial or tribal privacy) in making children the bearers of retribution and barbaric transmission: it is the children of American torturers who must carry the curse of their fathers by repeating the story of Abu Ghraib down the generations. There is, furthermore, an ethical ambivalence in condemning humiliation on moral grounds for the Iraqis and demanding it for the Americans. Thinking – and *feeling* – through the medium of ambivalence is a kind of strange global necessity, particularly in conditions of barbaric transmission. Ian McEwan's central character in his post-9/11 novel, *Saturday*, puts it this way:

> For or against the war on terror, or the war in Iraq; for the termination of an odious tyrant and his crime family, for the ultimate weapons inspection, the opening of the torture prisons ...; or against the bombing of civilians, the inevitable refugees and famine, illegal international action ... Does he think that his *ambivalence* – if that is what it really is – excuses him from the general conformity? ... *He's become dim with contradictory opinion* ...[23]

This gesture of ambivalence is not merely a contradictory experience. It counts, as in the case of the Abu Ghraib interpreter, for something more than the phenomenological *affect* of the conflict of cultural differences: it amounts to a demand for a discursive ethics that emerges from the movement of ambivalence by which you are drawn *into* the circle of evil and then *repulsed* by it to stand on the resistant rim; placed in a relation of proximity while taking up a position of oppositionality. Ambivalence is a condition of social and psychic conflict that nonetheless demands that a political and ethical 'choice' has to be made. It is a choice that is clearly heard in a speech-act that I may describe as an ethical mode of 'double' accountability in which the conditions of utterance require a dialogical dispersal of the sovereignty of self-recognition and the 'autonomy' of self-interest. How do I relate to myself – *hypocrite lecteur! – mon semblable – mon frère!* – when I *ambivalently* occupy the place of 'barbaric transmission' which is also the negative space of civilisation? How does my neighbour, my enemy, my Other, relate to me while standing knee-deep in the dispossessed, barbaric site of his or her own cultural property and possession?

Memory and story have made it possible for me to re-construct the narrative of the *Zeppelinfeld* upon the moral grounds of the twenty-first century, and thereby to open up 'the history of the present' to the interruptions of the past, and the projections of the future. The repetitions of a fallen past bring back traumatic, unresolved and unrepresented narratives, with a demand that the cultural record be re-written *from this moment on*; from the un-realised future comes the aspiration for equity and liberty that haunts the moral economy of the present and demands that its goals be revised. A global ethics demands that we take responsibility – imaginatively and actively – for a world that is caught between a past that refuses to die, and a future that refuses to wait to be born. A discourse of ethics that compels us to take responsibility for the remembered past while the future warns against the complicity and corruptibility of the present. Caught in the ambivalences of these double-lives of our times we tell each other our hybrid stories: part yours, part mine, a part that is written in a language of mixed bits and pieces that is as yet unresolved, caught in the midst of developing a vocabulary of values and wishes which engages the double aspect of the global ideal – an extensive historical achievement yearning for an elusive aspirational horizon.

Chapter 4

Culture and Captivity*

Amartya Sen**

The world has come to the conclusion – more defiantly than should have been needed – that culture does matter. However, the real question is: "*How* does culture matter?"[1] The confining of culture into stark and separated boxes of civilizations or of religious identities ... takes too narrow a view of cultural attributes. Other cultural generalizations, for example, about national, ethical, or racial groups, can also present astonishingly limited and bleak understandings of the characteristics of the human beings involved. When a hazy perception of culture is combined with fatalism about the dominating power of culture, we are, in effect, asked to be imaginary slaves of an illusory force.

And yet simple cultural generalizations have great effectiveness in fixing our way of thinking. The fact that such generalizations abound in popular convictions and in informal communication is easily recognized. Not only are the implicit and twisted beliefs frequently the subject matter of racist jokes and ethnic slurs, they sometimes surface as grand theories. When there is an accidental correlation between cultural prejudice and social observation (no matter how casual), a theory is born, and it may refuse to die even after the chance correlation has vanished without a trace.

Consider the laboured jokes against the Irish (such crudities as "How many Irishmen do you need to change a lightbulb?"), which have had some currency in England for a long time, and which are similar to equally silly jokes about the

* This piece is extracted from Amartya Sen, 'Culture and Captivity' in *Identity and Violence: The Illusion of Destiny* (Norton: New York, and Penguin: London, 2006), pp. 103–119.
** **Amartya Sen** is an economist and philosopher and a winner of the Nobel Prize in Economics for his contributions to welfare economics and social choice theory, and also for his analysis of inequality, poverty and famine. He is former President of the Econometrics Society, The American Economic Association, The Indian Economic Association, and The International Economic Association. His books have been translated into more than thirty languages. He is Lamont University Professor at Harvard University.

Poles in America. These crudities had the superficial appearance of fitting well with the depressing predicament of the Irish economy, when the Irish economy was doing quite badly. But when the Irish economy started growing astonishingly rapidly – indeed in recent years faster than any other European economy (Ireland is now richer in per capita income than nearly every country in Europe) – the cultural stereotyping and its allegedly profound economic and social relevance were not junked as sheer and unmitigated rubbish. Theories have lives of their own, quite defiantly of the phenomenal world that can actually be observed.

IMAGINED TRUTHS AND REAL POLICIES

Such theories are, often enough, not just harmless fun. For example, cultural prejudice did play a role in the treatment Ireland received from the British government, and had a part even in the non-prevention of the famines of the 1840s. Among the influences that had an effect on London's treatment of Irish economic problems, cultural alienation did count. While poverty in Britain was typically attributed to economic change and fluctuations, Irish poverty was widely viewed in England (as Richard Ned Lebow, the political analyst, has argued) as being caused by laziness, indifference, and ineptitude, so "Britain's mission" was not seen as one "to alleviate Irish distress but to civilize her people and to lead them to feel and act like human beings."[2]

The search for cultural causes of Ireland's economic predicament extends far back, at least to the sixteenth century, well reflected in Edmund Spenser's *The Faerie Queene*, published in 1590. The art of blaming victims, plentifully present in *The Faerie Queene* itself, was put to effective use during the famines of the 1840s, and new elements were added to the old narrative. For example, the Irish taste for potatoes was added to the list of calamities which the native had, in the English view, brought on themselves. Charles Edward Trevelyan, the head of the Treasury during the famines, expressed his belief that London had done all that could be done for Ireland, even though the famine killed rampantly (in fact, the mortality rate was higher in the Irish famines than in any other recorded famine anywhere in the world).

Trevelyan also proposed a rather remarkable cultural exegesis of Ireland's manifest hunger by linking it with the allegedly limited horizons of Irish culture (in contrast with putting any blame on British governance): "There is scarcely a woman of the peasant class in the West of Ireland whose culinary art exceeds the boiling of a potato."[3] The remark can be seen as an encouraging departure from the English hesitation about making international criticism of culinary art elsewhere (the French, the Italian, and the Chinese may be next). But the oddity of that cultural explanation of Irish hunger certainly merits a place in the annals of eccentric anthropology.

The connection between cultural bigotry and political tyranny can be very close. The asymmetry of power between the ruler and the ruled, which generate a heightened sense of identity contrast, can be combined with cultural prejudice in explaining away failures of governance and public policy. Winston Churchill made the famous remark that the Bengal famine of 1943, which occurred just before India's independence from Britain in 1947 (it would also prove to be the last famine in India in the century, since famines disappeared with the Raj), was caused by the tendency of the people there to "breed like rabbits". The explication belongs to the general tradition of finding explanations of disasters not in bad administration, but in the culture of the subjects, and this habit of thought had some real influence in crucially delaying famine relief in the Bengal famine, which killed between two and three million people. Churchill rounded things up by expressing his frustration that the job of governing India was made so difficult by the fact that the Indians were "the beastliest people in the world, next to the Germans".[4] Cultural theories evidently have their uses.

KOREA AND GHANA

Cultural explanations of economic underdevelopment have recently been given much ground. Consider, for example, the following argument from the influential and engaging book jointly edited by Lawrence Harrison and Samuel Huntington called *Cultural Matters*; it occurs in Huntington's introductory essay, called "Cultures Count", in that volume:

> In the early 1990s, I happened to come across economic data on Ghana and South Korea in the early 1960s, and I was astonished to see how similar their economies were then … Thirty years later, South Korea had become an industrial giant with the fourteenth largest economy in the world, multinational corporations, major exports of automobiles, electronic equipment, and other sophisticated manufactures, and per capita approximately that of Greece. Moreover it was on its way to the consolidation of democratic institutions. No such changes had happened in Ghana, whose per capita income was now about one-fifteenth that of South Korea's. How could this extraordinary difference in development be

explained? Undoubtedly, many factors played a role, but it seemed to me that culture had to be a large part of the explanation. South Koreans valued thrift, investment, hard work, education, organization, and discipline. Ghanaians had different values. In short, cultures count.[5]

There may well be something of interest in this way-out comparison (perhaps even a quarter-truth torn out of context), but the contrast does call for probing examination. As used in the explanation just cited, the causal story is extremely deceptive. There were many important differences – other than their cultural predispositions – between Ghana and Korea in the 1960s.

First, the class structures in the two countries were quite different, with a much bigger – and proactive – role for the business classes in South Korea. Second, the politics were very different too, with the government in South Korea willing and eager to play a prime-moving role in initiating business-centred economic development in a way that was not true in Ghana. Third, the close relationship between the Korean economy and Japan, on the one hand, and the United States, on the other, made a big difference, at least in the early stages of Korean economic expansion.

Fourth – and perhaps most important – by the 1960s South Korea had acquired a much higher literacy rate and a more expanded school system than Ghana had. Korean progress in school education had been largely brought about in the post-Second World War period, mainly through resolute public policy, and it could not be seen just as a reflection of culture (except in the general sense in which culture is seen to include everything happening in a country).[6] On the basis of the slender scrutiny that backed Huntington's conclusion, it is hard to justify either the cultural triumphalism in favour of Korean culture or the radical pessimism about Ghana's future to which Huntington is led through his reliance on cultural determinism.

This is not to suggest that cultural factors are irrelevant to the process of development. But they do not work in isolation from social, political and economic influences. Nor are they immutable. If cultural issues are taken into account, among others, in a fuller accounting of societal change, they can greatly help to broaden our understanding of the world, including the process of development and the nature of our identity. While it is not particularly illuminating, nor especially helpful, to throw up one's hands in disapproval when faced with allegedly fixed cultural priorities ("Ghanaians had different values", as Huntington puts it), it is useful to examine how values and behaviour can respond to social change, for example, through the influence of schools and colleges. Let me refer again to South Korea, which was a much more literate and more educated society than Ghana in the 1960s (when the two economies appeared rather similar to Huntington). The contrast, as has already been mentioned, was substantially the result of public policies pursued in South Korea in the post-Second World War period. But the post-war public policies on education were also influenced by antecedent cultural features. Once we dissociate culture from the illusion of destiny, it can help to provide a better understanding of social change when placed together with other influences and interactive social processes.

In a two-way relationship, just as education influences culture, so can antecedent culture have an effect on educational policies. It is, for example, remarkable that nearly every country in the world with a powerful presence of Buddhist tradition has tended to embrace widespread schooling and literacy with some eagerness. This applies not only to Japan and Korea, but also to China, Thailand, Sri Lanka, and even to the otherwise retrograde Burma (Myanmar). The focus on enlightenment in Buddhism (the word "Buddha" itself means "enlightened") and the priority given to reading texts, rather than leaving it to the priests, can help to encourage educational expansion. Seen in a broader framework, there is probably something here to investigate and learn.

It is, however, important also to see the interactive nature of the process in which contact with other countries and the knowledge of their experiences can make a big practical difference. There is every evidence that when Korea decided to move briskly forward in expanding school education at the end of the Second World War, it was influenced not just by its cultural interest in education, but also by a new understanding of the role and significance of education, based on the experiences of Japan and the West, including the United States.

JAPANESE EXPERIENCE AND PUBLIC POLICY

There is a similar story, early on, of international interaction and national response in Japan's own history of educational development. When Japan emerged from its self-imposed isolation from the world (lasting since the seventeenth century, under the Tokugawa regime), it already had a relatively well-developed school system, and in this achievement Japan's traditional interest in education had played a significant part. Indeed, at the time of the Meiji restoration in 1868, Japan had a higher rate of literacy than Europe. And yet the rate of literacy in Japan was still low (as it obviously was in Europe too), and perhaps most importantly, the Japanese education system was quite out of touch with advances in science and technical knowledge in the industrializing West. When, in 1852, Commodore Matthew Perry chugged into Edo Bay, puffing black smoke from the newly designed steamship, the Japanese were not only impressed – and somewhat terrified – and driven to accept diplomatic and trade relations with the United States, but they also had to re-examine and reassess their intellectual isolation from the world. This contributed to the political process that led to the Meiji restoration, and along with that came a determination to change the face of Japanese education. In the so-called Charter Oath, proclaimed in 1868, there is a firm declaration on the need to "seek knowledge widely throughout the world".[7]

The Fundamental Code of Education issued three years later, in 1872, put the new educational determination in unequivocal terms:

> There shall, in the future, be no community with an illiterate family, nor a family with an illiterate person.[8]

Kido Takayoshi, one of the most influential leaders of that period, put the basic issue with great clarity:

> Our people are no different from the Americans or Europeans of today; it is all a matter of education or lack of education.[9]

That was the challenge Japan took on with determination in the late nineteenth century.

Between 1906 and 1911, education consumed as much as 43 per cent of the budgets of the towns and villages for Japan as a whole.[10] By 1906, the recruiting army officers found that, in contrast with the late nineteenth century, there was hardly any new recruit who was not already literate. By 1910, Japan had, it is generally acknowledged, universal attendance in primary schools. By 1913, even though Japan was still economically very poor and underdeveloped, it had become one of the largest producers of books in the world, publishing more books than Britain and indeed more than twice as many as the United States. Indeed, Japan's entire experience of economic development was, to a great extent, driven by human-capability formation, which included the role of education and training, and this was promoted *both* by public policy and by a supportive cultural climate (interacting with each other). The dynamics of associative relations are extraordinarily important in understanding how Japan laid the foundations of its spectacular economic and social development.

To carry the story further, Japan was not only a learner but also a great teacher. Development efforts of countries in East and Southeast Asia were profoundly influenced by Japan's experience in expanding education and its manifest success in transforming society and the economy. The so-called East

Asian miracle was, to no small extent, an achievement inspired by the Japanese experience.

Paying attention to cultural interrelations, within a broad framework, can be a useful way of advancing our understanding of development and change. It would differ both from neglecting culture altogether (as some narrowly economic models do) and from the privileging of culture as an independent and stationary force, with an immutable presence and irresistible impact (as some cultural theorists seem to prefer). The illusion of cultural destiny is not only misleading, it can also be significantly debilitating, since it can generate a sense of fatalism and resignation among people who are unfavourably placed.

CULTURE IN THE BROAD FRAMEWORK

There can be little doubt that our cultural background can have quite a major influence on our behaviour and thinking. Also, the quality of life we enjoy cannot but be influenced by our cultural background. It certainly can also influence our sense of identity and our perception of affiliation with groups of which we see ourselves as members. The scepticism I have been expressing here is not about the recognition of the basic importance of culture in human perception and behaviour. It is about the way culture is sometimes seen, rather arbitrarily, as the central, inexorable, and entirely independent determinant of societal predicaments.

Our cultural identities can be extremely important, but they do not stand starkly alone and aloof from other influences on our understanding and priorities. There are a number of qualifications that have to be made while acknowledging the influence of culture on human lives and actions. First, important as culture is, it is not uniquely significant in determining our lives and identities. Other things, such as class, race, gender, profession, politics, also matter, and can matter powerfully.

Second, culture is not a homogenous attribute – there can be great variations even within the same general cultural milieu. For example, contemporary Iran has both conservative ayatollahs and radical dissidents, just as America has room for both born-again Christians and for ardent nonbelievers (among a great many other schools of thought and behaviour). Cultural determinists often underestimate the extent of heterogeneity within what is taken to be "one" culture. Discordant voices are often "internal", rather than coming from the outside. Also, depending on the particular aspect of culture we decide to concentrate on (for example, whether we focus on religion, or on literature, or on music), we can get quite a varying picture of the internal and external relations involved.

Third, culture does not sit still. The brief recollection of the educational transformation of Japan and Korea, with profound cultural implications, illustrated the importance of change, linked – as it often is – with public discussion and policy. Any presumption of stationariness – explicit or implicit – can be disastrously deceptive. The temptation toward using cultural determinism often takes the hopeless form of trying to moor the cultural anchor on a rapidly moving boat.

Fourth, culture interacts with other determinants of social perception and action. For example, economic globalization brings in not only more trade, but also more global music and cinema. Culture cannot be seen as an isolated force independent of other influences. The presumption of insularity – often implicitly invoked – can be deeply delusive.

Finally, we have to distinguish between the idea of *cultural liberty*, which focuses on our freedom either to preserve or to change our priorities (on the basis of greater knowledge or further reflection, or, for that matter, on the basis of our assessment of changing customs and fashions), and that of *valuing cultural conservation*, which has become a big issue in the rhetoric of multiculturalism (often providing support for the continuation of traditional lifestyles by new immigrants in the West). There is undoubtedly a strong case for including cultural freedom among the human capabilities people have reason to value, but there is a need also for a probing examination of the exact relation between cultural liberty and the priorities of multiculturalism.[11]

MULTICULTURALISM AND CULTURAL FREEDOM

In recent years, multiculturalism has gained much ground as an important value, or more accurately as a powerful slogan (since its underlying values are not altogether clear). The simultaneous flourishing of different cultures within the same country or region can be seen to be of importance on its own, but very often multiculturalism is advocated on the ground that this is what cultural freedom demands. That claim has to be scrutinized further.

The importance of cultural freedom has to be distinguished from the celebration of every form of cultural inheritance, irrespective of whether the persons involved would choose those particular practices given the opportunity of critical scrutiny and an adequate knowledge of other options and of the choices that actually exist. Even though there has been much discussion in recent years about the important and extensive role of cultural factors in social living and human development, the focus has often tended to be, explicitly or by implication, on the need for cultural conservation (for example, continued adherence to the conservative lifestyles of people whose geographical move to Europe or America is not always matched by cultural adaptation). Cultural freedom may include, among other priorities, the liberty to question the automatic endorsement of past traditions, when people – particularly young people – see a reason for changing their ways of living.

If freedom of human decision is important, then the results of a reasoned exercise of that freedom are to be valued, rather than being negated by an imposed precedence of unquestioned conservation. The critical link includes our ability to consider alternative options, to understand what choices are involved, and then to decide what we have reason to want.

It must, of course, be recognized that cultural liberty could be hampered when a society does not allow a particular community to pursue some traditional lifestyles that members of that community would freely choose to follow. Indeed, social suppression of particular lifestyles – of gays, of immigrants, of specific religious groups – is common in many countries in the world. The insistence that gays or lesbians live like heterosexuals, or stay inside closets, is not only a demand for uniformity, it is also a denial of the freedom of choice. If diversity is not allowed, then many choices would be rendered unviable. The allowing of diversity can indeed be important for cultural freedom.

Cultural diversity may be enhanced if individuals are allowed and encouraged to live as they would value living (instead of being restrained by ongoing tradition). For example, the freedom to pursue ethically diverse lifestyles, for example, in food habits or in music, can make society more culturally diverse precisely as a result of the exercise of cultural liberty. In this case, the importance of cultural diversity – instrumental as it is – will follow directly from the value of cultural liberty, since the former will be a consequence of the latter.

Diversity can also play a positive role in enhancing the freedom even of those who are not directly involved. For example, a culturally diverse society can bring benefits to others in the form of the ample variety of experiences which they are, as a consequence, in a position to enjoy. To illustrate, it can plausibly be argued that the rich tradition of African-American music – with its African lineage and American evolution – has not only helped to enhance the cultural freedom and self-respect of Africa-Americans, it has also expanded the cultural options of all people (African-American or not) and enriched the cultural landscape of America, and indeed the world.

Nevertheless, if our focus is on *freedom* (including cultural freedom), the significance of cultural diversity cannot be unconditional and must vary contingently with its causal connections with human freedom and its role in helping people to take their own decisions. In fact, the relation between cultural liberty and cultural diversity need not be uniformly positive. For example, the simplest way of having cultural diversity may, in some circumstances, be a total continuation of all the pre-existing culture practices that *happen* to be present at a point in time (for example, new immigrants may be induced to continue their old, fixed ways and mores, and discouraged – directly or indirectly – from changing their behaviour pattern at all). Does this suggest that for the sake of *cultural diversity* we should support *cultural conservatism* and ask people to stick to their own cultural background and not try to consider moving to other lifestyles even if they find good reason to do so? The undermining of choice that this would involve would immediately deliver us to an antifreedom position, which would look for ways and means of blocking the choice of a changed living mode that many people may wish to have.

For example, young women from conservative immigrant families in the West might be kept on a short leash by the elders for fear that they would emulate the freer lifestyle of the majority community. Diversity will then be achieved at the cost of cultural liberty. If what is ultimately important is cultural freedom, then the valuing of cultural diversity must take a contingent and conditional form. The merit of diversity must thus depend on precisely *how* that diversity is brought about and sustained.

Indeed, to plead for cultural diversity on the ground that this is what the different groups of people have *inherited* is clearly not an argument based on cultural liberty (even though the case is sometimes presented *as if* it were a "profreedom" argument"). Being born in a particular culture is obviously not an exercise of cultural liberty, and the preservation of something with which a person is stamped, simply because of birth, can hardly be, in itself, an exercise of freedom. Nothing can be justified in the name of freedom without actually giving people an opportunity for the exercise of that freedom, or at least without carefully assessing how an opportunity of choice would be exercised if it were available. Just as social suppression can be a denial of cultural freedom, the violation of freedom can also come from the tyranny of conformism that may make it difficult for members of a community to opt for other styles of living.

SCHOOLS, REASONING AND FAITH

Unfreedom can result also from a lack of knowledge and understanding of other cultures and of alternative lifestyles. To illustrate the main issue that is involved here, even an admirer (as this writer is) of the cultural freedom that modern Britain has, by and large, succeeded in giving to people of different backgrounds and origins who are resident in that country can well have considerable misgivings about the official move in the United Kingdom towards extension of state-supported faith-based schools.

Rather than reducing existing state-financed faith-based schools, actually *adding* to them – Muslim schools, Hindu schools and Sikh schools to pre-existing Christian ones – can have the effect of reducing the role of reasoning which the children may have the opportunity to cultivate and use. And this is happening at a time when there is a great need for broadening the horizon and understanding of other people and other groups, and when the ability to undertake reasoned decision-making is of particular importance. The limitations imposed on the children are especially acute when the new religious schools give children rather little opportunity to cultivate reasoned choice in determining the priorities of their lives. Also, they often fail to alert students to the need to decide for themselves how the various components of their identities (related respectively to nationality, language, literature, religion, ethnicity, cultural history, scientific interests, etc.) should receive attention.

This is not to suggest that the problems of bias (and the deliberate fostering of a blinkered vision) in these new faith-based British schools are anything as extreme in, say, the fundamentalist madrasas in Pakistan, which have become a part of the breeding ground for intolerance and violence – and often for terrorism – in that strained part of the world. But the opportunity of cultivating reason and the recognition of the need for scrutinized choice can still be far less in these new faith-based schools, even in Britain, than in the more mixed and less sequestered places of learning in that country. The actual opportunities are often rather less than even in traditional religious schools – particularly in those Christian schools which have had a long tradition of having a broad curriculum, along with tolerating considerable scepticism about religious education itself (though these older schools too can be made considerably less restrictive than they already are).

The move towards faith-based schools in Britain reflects also a particular vision of Britain as "a federation of communities", rather than as a collectivity of human beings living in Britain, with diverse differences, of which religious and community-based distinctions constitute only one part (along with differences in language, literature, politics, class, gender, location and other characteristics). It is unfair to children who have not yet had much opportunity of reasoning and choice to be put into rigid boxes guided by one specific criterion of categorization, and to be told: "That is your identity and this is all you are going to get."

In the annual lecture for 2001 at the British Academy which I had the privilege of giving (it was called "Other People"), I presented the argument that this "federational" approach has a great many problems, and in particular tends to reduce the development of human capabilities of British children from immigrant families in a significant way.[12] Since then the incidents of suicide bombings in London (in July 2005), carried out by British-born but deeply alienated young men, have added another dimension to the question of self-perception and its cultivation in Britain. However, I would argue that the basic limitation of the federationist approach goes well beyond any possible connection with terrorism. There is an important need not only to discuss the relevance of our common humanity – a subject on which schools can play (and have often played in the past) a critical role. There is, in addition, the important recognition that human identities can take many distinct forms and that people have to use reasoning to decide on how to see themselves, and what significance they should attach to having been born a member of a particular community.

The importance of non-sectarian and non-parochial school education that expands, rather than reduces, the reach of reasoning (including critical scrutiny) would be hard to exaggerate. Shakespeare gave voice to the concern that "some are born great, some achieve greatness, and some have greatness thrust upon them". In the schooling of children, it is necessary to make sure that *smallness* is not "thrust upon" the young, whose lives lie ahead of them. Much is at stake here.

Chapter 5

Realistic Cosmopolitanism
How Do Societies Handle Otherness?

Ulrich Beck*

What we call 'cosmopolitanization of reality'[1] is not the result of a cunning conspiracy on the part of 'global capitalists' or an 'American drive for world domination'; it is an unforeseen social consequence of actions directed at other results, within a network of global interdependence and its attendant risks. These cosmopolitan side-effects, often forced, mostly unforeseen and unintended, frustrate the equation of the national state with national society and create new transnational forms of living and communicating, new ascriptions and responsibilities, new ways in which groups and individuals see themselves and others. Countries are, so to speak, increasingly besieged and penetrated by global interdependence, by ecological, economic and terrorist risks that bind together the separate worlds of underdeveloped and developed nations. And, in so far as this historical situation is reflected at the level of world opinion, it gives rise to a new cosmopolitan vision, in which people see themselves both as part of an endangered world and as part of their local histories and situations.

This is the starting point from which to approach realistic cosmopolitanism. But what distinguishes this realistic cosmopolitan outlook from a universalist, relativist or multicultural perspective?

To simplify matters, the term 'realist' should be understood here as equivalent to 'social-scientific'. We may say that realistic cosmopolitanism, removed from a philosophical prehistory, refers to a fundamental problem of the second modernity: how do 'societies' handle 'otherness' and 'boundaries' amid the global interdependency crisis?

* **Ulrich Beck** is Professor of Sociology at the University of Munich, and the British Journal of Sociology Professor at the London School of Economics and Science.

We shall distinguish various ways in which societies handle otherness – universalism, relativism, ethnicism, nationalism, multiculturalism, cosmopolitanism etc. – and relate each of these in turn to the historical social formations of premodernity, modernity and postmodernity.

THE TWO FACES OF UNIVERSALISM

At the beginning of the twenty-first century, someone looking within a long historical perspective at the discussion of how the Western world should handle the otherness of others – a discussion exemplified by such influential books as Samuel Huntington's *The Clash of Civilizations and the Remaking of World Order*[2] or Francis Fukuyama's *The End of History*[3] – cannot fail to be struck by its resemblance to the debates at the legendary conference in Valladolid in 1550, when the issue in dispute was the extent to which the American Indians were different from and therefore inferior to Europeans.

Huntington's argument is that, whereas the main lines of conflict during the Cold War were openly political and derived their explosive nature from considerations of national and international security, the lines of conflict today correspond to major cultural antagonisms involving a clash of values between civilizations. The culture, identity and religious faith that used to be subordinate to political and military strategies now define the priorities on the international political agenda. We are witnessing the invasion of politics by culture. Divisions between civilizations are becoming threats to international stability and world order. The democratic values of the West and the premodern values of the Islamic world stand opposed to each other in ever more menacing and hostile ways, both within individual countries and between different regions of the world.

As to Fukuyama, his simplistic view is that, since the collapse of the Soviet Communist system, there is no longer any alternative to the Western model of liberal democracy and the American-style market economy. 'Democratic capitalism' is the only real vision of modernity, which by its own inner logic spreads through and refashions the entire world. This will give rise to a universal civilization that brings history to an end.

These two ways of handling otherness already confronted each other at that conference in Valladolid nearly five centuries ago, where the Aristotelian philosopher Juan Ginés de Sepúlveda and the Dominican priest Bartolomé de Las Casas represented, respectively, the universalism of difference and the universalism of sameness. Sepúlveda, like the political theorist Huntington today, argued that the defining characteristic of humanity was the hierarchy of values, while Las Casas, like the political scientist Fukuyama, maintained that it was the basic oneness of civilization. The philosopher, then, emphasized the differences between Spaniards and Indians: the fact that the latter went around naked, sacrificed human victims, made no use of horses or asses, or were ignorant of money and the Christian religion. He accordingly structured the human species into peoples living at the same time but at different cultural stages. In his eyes, difference meant the same as inferiority – from which it followed (looking at 'barbarian' America from civilized Europe) that man was the god of man, and that subjugation and exploitation were a pedagogic task.

Similarly, Huntington today conceives the relationship of the Western world to its cultural Other, Islamic civilization, as one of vertical difference consisting of two aspects: 'Others' are denied sameness and equality, and therefore count in the hierarchy as subordinate and inferior. From here it is only a short step to treat the cultural Others as 'barbarians' – whether this means that one has to convert them to the true values of Christianity or democratic capitalism, or to resist with military force the threat that they allegedly pose. The self-assured superiority radiating from the Aristotelian philosopher certainly stands out today, whereas the most striking thing about Huntington's diagnosis is its apocalyptic overtones. A new 'decline of the West' seems to be on the cards, unless we all shake hands and march off to battle against the 'Islamic threat' and for the values of the West.

The Dominican priest Las Casas eloquently defended the rights of the Indians and saw them as remarkably similar to Europeans. They fulfilled the ideals of the Christian religion, which recognized no difference in terms of skin colour and racial origin. Moreover, they were friendly and modest, respected interpersonal norms, family values and their own traditions, and were thus better prepared than many other nations on earth to hear God's word and to practise his truth. The priest vehemently opposed hierarchical difference, in the name of a Christian universalism. Against the principle that saw Others as hierarchically subordinate and inferior, he argued for the dissolution of differences – either as an anthropological fact, or as part of the forward march of civilization (modernization).

Two ways of handling the otherness of others are apparent in the case of universalism. We can already see this in the position of the Dominican priest, for whom it is not otherness but sameness that defines the relationship between us and the other. Under the universalizing gaze, all forms of human life are located within a single order of civilization, with the result that cultural differences are either transcended or excluded. In this sense, what is involved is a hegemonic project, which the Other's voice is permitted to enter only as the voice of sameness, as confirmation of oneself, contemplation of oneself, dialogue with oneself. Translated into an African universalism, this would mean that the true White has a Black soul.

Even the American nation, which provides a home for all ethnicities, peoples and religions, has an ambivalent relation to difference. To be an American means to live in the immediate proximity of difference; and that often means to live in the 'Huntingtonian' fear that a stress on ethnic difference will spell the decline of the West, that ethnic differences can never be bridged, and that, without national assimilation in which difference is transcended, the chaos raging beneath the surface will break through. Precisely because ethnic difference is an integral part of the American national consciousness, the fear keeps re-emerging that the American people consists of peoples who cannot be mixed together in the 'melting pot'. And this fear both demands and promotes a compulsion to sameness and conformism. This is the basis for that dialectic of difference and conformity with which nationalism opposes the danger of ethnic dissolution. The greater the diversity, and the more unbridgeable the differences that appear and are staged, the louder are the calls for conformity that proclaim the national ethos (communitarianism).

From Paul of Tarsus through Kant and Popper to Lyotard and Rorty, variants of the same dialectic serve to limit the danger of ethnic difference by stressing a common humanity binding on all – that is, by having recourse to Western universalism. In this perspective, ethnic diversity does exist but has no intrinsic value such as universalism naturally claims for itself. What is asserted is not that we must recognize the otherness of others, but that in the end we are all human beings and have a claim to equal rights. In the event of conflict, where ethnic diversity calls into question the universal value of the human, it is essential to defend universalism against particularism.

Let us clarify this by again taking the case of Christian universalism and the opposition between 'Christian' and 'heathen'. It draws its strength from the fact that it releases everyone from their seemingly rigid attachment to skin colour, ethnic origin, gender, age, nationality and class, and addresses them as equal before God, in the existential community of the Christian faith. The duality thus belies the asymmetry that it posits. 'The opposition between all men and all the baptized is no longer quantifiable as the previous tokens were, but involves a reduplication of the reference group itself. Everyman must become a Christian, if he is not to sink into eternal damnation.'[4]

Imperial Christian universalism thereby releases emancipatory impulses that can be traced back to the movement for liberation from slavery. Feminist movements have also made reference to Paul the Apostle. But here too the dual face shows itself. Only within the confines of a negating universalism – based on Christianity or the Enlightenment – does the blackness of Blacks, the Jewishness of Jews or the femininity of women become a 'particularism' that is considered morally inferior. To deny equality is to shut out, or snuff out, the otherness of others. All who claim anything other than universalism exclude themselves, and whenever universalism is called into question the promulgators of universal truth and morality sense chaos and disorder, or even the destructive power of ethnic particularism. Anyone who rejects universalism supposedly fails to recognize the higher morality that distinguishes it, thereby becoming liable to a verdict of amoral or anti-moral particularism.

By these means, one's own particularity becomes transfigured and displaced in a universalist direction; the majority raise their own ethnicity to excessive heights and declare their own norms to be universal. In countries where whites are dominant, being white is the privilege of not noticing that one is white. The postulate of abstract identity sets up pressure on the ethnic Other to yield to this particular identity claim – that is, to give up the positing of difference. Within a national framework, all attempts to combine universalism and particularism lead to the supposition (or imposition) that the true Black is the non-Black, the true Jew is the non-Jew, the true woman is the non-feminine woman. If Blacks, Jews, Chinese, Japanese and women then call themselves Black, Jewish, Chinese, Japanese or female, they lack theoretical and philosophical authority: they are not up-to-date; they are structurally conservative, imprisoned in an antiquated self-image. The self-understanding of 'particulars' is 'ethnically correct', and thus not ethnically human, only when people emancipate themselves from their ethnicity and bow to the official model of the non-Black Black, the non-Jewish Jew, the non-female woman.

To put it in the terminology of the mainstream sociology of modernization, the otherness of others is a relic that modernization whittles down to eventual insignificance. Both Las Casas and Fukuyama conceive this disappearance of diversity as a civilizing process – in the one case through Christian conversion and baptism, in the other through the infectious superiority of Western values (market economy, democracy). Then as now: No alternative! The only way forward is Christian-Western universalism. Seen in this way, the so-called 'end of history' began some five hundred years ago.

But the twin face of Western universalism also means that it promotes the principles of liberty and equality throughout the world. It is not possible to proclaim global human rights on the one hand, and to have a Muslim, African, Jewish, Christian or Asian charter of human rights on the other hand. To respect the otherness and the history of others, one must consider them as members of the same humanity, not of another, second-class humanity. Human rights infringe the right to screen off traditions from 'external attack'. Respect for traditions that violate human rights is tantamount to disrespect for their victims.

THE TWO FACES OF RELATIVISM

To vote against universalism is to argue in favour of relativism: this is how things appear to those who think in terms of either/or alternatives. Whereas universalism removes the boundaries around the cultural Other, relativism permits, imposes and constructs new boundaries. Where and how these run or are drawn will depend on what relativism is associated with: nationalism (national relativism), local units (local relativism) or culturalism (cultural relativism). If universalism aims at the overcoming of differences, relativism aims at their underlining. It therefore categorically rejects what universalism affirms: the very possibility of developing and recognizing general norms. Recognition of such norms presupposes Nietzsche's will to power. Within a relativist perspective, then, universalism and hegemony are two sides of the same coin.

Relativism, like universalism, shows two faces. As we have seen, universalism has the drawback of imposing its standpoint on others, but offers the advantage of taking the fate of others seriously, as if it were its own fate. The two faces of relativism may be conceived in a complementary manner. On the one hand, a certain dose of relativism may serve as an antidote to the hubris of universalism. Relativism and contextual thinking sharpen our respect for cultural difference and can make it both attractive and necessary to change perspectives with the Other. But, if relativism and contextualism are absolutized, this attentiveness to others turns into its opposite and any change of perspective is rejected on the grounds that it is quite simply impossible. The instrument for closing oneself to others as well as for rejecting the Other's gaze upon one's 'own' culture is the incommensurability principle. If everything is relative, then the conqueror has one standpoint and the vanquished another standpoint; the watching public takes up further standpoints of its own. More or less unbridgeable gulfs yawn wide between all these positions. Everyone is simply like this or like that. The result is a disorientated relativism for which navel-gazing becomes a gaze upon the world.

The unintentional irony of the relativist incommensurability thesis is that it is the spitting image of an essentialist world-view. It leads (astray) to a postmodern quasi-essentialism, which shares with univocality a compulsion to accept things as they are.

THE TWO FACES OF NATIONALISM

The way in which nationalism strategically handles otherness may be understood as a combination of the strategies discussed so far: hierarchical otherness, universalism of sameness and relativism. Hierarchical otherness applies in external relations and universalism of sameness in internal relations, while the relativism is a territorial relativism coinciding with national boundaries. Nationalism denies the otherness of others internally, while claiming, producing and fixing it externally. To be sure, there can be politically effective solidarity with like others, therefore a duty to pay taxes and an entitlement to social support, educational facilities and political participation; but this stops at the garden fence, and may serve to deny other nations equal rights, to classify them as barbarian, or even to make one's own nation barbarian.

This territorially restricted historic 'compromise' among universalism, otherness and relativism is the typical way in which otherness is handled in the first modernity. It is well known that the dual face of nationalism shows itself not only in its use of the opposition between us and barbarians to produce national sameness and integration, but also in the relation of the 'majority' (as defined in national eyes) to 'minorities'.

THE TWO FACES OF ETHNICISM

One argument that has recently been mobilized to fend off global interdependence comes from the arsenal of anti-colonialism: South America for South Americans, Cuba for Cubans, Algeria for Algerians, Africa for Africans. Paradoxically, these solutions involving ethnic territorial autonomy are also taken up by Europeans, so that the slogan 'Europe for Europeans' becomes a means of mobilizing people against an imminent invasion by 'Turks', 'Russians', and so on. Here the two faces of ethnicism are all too apparent, as common ground between ethnic groups has to be constantly removed. If the intense modern sense of freedom becomes part of one's own self-image while coinciding with extreme poverty and discrimination, those who suffer social exclusion may turn the tables and shut themselves off in turn. This overlapping of a sense of freedom with systematic violation of human dignity marks the historical birth of the 'ugly citizen' – a figure which should not be overlooked in analysis of the historical rise of the citizen, although political theorists and philosophers have nearly always traced this in terms of the 'good citizen'. In many parts of the world, there is a danger that autistic ethnicism, charged with a modern consciousness of freedom, will deliberately wreck the national compromise that at least recognizes minority rights.

Non-violent coexistence with those who are culturally other is something that absolutely everyone in a civilized society must accept. Anyone who thinks they have the human right to make aliens of their neighbours, and to justify their forcible expulsion by reference to some wrong suffered in the past, cannot count on being shown the tolerance they deny to others. Neither talk of counter-violence nor mention of violations to one's own dignity can give anyone the right suddenly to treat neighbours as aliens and to use violence against them.

If a Palestinian woman blows herself up in a café where Israeli women are sitting with their children, this certainly cannot be excused (as we sometimes hear). But, in order to understand, we should take it into account that by such actions the 'poor devils' are reflecting their own history of repression; and that people so deeply wounded in their dignity cannot be simply expected to see that it is impermissible to blow children up with a bomb. The differentiation and exclusion involved in the emphasis on ethnicity release a dynamic of violence in which the minimum of civilization no longer applies.

Cosmopolitanism essentially means recognition of otherness, both externally and internally; differences are neither ranged in a hierarchy nor dissolved into universality, but are accepted. From the viewpoint of cosmopolitan realism, this 'either universalism or relativism' or 'either sameness or diversity' is a false debate between false alternatives, which can be overcome if the various strategic ways of handling diversity are reconsidered, demarcated and related to one another in accordance with the both-and principle. Realistic cosmopolitanism should not be understood and presented in opposition to universalism, relativism, nationalism and ethnicism, but as a summation or synthesis of all four. Contrary to their own usual understanding of themselves, the different strategies for the social handling of otherness do not exclude but presuppose one another; they are mutually correcting, limiting and protecting.

Cosmopolitanism acquires its realism and historical specificity, its persuasiveness and seductiveness, from the interpenetration of different modes of socially handling the otherness of others. The resulting fusion of these modes is such that their cosmopolitan impulses are strengthened and their anti-cosmopolitan impulses weakened and curtailed.

Chapter 6

Religious Tolerance – The Pacemaker for Cultural Rights*

*Jürgen Habermas***

[...]

Only from a basis of a *reciprocal* recognition of the rules of tolerant behavior can we find a solution to the ostensible paradox that each act of toleration must circumscribe the range of behavior everybody must accept, thereby drawing a line for what can *not* be tolerated. There can be no inclusion without exclusion. And as long as this line is drawn in an authoritarian manner, i.e., unilaterally, the stigma of arbitrary exclusion remains inscribed in toleration. Only with a *universally convincing* delineation of the borderline, and this requires that all those involved *reciprocally* take the perspectives of the others, can toleration blunt the thorn of intolerance. Everyone who could be affected by the future practice must first voluntarily agree on those conditions under which they wish to exercise mutual toleration. The usual conditions for liberal co-existence between different religious communities stand this test of reciprocity. They refer in the first place to prohibiting the use of political power for missionary purposes, and to the freedom of association that also prevents religious authorities being able to influence their members' conscience compulsorily. Only if they find intersubjective recognition across confessional boundaries can such specifying norms provide justifications that *out-trump* those personally maintained reasons for rejecting alien religious convictions and practices. Even if

* This was the Royal Institute of Philosophy Lecture for 2003 and the full version was originally published in *Philosophy* 79 (2004), pp. 5–18.
** **Jürgen Habermas** is Professor Emeritus, Johann Wolfgang Goethe-Universität, Frankfurt am Main. He is the author of numerous texts on philosophy, law and social theory.

there is no historical substantiation for Jellinek's suggestion that all human rights are rooted in religious freedom,[1] there is certainly a conceptual link between the universalistic justification for religious tolerance, on the one hand, and democracy as the basis for legitimation for a secular state, on the other.

The purported paradox dissolves if we conceive of religious freedom – covering both the right to free expression of one's own religion and the corresponding negative freedom to remain undisturbed by the others' practicing their respective religions – as part of a democratic constitution. Religious tolerance can be practiced in a tolerant manner precisely under those conditions which the citizens of a democratic community mutually accord one another. From the viewpoint of the democratic lawmaker who makes the addressees of such a law likewise the authors thereof, the legal act of mutual toleration melds with the virtuous self-obligation to behave tolerantly.

However, the paradox does not seem to be fully resolved by the reciprocal generalization of religious freedom, since it appears to re-emerge, in secular terms, at the very core of the constitutional state. A democratic order that guarantees tolerance also in terms of political freedoms, such as free speech, must take preventive protection against the enemies of that very core of the constitution. At latest since the 'legal' transition from the Weimar Republic to the Nazi régime we in Germany have become aware of the necessity of self assertion – but equally of that strange dialectic of the self-assertion of a 'militant' democracy that is 'prepared to defend itself'.[2] Courts can on a case-by-case basis pass judgment on the limits of religious freedom, basing their conclusions on the law. However, if the constitution faces the opposition of enemies who make use of their political freedom in order to abolish the constitution that grants it, then the question arises as to the limits of political freedom in a self-referential form. How tolerantly may a democracy treat the enemies of democracy?

If the democratic state does not wish to give itself up, then it must resort to intolerance toward the enemy of the constitution, either bringing to bear the means afforded by political criminal law or by decreeing the prohibition of particular political parties (Article 21.2 of the German Constitution) and the forfeiture of basic rights (Article 18 and Article 9.2 of the same). The 'enemy of the state', a concept originally with religious connotations, resurfaces in the guise of the enemy of the constitution: be it in the secularized figure of the political ideologist who combats the liberal state, or in the religious shape of the fundamentalist who violently attacks the modern way of life *per se*. Today's terrorists seem to embody a combination of both. Yet it is precisely the agencies of the constitutional state itself who define what or who shall be classified as an enemy of the constitution. A constitutional state must perform a twofold act here: it must repel the animosity of existential enemies while avoiding any betrayal of its own principles – in other words, it is exposed in this situation to the constantly lurking danger of itself being guilty of retrogressively resorting to an authoritarian practice of *unilaterally* deciding the limits of tolerance.

Those who are suspicious of being 'enemies of the state' might well turn out to be radical defenders of democracy. This is the problem: whereas the task of a seemingly paradoxical self-limitation of religious tolerance can be ceded to democracy, the latter must process the conundrum of constitutional tolerance through the medium of its own laws. A self-defensive democracy can sidestep the danger of paternalism only by allowing the self-referentiality of the self-establishing democratic process to be brought to bear on controversial interpretations of constitutional principles. In this regard, it is something like a litmus test, how a constitutional state treats the issue of civil disobedience. Needless to say, the constitution itself decides what the procedure should be in the case of conflicts over the correct interpretation of the constitution. With a legal recognition of '*civil disobedience*' (which does not mean it does not punish such acts), the tolerant spirit of a liberal constitution extends even beyond the ensemble of those existing institutions and practices in which its normative contents have become actually embodied so far. A democratic constitution that is understood as the project of realizing equal civil rights tolerates the resistance shown by dissidents who, even after all the legal channels have been exhausted, still insist on combating decisions that came about legitimately. Under the proviso, of course, that the 'disobedient' citizens plausibly justify their resistance by citing constitutional principles and express it by nonviolent, i.e., symbolic means.[3] These two conditions again specify the limits of political tolerance in a constitutional democracy that defends itself against its enemies by non-paternalist means – and they are limits that are acceptable for its democratically minded opponents, too.

By recognizing civil disobedience, the democratic state copes with the paradox of tolerance that reoccurs at the level of constitutional law in a tolerant manner. It draws a line between a tolerant and a self-destructive handling of ambivalent dissidents in such a way as to ensure that these persons (who could in the final analysis transpire to be enemies of the constitution) nevertheless have the opportunity contrary to their image to prove themselves to actually be the true patriotic champions of a constitution that is dynamically understood as an ongoing *project* – the project to exhaust and implement basic rights in changing historical contexts.

Pluralism and the struggle for religious tolerance were not only driving forces behind the emergence of the democratic state, but continue to stimulate its further evolution up to now. Before addressing religious tolerance as the pacemaker for multiculturalism, in the correct sense of the term, allow me to analyse the concept of tolerance a bit further.

(a) The religious context of discovering tolerance brings first to mind the key component of a 'rejection based on existentially relevant conviction.' That rejection is a condition necessary for all kinds of tolerant behavior. We can only exercise tolerance toward other people's beliefs if we reject them for subjectively *good* reasons. We do not need to be tolerant if we are indifferent to other opinions and attitudes anyway or even appreciate the value of such 'otherness'. The expectation of tolerance assumes that we can endure a form of ongoing non-concurrence at the level of social interaction, while we accept the persistence of mutually exclusive validity claims at the cognitive level of existentially relevant beliefs. We are expected to neutralize the practical impact of a cognitive dissonance that nevertheless calls for further attempts to resolve it within its own domain.

In other words, we must be able to socially accept mutual cognitive dissonances that will remain unresolved for the time being. Yet such a cognitive difference must prove to be 'reasonable' if tolerance is to be a meaningful response here. Tolerance can only come to bear if there are legitimate justifications for the rejection of competing validity claims: 'If someone rejects people whose skin is black we should not call on him to be "tolerant toward people who look different" ... For then we would accept his prejudice as an ethical judgment similar to the rejection of a different religion. A racist should not be tolerant, he should quite simply overcome his racism.'[4] In this and similar cases, we consider a critique of the *prejudices* and the struggle against *discrimination* to be the appropriate response – and not 'more tolerance.'

The issue of tolerance only arises after those prejudices have been eliminated that led to discrimination in the first place. But what gives us the right to call those descriptions 'prejudices' that a religious fundamentalist, a racist, the sexual chauvinist, the radical nationalist or the xenophobic ethnocentric have of their respective 'other'? This points to the second kind of reasons. We allow ourselves those stigmatizing expressions in light of the egalitarian and universalistic standards of democratic citizenship, something that calls for the equal treatment of the 'other' and mutual recognition of all as 'full' members of the political community. The norm of complete inclusion of all citizens as members with equal rights must be accepted before all of us, members of a democratic community, can mutually expect one another to be tolerant. It is the standard of non-discrimination that first provides this expectation with moral and legal reasons that can *out-trump* the epistemic reasons for the persisting rejection of those convictions and attitudes, we merely tolerate. On the base of that normative agreement, the potential for conflict in the cognitive dimension of ongoing contradictions between competing worldviews can be defused in the social dimension of shared citizenship. Thus, tolerance only begins where discrimination ends.

(b) Keeping in mind both kinds of reasons, reasons for rejection at the cognitive, and for acceptance on the social level, we can better answer the question of which sort of burden the tolerant person is expected to carry. What exactly must this person 'endure'? As we have seen, it is not the contradiction between premises and perspectives of different worldviews that has to be 'accepted' as such: there is no contradiction in one's own head. An unresolved contradiction remains only in the interpersonal dimension of the encounter of different persons who are aware that they hold contradictory beliefs. The crux is rather the neutralization or containment of specific practical consequences of unresolved contradictions. To tolerate that pragmatic contradiction means a twofold burden: She who is tolerant may only realize the ethos inscribed in her own worldview within the limits of what everyone is accorded. The way of life prescribed by a particular religion or worldview may be realized only under conditions of equal rights for everybody. And, within these limits she must also respect the ethos of the others. This burden is of a cognitive kind to the extent that those beliefs in which each person's ethos is rooted must be brought into harmony with the liberal norms of state and society. What this requires can be seen from the accommodation of religion in modern Europe. Every religion is originally a 'worldview' or, as John Rawls would say, a 'comprehensive doctrine' – also in the sense that it lays claim to the authority to structure a form of life in its entirety. A religion has to relinquish this claim to an encompassing definition of life as soon as the life of the religious community is differentiated from the life of the larger society. A hitherto prevailing religion forfeits its political impact on society at large if the political regime can no longer obey just one universal ethos. Emancipated minority religions face a similar challenge. By having to deal with the fact of pluralism, religious doctrines are forced to reflect on their own relations to the environments of the liberal state and a secularized society. This results, among other things, in the renunciation of violence and the acceptance of the voluntary character of religious association. Violence may not be used to advance religious beliefs, both inside and outside the community.[5] However, the major religions must appropriate the normative foundations of the liberal state under conditions of *their own premises* even if (as in the European case of the Judeo-Christian legacy) both evolved from the same historical context.

[...]

The cognitive demand we make of someone in expectation of tolerance is the following: he shall develop from his own worldview reasons that tell him why he may realize the ethos inscribed in that view only within the limits of what everyone is allowed to do and to pursue. Of course, these limits themselves are often up for discussion, at which point the courts decide who must accept whose ethos – the majority that of a minority, or vice versa.[6]

This brings me, following the reasons for rejection and acceptance, on to the third kind of reasons. The legal *reasons for excluding intolerant behavior* provide the yardstick for measuring whether the state adheres to the imperative of remaining neutral and whether legislature and jurisdiction have institutionalized tolerance in the right way. Let me first discuss some familiar examples (a) and then introduce the notion of a cultural right (b).

(a) Sikhs in Great Britain and the United States gained exceptions from generally binding safety regulations and are permitted to wear turbans (rather than crash helmets) and daggers (kirpans). In Germany Jehovah's Witnesses successfully fought for being recognized as a public-law entity ('Anstalt öffentlichen Rechts') and thereby gained the same legal privileges our large churches enjoy. In these cases when minorities call for equal standing, for exceptions from established laws, or for special subsidies (e.g. for curricula transmitting the language and tradition of a minority culture), in many cases the courts must decide who has to accept whose ethos or form of life. Must the Christian inhabitants of the village accept the call of the muezzin? Must the local majority for strict animal protection accept the ritual slaughter of poultry and cattle by Jewish butchers? Must the non-confessional pupils, or those of different confessions, accept the Islamic teacher's head scarf? Must the owner of the grocery shop accept the decision of his employee to wear what to the customers appear conspicuously strange symbols or clothes? Must the Turkish father accept coeducational sports for his daughters at public schools?

In all these cases religious freedom tests the neutrality of the state. Frequently neutrality is threatened by the predominance of a majority culture, which abuses its historically acquired influence and definitional power to decide according to its own standards what shall be considered the norms and values of the political culture which is expected to be equally shared by all.[7] This implicit fusion of the common political culture with a divisive majority culture leads to the infiltration of the manifest legal form by inconspicuous cultural substance, thus distorting the very procedural nature of a democratic order. After all, the moral *substance* of democratic principles is spelled out in terms of legal *procedures* that can only build up legitimacy because they enjoy a reputation of granting impartiality by focusing consideration on all interests equally.

Legal procedures thus stand to lose the force to found legitimacy if notions of a substantial ethical life slowly creep into the interpretation and practice of formal requirements. In this regard, political neutrality can be violated just as easily by the secular or laical side as by the religious camp.

For the one side, the paramount example is the *affaire foulard*, for the other, the response of the Bavarian State government to the German Supreme Court's judgment on whether crucifixes should be mandatory for classrooms in elementary schools. In the former case, the headmaster of a French school prohibited Muslim girls to wear their traditional head scarves; in the other, the German Supreme Court agreed with the complaint brought by anthroposophical parents that there should be no crucifix in the classroom in which their daughter had to sit for lessons. In the French case, positive religious freedom is called into question; in the German case, it is the negative version which is cast into doubt. The Catholic opponents of the crucifix verdict of our Supreme Court defend the religious symbol of the crucified Christ as an expression of 'Occidental values' and thus as part of a political culture which all citizens may be expected to share. This is the classical case of a political over-generalization of a regionally dominant religious practice, as it was reflected in the Bavarian Public Primary School Order of 1983. By contrast, in France the Muslim pupils were forbidden from wearing head scarves – the laical argument given was that religion is a private matter that has to be kept out of the public domain. This is the case of a secularist interpretation of the constitution that must face the challenge whether the republican interpretation of constitutional principles that prevails in France is not too 'strong' and is thus not able to avoid violating due neutrality of the state vis-à-vis legitimate claims of a religious minority to enjoy the right of self-expression and to receive public recognition.

These legal conflicts show why the spread of religious tolerance – and we have seen that it was already a driving force for the emergence of democracies – has now become also a stimulus for developing further cultural rights. The inclusion of religious minorities in the political community kindles and fosters sensitivity to the claims of other discriminated groups. The recognition of religious pluralism can fulfill the role of a pace-maker in legal development, as it makes us aware in an exemplary fashion of the *claims of minorities to civic inclusion*. One might object that the debate on multiculturalism hinges less on neglecting religious minorities than on other issues such as defining national holidays, specifying official language(s), promoting instruction for ethnic and national minorities, set quotas for women, coloured people, indigenous populations at the working place, in schools or politics. From the viewpoint of equal inclusion of all citizens, however, religious discrimination takes its place in the long list of forms of cultural and linguistic, ethnic and racial, sexual and physical discrimination, and thus function as a pacemaker of 'cultural rights'. Let me explain what I mean by this term.

Inclusion refers to one of two aspects of the equal standing of citizens, or civic equality. Although the discrimination of minorities is usually associated with social under-privileging, it is well worth keeping these two categories of unequal treatment separate. The one is measured against the yardstick of *distributive justice*, the other against that of *full membership*.[8] From the viewpoint of distributive justice, the principle of equal treatment of everybody requires that all citizens have the same opportunities to make actual use of equally distributed rights and liberties in order to realize their own particular life plans. Political struggles and social movements opposing status deprivation and fighting for redistribution are fueled by the experiences of injustice at the level of distributive justice. By contrast, the struggles that relate to the *recognition of a specific collective identity* are based on a different kind of experience of injustice – not status deprivation but disregard, marginalization or exclusion depending on membership in a group, considered as 'inferior' according to prevailing standards.[9] From this aspect of incomplete inclusion, overcoming religious discrimination is the pacemaker for a new kind of cultural rights.

Cultural rights serve, as does the freedom to practice one's religion, the purpose of guaranteeing all citizens equal access to those associations, communication patterns, traditions and practices, which they respectively deem important in order to develop and maintain their personal identities. Cultural rights need not in each case refer to the ascribed group of origin; the personal identity in need of protection can just as well be based on a chosen and achieved environment. Religious convictions and practices have a decisive influence on the ethical conception of believers in all cultures. Linguistic and cultural traditions are similarly relevant for the formation and maintenance of one's own personal identity. In light of this insight we need to revise the traditional conception of the 'legal person'. The individuation of natural persons occurs through socialization. Individuals socialized in this manner can form and stabilize their identity only within a network of relationships of reciprocal recognition. This should have consequences for the protection of the integrity of the legal person – and for an intersubjectivist expansion of a person concept that has to date been tailored to the narrow lens of the tradition of possessive individualism. All rights protecting the integrity of an individual define the legal status of that person. These rights must now extend to the access to that community's matrix of experience, communication, and recognition, within which people can articulate their self-understanding and maintain their identity.

From this angle, cultural rights are introduced as individual rights in the first place. In line with the model of religious freedom, they are what German lawyers call 'subjective rights', designed for the purpose of granting full inclusion.[10] The point of cultural rights is to guarantee all citizens equal access to cultural environments, interpersonal relations and traditions as far as these are essential for them to form and secure their personal identity.

Yet cultural rights do not just mean 'more difference' and 'more independence' for cultural groups and their leaders. Members of discriminated groups do not enjoy equal cultural rights 'free of charge'. They cannot benefit from a morality of equal inclusion without themselves making this morality their own. The cognitive demand the liberal state makes of religious communities is all the same for 'strong' secular communities (such as national or ethnic minorities, immigrant or indigenous populations, descendants of slave cultures, etc.).[11] The traditions they continue open up 'world perspectives' that, *like* religious worldviews, can come into conflict with one another.[12] Therefore, cultural groups are equally expected to adapt their internal ethos to the egalitarian standards of the community at large. Some of them may find this even tougher than do those communities who are able to resort to the highly developed conceptual resources of one or the other of the great world religions. In any case, the leap in reflexivity that has come to characterize the modernization of religious consciousness within liberal societies provides a model for the mind-set of secular groups in multicultural societies as well. A multiculturalism that does not misunderstand itself does not constitute a *one-way street* to cultural self-assertion by groups with their own collective identities. The coexistence of different life forms as equals must not be allowed to prompt segmentation. Instead, it requires the integration of all citizens – and their mutual recognition across cultural divisions as citizens – within the framework of a shared political culture. Citizens are equally empowered to develop what is for them their cultural identity and might appear to others as cultural idiosyncrasies, but only under the condition that all of them (across boundaries) understand themselves to be citizens of one and the same political community. From this point of view, the very same normative base of the constitution that justifies cultural rights and entitlements likewise limits a kind of aggressive self-assertion that leads to fragmenting the larger community.

PART II

Cultural Technologies and Social Transformations

INTRODUCTION

Cultural technologies engender social transformations, and vice versa. This section examines the scale, structure and organisation of cultural organisations, including the media, the film industry and the internet, and in so doing examines how the financing, institutional structures, management and political involvements of these industries shapes the nature of cultural production and cultural flows. People's values, aspirations and expectations are changing; their symbols, life ways and ideals are altering; and their identities, self-understandings and perspectives are being transformed. Cultures have never been static, but the scale of change, its interconnected and media mediated nature are new.

The means through which we achieve symbolic production, and the social contexts of production are often argued to have an impact of how we imagine ourselves and others. In what ways is globalisation affecting this mediation process? What cultural changes can be ascribed to this process? **John Tomlinson** approaches the question of cultural change and globalisation by bringing our attention to the question of how routine practices and experiences with electronic media technologies 'transform the texture of everyday life in a globalized world'. He discusses how the speed and proximity of symbolic production is changing the way we perceive not only work-life boundaries, but also relationships between ourselves and others. Discussing a number of contemporary examples of how different communities around the world are mediated by and through ICT technologies, **Don Slater** argues that if our task is to understand something of how 'culture' constitutes 'globalisation', then this necessitates an understanding of the internet as a cultural artefact, in all its deep complexity. In this regard, an understanding of the relationship of culture to this particular technology requires us to envisage how and what people see in the internet, and what they perform through it. Slater highlights a paradox – namely that the terrain of the internet and ICTs in general has prompted very aggressive claims about the production and multiplication of diversity, yet there is a certain expectation and language of irresistible uniformity.

Reflecting on the role of the media in shaping practices and perceptions of globalisation, **Danny Schechter** reminds us that the shaping of political issues and attitudes has much to do with the way in which the experience of politics is transmitted, mediated and explained by the media. It does so, Schechter contends, through entertainment programming that influences the discourses in our imaginations, frames the agendas we consider, and informs our modes of habitation. Despite acknowledging the transformative capacities that contemporary media provides, Schechter nevertheless remains boldly critical of how many (dominant) media products 'depoliticizes our politics' and argues that the 'media problem is at the heart of the political crisis in America'.

How can we understand the relationship between technological mediation of culture, the manifold challenges that globalisation brings, and cultural responses to this process? Moreover, how might culture itself be mediating this process? **Augustus Casely-Hayford** examines the role of changing communications technologies on cultural interpretation and participation. He gives us a rich account of how technological change – and its social mediation – is augmenting traditional modes of communication. Casely-Hayford compares the digital arena to a Ghanaian piece of cloth passed on within his family; fluid, open and malleable through which we are empowered to participate and re-negotiate in the sense of augmenting traditional modes of communication with the new digital possibilities on offer. He forces us to consider the ways in which changing technological spaces are mediums for selective social interaction and symbolic belonging, and in this regard asks us to reflect on whether or not the greater fluidity of interpretation and collective experience provided by the digital arena allows individuals to perhaps better navigate the decisions about how they engage with and interpret their experiences.

Performance, film, and music are crucial cultural technologies that amplify, shape and create new manifestations of cultural interpretation, new arenas of meaning. Through what frame can we understand the role of film and music in this process? **John Hutnyk** focuses on the hybrid fora of digital music combined with classical cinematic traditions in the Asian Dub Foundation's performances. Examining this case through a Heideggarian lens, where technology is thought of as something more than simply an instrumental tool, Hutnyk asks what to make of this combination, and offers a series of reflections on how technology frames the world for us yet still endows us with responsibility for that reflection. Hutnyk situates himself in this debate such that technology is seen as constitutive and empowering of subjectivity.

Chapter 7

Global Immediacy

*John Tomlinson**

N
o enquiry into contemporary globalization can get far without discovering media and communications systems and their associated technologies deeply and complexly embedded within the processes that are reshaping our world. But how can we best understand this ubiquitous implication of the media in the globalization process? The problem is made difficult not only because of the complex interaction between the media and other dynamics of global modernity – in particular global capitalism – but because 'the media' refers in a deceptively familiar way to a rather complicated entity: an *ensemble* of technologies and institutions which have at the same time become the dominant cultural form of our time, the mode and context of an increasing proportion of human experience.

There are of course many ways of approaching the analysis of such a complex entity: interrogations of its institutional structures, its political economy, its technological ramifications and trajectory, its professional practices, values and informing ideologies, the impact of media 'texts' on consumers and audiences, the integration of media into the political process and so on. But I want to pose a question, as it were, to the *totality* of the media ensemble as it is integrated into the globalization process. Can we identify any emergent properties of the culture distributed by globalization that are attributable to, or at least significantly inflected by, the routine 'mediatization' of everyday life?

* **John Tomlinson** is Professor of Cultural Sociology and Director of the Institute for Cultural Analysis, Nottingham Trent University, and is head of research in Communications, Media and Cultural Studies and Director designate of NICA. His books include *Cultural Imperialism* (Pinter, 1991) and *Globalization and Culture* (Polity Press, 1999). His latest book, *The Culture of Speed: The Coming of Immediacy*, is published by Sage in October 2007. His current research includes work on the impact of globalization in China and the analysis of contemporary values. He has published on issues of globalisation, cosmopolitanism, modernity, identity, media and culture across a range of disciplines from sociology, anthropology and media studies to geography, urban studies and development studies.

It is important to distinguish this question – rough hewn and speculative though it is – from the rather more common one of whether a globalized media is leading to the emergence of a 'global culture'. When this is posed, what is almost invariably intended is a speculation on the coming to dominance of one particular existing culture. Predominantly this speculation is couched in a pessimistic critique: of global consumer capitalism, Americanization, Westernization and so on. Occasionally we find it expressed in a more optimistic light, in the search for common 'post-territorial' cultural values and identity positions which may give the clue to a progressive cosmopolitan disposition, freed from national, ethnic or sectarian agendas. But in either case speculation on an emergent global culture tends to focus on the *contents* of culture, be these artefacts and their symbolic meanings, myths and beliefs, tastes, styles, values and attitudes.

There are well known problems with this sort of speculation over the universalizing of a particular cultural content which need no rehearsal here.[1] But what is important to notice is how this approach casts the media in the simple role of messenger delivering a determinant content. This is not what I have in mind. I want to direct a question at the media themselves, not at the cultures they are assumed to 'transmit'. It is a question of what implications the global distribution of a mediated culture *itself* might have. Specifically, how do the routine practices, experiences and protocols associated with electronic media technologies and their operative institutions transform the texture of everyday life in a globalized world?

To begin to answer this question I shall first try to encapsulate the quality of our routine interactions with a globalized and globalizing media by introducing into the discussion a new general concept that I will call 'global immediacy'. What I mean by global immediacy is not an emergent culture as such; the term it is better understood as expressing a general *condition* attaching to cultural experience, particularly by dint of its association with media institutions and technologies.

What is immediacy? For our purposes the term has two relevant connected meanings. In relation to space, as the *Oxford English Dictionary* gives it, 'direct relation or connection ... proximate, nearest, next, close, near'; and in relation to time, 'pertaining to the time current or instant ... occurring without delay or lapse in time, done at once; instant'. In the most abstract terms then, immediacy is a condition recognizably linked to the time-space compression of globalization. And the terminological felicity that places 'media' literally and exactly at the word's centre invites us to see these compressions as deriving, in some proportion at least, from the impact of media technologies and institutions. Let's accept this invitation and return later to the question of proportion.

Putting a little more flesh on the bare bones of time and space compression we can say that immediacy implies, firstly, ideas of the acceleration of the pace of life and a culture of instantaneity, adapted and accustomed to the rapid delivery of goods and (particularly) information. And underpinning this, an economy and an associated work culture geared not just to sustaining, but to constantly increasing this tempo of life. Simultaneously, however, immediacy can be taken to imply a sense of directness, of cultural *proximity*. Etymologically this is, indeed, the primary sense: from the late Latin 'immedia-tus', 'not separated'. In this second sense immediacy suggests not just an accel-eration in culture, but a distinct *quality* to cultural experience. This may be grasped as an increasing routine connectedness both with other people and with the access points (typically now, websites) of the institutions that afford and govern modern social existence. Daily life becomes increasingly saturated in communicational practices and increasingly dependent on the ubiquitous presence-availability, via electronic media, of informational and human resources. And this density of communicational connectedness promotes a new kind of intensity in everyday experience, mixing pace and vibrancy with an increase in communicational demands on the individual and, arguably, a new sense of compulsion and 'drivenness' in life.

'FAST CAPITALISM'

To help develop these twin themes of speed and proximity in the condition of immediacy we can begin with a brief example. BlackBerry hand-held mobile wireless devices are high-end examples of what we can call globalizing media technologies. In their 2006 advertising campaign the marketers of the BlackBerry 8700 series describe the product as 'Faster than the speed of life'. This claim is redeemed in the advert by a list of the functions the BlackBerry can perform, inter alia, 'Open attachments, Get football results, Review contract arrangements, Book restaurants, Follow share prices, Search on Google, Update travel arrangements, Track competitors'. Even allowing for the tailor-ing of the advertisement to the product's distinct target consumer profile, we can draw some general inferences.

The BlackBerry 8700 is presented as a way of keeping pace with an acceler-ating modern life, indeed of staying ahead of the game. The assumption that modern life is intrinsically fast moving is of course crucial to a marketing strat-egy which attempts to establish the product as essential to social competence. But this ratcheting up of the pace of life owes much to the widespread use of the mobile integrated media technologies of which BlackBerry is a part. The device might then be seen as a sort of *pharmakon* object, at once the poison and the cure.

Well not quite. For although this sort of media technology is at the same time an instrument, a commodity and a cultural form – and so plausibly interpreted as having a cultural impact on its own account – there are other important contexts to be considered. The most obvious one, highlighted in the rhetoric of the advertisement, is what has been recently dubbed – to the extent of becoming the title of an online journal – 'Fast Capitalism' (www.fastcapitalism.com).

In an obvious sense, increasing speed in the circulation of capital has been a defining feature of modern industrial capitalist economies ever since their inception. But the idea of fast capitalism points us towards something new, a step change in pace facilitated by the integration of media and communications systems into the operations of capitalist production, exchange and indeed culture.[2] In the most general sense this can be seen as an increase in the intensity, energy and mobility of the capitalist order overall. In its global scope, impatient with various forms of constraint and regulation, this 'turbo-capitalism' might look like a recrudescence of the original impulses of nineteenth-century free-market liberalism.[3] But what has enabled this to occur are some qualitative changes in the nature of capitalism. Some of these are changes in the techniques of the production and exchange of actual commodities, particularly those attributable to the wider connectivity of globalization – flexible, global sourcing of materials and components, a global distribution of labour. Others are essentially sophistications in the manipulation of the capitalist market, particularly in the sphere of finance capital where we see increasing speculation on the future value of commodities ('futures') and financial trading at a high level of abstraction from the actual exchange of commodities through the use of synthetic instruments collectively known as 'derivatives'. Such financial instruments and the associated use of high-risk financing from outside the conventional bonds, equities and currency markets are deeply implicated in both the intense high-speed speculative activity of the contemporary global market and in the turbulence and frequent threats of crisis that accompanies this.[4]

What is significant for the present argument is that, whether in the conventional operations of the capitalist market or in these parasitic forms, it is media and communications systems that provide their essential *modus operandi*. What makes contemporary capitalism fast are communication-rich systems: from Web-based work flow systems and 'just-in-time' delivery logistics to the near-instantaneous speed of computerized, networked fund-transfer systems combined with the speed of market intelligence via the internet. It is this integration of media systems into global capitalism which provides the key dynamic behind the 'market reality of increased global competitiveness' – a phrase which has become so familiar in the mouths of politicians chastising dissent from neo-liberal economic policies.

What sort of cultural experience accompanies these economic trends? The BlackBerry advertisement gives us another clue to this, in the way that its list of attractions integrates 'hard' and 'soft' activities: 'Track competitors' and 'Get football results'. The condition of immediacy seems to involve a curious mixing of work and leisure. A good example of this is the creeping encroachment of work activities into home and family time and space, particularly via the use of networked computers. For example, the tendency to send or to pick up work-related emails outside normal working hours is now widespread (not least among academics). There is a straightforward sense in which this is exploitative in simply extracting more labour time from employees than is contracted for. And of course, though this practice may be regarded, contractually, as voluntary, it is not cynical to see it as a tacit requirement of performance in competitive work environments. Thus the sending off of emails time-stamped late in the evening or early in the morning may be regarded as a practice of career 'image management'. And yet, on the other hand, it would be uselessly cynical not to allow that for some – many – people and in many circumstances, this sort of flexible integration represents a genuine exercise of autonomous time use and convenience.

One way of regarding this blending of work and home life is, reversing the terms of E.P. Thompson's classic discussion, as a rather ironic shift away from the 'time orientation' to labour imposed within clock-regulated, Taylorist factory capitalism back to the 'task orientation' of pre-industrial work culture in which, 'social interaction and labour are intermingled – the working day lengthens or contracts according to the task.'[5] And if this does grasp the experience of many people of the reach of capitalist-inflected work relations into private life, it points us to another interesting feature of the condition of immediacy: its qualities of 'lightness' and 'softness'.

In this context it is the comparative softness of work schedules that demand and obtain more of us without imposing the harder disciplines of the time clock and the factory whistle. But there is also a certain lightness and softness in the actual exertions and manipulations associated with the use of media and communications technologies – in the acts of typing, clicking, scrolling and texting and the immediacy of the responses that these elicit – which in a sense also blur the boundaries of work and play. For what really differentiates a work-oriented email from a message sent about, say, a sports fixture, or web-research for a work project as opposed to that done to help the children with their home-work? Surely little other than, as Thompson puts it, 'a distinction between [the] employer's time and [the worker's] "own" time'.[6] And this is a distinction that, with so little actual task differentiation involved, is often hard to maintain.

I don't, however, want to give the impression that the condition of imme-diacy is all sweetness and light, that it somehow resolves the alienations of labour by blending them with playfulness. Fast capitalism has lightened its structures and processes, notably by shedding some of its older encumbrances – heavy plant, large permanent and often powerfully unionized workforces. But as Zygmunt Bauman insists in employing the metaphor of 'liquid' moder-nity – this has not made modern experience 'light' in the sense of being easy, comfortable and anxiety-free, even for those who are, as it were, the economic winners in capitalist globalization.[7]

But what can be said is that the sharp differentiations between the culture of work and the culture of consumer-inflected leisure are blurring as societies emerge from an era in which heavy, labour-intensive industry dominated and organized daily life into clear-cut time-space regimes. Indeed some have argued that consumption itself has become a form of labour. Teresa Brennan, for instance, claims that consumer practices in fast capitalism involve a significant element of unpaid labour, an element that is necessary to offset escalating costs of distribution needed to match an accelerating speed of production:

> To go online and buy products, or book airline tickets, is to perform deliv-ery work. Such work is squeezed into the time once given to rest and revival. The turn of the century has witnessed a shift in the burden of ser-vice labour, from producer to consumer.[8]

Such online consumer practices take time and a certain level of skill, and are often frustrating. And yet they don't quite seem like 'work' in the way we have become accustomed to view it.

LEGERDEMAIN

Attempting to apply a little more precision to the way in which routine media practices are implicated in immediacy, we can retain the general notion of lightness but characterize this as both a literal and a figurative *legerdemain*. This sleight of hand can be understood both as a lightness of touch and as a mystification.

In the first sense it refers us to a new set of commonplace bodily practices which are particularly underlined by the lightness of our interaction with new communications technologies: with keyboards, keypads, screens, handsets and remote controls. These manipulations are deft and smoothly choreographed into our working (and playing) rhythms, almost seeming less physical operations than gestures. And this lightness of touch is closely associated with the perception of immediate and ubiquitous access. Things – and particularly people – do often seem to be pretty much immediately available simply by the lightest pressure on a keypad. (To the extent that we may feel an unreasonable resentment when, occasionally, the communication is not instantaneously effected: when someone's mobile phone is switched off, or the email response does not appear by return in our inbox.) This association of physical lightness and (near) effortlessness in the operation of communications technologies with a tacit assumption of the instant and constant availability of things and people – of a world, as it were, waiting to be accessed – is characteristic of the experience of immediacy.

But this perception raises the other sense of a *legerdemain* – something like an act of conjuring which, while offering delights, nonetheless involves certain concealments and deceptions. One of these is the concealing of the costs and consequences of the immediate satisfaction of consumer desire. For the routine expectation of immediate connectivity is closely related in the context of fast capitalism with an expectation of open-ended growth in consumption. This is not, of course, to say that wealth distribution becomes more equal. Nonetheless, in developed economies, and for larger sectors of the population within these economies, there exists a broad assumption that goods and particularly technological advances, will simply and continuously be delivered, become affordable, morph from luxuries into necessities. Whatever else may be taking place in our personal biographies, and whatever uncertainties and anxieties are born out of the turbulence of global modernity, the promise of global immediacy is that 'stuff arrives'. There is then arguably a new complacency in consumer culture that matches the insouciant style of contemporary communicational practice. What this conceals of course is the inescapable material cost of unrestricted consumption growth, in the exploitation, somewhere in the world, of the natural environment and of human labour.

When such issues are broached in relation to the media, the most common assumption is that it is the saturation of media content with images of the good life as one of high consumption – be this in advertising or in actual programming – that is the culprit. The problem is posed as one of ideology. While not denying this effect, I am suggesting something rather different. It is that we might trace some of the responsibility for promoting broad expectations of the open-ended and consequence-free delivery of new consumer goods to the nature of mediated experience itself. That the experience of instant and effortless access and delivery in telemediated communication may be encouraging unrealistic expectations of unproblematic abundance and ubiquity in the other orders of everyday life.

This thought brings us back, in conclusion, to the question of proportion that I raised earlier. The media without doubt occupy a central place in globalized cultures, and indeed constitute the most important modality though which most people now access the world. But, set against the huge range of benefits that this brings, is the danger that this modality comes to assume a disproportionate role in our cultural self-understanding; that we come to mistake an immediacy of contact limited to the modality of electronic communication for a more general and dramatic evolution. The risk is that we come, via the routine accomplishments of telepresence, to a confused understanding of the nature and limitations of the human condition, particularly of the existential primacy of embodiment.[9] In an earlier era of modernity the constraints of embodiment and the concrete realities of physical distance were preserved in a set of relatively stable distinctions: between here and elsewhere, now and later, desire and its fulfilment. The challenge of responding to global immediacy is to ensure that these ontological distinctions – which have also been the grounds of significant human values – do not, in the process, slip from our grasp.

Chapter 8

Glimpsing God in the Internet

*Don Slater**

There is one overriding sense in which 'culture' appears to be a driver behind 'the internet' as a 'globalizing' agent: new media technologies offer themselves as prestige objects of material culture through which people exchange, objectify and perform diverse notions of 'the global', of 'the future' and of translocal interconnection. This is very far from saying that we can identify 'a culture' that stands behind the internet, let alone a new culture that has been produced by it. Rather, we might simply say – in Lévi-Strauss's old phrase – that many people have found the internet 'good to think with', and that the things they think with it tend to be about the globe and about the future. Let me give a few examples from my past research:[1]

Trinidad, 1999: a Catholic charismatic eloquently argues that she experiences in the global scale and complexity of the internet a 'sense of transcendence' that brings the user closer to God. Similarly, an Apostolic Christian feels deeply that God *had* to give humanity the internet so that they could finally envisage the coming future of global salvation: 'since the net is so global it immediately allows the church to feel global', and is therefore given by God to realize his plans. And a Pentecostal with much media experience was clear that the internet, along with TV and radio, were 'closer to the structure of a Pentecostal mind in terms of the relationship they have got: God is immediate'.[2]

* **Don Slater** is a Reader in Sociology at the London School Economics. His research interests include theories of consumption (*Consumer Culture and Modernity*, Polity, 1997); sociology of economic life (*The Technological Economy*, with Andrew Barry, Routledge, 2005); and visual culture (photography). For the past seven years he has been engaged in ethnographies of new media use in non-northern places (e.g. *The Internet: An Ethnographic Approach*, with Daniel Miller, Berg, 2000), and is currently completing a book-length treatment of this research agenda, *New Media, Globalization and Development* (Polity).

Trinidad, June, 1999: Canadian representatives of IBM and KPMG hold a breakfast seminar for Trinidadian business leaders. The message they deliver is that the internet and information-based economy is the last train to global modernity, productivity and profit. It has already left the station, but if the Trinidadian elite run very quickly they might just jump on the caboose. The Trini response is both feverish and self-castigating: the participants already entirely accepted that the internet is the inevitable future; the seminar simply stunned them with the amount of ground they had already lost, yet again, in securing their proper place on the global stage; they felt (and were told) that this was their 'last chance'.

Ghana, 2002–4: the Ghanaian government launches a series of ICT (information and communication technology) policy documents that envisage transforming the country from agricultural society to information society within twenty years, leaping over the industrial age. This embrace of informationalization is both an alliance with prevalent development and business discourses, and a thorough break with previous Ghanaian development narratives. The documents build on deeply internalized concepts of information society drawn from international academics, development agencies, business experience and consultants; these concepts are performed through, inter alia, policy documents, seminars, informal contacts, enforcement through 'conditionality', rhetorical constructions and so on. The resulting documents project a top-down transformation of every aspect of Ghanaian governance and society, covering everything from health and education services to the generation of a software programming elite and off-shoring operations.

Ghana, 2003, fieldsite in Accra: in an extremely poor migrant area, there is large-scale and enthusiastic internet use, particularly by young people, in up to ten internet cafes along the local high street. Almost none of these skilled users has ever knowingly visited a website, let alone obtained through any internet facility anything that would be construed as 'information' by their government or by ICT and development professionals. For these young users, 'the internet' is almost exclusively a chat facility (MSN, Yahoo) through which they seek to accumulate foreign contacts that might yield various values: money, help with visas, tickets abroad, invitations, help in getting a foreign education, a marriage partner, or simply a long list of foreign contacts to show one's friends. A Ghanaian academic colleague describes internet use simply as the latest 'cargo cult': if all value is abroad, the internet enables both practical and symbolic enactments of escape. More concretely, people understand the new technology in terms of a very old logic in which 'success in life depends on being enmeshed in a web of relationships';[3] the internet is a means by which that 'web' might more effectively enmesh northerners.

North America, early 1990s: cyberculture activists perceive in the internet the achievement of both virtuality and disembedding, whereby identity is detached from the essentialism of the body on the one hand and physical social context on the other. Through the internet we might thereby achieve or demonstrate the truth of identity, which is its lack of truth, its constructed and performed nature. 'You are what you type': culminating a long tradition that perhaps starts with psychedelia, and persists through poststructuralism, they recognize that identity fixed by notions of authenticity and normativity is oppressive, and liberation lies in reflexively enacting identity as fluid, contradictory and constructed in performance.

Berkeley, mid-1990s: while 'networks constitute the fundamental pattern of human life at all stages', it is only with the advent of the internet that this form of social organization can transcend the limitations that have so far subordinated it to hierarchical structures. The internet now enables and epitomizes the emergence of a new network society, which potentially resolves three social processes: a crisis in the industrial mode of production; the profusion of 'freedom-oriented cultural social movements'; and the rise of technically-driven informationalism.[4]

The point of telling these stories is obviously not to decide which are true or false, let alone to opt for any one of them (though the Catholic charismatic was rather persuasive). Rather, they suggest that if our task is to understand something of how 'culture' constitutes 'globalization', then we need to confront 'the internet' as a cultural artefact in all its deep complexity: what do people *see* in the internet, and therefore what do they seek to make it into and what do they try to perform through it? Whether they glimpse God, network society or the truth of human identity there, the internet evidently evokes some very epic visions.

There are two simple responses to this approach, each of which is partially true: perhaps it is obvious that the internet would serve people as an idiom for thinking global futures because, on the one hand, the internet is in fact capable of connecting anyone to anywhere, instantaneously; and on the other hand, because these affordances have been relayed through highly prestigious global discourses (particularly American ones, as usual) so that the story of the inevitable coming of the information age has simply become global common sense. That is to say, the internet is 'good to think' global futures because this is either, or both, an intrinsic technical property or the upshot of global ideologies.

Neither point is wrong as such, but they don't take us very far. Any two people connected up to the internet (or viewing it at a remove) are alike only in that they are using an apparatus that is indeed capable of translocal connections. Beyond that, their understandings of the global, the internet and connection itself are likely to be consequentially different (e.g. religious 'transcendence' versus 'last train to profitability'). By the same token, their relationship to internationally pervasive discourses is likely to be mediated through very different histories and diverse institutional relays, power differentials and political stances (e.g. donor dependence in Ghana versus oil-based industrialization in Trinidad).

In both cases, if we were to focus on the commonality ('through the internet everyone is somehow bound up with globalization') rather than the differences ('both internet and relations to the global are always performed quite differently') then we would be merely replicating what we are supposed to be analysing: we would be simply globalizing the concept of 'globalization', using the image and practice of 'internet' to concretize and perform the idea of a globalized world or a network society.

However, there is another problem with both points, one which takes us more explicitly to the issue of culture. The first of these points is a realist argument about the nature of the technology and its effects; the second is an argument about discourse, representation or ideology. The tendency is to keep them separate, and identify the latter as the 'cultural' aspect: there is the global spread of new mediations on the one hand, and on the other hand there is the 'hype' (from cyberculture, to vice-presidential proclamations about information superhighways, through dot.com booms and busts, to WSIS, to Web2.0). Indeed much of my own research gets funded on precisely this basis: overseas development agencies want research that will 'separate the hype from the reality', and prove, unambiguously, whether or not ICTs really do have an impact on development goals.

However, the stories above are *not* about 'hype', or about culture as systems of representation or discourse. They are about cosmologies, or the 'webs of significance'[5] that permeate practical forms of action, whether logging onto the internet in Accra or writing World Bank documents with a view to rationalizing global ICT and development policy. In this sense, the stories above are all snapshots of 'thick descriptions'. What they suggest is that it is 'culture' all the way down: these cosmologies are practical engagements with the world through which ICTs are understood and constructed; conversely, ICTs are deployed to reproduce and enact quite large-scale understandings of the world. 'Separating the hype from the reality' is precisely what one cannot do if the internet, as material culture, is largely constituted in, and as, cosmological thinking about the nature of a changing globe, thinking carried out in diverse ways by diverse people, northern and southern.

If the cosmologies are diverse in that people 'see' in the internet (and rationally act upon) anything from the presence of God to epochal social transformation, then there is at least equal diversity in what they actually take 'the internet' to mean. In fact, 'the internet' only appears as one thing (*the* internet) when people are looking at it from within a particular cosmology. We can approach this from several angles.

Firstly, 'the internet' is never the same object in different places, even in the most mechanical sense. For the Ghanaian government, buying into transnational programmes of informationalization, 'the internet' was e-government: they were clear that 'the internet' *is* web-sites for public information access plus email and intranets for more effective government. However, for Ghanaian youth websites barely existed and were simply not part of *their* internet, which they defined as a chat medium. The farce of much ICT in development is often that users and policy-makers, 'beneficiaries' and elites, are not even talking about the same machine, yet both may be skilled users of their own machine.

Secondly, the problem is more complicated because 'the internet' is usually a proxy for much wider constructions, such as 'ICTs', 'IT' or 'information society'. Use of the word 'internet' marks out particularly prestigious narratives of emergent information societies, but then often scoops up other technologies into the same narrative, producing great confusion. For example, Ghanaian plans for their coming information society focused on the internet but then pointed to mobile phones as if they were part of the same story. Our own research indicated that internet and mobile phone use in Ghana represented two different and fundamentally opposed processes: whereas internet was focused on a somewhat 'magical' connection to northern values, mobile phones were already profoundly embedded in the practices of daily life and in maintaining existing social networks.[6] Internet, as a proxy for information society, was also defined so that it excluded older ICTs that had no place in the prestige northern cosmologies of the globe and its future: radio was hugely popular and embedded in everyday life, was seen as central to the recent democratization of Ghana, and had close community ties through local language broadcasting, connection to church networks as well as music culture, and a very creative earlier generation of community radio activists. Yet radio had no place in government ICT policy, was largely excluded from Ghanaian preparations for WSIS, and was not connected to ICT (read 'internet') projects. We can go further: the most important ICT in rural Ghana was clearly roads and buses, and any medium which does not connect with the movement of people-with-messages can have very little impact or relevance. Yet within cosmologies of 'information society', it provoked a sense of ritual defilement even to put roads and internet in the same sentence let alone the same plan.

This situation prompts recourse to Actor Network Theory.[7] Crudely put, entities like 'the internet' are given a false unity and stability within these various cosmologies – they are 'black boxed' – whereas their productive use depends on opening them out to interconnection, to extensive enrolment of the materials and people to hand, to taking new material and institutional shapes, and to the construction of contingent assemblages (e.g. internet + radio + roads = a useful ICT). The guiding concept in all the studies on which this chapter is based was 'communicative ecology': instead of studying the 'impact' of a new communicative machine ('the internet') on 'a culture', or of a local culture on a new machine, let us look at what actually counts as an act of communication, or a medium, or information in a particular place. Taking this approach, it is easier to open the black boxes. Instead of assuming that we know in advance what the internet is (let alone what the local culture is), we instead focus on the diverse things that actual people assemble into systems for communicating: machines, roads, social networks, theories, global discourses and much more.

Thirdly, even where we can reasonably assume that we are talking about a similar feature of the same object ('the internet'), the differences overwhelm the similarities. It is clearly true that most people understand the internet in terms of global connectivity (for example, rural Sri Lankan children, who had often never seen a computer, regularly described the internet as extremely fast mail that you can send anywhere). But consider how 'the globe' and 'globalization' are constructed through the material culture of the internet in the following cases, all focused on youth. In Ghana, the internet is seen by poor young users as a conduit to northern goods that replicates histories of donor dependency, post-colonial migration and structural adjustment livelihood strategies: for these users, 'the global' is identified with specific geographical routes to poverty reduction, and these are developed through internet, but not mobile phone, use.

By contrast, rural Sri Lankan youth, steeped in a village-centred moral universe, regarded global connectivity as a means by which 'the globe' can be accorded the privilege to see website photographs of their village shrines and local landscape; and by which migrant Sri Lankan labourers in the Middle East could see and hear the village. Young Trinidadians, on the other hand, see themselves as naturally global actors who have been marginalized by global scenes (educational, economic, musical, whatever), or have had to leave Trinidad for London, Toronto or New York in order to realize their cosmopolitan sense of themselves. They prided themselves on their knowledge of other places, and their ability to operate anywhere, absorb anything on their own terms. Unlike with Ghanaian youths, for example, it was definitely not cool to copy northern hiphop styles: soca music had always absorbed whatever it encountered within its own aesthetic structures, and the expanded contacts afforded by the internet developed along precisely the same lines.

All these stories involve 'the global', perform the global; they even globalize. But they are obviously more than a matter of local instantiations of something global called 'globalization' or 'the internet'. They also signify more than the mediation of the global through local conditions. They are about the production of different globes and global connections, different maps and different journeys. And this leads to a fourth issue: these different maps and journeys, these different internets, are not 'culture' in the vague sense that the internet is somehow moulded by local or indigenous or traditional values and beliefs, or that culture forms a 'context' for assimilating a given object. What people glimpse in the internet is both theoretical and practical, models of how the world works (or could work) and strategies for achieving goals within the kind of world they perceive.

Let's pursue this final point through another example: Meenakshi was a member of a women's self-help group (SHG) in a village in southern India. The group participated in a UNESCO project through which it received ICT equipment, plus a researcher/project worker for a year; equipment and worker were to be located in one of their member's houses. The original project proposal intended that the SHG should focus their ICT use on 'income generating activities': in this development discourse, ICTs should feed into income generation by various routes such as designing and printing marketing materials, learning skills online and by CD, email communication with experts, access to market information and so on. This initially framed the technologies as directly instrumental 'tools' within a vision of technical modernization.

Meenakshi and her colleagues had not previously encountered ICTs directly, but they had been represented to her in many ways: glimpsed in Bollywood films, in billboard ads for local private computer schools (one in her village carried the tag-line, 'computer education: boon for middle class'), from family connections in the cities, from local NGOs, from educated local people, from prior UNESCO visits and so on. In all these encounters, ICTs were self-evident framed as the inevitable future of the world, from local to national to regional to global scale; they summed up what it will now mean to be 'modern' and to survive in yet another new modernity. As the project developed, all of this was also negotiated, debated and rethought in engagements with other self-help groups, with the project worker and with UNESCO workers like myself. Indeed, Meenakshi and others were very clear that ICTs generally brought them into extensive global connections by means other than actually using them: the *transaction* of these technical objects involved conversations, networks, institutional ties that forged new geographies (and frankly the internet connection itself often didn't work).

In this context, Meenakshi to a great extent experienced ICTs as a new burden. She was an extremely poor woman, separated from her husband (and therefore of very problematic status), with a ten-year-old daughter, employed in coolie labour on roads and fields. She was already investing a staggering proportion of her income on private school tuition for her daughter. She would now have to invest in computer literacy in addition, because it was now accepted as an essential survival skill within any responsible mother's familial livelihood strategy.

Meenakshi accepted this level of sacrifice because she accepted the place of ICTs in the global future. However, she was very unclear as to how precisely these ICTs actually connected up to that future, let alone to particular career paths or other modes of advancing her daughter. That is to say, she was in precisely the same situation as UNESCO and me; indeed, the only reason I met her was that all of us were sure that ICTs were part of the future, in some sense, but could not specify quite how. We all had to generate development theories and strategies.

Meenakshi's theorization of the future through the idiom of ICTs followed two contrary routes, and she was quite typical in this respect. On the one hand, she assimilated ICTs to a much older development narrative: people advance their children by helping them to get educational credentials that should lead to secure white collar office jobs. Meenakshi had at this point never seen the inside of an office, but knew this to be the gold standard of social advancement. Whereas previously she would have had to invest in English language lessons and secretarial courses for her daughter, now it would take computer literacy as well.

On the other hand, Meenakshi's own encounter with ICTs – as opposed to her theorizing of development on her daughter's behalf – pointed towards a different line of analysis: Meenakshi loved this technology and was extremely adept. Although entirely illiterate, she could always find the right menu commands, produced very inventive drawings, wrote her name on screen, loved using a digital camera, and could run all the peripherals, such as the printers. Meenakshi perceived and acted upon a potential for empowerment and democracy, in which her access to technology and status within the group depended on her energy and skill in the matter at hand. The similarity to new economy visions of ICT-driven flattening of hierarchies, innovation and meritocracy is hard to avoid. However, this vision got her into trouble, and led to her and her daughter's temporary expulsion from the group: Meenakshi easily got the printer to work when the highest status woman (who also had a powerful relative and a college degree) floundered and failed. She was labelled as aggressive and insubordinate, and finally as corrupt.

Meenakshi therefore constructed not one but two configurations of technology, development theory and practical strategy. One assimilated new technology to a very old view of social structure while the other saw in technical relations the means for overturning social structures. One started from conventional narratives of social mobility through education; the other started from practical engagements with the technologies and with social relationships around the technologies. In both cases, however, particular objects (printers, computers) and models of social process are directly connected up because what is at stake are strategies and practices: again, both UNESCO and Meenakshi were concerned with ICTs in the first place because they are framed as 'the global future'; and in order to see how ICTs might be practically mobilized to achieve desired futures and connections, both had to act as development theorists. Whether it is useful to describe all this under the notion of 'culture' is another matter.

The whole terrain of internet and ICTs is seriously paradoxical. On the one hand, it has prompted the most extravagant claims about the production of diversity: visions of a world of promiscuous and unbounded interconnection, dissolving identities, allegiances and institutions into fluid and multiform networks, and based on a technical imaginary of centreless aggregations of semi-autonomous nodes. On the other hand, academic and public discourse has spoken a language of extreme uniformity, universalism and technological determinism: it is somehow inherent in the very nature of the internet to produce such a new world, wherever it is instantiated; and this process is somehow so irresistible that, despite local resistance or mediation, 'we' can glimpse the global future in this bit of material culture. In this sense, the cosmologies of internet spilling out of the north have also provided much of the energy and imagery for the idea of 'globalization' itself (after all, the term appeared at about the same time that the internet became a public obsession). It is probably also not a coincidence that internet-based visions of information society are arguably the first since nineteenth-century romantic nationalism to portray total and epochal social transformation in largely 'cultural' terms, in that a new communicative machine has become extrapolated into a new social order.

What is missing from these accounts is something simpler: the profusion of cultures, globes, technologies that arises from diverse people's attempts to make sense of what the world now is, how it works and how to live within it through their encounters with an object that seems capable of both representing and producing the world.

Chapter 9

The Politics of Culture and Culture as Politics

*Danny Schechter**

Culture and politics. Politics and culture. The two are entwined like twins to a not always visible umbilical chord. Modern politics operates in a cultural environment and is ultimately shaped by one as well. The same, of course, is true of the way politics impacts on and influences the cultural environment. The two interact in a symbiotic and mutually reinforcing framework.

In every society there is an official and mainstream culture broadly accepting of the status quo and defined by its values, rules, traditions, and assumptions. It is often guided by an elite operating within a well-understood power structure driven by written and unwritten rules. The rules of the game are not just set by rulers but are influenced by historical precedent and organizational procedures as in legal protocols and parliamentary or Congressional rules.

Most discussions of political culture revolve around formal documents and institutions. They establish the terms for elections and decision-making. In the United States, the system brands itself a democracy, an idea reinforced by our educational system and enshrined in our official ideology.

"A political culture is a distinctive and patterned form of political philosophy" explains the dominant view echoed in the Wikipedia:

> Most schools in the United States teach the Declaration of Independence, Constitution, Bill of Rights, and the writings of the Founding Fathers as the definition of the country's governing ideology. Among the core tenets of this ideology are the following:
>
> The government is answerable to citizens, who may change it through elections. The government's power in matters of religion, expression, and

---

* **Danny Schechter** is an American filmmaker, journalist, author and editor of Mediachannel.org, the world's largest online media issues network. Comments to dissector@medichannel.org.

law enforcement should be limited to prevent abuse of power. The laws should attach no special privilege to any citizen (that is, citizens should be equal before the law).

Individuals and political parties debate how this ideology applies to particular circumstances, and may disagree openly with any of it.

These religious-like axioms have become the cornerstone of a conventional wisdom, a mythic expression of an official ideology projected as the building block of a larger political culture. This traditional view may have been partially true at one point in our history, but not any more.

Politics is no longer just the preserve of politicians or the property of political institutions if it ever was. Politics today is driven less by ideas and institutions than powerful and extra-parliamentary corporate interests represented by highly paid lobbyists with the ability to shape legislation and finance political campaigns.

The way modern political life and its issues are formed and behaviors guided has a lot more to do with how the experience of politics is transmitted, mediated and explained by a powerful set of institutions that were not around in any significant way when the country was founded: our media.

The culture of media dominates political culture. Critic Douglas Kellner, who has studied media culture, concludes "that images sounds and spectacles help produce the fabric of everyday life, dominating leisure time, shaping political views and social life, and providing the material out of which people forge their everyday identities."[1] He contends that vast culture industries help us construct our ideas about our nationalities, ethnicities, races, and religions.

These cultural industries dominate the political system in many ways – with entertainment programming that influences the discourse in our imaginations, as well as with news that frames the issues that we think about (and the way we think about them) along with the advertising that sells us products and our consumption-driven lifestyle.

This techno-transmitted culture produces "platforms" for the dissemination of vast arrays of cultural products from films and recorded music to video games and on-line websites. TV, radio, and now the internet disseminate information, ideals, ideologues in a way that is far more powerful and pervasive than the decisions reached by politicians, parliaments and Congresses. In many ways, these media products depoliticize our politics turning political races into personality contests and important issues into simplistic choices and message points.

A democracy which in theory is accountable to its voters has become a mediaocracy that is answerable to the market when it is answerable at all. Classical democratic theory posits that a free press is a guardian of democracy, a "fourth estate" designed to inform the public and play a watchdog role to keep politicians and political institutions honest. In theory the media is supposed to be the transmission belt of a robust political culture.

In practice, as media outlets become more powerful, they become the agenda setters and the framers of debate. When issues are not on TV they don't exist for most people. When political advocates are not heard or reported, their impact is nil. That's why politicians spend as much time as they do raising money to advertise on TV or on consultants to craft their messages and position their candidacies.

Governments don't have to buy time but their media operations have even bigger budgets to hire small armies of strategists and speechwriters, spin doctors and PR specialists. Increasingly, anyone interested in transforming the practice and culture of political institutions has to confront the power and dominant role of media power.

MEDIA AS OUR POLITICS

We live in an age of media politics, governed not just by politicians but by what is a mutually dependent and interactive relationship between major media and politics, a nexus of power in which political leaders use media exposure to shape opinions and drive policy while media outlets use politicians to confer legitimization and offer what *TIME* magazine called "Electotainment."

The news media has become the fulcrum of political life throughout the West and the driver of economic life as well. Debt drives consumption. Commercials excite demand. TV celebrities become commodities. Marketing strategies sell products, and programs focused on markets also sell ideology. The ups and downs of share prices get more attention than the rate of unemployment or indices of social misery. Young people spend more time in the living room learning from TV than in the classroom learning from teachers. Many scholars believe that television has become their principal socializer. Some critics call TV a "plug in drug."

U.S. media, given Constitutional sanction by the U.S. Constitution under the First Amendment now often degrades democracy, promoting the business system over the culture of civil society. The biggest businesses they boost are their own brands, as media companies become billion dollar businesses thanks to government sanctioned deregulation, mergers, and acquisitions. This has led to unprecedented consolidation and concentration of ownership in fewer and fewer hands.

As commercial media expands, infiltrating into every corner of life, public service media clones its formulas for survival joining in the dumbing down of content and loosening of public interest standards. Bottom line pressures impact on every side as competition leads to splintering of the audience into smaller and smaller demographically designed niches. At the same time, larger economic problems limit state subsidies to public broadcasters and depress advertising revenues for commercial purposes. The result: a drop in quality.

One problem is that many prominent political leaders or political activists don't recognize that the media problem is at the heart of the political crisis in America. The Democratic leader Al Gore had avoided discussing the role of the media during his failed bid for the Presidency in 2000.

Two years later and just before he decided to drop out of politics, he finally spoke out. It was as if he had finally seen the power of a media system that Marshall McLuhan once called "transparently invisible." In an interview with the *New York Observer*, Gore pointed to an institutional imbalance in the media system that tilts in favor of conservatives and conservative values.

According to writer Josh Benson in the *NY Observer*:

> Mr. Gore has a bone to pick with his critics: namely, he says, that a system-atically orchestrated bias in the media makes it impossible for him and his fellow Democrats to get a fair shake. "Something will start at the Republican National Committee, inside the building, and it will explode the next day on the right-wing talk-show network and on Fox News and in the newspa-pers that play this game, *The Washington Times* and the others. And then they'll create a little echo chamber, and pretty soon they'll start baiting the mainstream media for allegedly ignoring the story they've pushed into the *zeitgeist*. And then pretty soon the mainstream media goes out and disin-genuously takes a so-called objective sampling, and lo and behold, these R.N.C. talking points are woven into the fabric of the *zeitgeist*."

And during a lengthy discourse on the history of political journalism in America, Al Gore said he believed that evolving technologies and market forces have combined to lower the media's standards of objectivity. He also said:

> The introduction of cable-television news and Internet news made news a commodity, available from an unlimited number of sellers at a steadily decreasing cost, so the established news organizations became the high-cost producers of a low-cost commodity. They're selling a hybrid product now that's news plus news-helper; whether it's entertainment or attitude or news that's marbled with opinion, it's different. Now, especially in the cable-TV market, it has become good economics once again to go back to a party-oriented approach to attract a hard-core following that appreciates

the predictability of a right-wing point of view, but then to make aggressive and constant efforts to deny that's what they're doing in order to avoid offending the broader audience that mass advertisers want. Thus the Fox slogan "We Report, You Decide," or whatever the current version of their ritual denial is.[2]

Gore is right but his response to the problem was to help finance Current, a youth-oriented TV channel that in the interests of satisfying its investors became an MTV without the music. It quickly denied any social mission and uses gimmicky entertainment modules or "pods" to offer storytelling and fun with occasional serious content. Market logic turned "his creation" into the very cultural product he decried.

Some conservatives like Edward Luttwak realize this too, asking at a 2004 Arts and Ideas Festival at Yale, "Can Democracy Survive The Media?" He and other critics point to the lack of diversity of viewpoint in the media reporting and shrinking substantive issue-oriented coverage during elections. They note that the focus on polls and personalities leads to what media critics call "Agenda cutting," weaning the public off factual issues and policy choices. The result is growing cynicism and dropping out of politics.

Concludes Roland Schatz of Media Tenor, a media firm that studies political coverage in many different countries, "the people's reaction to this is to turn their backs on the ballot boxes. The party of non-voters has grown to become the most important group in all Western democracies, a fact that has not been given sufficient attention by the media." That may be because it is the media itself that is encouraging this anti-democratic trend.

There are libraries full of very good books documenting how this has happened. Most explain how market pressures tend to drive out public interest obligations. They show through case studies and well-documented narratives how news has been sanitized, journalists censored and important stories suppressed. They have described a merger of news business and show business in an era of growing concentration of ownership that has led to a "dumbing down" of content. They decry packaging over substance and claim that we are in a "post-journalism" era where information is a commodity but facts no longer matter.

They describe the ever-increasing transformation of the news into a corporate commodity. Thoughtful newspaper editors like John Carroll fear that corporate ownership is eroding the quality of our newspapers telling an interviewer: "Newspaper-owning corporations – and I mean all of them, not just my own employer – have an unwritten pact with Wall Street that requires unsustainably high profit levels. Each year, newspapers shed reporters, editors, photographers, designers and their 'news holes' [an insider term referring to space allocated for news coverage]. Each year, readers get less. Each year many of those readers turn elsewhere for their news."[3]

Media workers, especially journalists, know how seductive this corporate pressure and, its corollary, the daily routines of creeping personal co-optation can be. Most feel they have few means of resistance, "This is the deepest censorship of the self," writes the critic John Leonard, "an upward mobility and a downward trajectory."[4]

Even media moguls like CNN founder Ted Turner now admit that big media is a threat to providing Americans with the news we need. Writing in the *Washington Monthly*, he turns on the industry he was once part of:

> These big companies are not antagonistic; they do billions of dollars in business with each other. They don't compete; they cooperate to inhibit competition. You and I have both felt the impact. I felt it in 1981, when CBS, NBC, and ABC all came together to try to keep CNN from covering the White House. You've felt the impact over the past two years, as you saw little news from ABC, CBS, NBC, MSNBC, Fox, or CNN on the FCC's [Federal Communications Commission] actions. In early 2003, the Pew Research Center found that 72 percent of Americans had heard "nothing at all" about the proposed FCC rule changes.
>
> Why? One never knows for sure, but it must have been clear to news directors that the more they covered this issue, the harder it would be for their corporate bosses to get the policy result they wanted. A few media conglomerates now exercise a near-monopoly over television news.[5]

On the occasion of CNN's twenty-fifth anniversary in June 2005 Turner told a reunion of staffers that he yearned for a "return to a little more international coverage on the domestic feed and a little more environmental coverage and, maybe, a little less of the pervert of the day."[6]

At the same time that media outlets fragment the audience and pursue the lowest common denominator, corporations with vast marketing and research budgets and even the military has recognized the importance of shaping a culture that is supportive of its needs and objectives.

In the summer of 1997, Major P. Ralph Peters, a graduate of the U.S. Army Command and General Staff College assigned to the Office of the Deputy Chief of Staff for Intelligence, where he was responsible for future warfare wrote the following about culture:

> Culture is fate. Countries, clans, military services, and individual soldiers are products of their respective cultures, and they are either empowered or imprisoned. The majority of the world's inhabitants are prisoners of their

cultures, and they will rage against inadequacies they cannot admit, cannot bear, and cannot escape.

Hollywood is 'preparing the battlefield,' and burgers precede bullets. The flag follows trade. Despite our declaration of defeat in the face of battlefield victory in Mogadishu, the image of US power and the US military around the world is not only a deterrent, but a psychological warfare tool that is constantly at work in the minds of real or potential opponents ...

Everybody is afraid of us. They really believe we can do all the stuff in the movies. If the Trojans 'saw' Athena guiding the Greeks in battle, then the Iraqis saw Luke Skywalker precede McCaffrey's tanks. Our unconscious alliance of culture with killing power is a combat multiplier no government, including our own, could design or afford. We are magic. And we're going to keep it that way.[7]

"Go America Go!" is the subtext here but what seems clear is that political leaders and military strategists make an effort to study culture and influence its direction. The Pentagon relies on input from Hollywood producers in shaping its propaganda narratives. TV ads for military recruitment rely on rock music and video game techniques. Many are used on MTV and other music television stations. Political messages are keyed to cultural prejudices and symbolic issues like fear of gay marriage and flag burning. Many of the ads are not used but played on MTV to youth outlets, including alongside films directed at young people.

The military's ad agencies place their recruitment spots in theaters and on TV programs aimed at young people. Of course, there is no competition from anti-military groups or peace organizations. This is all part of a strategy of "information dominance."

The September 11 attack on the World Trade Center was an attack on urban culture. Many cultures that oppose Western culture perceive diverse urban cultures as a threat. For example, the Serbs who attacked Sarajevo attacked a mixed society in which Muslims were very much present but also intermarried and European. This was an attack on a cosmopolitan culture, an attack on the idea of people from different backgrounds being together. It was a blow from a traditional, rural-based culture against the power of the city and the power of its ideas.

Likewise, the Islamic fundamentalists, if that's what they are, the people presumed to be behind the attack on the World Trade Center, saw these buildings as the physical manifestation of a globalized economy and society. Benjamin Barber wrote a book called *Jihad Against McWorld*. This holy war pits the forces of Islamic fundamentalism against a different fundamentalism, the forces of market capitalism. "McWorld wants to concentrate power in global corporations, symbolized by those at the very top of the World Trade Center," he writes.

> The World Trade Center was selling the power of affluence on top of the world, an image that peoples from poorer cultures really resent. They resent the arrogance associated with it, they resent the fact that these people are looking down and don't really see them. Hence, the buildings and their occupants become the target in a symbolic battle.[8]

The 1993 bombing and the September 11 attacks were strikes against these symbols of financial power and of America as a cultural force in the world. If they knocked down those buildings, they believed, they would show the society's weaknesses. Knocking the World Trade Center down was striking a blow against the values that underlie it, which in many ways are urban values. James B. Goodno, editor of *Urban Ecology*, adds:

> Fear is an anti-urban sentiment and to the extent that the terrorists were out to sow fear, they were attacking urban culture. Contemporary urban life depends upon the interaction – not always comfortable – of people from different cultures, classes, races, and faiths. This interaction creates the cultural dynamism that we associate with the best of urban life. It allows us to move forward as a society. The city provides a stage on which this interaction takes place.[9]

So even an event like September 11 has a cultural subtext to debate. The interface between culture and politics is omnipresent but also often invisible because media outlets rarely raise or discuss them, just as they do not call attention to their own techniques and the ways they structure the issues we care about.

Our culture forms our politics, and politics is increasingly about culture and cultural difference as the Red State/Blue State debate shaped by religious sentiments, values and lifestyle differences define and underlie political campaigning. Increasingly, the politics of culture and the culture of politics are merging.

Chapter 10

Navigating Digital Geographies

*Augustus Casely-Hayford**

In 1966 32.3 million British people tuned in to see England's 4–2 victory over West Germany in the World Cup final, the most watched TV broadcast in British history. These viewer figures are all the more remarkable because only 15 million households owned a TV at the time. My father often told me how he hired a television set especially to watch the game. When Geoff Hurst's goal went in off the bar, all the neighbours poured out of their houses. Every word of Kenneth Wolstenholme's commentary could be heard echoing off the brick facades of the houses, *"and here comes Hurst he's got … some people are on the pitch, they think it's all over. It is now! It's four!"* – England had put the game beyond doubt. Possibly the definitive British television moment; the analogue age of buzzing valves, big Bakelite dials and *received pronunciation* defining the scope and imagination of the English-speaking world had reached a romantic, but decades late, high.

In the summer of 2006 about 20 million British people tuned in to see the World Cup final on television, fewer than any previous final since the 1960s. To many in the British television industry it was no surprise. The relative drop in audience figures was not driven by attitudes to football or television content; the fall in viewers was created by a subtle but decisive renegotiation of the dynamics

* **Augustus Casely-Hayford** is Executive Director Arts Strategy, Arts Council England, and is ex-Director of inIVA (Institute of International Visual Arts), a London-based arts organisation with a particular emphasis on international practice. Prior to this he was Director of Africa 05, the largest and most successful African arts season ever hosted in Britain. A curator and cultural historian, he has presented award-winning television programmes and written and curated widely. He lectures on world art, and is a consultant for the Arts Council England and the BBC. He is a Clore Fellow and sits on a variety of cultural committees including Tate Britain Council.

of Western communications. More people than ever watched the game via broadband, on mobile phones, were updated by text and RSS (Really Simple Syndication), downloaded images and updates, blogs and podcasts, kept updated via chat rooms and digital fora. The most forward-thinking communications companies have begun to acknowledge that the first and perhaps final age of television is drawing to a close; in the parts of the world with the highest density of televisions, viewers have begun to decline and in the areas of the globe with the highest advertising revenues, the hours that viewers spend in front of their TVs has fallen steadily.

Analogue television occupied an interesting window in the history of communication. Many of my earliest memories are television related. From childhood, it was my intellectual dummy, an anaesthetizing lullaby from which I was never really weaned; Ali standing over Foreman's crumpled body, the World Cup debutant Pele on his knees after scoring, Neil Armstrong's one small step, were my wizards and fairy tales, my devils and moral guide. TV is unarguably a powerful and romantic medium, the hearth of the late twentieth-century Western home. But television was also the witch's apple; a highly corrosive and corrupting force that inveigled its way into our lives, to addict our children and lobotomize our parents. The scale of its reach, influence and impact combined with the alienatingly serialized homogenization of the viewer experience, its synthetic first-person relationship with us, its one-way flirtation, commanded almost complete passivity of the viewer. It facilitated the commercialization of every other art form and presented a barely negotiated intellectually reductive simplification of the world, making us feel powerful while disempowering us; we knew all of that, yet still loved it. At the heart of television's demise was not a recognition of its inherent problems, but a growing awareness of its inflexibility when compared to the unfathomably powerful potential of the digital alternatives.

For some years after I heard the story of the 1966 World Cup, I wondered why when the game was about to reach its climax people left their homes. Then one Christmas two of my Ghanaian aunts came to stay. They brought with them our West African family history woven into pieces of cloth. They introduced me to a different kind of creative interaction. Over a single Christmas holiday they held the house spellbound with family stories illustrated by cloth. The stories opened up a new mode of communal discourse to me. The narrative that my aunts wove through cloth was not like the linear narrative of television, it didn't use the epistemological systems of written history. These stories had a kind of shared subjectivity; they formed a place where our imaginations could meet, they encompassed us, and gave us a coherence and an exoskeleton for our conjoined history. When my aunts spoke we felt like we were wrapped in the space created by the narrative of those pieces of cloth. If they picked up a piece of indigo-dyed cotton, they could attach every stain and loose thread attached to a particular story and almost read it like a diary. Yet, they were more than records, they yielded a corroborative testimony. We were encouraged to add to the narrative, embellish the stories, but the cloth remained the point where we met. Cloth in my aunts' hands could link processes and means, join causality and praxis. Scraps of a nineteenth-century magenta Yoruba imported cloth created a fluid framework for particular oral histories that anchored words with empirical evidence, while being fluid enough for us all to feel that we might all contribute. An old piece of resist-dyed Yoruba cloth did not represent a historical superstructure or particular causal end; fabric was the fluid that eased the causality between events.

Very often, these pieces of material were the only enduring witnesses that could link disparate and momentous events over decades, across generations. A faded piece of funeral cloth, its weft-face faded from laying on a dozen family coffins, during a generation of wakes, was more than an archaeological remnant of a family's mourning processes. You could smell in its fibre a meal cooked in palm oil a generation ago, see on its surface how pearly globules of candle wax spilt when the cloth was new had trapped the intensity of fresh cobalt blue forever. The cloth had written into its fabric the collected forensic evidence of the family's continuity; it reminded us of our part-Nigerian ancestry, its fabric gave focus and coherence to the lives of people united by blood, but separated by geography and death. The material had become substantiated history. Yet, one knew that without the animating force of conscious, appropriate and continued use, without activating the cloth through discussion, the fabric's particular metaphysic would drain away, leaving it as little more than old material.

What these cloth narratives importantly offered was a space where we could create the connections and hyper-linkages that became oral histories, and we felt that space really belonged to us as a group. That space was unlike the forum created by traditional analogue television that represented a one-way semi-permeable narrative, relayed complete, edited, remote and perhaps disempowering to its audiences. It allowed us to be involved, connected in a way that could make a significant difference. I began to reflect on the reasons why people left their houses at the climax of the 1966 World Cup; they wanted to be able to define the moment for themselves, not to have the match solely curated by the BBC, but to co-curate and truly interact with the event, to make it their own. During the 2006 World Cup hundreds of thousands of Germans chose to leave their homes to watch the match on large screens in parks and city squares. The real event became the fans' interaction; the passage and result of the game became its commentary. Being involved with something momentous and global was the event, it created a dynamic medium that connected individuals to a huge global community. Similar acts of engagement and involvement have today become an everyday by-product of digital communications.

The internet and digital television have offered us a means to communicate and be entertained in ways that were science fiction a generation ago. We need not be defined by where we live, or who we might choose to support in the World Cup. Increasingly how we choose to share information sets out the parameters of our world. In a digital context our means of communication can pull us into communities beyond our geographic neighbourhood into broader networks that might reflect specificity of interest and affiliation in ways that were previously unimaginable. These groups might well reflect global economic trends or socio-religious affiliations that could sit in tension with the politics of our immediate localities. This has created an interesting tension between rigid old-fashioned sociologies, their concomitant marketing categories and our individual identities that may well be under constant parallel renegotiation.

Digital interactivity allows identity to be much more easily redefined by new global polarities, fostering localized sociological flux and a transnational fluidity. Both as individuals and groups we are leaving behind the sociologies that bred the twentieth century's economic allegiances, and we are finding a new sense of identity that is given coherence not by our national politics, but by the relationship between personal or localized beliefs and global politics. In that landscape everyone can feel like a minority, we are all *culturally diverse* in that broad context; our sense of identity is defined by dialectic of regional and international issues, by an equation of personal and the global agenda, and no longer by our national anthem. National issues can be supplanted by pan-national and super-regional agendas and macro-ecological concerns. And even if in the West, we are voting in lower and lower numbers, our electorates remain deeply politically engaged, grappling for control of change, but change at a local and a notionally international level. We are in a polite way, as mad as hell, but we seem to want to articulate our outrage in community centres and through broadband connections, in chat rooms and coffee shops and not necessarily at the ballot box. We are bypassing national fora and tapping directly into the macro agenda – religion, climate change, human rights, freedom – but we are using the digital arena to make these issues highly particular to us. The parochialization of global issues has created a massive serialization of effort dissipating the effectiveness of our campaigns. But I have the sense that we are quite happy with this. I think we are slowly growing to consciously embrace difference and dissonance. We have created a dynamic symbiosis with those we oppose – they give us the context in which to judge the effectiveness of the informal digital communications strategies that broadcast our beliefs; new beliefs that are fighting to define a nebulous changing political landscape and building a new kind of digital community and a politics that is inherently uncoordinated.

The new interactive digital arena allows us to build and hold these narratives, to leave traditional affiliations and sociologies behind and become different people in different spaces. For the digital generation cultural affiliation can be inverted, their geographically local sociology need not define them, they have the freedom and ability to choose and define their broader culture, curate their own space. Today the most successful internationally well-visited cultural arena are not the Louvre or the British Museum, they are: iTunes, MySpace or Flickr – these new spaces allow us, everyone of us, to become a curator and they allow us both to talk to the world, to remodel it to suit us and, if we wish, to exist in an audience of one. This technology facilitates the expression of massive individuality and also gives us each the ability to communicate directly with millions of people. Most of us may choose to listen to music alone most of the time.

To some extent the headphone has replaced the concert hall, iTunes the record store. If we log onto Amazon, it will suggest something for us to buy based on our previous purchases. We can be in a virtual demography of one. But the virtual chart, the digital message boards and chat rooms offer spaces to contribute to global debates that might place us in an active relationship with a community of millions, meaningfully in dialogue with as many people as we wish. Within that context race, religion, sex, sexuality are important to who we are, in that they define the communications that surround the culture, but as we consume and digest culture, we can choose to be who we wish. In the West many of the generation that grew up with these digital possibilities feel that they can proactively define or redefine their cultural affiliations, if they choose. Their "culture" as it might conventionally be conceived does not define or contain them in the way that it did their parents. Culture does not have to sit as a concomitant of classical sociological structures, it can manifest itself through the nebulous digital relationships that are negotiated by individuals who make and consume it. This kind of interaction is highly complex and fluid because it allows us to choose to subscribe to it at personal levels of negotiation.

This world is hard to penetrate when looked at as geo-politics and macro-sociology because, under the skin of the digital ecology, there are not hordes of homogenous football supporters rooted to one locality and happy to be defined in that way; we know this space is driven by a conglomeration of individual and distinct human beings. And technology allows us to unravel the demographic and marketing data and drill down to tease out the taste of each and every internet customer. While this might be challenging for traditional politicians who work at a macro level within geographic boundaries it is emancipating for their constituents; fundamentalists and the non-conformists, liberals and conservatives, can each broker their own relationships of enfranchisement and build communities that bypass parochial pressures and geographically localized politics, or if they choose they can absorb and drive those agenda in ways that were never previously possible. There does not need to be an average consumer of culture, no generic marketing; we will be able to individually negotiate the definitions or conglomerated particularities by which we are categorized, creating a completely new set of relationships between consumer and marketplace.

Perhaps this could be the beginning of the end of the Western notion of "mainstream", as the fixed frame through which we can judge difference collapses, replaced by a sea of complex, overlapping cultural gravities, absorbing and repelling, collapsing and expelling. This greater fluidity allows individuals to navigate the possibilities and make decisions about how they engage. The digital arena is a piece of cloth in an aunt's hands, fluid, open and malleable; we can to some extent all be part of the renegotiation of this space. People all over the world are augmenting their traditional modes of communication with the new digital possibilities on offer. This might mark the relegation of the author and the curator as the audience increasingly becomes the event, as participation becomes the focus and communications the art form.

Chapter 11

Martin Heidegger Goes to the Movies

*John Hutnyk**

'Music is a weapon of mass destruction' – ADF (Asian Dub Foundation)

Cinema and sound sync/mix technology seems to come and go in leaps and loops. Where once the screen image required accompaniment by a live performer at a piano, today, such a 'throw back' to the old black and white days of immediately present live sound is rare, even nostalgic. A calculated and curious staging renews our appreciation of the artifice of sync sound, although the piano is electric and the 'live' now requires mixing desks, digital precision, planned sequencing and programmed synthesisers. It requires all this, at least, in the case of recent performances over film by the drum and bass outfit ADF, who have been filling cinema halls with new audiences for old films. I am impressed by this revival of a past format, and thinking about how this technology is used perhaps helps our understanding of the pursuit of innovative modes of political activism. So I want to approach this scene informed by a more nuanced notion of technology than is often required – taking my cue from an essay by Martin Heidegger, where technology is thought of as something more than mere instrumental tool. As culture crashes into the

* **John Hutnyk** is Academic Director of the Centre for Cultural Studies at Goldsmiths College and the author of a number of books including *The Rumour of Calcutt* (1996 Zed); *Critique of Exotica: Music, Politics and the Culture Industry* (2000 Pluto Press); *Bad Marxism: Capitalism and Cultural Studies* (2004 Pluto), and recently co-authored with Virinder Kalra and Raminder Kaur, *Diaspora and Hybridity* (2005 Sage). He is also the editor of several volumes of essays, including *Dis-Orienting Rhythms: the Politics of the New Asian Dance Music* (1996 Zed, co-ed. with Sharma and Sharma) and most recently a festschrift for Klaus Peter Koepping called *Celebrating Transgression* (2006 Berghahn, co-ed. with Ursula Rao). He writes irregular prose at http://hutnyk.blogspot.com

technological, I wonder what motivations might be heard when the echos of days gone by are radically reworked in this way.

ADF screen movies with intent. For several years they had used the 1995 Kassowitz film *La Haine* as a vehicle for a cinema-music experiment, where the story of three youths caught up in suburban unrest (which is itself largely off screen), in the suburbs of Paris, is presented in performance with a new *live* ADF soundtrack. This film has particular relevance given events in the Paris suburbs in November 2005, but I do not want to focus upon representation and the repetition 'in the real' of the events 'in the film'. Rather, I am more interested here in the scene of the screening of a French film replayed in Britain, a film which itself is very much alert to the politics of representation, to the reverberation of screens, such that when shown in the UK it is meant to evoke parallels and differences in terms of race, suburban alienation and the politics of the imagination, especially with regard to thinking about technology and terror.

La Haine begins with a Molotov cocktail, set across the background of a shot of the planet as seen from space. The incendiary device is falling, and spinning as it falls, towards the earth as pictured from afar. A voice recounts a story of someone who fell from a tall building, and as he passed each floor on the way down, he said aloud: 'So far, so good, so far, so good.' Ash and Sanjay Sharma wrote perceptively on this film, suggesting that this 'anxious repetition of assurance' might be dubbed 'the inner voice of liberal democracy'.[1] The Sharma brothers link this reassurance to the critical scene of the journalists visiting the suburbs only to be confronted as intruders by the youth, chased with their television cameras back to the safer boulevards. When the three youths themselves are stranded in the centre of the city, caught without tickets to the metro, they see reports from the 'riots' on a public multi-screen, and learn of the death of one of their comrades.

ADF want the film to provoke discussion. They screen it for new audiences and it is discussed in detail on the interactive activist/fan website that is part of the ADF Education Foundation (ADFED), itself an activist-oriented youth politics forum. Workshops organised by ADFED included one by Sonia Mehta in 2003 involving Ash Sharma on the development of ADFED as a music technology training provider working with visual media and exploring the politics of sound.[2] Discussion within ADFED and on the ADF chat site is not uncritical. For example, the politics of screening action cinema as entertainment is measured against questions about the best ways to organise, and politicise, the music industry, organisations like Rich Mix (an arts centre and venue for music, cinema, performance and training with which ADFED is associated[3]) and anti-racist campaigns. Concerns about street and police violence are aired and the testosterone-fuelled adventurism of the Paris uprisings are compared with events in the UK that echo those shown in *La Haine*. The film, as ADF intend, also articulates these concerns. The absence of women in the film is striking, but as the Sharmas argue, the pathologising of the suburbs is an old sociological, anthropological and Hollywood standard, where inner urban tradition demands alienation and decay, disaffection and lawlessness, reinforcing the racism, even as *La Haine* challenges these easy moves.[4]

In 2002 ADF initiated similar concert-screenings of another film, this time the revolutionary cinematic extravaganza of *The Battle of Algiers*, directed in 1964 by Gillo Pontecorvo (music by Ennio Morricone). This film tells the story of the clandestine resistance movement against the French occupation of Algeria and works well when screened for new audiences with a live ADF soundtrack. Bringing a new audience to an old film, a part of the third cinema movement, quite often overlooked by drum and bass fans, carries a powerful allegorical charge at a time when issues of colonial occupation – Afghanistan, Iraq, Lebanon – are prominent in the media.

I am interested in what a British Asian music activist outfit, with a record of anti-racist, anti-imperialist organising, can achieve with the technology of sound and film as propaganda device. What does this tell us about activism, media, and the intended audience for ADF's experiments at the movies? Some will of course say that the ADF update track for *Battle of Algiers* is no improvement upon Morricone's score; some will quibble about the sanctity of creative work in the age of digital reproduction; some might suggest that ADF cash in with a radical pose, presenting themselves as advocates of any and every left cause going. It is of course possible to discuss these matters, but I think these are the wrong questions. To explain, I want to turn to a German philosopher who knew very little about *this* kind of drum and bass.

Martin Heidegger, were he to come down from his mountain retreat, might have us examine the way our thinking about technology hands us over to a calculated, and so compromised, entrapment. Concerned that we may 'have ears only for the noise of media',[5] Heidegger makes a distinction, in a 1955 address in his home town, between calculative and meditative thought.[6] It is meditative thought that is lost in the modern world for Heidegger. Calculation well suits the opportunist mind-set of capitalism. He complains of those who 'hourly and daily ... are chained to radio and television' and 'week after week the movies carry them off into uncommon, but often merely common, realms of the imagination, and give the illusion of a world that is no world.' '... Picture magazines' and 'modern techniques of communication' assail us.[7]

No doubt the mid-twentieth-century philosopher would have thought

ADF noisy, and that they were gratuitously given over to calculation (of record sales, of internet hits on their website). So far as I know, he expressed no position on Algeria or on Pontocorvo's film, if he ever saw it. But nevertheless it might be interestingly provocative to ask if he would have approved of ADF's attempt to get the youth to question, to 'meditate' (not at all in the yogic sense) upon questions of politics, violence, resistance, and on alternate ways of viewing the world. *Battle of Algiers*, in Pontocorvo's third cinema way, was already a moment of consciousness-raising, which ADF now update according to their want. ADF are not sentimental, and they are never in denial about the culture industry as a sapping vortex of commercialisation, but their engagement with the media cannot be described simply as an issue of chains or noise.

Given what we know (or think that we know[8]) of Heidegger's declared politics, it may seem strange that I can imagine ADF at least agreeing with him when he says:

> The power concealed in modern technology determines the relation of man to that which exists. It rules the whole earth. Indeed, already man is beginning to advance beyond the earth into outer space ... gigantic sources of power have become known through the discovery of atomic energy.[9]

Heidegger warns of a danger in calculative thinking's triumph 'in the sense that the approaching tide of technological revolution in the Atomic age could so captivate, bewitch, dazzle, and beguile ... that calculative thinking may someday come to be accepted and practised *as the only* way of thinking' (Heidegger, 1955/2003:93).

ADF would want to promote a revolutionary consciousness. I wonder if we can grant them the luxury of thinking so differently?

'The Question Concerning Technology' was first given as a talk in 1949 and expanded in 1954. In this essay, Heidegger advocates a questioning that concerns itself with technology in a particular, political, way. Since we are not free, but are caught in a mode of thinking where we are mostly unable to think in any other than a calculative way about technology, Heidegger takes great pains to explain his way of questioning concerning technology. He will work through various ideas – cause, bringing forth, revealing, enframing, standing reserve and clearing – to prepare the possibility of escaping from the dangerous trap of conventional thoughts about technology. To do this he first goes back to Greeks to think about the meaning of words, not about the technological. Here, as ever, Heidegger teaches etymologies like no other – he asks us to think of *verstehen*, understanding, knowledge. To properly think this he asks that we look at assumptions; for example, about how we think of technology as an activity; as a way of doing something; and as means to an end – as an instrumental thing that we try to control, and how our attempts to control technology as a tool keeps us still firmly in the grip of unexamined instrumentalism. For Heidegger, it is a first step of questioning (itself a kind of technology) that we need to examine our assumptions in a rigorous way, and he does so through an examination of the roots of the notion of cause. There is a long exploration of Greek and Latin terms, and of the creative intentionality that lies behind bringing something or causing something to be. The discussion moves from how we get things done, through consideration of cause as bringing forth, to a notion of the revealing, or the presence, of something. Then Heidegger offers a discussion of *techne* – as manufacturing technique *and* art (*poeisis*) – as a kind of know-how – the art of doing that brings something to presence.

Looking for parallels with the thinking behind the performances by ADF, I have in mind the ends of activism, including those more abstract 'oppositional-creative' aims of ADFED as educational foundation that reveal a kind of community activism and a politics itself. The built-in radical charge of this makes me want to ask what might be added to our understanding of activism if this sort of evaluation and thinking were to become common practice?

So – hypothetical and experimental as it is – what if we bring forward this multifaceted, Heideggerian understanding of *techne* to Pontecorvo's film, insofar as it is brought forth into the sometimes discordant, sometimes lyrical, but overall creative context of an ADF screening performance? Perhaps in this way we can better understand something about what ADF's rendition of *Battle of Algiers* achieves. The event is never simply the cause of bringing about a critical anti-colonialist consciousness in the youth that are attracted to ADF performances. Ostensibly this would be one of the simple planned, even calculated, ends, but no one would be so foolish as to think there is a one-to-one equivalence between planned intention and effect. Indeed, there is no simple or singular intention possible when an audience, by definition, comes from a wide range of disparate positions. There are plenty of debates about ethics and motivation, even inspiration, in the literature on propaganda, promotion and politics. There is much to be said for difference and for multiple modes of thinking. ADFED itself is a broad 'church', open to many, and ADF have long pointed out their wide 'consciousness-raising' orientation and commitment to diversity.

Perhaps what ADF and Heidegger share then is not just any kind of politics, nor any greater or lesser disguised evangelical mission, but a common push towards a more fundamental form of thinking; the realisation that a limit to thinking, a narrowing, is a baleful consequence of an unexamined attachment to the silver screen. The jangling soundtrack ADF provides for *La Haine* or *The Battle of Algiers* is intended to provoke a meditation, a rethinking. To resist what comes to presence in conventional everyday chit-chat versions of media consumption requires provocation if it is to open up any chance of radical thinking. Heidegger elsewhere is contemptuous of idle-talk and rumour as a substitute for thought, and in many ways I hear this idea resonating in ADF's politically motivated use of film.

Unfortunately, this does not mean that film itself, with added live music, is by and by an automatic consciousness-raising tool. One particular story drives this point home. In 2002 it was reported that Pontocorvo's film was to be screened (with the original score) at the Pentagon as an instructional text for the generals of the low intensity warfare operations unit, with the intention of aiding the generals in their thinking about how to win the war in Iraq, and how to deal with a militant insurgency without losing the 'battle for hearts and minds', as the French so clearly did in Algeria. It seems the generals watched less than carefully. The point is not to suggest only that any text – film, event – can be turned to any politics whatsoever (though I am sometimes convinced that all things can be recuperated and co-opted to do service for capital) but that what is required to achieve a radical thinking is something more than the conventions of calculative thought that usually belong to technology, especially technology in the hands of the generals bombing Afghanistan, Lebanon and Iraq.

It is here that things become complicated. Revealing – bringing forth – goes down a wrong path if we are in thrall to technology and do not question it. I do not want to simply say that the film is a technology, to be given over to a certain view and fixed, or simply that it is something to be interpreted by whatever group – ADF or the Pentagon – that wants to make use of it. Sure, the figure of Martin Heidegger is not unlike the film – the old Nazi philosopher can be provocative as material support for left *and* right wing ends – that is not the point, the point is to watch over the calculation machine and see where it leaves us; thinking or stuck.

ADF use technology to make us think, not simply consume. In this, they are, I feel, an advance insofar as they do more than simply offer a critical note against colonialism, revealing some of the truths about colonial history; rather, revealing plus an activism that militates *for* critical thinking. It is no accident that ADF called an earlier EP *Militant Science*. They explain:

> Whatever anyone says about ADF's so called 'political' lyrics, no one would have taken any notice if it wasn't for ADF's sound and its inherent energy: ragga-jungle propulsion, indo-dub basslines, distorted sitar-like guitars and samples of more 'traditional' Asian sounds.[10]

When Heidegger moves to the conclusion of his essay, he tries to clarify the relationship between two opposing orientations contained within what he calls *Gestell* or enframing, where enframing means something like a framework through which we look towards the world (we might remember here the opening scene in *La Haine* which pictures the world). Thus, for Heidegger, questioning concerning technology reveals both ordering and revealing as parts of our understanding of technology. But revealing is in danger and may be lost if questioning does not stay alert to this danger, and in questioning provoke us to watch out for ways revealing might become limited to or reduced only to ordering. It is not enough to know the facts of Afghanistan, Iraq or Lebanon (indeed, the generals know so much more, and no doubt hide more, than the rest of us), the danger is in *how* knowing is used. What do the generals do with their facts (their intelligence and counter-intelligence)? Clearly, knowledge is not neutral.

When ADF, by their efforts, enframe activism and resistance within the same screen format that houses the propaganda effort of the evening news, the Pentagon private screenings and the third cinema aesthetic tradition, then can we be sure that a common instrumentalisation has not captured all perspectives?

Heidegger expresses his concern that humanity's effort to 'bring order to the globe' is in vain so long as the language of what he calls 'the pathway' is not heard. But this is where Heidegger gets too rustic. Something that would be anathema to drum and bass militant rhythm scientists like ADF. Against the calculative, Heidegger would privilege crafts, and technologies like a water wheel that does not store up energy, does not dam the river (he learned a river obsession from Holderin – see *The Ister*[11]). This rustic sleepy village scenario is one that ADF abhor since it buys into the entire romantic pre-colonial fantasy that keeps three-quarters of the world in underdevelopment. On their album *Rafi's Revenge*, ADF offer a lyric that condemns those who imagine India remains a 'mass of sleeping villages' – as such imagery fixes the idea of India in a rustic nostalgia, automatically or naturally excluded from modern development; homogenised and historicised as a manifestation of a eurocentric past.

All of which raises the question of whether we can think outside this frame. Is it right to try to do so by going 'back' to techniques that do not store up and count? Can we think outside an instrumental mode, i.e. can we commit to a mode of thinking that does not calculate the world and us in it, in terms of *use*, that makes us and our world simply standing reserve, available, only in this way? The very possibility of asking this question is the critical hermeneutic. The danger would be that we confirm that we are merely standing reserve, and so we will be denied a more fundamental revealing of our world. We would instead be lost in worrying about control, controlling technology that gets out of control – but we would never have the critical perspective and possibility of thinking outside the frame that would be needed to comprehend the essence of technology.

The threat does not come in the first instance from the potentially lethal machines and apparatus of technology. The actual threat has already affected man in his essence. The rule of enframing threatens man with the possibility that it could be denied to him to enter into a more original revealing and hence to experience the call of a more primal truth.[12]

But if we are to reject the rustic pathway, this truth would be what? Would it be that technology, sound and film is not a necessary, forever unidirectional or fixed, received wisdom, but can be tampered with by militant science, by a political consciousness that disrupts every received verity? Be it the sanctity of the original motion picture (those that criticised ADF for spoiling Pontercorvo's film and displacing Morricone's soundtrack) or be it the Leftist purists who would dare not use Heidegger to make an anti-colonial point, thus closing their ears to ideas in favour of blind narrowness.

That Heidegger and ADF use questioning or noise to provoke us towards the possibility of thinking in a way not merely caught in repletion of our received and ordered enframing is all important. Maybe then we *should* feel uncomfortable, since the essence of technology shows us the (dangerous) way in which a technology, or technology in general, frames the world for us. Our responsibility will be to watch over this revealing so as to always seek – catch sight of – a more primordial revealing – of that which technology does, and that which we might do with technology, a soundtrack for instance. And so, to ask if questioning is enough may be the important question. The one that motivates a deeper thinking? It would not be wrong to ask if the danger of falling for enframing is greater than the physically existing lethal machines. Yet, is questioning enough? Is dancing in the aisles to Pontocorvo's images of Algeria radical enough? In the face of the war of terror, what is?[13]

PART III

The Crisis of Liberalism and Secularism

INTRODUCTION

Liberalism and secularism are being challenged in public discourse in different contexts around the world. What are these challenges? How significant are they? How can we conceptualise a response to them? The authors in this section offer a number of frameworks for thinking through these questions, and, in so doing, contribute a rich set of reflections about how to both weigh, and respond to the cultural challenges to liberalism and secularism. As noted in the Introduction, there are grave dangers here, as well as political and cultural opportunities, for instance, to reconstitute the nature and form of democratic life itself.

A carefully argued defence of liberalism and secularism is offered by **Paul Kelly**, who provides several reasons for why liberalism might be considered the best candidate for accommodating the claims of different religious groups in diverse democratic societies. Connecting to a theme running throughout this volume, his argument is founded on the notion that individuals are never simply composed of their beliefs or identities, and identities are rarely fixed over time. Moreover, secularism can be defended on the grounds that it is a basic requirement of modern citizenship whereby individuals understand themselves as existing in a shared public space with others who inevitably have different views and accounts of the world. If people are to live with minimum resort to coercion, they must accept general rules which underpin their, and others' capabilities to choose and act.

Engaging with the debates surrounding multiculturalism, liberalism and cultural autonomy, **Kok-Chor Tan** argues that with regards to engaging non-liberal cultures, it is possible to 'have it both ways'; that is, it is possible to protect cultural autonomy and individuals at the same time. Tan seeks to clarify the oft flagged contradiction in multicultural thought and public discourse between the cultural rights of peoples and an individualist commitment. He does so by differentiating among different forms of individualism, and among different cultures and specific cultural practices. These distinctions help him go some way towards casting new light on and resolving the tensions between group and individual rights.

Pheng Cheah argues that recent cultural forces and conflicts should not be understood as threatening or opposed to liberalism. Engaging with several classical liberal texts such as those of Locke and Mill, Cheah explores the origins of the conceptual separation so popular today between liberalism, religion and culture, and offers some thoughts on how globalisation challenges this separation. Turning the secular-religious-liberal discussion on its head, Cheah contends that neoliberal economic globalisation 'is suffused by a religious aura', a 'religion of instrumentality' and a 'new religion of business management science and technological innovation that continually re-enchants the world with its promises of exponentially increasing efficiency, creative productivity and perfect control of an increasingly miniaturized and systematized world'. Further inverting our sense of the religious and the secular, Cheah links the rise of East Asian capitalism with a re-constellation of Chinese culture with liberal values and technologies.

Cosmopolitanism is the defence of liberal principles on a general and universal basis. It seeks to set out an ethical and political framework that would enable all human beings, irrespective of territory, to live under basic common rules and conditions. Cosmopolitanism has a cultural dimension too, thought of as the emergence of a political orientation that identifies with, and prioritises humanity above and beyond particular social or national identities. **Montserrat Guibernau** begins her essay by examining the cultural dimension of cosmopolitanism, and providing a distinction between global and cosmopolitan culture. Guibernau argues that proponents of cosmopolitanism and the idea of a cosmopolitan culture should consider national identity's proven capacity to generate solidarity bonds and a sense of community among fellow nationals and that these are unlikely to be matched by the rise of cosmopolitan identity. Cosmopolitan sentiment of belonging 'to humanity' will never be outweighed by the mobilising, binding identity of nations. Guibernau concludes by reflecting on the quest for cosmopolitan identity and suggesting that it is best understood as an attitude in favour of freedom and equality among human beings – an attitude that should add a vital new moral dimension to national identity, rather than supersede it.

David Held concludes this section by outlining and defending the basic tenets of cosmopolitanism, emphasising that the political ideals on which cosmopolitanism is based are comprised of norms which, in part, have already taken form, and rule systems and institutions that are in interesting ways already embedded in the global order. Held outlines a number of interrelated principles. Responding to the critique of cultural and value heterogeneity in the world, Held emphasises that cosmopolitan principles are in fact the conditions of taking cultural diversity seriously and of building a democratic culture to mediate clashes of the cultural good. Groundrules for communication, dialogue and dispute settlement are essential, Held argues, precisely because moral-political questions will conflict and forms of life are irreducibly plural. Responding to the notion that cosmopolitan principles are quintessentially Western in extraction and content, Held contends that they disclose the most universally acceptable framework for the pursuit of argumentation, discussion and negotiation about particular spheres of value, spheres in which local, national and regional affiliations will inevitably be weighed.

Chapter 12

Liberalism, Secularism and the Challenge of Religion – Is there a Crisis?

*Paul Kelly**

Although there are many signs of a resurgence of the influence of religion in the public sphere of many societies and states across the globe, liberal intellectuals have tended to ignore religion as it has come to play less and less of a role in their own lives and in the cosmopolitan cultural communities that they (we) inhabit. Yet religion has hardly been on the decline. We have been challenged by the more vocal assertion of Islam among recent generations of immigrants to Western European societies, especially illustrated by the controversy over Salman Rushdie's *The Satanic Verses*[1] and most recently the publications of the infamous cartoons in the Danish *Jyllands Posten* newspaper.[2] Some British Sikhs have also demonstrated against the play *Bezhti*,[3] while Christians of all varieties regularly raise their voices to complain about everything from *Jerry Springer the Opera* to civil partnerships.

The danger for those of a liberal persuasion is to see these instances as the eruptions of a minority and declining voice from the margins of society. Yet other factors suggest that religion (in all its varied forms) is far from marginal in many people's lives, and is far from being in decline. There may well be fewer practising Anglicans in the United Kingdom and the Catholic Church may be

* **Paul Kelly** is Professor of Political Theory at the London School of Economics. He has published books and articles on the history and theory of utilitarianism, Liberalism and multiculturalism. He is currently completing a book on John Locke and a book on Ronald Dworkin as well as a book on challenges to Liberalism in the twenty-first century. His most recent books are *Political Thinkers* (ed.) (Oxford University Press 2002), *Multiculturalism Reconsidered* (ed.) (Polity 2002), *Liberalism* (Polity 2005) and *John Locke's Second Treatise of Government* (Continuum 2007).

in decline throughout Europe, but there are approximately 900 million Catholics worldwide and if one includes all Christian denominations then there are over a billion Christians. Islam is somewhat smaller than Christianity, but its numbers remain considerable and growing. It is certainly a global religion with significant populations in most European countries and throughout Asia, as well as its more traditional concentrations in the Middle East, Africa and the subcontinent. Then there is the curious phenomenon of the United States, a secular republic with one of the highest levels of active religious affiliations of any Western democratic state. The US has a strict separation of Church and State, but no serious politician can hope to succeed there without at least some superficial public commitment to religious belief and practice.

Faced with the prevalence of religion and its seeming resilience (as yet) to patterns of modernisation that were supposed to result in the secularisation of democratic and technologically advanced societies, it is Liberalism and the political culture of secularism that is in crisis and under attack. Increasingly Liberalism and secularism in politics are seen as merely the partial interest and perspective of an intellectual elite. Liberalism and secularism, in so far as they go together, is merely one perspective among many that can be applied in the public realm to politics, morality and law. Multiculturalism and the growth of identity politics has emphasised the need to accommodate group identities and this includes not only the toleration of religion or its benign neglect, but rather its positive recognition in the public sphere as part of the equal recognition of individuals and groups.

The democratic challenge facing pluralistic societies is how we can negotiate the terms of integration of the wide variety of perspectives and beliefs in such societies. The specific challenge for Liberals is why their perspective should regulate the public sphere? Many defenders of the claims of culture or religion will argue that there is no special reason for privileging Liberalism.[4] In what follows I will give some (what I consider compelling) reasons why Liberalism is the best candidate for accommodating the claims of different religious groups in diverse democratic societies.

THE PROBLEM OF LIBERALISM

One reason why Liberalism is challenged as the basis for accommodating the claims of religion and cultural groups in plural democratic societies is that it has a chequered history in terms of its relationship to religion and its claims. Early Liberals such as John Milton and John Locke were committed Protestant Christians who saw no obvious contradiction between their political beliefs and their religious commitments. Locke believed that there should be wide ranging toleration of different religious beliefs, but he drew the line at Catholics who, due to their adherence to the political authority of a foreign prince (the Pope), were potential terrorists.[5] He also thought that there could be no society with atheists. Locke's Christianity was a rational religion that made few demands that could not be discovered by the exercise of natural reason. Consequently many of his contemporaries regarded him as barely a Christian at all and ever since his time Liberals have been seen as a potential threat to religion, whatever the profession of Liberal thinkers.

The Liberal reliance on the power of reason and the consequent challenge to the claims of revealed religion as well as its suspicion of the supernatural was shared by many Enlightenment intellectuals and has subsequently shaped the modern understanding of Liberalism as a godless doctrine. Indeed the political epithet 'Liberal' was imported into Britain from Spain and applied to Benthamite utilitarians precisely because of their reputation as anti-clerical freethinkers. Liberalism grew up in Europe in opposition to the political claims of religious authority and that still shapes its contemporary understanding by many religious groups, however much it might claim to be a doctrine based on liberty or equal recognition. It is no surprise then that in a society as religious as the United States the term Liberal should be often invoked as a term of political abuse. Viewed in this way, Liberalism is a doctrine that is committed to the secularisation of civil and political society. This freethinking and anti-clerical legacy is in many ways more deep seated than the perception held by many on the left, of Liberalism as a doctrine solely concerned with free-trade and the rights of contract and private property. However much contemporary Liberalism has succeeded in shedding the reputation as the ideology of capitalism, it has failed to address the more fundamental problem of its reputation as a godless anti-clerical philosophy: a reputation that has also recently attracted the attention of many traditional Muslim clerics.

THE CHALLENGE OF RELIGION

Militant Liberal secularism is based on a challenge to the epistemological claims of religion. In this view religions are seen to make demanding political, social and ethical claims about how others should live, based on dubious or controversial premises and arguments. At its most extreme this argument claims that religion is based on superstition, credulity and tradition. This is a charge that is reciprocated by many sensitive and intelligent adherents of religion, especially in light of Liberalism's inability to provide any unchallengeable philosophical foundations for its core ethical commitments.[6] Yet, this debate about epistemological foundations has largely missed the point of the contemporary challenge to Liberalism which is based on recognition and identity. We can illustrate this point with the example of recent public controversies over the portrayal of religious imagery and the sacred in the case of *Jerry Springer the Opera* and the *Jyllands Posten* cartoons. In both cases, freedom of expression has been used to mock and ridicule sacred beliefs and images of Christians and Muslims. Liberals defend this kind of behaviour on the basis of a distinction between the individual believer and the belief. It would not be acceptable to persecute Islamic or Christian believers as such, but it is a different matter if one insults their beliefs. In the first case we have harm to the person, in the latter case only offence. Yet many egalitarians have come to argue that this Liberal distinction is simplistic and that some forms of offence are harms that require legal restriction. The reason for this is that certain beliefs, values and commitments are not merely contingent appendages of a person but are central to their identity as a person. Thus it is argued that to blaspheme against God or to insult the Prophet is not merely to offend the sensibilities of a person but is to attack their conception of themselves. It is every bit as harmful as a physical injury or the imposition of a civil punishment, and just as a physical attack inspires a defensive response so does an offence against the fundamentals of one's beliefs. On this view we should not be surprised at the anger of those whose conceptions of the sacred are insulted by Liberal free speech or the form that their anger takes. The harm is not just to the idea of a God, who for the Liberal may or may not exist: the harm caused by the denial and marginalisation of one's identity is a denial of equality of concern and respect. This form of egalitarian argument has been used to defend the idea of 'group libels' as actionable offences. Examples of group libel include 'Holocaust denial', 'Blasphemy laws' and restrictions of various kinds of 'hate speech'; some radical feminists even argue that pornography can be seen as a group libel against women.

But the religious challenge to Liberal secularism is not merely that Liberals allow members of religious groups to be harmed and marginalised by misrepresentation and insult. Increasingly the claim is that the Liberal emphasis on the secularisation of the public realm silences those who do not share a Liberal sensibility just as much as overt discriminatory laws and civil restrictions on participation. By insisting on the secularisation of the public realm, Liberal thinkers not only dismiss the use of religious language but also exclude those whose political claims and interests can only be articulated in religious terms, or else it puts additional political burdens upon the religious believer that are not imposed on others. Religious believers are expected to bear the cost of their day of rest or observance when they do not coincide with the public rest days whereas the secular are the beneficiaries of a cost-free good. In Liberal societies religious believers are expected to bear the considerable cost of insult to the sacred as a burden of social cooperation that has no parallel for those who are of a secular disposition.

Consequently, if we use the Liberal language of sharing the benefits of social cooperation as a burden of citizenship, it is clear that there is no question of reciprocity or fairness between those who are religious and those who are secular. Again the Liberal hostility to religion has the effect of institutionalising inequality, at least according to multiculturalist egalitarians such as Bhikhu Parekh and Tariq Modood,[7] among many others.

LIBERALISM AND SECULARISM

The challenge of secularism is presented as a challenge to the foundations of religious belief and practice. This view is perhaps warranted when applied to the ideas of some Liberal apostles of the Enlightenment who did indeed see religion as a bastion of superstition and false reasoning. However, such a top down secularism which aims at secularisation or the eradication of religion based on epistemological claims to authority, is a politically precarious and philosophically controversial basis for regulating the public realm as it turns every political question into a question of philosophical and moral foundations. Whatever militant secularists such as the biologist Richard Dawkins may argue,[8] the epistemological foundations of all social and political theories are controversial and open to challenge. This is not to conclude that Liberalism is no more than a philosophical preference, alongside equally valid preferences such as theism or nihilism, but it is to acknowledge that issues of foundational justification are philosophically complex, rarely conclusive and are a poor place to begin thinking about politics. If there is an argument for secularising the public realm it has to be different from the claim that religious beliefs are probably all false.

Contemporary Liberal theory has offered two approaches to the problem of accommodating religious, cultural and ethical difference that have a bearing on how we should conceive of secularism in the public domain. The early work of the philosopher John Rawls, sought neutral principles to regulate social cooperation between different conceptions of the good-life.[9] In its most extreme interpretation, Rawls' theory was supposed to abandon any appeals to controversial ethical and political ideals in justifying its basic principles. The argument in favour of this view was that it would therefore be strictly neutral and not privilege one ethical, political or religious view over any other. This simplistic interpretation of Rawls' admittedly complex and subtle argument, invited the obvious response that either no such neutral ground existed, or else that Rawls introduced a Liberal individualist ethic under the misleading guise of a neutral theory. Rawls' subsequent work, and that of his more able defenders, has gone a long way to showing that this criticism is mistaken and that his position was never so simplistic. To avoid the confusion engendered by the language of neutrality, other Liberal philosophers who share much with Rawls have turned instead to the concept of equality. Ronald Dworkin's theory of resource-egalitarianism is such a view.[10] Dworkin's theory distributes equal bundles of resources to individuals with which they can then pursue their own conceptions of the good. Resources are the external conditions of various life choices or option sets, and as such they will normally include income and wealth but they will also include sets of rights and liberties. Dworkin's theory is complex and hypothetical and it includes a baseline principle of freedom, which is necessary for each participant in the hypothetical decision-procedure to choose or endorse the conception of the good that they pursue.

One obvious consequence of this Liberal approach is that it builds an idea of individualism into its fundamental presuppositions. Consequently, this individualism will not be compatible with religious or ethical views that put the good of the group above any consideration of the interests of the individual. The other important point about the Liberal resource-based conception of equality is that it focuses on external goods as the object or dimension of equalisation. It does not require that everybody respect the value of everyone else's life choices, beliefs or values. Thus again we have a conception of equality of respect for the person, but not for the person's beliefs, values and commitments. This commitment is precisely the position that advocates of equality of recognition, multiculturalism and identity politics challenge, because it respects an abstract person not a real person with gender, race, ethnicity, religious beliefs etc. Yet this commitment to abstraction is not a mere accident, it is central to the Liberal vision and it is there – and should remain there – for two good reasons.

Firstly, the idea that an individual is identical with their ends, goals or beliefs is simply false. Personal coherence can withstand considerable changes of belief, culture and values. Such change can be costly to the person but it just is not the case that anyone who loses her faith (religious or political) ceases to be the same person in anything but a metaphorical sense. Abstraction, therefore, only requires that we see no set of commitments as being definitive of a person over time.

The second reason for rejecting the idea that the person is defined by her beliefs or values is that this would preclude the idea that the person can adopt the perspective of a citizen. Citizen equality requires that people see themselves not only as belonging to a variety of substantive and identity conferring groups, but that they are such in a shared public space where not everyone will hold the same views, beliefs and values as they do. Consequently, citizen equality (or civility) requires us to be able to stand back sufficiently from our beliefs and values to live a common and minimally coercive life with others. This is the primary reason for the Liberal preference for secularism in the public realm. If a state is a confessional state then people who do not share the religious view of the majority will either be marginalised and denied the equal protection of the law, or they will be required to falsely comply with doctrines and practices which they do not believe. This form of sullen submission is precisely the kind of false religiosity that the Enlightenment challenged and something that most religions would consider valueless.

Of course there will be some with a militant religious outlook who will argue that they should never compromise with others who are infidels and apostates. Let me stress that this is by no means a peculiarly Muslim problem, as is sometimes intimated in public discourse of late. The Liberal conclusion when faced with militant defenders of religion is that if they are not prepared to accept the burdens of civility then they cannot expect the protections of Liberal laws. Liberals have no obligation to protect those who act in an anti-Liberal fashion. They do of course have an obligation to protect those who hold anti-Liberal views but who pursue these peacefully. This might seem a paradoxical position, but Liberals are not committed to the forcible maintenance of a Liberal society. If all Liberals were to be convinced of the truth of anti-Liberal religious views, Liberalism would die out. However, Liberalism is not a religious belief and has no value unless people actually differ about how to regulate social interaction. It is an ethic that applies to politics, and the political realm is always characterised by disagreement.[11] It is of course possible that religious communities will bear the burdens of a Liberal order until they hold the monopoly of power. In the end Liberalism does not have any conclusive argument that will give a religious community a reason for adhering to Liberal civility in the absence of a motive to seek fair terms of social cooperation with others with whom they disagree. But if a religion or ethical view does persist in claiming that it is not bound by the long-term obligations of Liberal civility, then it can hardly complain if it is criticised and vilified as a dangerous and backward doctrine by those who do not share its beliefs and values. Such was the position of the Roman Catholic Church in Europe for much of the last four centuries, and it is a perception it has struggled hard to overcome in the last fifty years.

ACCOMMODATING RELIGION: LIBERALISM AS AN OPPORTUNITY

The Liberal conception of equal treatment that I have sketched above has still attracted criticism by some egalitarian philosophers who argue that it assumes a primitive and hostile view of religion as something that needs to be excluded from the public domain. The idea here is that Liberals see religion as an uncompromising and static view of the world and therefore something that cannot have a place in a plural political world. Such egalitarian theorists claim that this is a caricature and that the proper way to seek fair and equal terms of social cooperation is to negotiate away our differences.

The problem with this view in contrast to the Liberal view is that it assumes too much of religious positions and fails to offer them true respect. Of course it would be a failure of understanding to see all religions as being in some kind of conflict or struggle, one with the other. But it is equally disingenuous to require religious beliefs to avoid confronting, challenging and criticising others' political, ethical and religious views. Disagreement, disapproval and denial do form part of many religions, as well as non-religious ethical positions. If we are to respect religious groups and religion then we need to respect it on its own terms, and that involves allowing it to speak for itself in its own way and to make its own exclusive truth claims. Such a strategy will indeed be controversial, challenging and sometimes offensive to others, but it is also part of the exchange of ideas. To seek peaceful reconciliation of beliefs and practices whereby no one is allowed to offend anyone else, would not be to afford it recognition and respect but would be to effectively silence religion altogether. Of course, if religion is afforded this liberty to be itself and offend the sensibilities of others, then it must accept that others will be offended by it and criticise and challenge it accordingly. This offence will no doubt be irksome and challenging, but it remains offence and not harm as long as it cannot be translated into political and social marginalisation and exclusion, and that is prevented by the Liberal commitment to equality of respect and not merely formal equality of rights.

Liberal secularism, by excluding the protection and privileging of religion in the public domain does, in a paradoxical way, protect religion by freeing it to speak in its own voice and not trying to shape it to a political agenda. To achieve this, religion does not have to be rejected or denied. Liberalism is secularist in terms of the relations that hold between groups and individuals in society, that is that they are all equal. It may well also be a godless doctrine in the sense that it does not appeal to theological premises, but it need not be a doctrine that attempts to eradicate religious belief. In this sense contemporary Liberalism is perhaps closer to its seventeenth century forebears in its toleration of religion than is sometimes acknowledged.

Chapter 13

The Problem of Oppressive Cultures*

Kok-Chor Tan**

Aliberal global order can endorse the cultural rights of peoples without compromising on its individualist commitments.[1] Indeed it does so *because* of its individualist commitments in that its concern for individual good entails a concern for the cultural context within which individuals form and pursue their ideas of the good life. And granting cultural communities special protection in the form of group rights does not offend against the liberal stipulation that political institutions treat individuals with "equal concern and respect" when it can be shown that the objective of these rights is to compensate for institutional background *inequality* between cultural groups.[2]

But for most liberal multiculturalists, the liberal protection of culture does not extend to illiberal and nonliberal cultures.[3] It is how cultures promote individual liberal good rather than cultures in themselves that makes cultural membership an important liberal good, and so cultures which contradict liberal values undermine the very reason why liberals give cultures moral weight in the first place. In other words, for liberal multiculturalists the reconciliation of liberal individualism and cultural rights succeeds only in the case of characteristically liberal cultures.

* This chapter contains excerpts, edited by the author, from 'The Problem of Oppressive Cultures', in Kok-Chor Tan, *Toleration, Diversity, and Global Justice* (Copyright 2000 The Pennsylvania State University). Reprinted by permission of The Pennsylvania State University Press. Some discursive footnotes have been omitted. Thanks to Kevin Young for his assistance in both facilitating and editing this reprint.

** **Kok-Chor Tan** is an Associate Professor in the Department of Philosophy, at the University of Pennsylvania. He is the author of *Toleration, Diversity, and Global Justice* (2000), and *Justice Without Borders* (2004). He is currently working on the problems of global justice under non-ideal conditions, especially in areas such as reparations for past injustices, intervention, war and humanitarian aid.

There is, therefore, a potential difficulty with this reconciliation project. If we take cultural membership to be an important liberal good because it situates individual choice, then would the rejection of nonliberal or oppressive cultures not undermine the context of choice for some persons (i.e., those who find these nonliberal cultures worthy)? We have here, it would seem, a tension between our commitment to individual rights and freedom on the one hand, and our commitment to cultural protection on the other. This difficulty posed by oppressive cultures for liberal multiculturalism will be the focus of the present chapter.

PROTECTING CULTURES AND INDIVIDUALS: HAVING IT BOTH WAYS

The above challenge assumes that a dual commitment to both individual rights and culture lies in a certain tension in the case of oppressive cultures and that there is no possibility of fulfilling both commitments. However, I believe this value conflict to be for the most part avoidable. One reason why I think this to be the case is that most cultures can be reformed or "liberalised" without actually being destroyed. In other words, few cultures are *irremediably* nonliberal in the sense that liberalising them entails changing their very cultural *identities*; or, if we like, few cultures are *inherently* nonliberal such that their defining institutions and practices are nonliberal. If this observation is correct, reforming nonliberal cultures (in favour of some) need not necessarily diminish the worth of these cultures (for others).[4]

To accept this compatibility of culture and liberalism, we need only accept the rather modest premise that few cultures are entirely nonliberal (or even entirely liberal for that matter). Instead, more precisely, "liberalness" is largely a matter of degree rather than an all-or-nothing affair – some cultures exhibit more nonliberal cultural *practices* than others, and vice-versa – and, consequently, most cultures will have liberal elements in some of their practices.[5] (Labelling some cultures as liberal or nonliberal is quite a misnomer then. More accurately, a culture is *more* or *less* "liberal" than another if it has more or fewer liberal practices than the other, but with this point securely in mind, I continue to use these labels as useful approximations). It follows, therefore, that reforming a culture is *not* necessarily a zero-sum scenario wherein either supporters or reformers of the nonliberal cultural group have to lose out altogether. We can reform certain aspects of a culture, namely its nonliberal practices, without eliminating other of its inoffensive practices. Indeed we should see how much of a culture's own potential (by appealing to its liberal aspects) we can draw on and expand when advocating changes.

That the nonliberal practices of a culture are often distinct from its cultural identity, and can be reformed or even eradicated without significantly altering the latter, is confirmed by numerous well-known historical examples. Just to cite two, ending foot-binding in China or Sati (widow-burning) in India did not in any significant way alter Chinese or Hindu national cultural identities. These are *specific* cultural practices which do not by themselves distinguish Chinese and Hindu cultures from other national cultures, and so discontinuing them did not undermine the basic cultural identity and institutions of these societies.

Thus even as liberal multiculturalists criticise nonliberal cultural practices, they should operate on what Charles Taylor calls the "presumptive worth of cultures" and not assume that the cultures in question are fundamentally flawed and worthless.[6] As a practice then, when faced with a so-called nonliberal culture, liberals should train their objections on its *specific* nonliberal practices and avoid condemning the culture as a whole with such broad brushstrokes.[7] Moreover, I would argue that criticism does not preclude recognising and supporting positive aspects in other areas of that cultural way of life, by way of institutionalised group-specific rights. Focusing and balancing their criticisms in this way, liberals can hope to defend individual rights without undermining a culture's overall worth and the context of choice that it provides for its adherents. But, very importantly also, focused and balanced criticisms will be seen as more sincere and well-meaning from the point of view of the groups being judged and hence more constructive. This is an especially important point to bear in mind when advancing liberal ideals globally.

The above discussion suggests that what sets apart one culture from another is not some certain fixed and particular set of traits and practices, but varying sets of evolving, fluid and negotiable features that are open to continued evaluation and assessment. A culture is not defined in terms of some fixed and static set of practices and patterns of behaviour and values. As David Miller points out, speaking of nationality,

> [n]ational identities are not cast in stone ... [T]hey are above all 'imagined' identities, where the content of the imagining *changes* with time. So although at any moment there will be something substantial that we call our national identity, and we will acknowledge customs and institutions that correspond to this, there is no good reason to regard this as authoritative in the sense that excludes critical assessment.[8]

For liberal multiculturalists, it is ultimately *members* of a cultural community who are to determine how the community's practices could be reformed without compromising its cultural identity. The aim of liberal multiculturalism is not to sustain cultures as static and rigidly bound entities but to ensure that any change in a given culture is not forcibly imposed (from without) but is instigated by members of the culture themselves. Consequently, the more individual participation evident in the formation and evolution of a culture, the more confident we can be that changes are not changes that will undermine the given cultural context of choice but are changes freely assented to and so are choice-enabling rather than choice-restricting. Thus Bhikhu Parekh writes that "ethnic communities do, of course, run the risk of becoming internally oppressive and reactionary, but that requires their constant *internal self-regeneration*, not extinction".[9]

Thus, rather than snuffing out oppressive cultures, liberal multiculturalism can engender their evolution and transformation. Liberal freedom not only defends a culture from outside incursions, but also insures that there is option for growth and reform from within.[10] As David Miller stresses, the identity of a nation is continuously being renegotiated and regenerated as part of an ongoing "conversation" among conationals. As he puts it,

> liberal freedoms play a vital role in providing the conditions under which the conversation can continue. Without freedom of conscience and expression, one cannot explore different interpretations of national identity, something that takes place not only in political forums, but in various associations that make up civil society ... These discussions must proceed on the basis that no one should be penalized or excluded for expressing views that challenge the traditional understanding of national symbols and historic events.[11]

THE CHALLENGE OF ASIAN VALUES

In response to my attempt at circumventing the tension between protecting rights and culture, one might argue that there are some prominent and widely adhered to cultural ways of life which are irremediably or inherently nonliberal and so we may not "liberalise" these cultures without *also* destroying the cultural preconditions of choice for a large number of people.

As a case study, let us examine the well-known Asian Values argument against liberal universalism. Proponents of Asian Values claim that liberal ideals like the freedom of expression and association, equality between the sexes and the equal right to dissent are values foreign and even hostile to their (Confucian) cultural tradition.[12] Moreover, they point out that the recent economic successes of their countries are the result of these very values and hence all the more reason to preserve them.[13] Bilahari K. H. Kausikan writes: "In talking about Asian values [their proponents] are often only examining issues such as the responsibility of individuals to society, the role of the family and the maintenance of law and order."[14] But because, so Kausikan believes, liberalism relegates these social issues to the background by stressing individualistic values, it is a political morality which is inapplicable and unacceptable in the Asian context.

But this cultural rejection of liberalism is groundless. First of all, its asserted incompatibility with liberalism is based on a fundamental misinterpretation of liberal morality. Kausikan's critique ignores the fact that individual responsibility, the family, and law and order are vital liberal concerns as well. For instance, the liberal conception of individual rights makes sense only if it presupposes that other individuals have some sort of responsibilities corresponding to these rights. So Kausikan's claim that the "exaggeration of liberal values and individual rights, devaluing the notion of [social] 'values,' has led to serious problems"[15] seems to me to be at best a criticism (and a well-taken one at that) against nominally liberal societies for failing to live up to liberal demands and social responsibility, but is not itself a criticism of liberal principles.

The fundamental mistake underlying the Asian Values opposition to liberalism, a mistake commonly made by critics of liberalism, is the confusing of liberal individualism with *egotism* understood commonsensically as selfishness or self-centredness *à la* MacPherson's "possessive Individualism".[16] Understood in this way, individualism is obviously an unattractive aspiration, encouraging the privileging of one's narrow self-interests over the interests of others in society. Without doubt, a political morality premised on this view of human nature and/or which encourages and engenders this nature is highly undesirable for all societies, let alone those which take collective goals and responsibilities seriously.

But individualism as a liberal ideal properly conceived enjoins quite a different account of individual aspiration. Liberal individualism is the view, firstly, that the individual is the ultimate unit of moral concern in that very non-contentious sense that persons are what matter ultimately, as opposed to some abstract entity like the collective or society. More significantly, it is also individualistic in that it holds individuals to be capable of evaluating and revising their socially conceived ends in life, and as having the highest-order interest to do so. And nothing about thus conceiving individualism entails selfishness, self-centredness, atomistic individualism, unresponsiveness to the needs of others or that one lives an aimless, discontinuous and disjointed life. And it certainly does not entail the belief that an individual may do as she wishes; nor does this understanding of individualism preclude the idea that individuals must have abiding communal ties and commitments, that they have important responsibilities to their society and other individuals, and that justice may require certain sacrifices and self-restraint on their part.

Thus, once the difference is acknowledged between the individualism of liberalism and egotism (or "excessive individualism") often mistakenly associated with liberalism, it will be clear that a rejection of liberal individualism does not follow from a rejection of egotism.[17] Objecting to excessive individualism or egotism is a sound critique of liberalism if it is indeed true that liberal individualism when put into practice invariably breeds egotism. And, to be fair to liberalism's critics, it is unfortunately true that egotism is on the rise in many liberal countries, in no small measure due to *laissez-faire* capitalist practices in these societies. But, again, we must be careful not to mistakenly treat avoidable practical failures within liberal societies as evidence against liberal theory.

Contrary to the claims of some "communitarian" societies then, the rule of law, order, individual social responsibility, the family, and social values are also important liberal interests. After all, the liberal idea of individual well-being does not imply that individuals are asocial beings unable to appreciate the value of family or other special social relationships that give meaning and worth to a person's life. More generally, the individual pursuit of the good presupposes a stable social order within which persons' understanding of the good makes sense and acquires its value. Thus liberals do appreciate the importance of social order, and the rule of law and ideals of social responsibility that characterise such an order.[18] Now, there may be disagreement between liberals and nonliberals over *how* these interests can be legitimately realised and enforced, but this is quite different from saying liberals do not care about these social issues.

It could be retorted here that Asian societies have been forced into this individualist moral framework (the history of Western conquest and colonialism being the main reason), that individualism is conceptually alien to the Confucian worldview. But Confucian scholars have argued that the inherent anti-individualism so commonly associated with Confucianism is a misconception, or at best a one-sided interpretation, of the tradition. On the contrary, they point out that the idea of individual rights and freedom is latent, albeit in a nascent form, in Confucian thought. According to Julia Ching, the seeds of individual freedom and democracy were already sowed in ancient China. "[T]he belief in human perfectibility, a cornerstone of Confucian philosophy, implied a belief in personal freedom." Though "this was more an interior, spiritual freedom to improve one's own moral character ... [and] the conception of freedom as a right ... was never clearly articulated until modern times, and then under Western influence" it strongly indicates nonetheless "that traditional Chinese culture contains 'seeds' for concepts like ... democracy which have come more directly from the West".[19] Some East Asian leaders, in opposition to the dominant ideology of the region, have openly endorsed this more liberal interpretation of Confucianism.[20]

My point here is not that this liberal interpretation of Confucianism is definitive; rather I meant only to show that the tradition (particularly concerning its receptiveness of individualistic ideals) is open to competing interpretations, which should give us pause before accepting uncritically any one interpretation over another. Indeed it may be well worth asking why one particular version is invoked and enforced rather than another. This has prompted some critics and observers to suspect the repressive interpretation of Asian Values currently in force to be "very much a political construction" rather than a popular expression of a cultural view.[21] As one commentator notes, "If Asian values are used to deny human or civil and political rights, such denial does not reflect cultural values, but a selective practice of political philosophy."[22] That is, we cannot with confidence accept that a set of "values" in force in a society are truly assented to cultural values (by all reasonable participants) when there is simply no avenue for persons to voice their assent to or dissent from these values. If a politically enforced "cultural view" quells internal dissension within a community, its claim that it is representative of that community's culture is immediately called into doubt. Liberal multiculturalists need not, therefore, take all cultural claims at face value but ought to determine whether these are truly culturally based claims or whether they are ideologically and politically "constructed" ones.

Hence it is open to question, in the case of an oppressive society, whether that which is put forth as a cultural view is indeed genuine and not merely a "political construct" imposed by a dominant class. How else should we react when a large segment of a population is prevented from participating in the formation and preservation of their own cultural identity in a variety of ways? It is plain that those who insist on the inherently nonliberal nature of their culture have the onus of showing that *this* very claim has a cultural basis, that it is not just a claim endorsed and enforced by the political elites.

The examination of the Asian Values position shows us the general strategy to adopt when confronted by so-called nonliberal cultures. But my more fundamental point is that *real examples* of irremediably nonliberal cultures are harder to come by than critics of liberalism and liberal multiculturalism might think. Consequently, the potential tension between individual rights and culture is less grave in reality than at first appears. Of course, I do not deny that there could be, however rare, genuinely nonliberal cultures. In the face of this challenge, liberal multiculturalists will be forced to make the difficult choice of letting the irremediably illiberal culture pass on, and even encourage its passing on. But the saving grace for the multiculturalist is that these hard cases are rare exceptions rather than the general rule.

Chapter 14

Cultures and Religions of Liberalism in a Global Era

*Pheng Cheah**

The crisis of liberalism and/as secularism in the contemporary era was probably first brought into prominence by Samuel Huntington's lurid argument that culture has become the primary determinant of global political conflict in a post-Cold War world.[1] Huntington suggested that instead of leading to the *Bildung* (my word) or cultivation of the world in the image of Western universalistic ideals, the global spread of economic and social modernity has brought about various forms of cultural and religious assertions – exemplified by the rise of Islamic fundamentalism and neo-Confucianism – that challenge the hegemony of Western civilization with its universalistic political values of liberalism and secularism, thereby forcing this formerly universal culture to retreat into a particularism that must strive to protect itself.[2]

In a post-September 11 world where the war against Islamic terrorism has become a routine part of the quotidian, Huntington's thesis of the culturalization of global politics with its implicitly xenophobic premise of the incommensurability of cultures seems to have become a self-fulfilling prophecy. Yet, the extent to which culture can be said to have brought liberalism into crisis in contemporary globalization is an issue that requires more careful theoretical reflection. For economic liberalism at the global level – the global spread

* **Pheng Cheah** is Professor in the Department of Rhetoric, University of California at Berkeley. He is the author of *Spectral Nationality: Passages of Freedom from Kant to Postcolonial Literatures of Liberation* (Columbia University Press, 2003) and *Inhuman Conditions: On Cosmopolitanism and Human Rights* (Harvard University Press, 2006), and the co-editor of *Cosmopolitics – Thinking and Feeling Beyond the Nation* (University of Minnesota Press, 1998) and *Grounds of Comparison: Around the Work of Benedict Anderson* (Routledge, 2003). He is currently working on a book on theories of money and the possibility of world literature in an era of financial globalisation.

of the practices, institutions, and technologies of capitalist accumulation as a result of the liberalization of world trade and the rise of a genuinely global mode of production – is in fact the material condition for the culturalization of politics. In Huntington's own words, "economic power is rapidly shifting to East Asia, and military power and political influence are starting to follow. India is on the verge of economic takeoff and the Islamic world is increasingly hostile to the West. The willingness of other societies to accept the West's dictates or abide its sermons is rapidly evaporating, and so are the West's self-confidence and will to dominate."[3] This indicates that cultural reassertions and liberalism are not intrinsically opposed or inimical to each other. In this essay, I explore the origins of the conceptual separation of liberalism from religion and culture before turning to consider how globalization challenges this divorce by demonstrating the compatibility and complicity of liberalism with religion and culture.

Why are religious and cultural reassertions and the return of religion to the public domain automatically interpreted as the crisis of liberalism? The sharp opposition between culture and religion and liberal values is a legacy of liberal political philosophy. The fundamental axiom of the natural liberty of human beings – the right "to be free from any Superior Power on Earth, and not to be under the Will or Legislative Authority of Man, but to have only the Law of Nature for his Rule" – leads logically to a restriction of political power *qua* power that individuals have ceded to society or collective authority to power that is exercised only for the common or public good and the preservation of the life, liberty and property of all members of society.[4] Hence, for Locke, the power of political or civil society "is a Power, that hath no other end but preservation, and therefore can never have a right to destroy, enslave, or designedly to impoverish the Subjects."[5] What is established is the conventional distinction between the state, which is only concerned with the public good, and a private realm that holds in reserve all remaining liberties and must be vigorously protected from state encroachment.

For various historical reasons, the separation of public and private realms led to the secularization of the state because religious freedom emerged as a paradigmatic example of individual liberty and the use of political power by majority groups to pursue religious intolerance was regarded as epitomizing the invasion of the private realm by the public realm.[6] Hence, Locke pronounced that it is

necessary above all to distinguish between the business of civil government and that of religion, and to mark the true bounds between the church and the commonwealth ... The commonwealth seems to me to be a society of men constituted only for preserving and advancing their civil goods. What I call civil goods are life, liberty, bodily health and freedom from pain, and the possession of outward things, such as lands, money, furniture, and the like ... The whole jurisdiction of the magistrate is concerned only with these civil goods, and ... all the right and dominion of civil power is bounded and confined solely to the care and advancement of these goods; and ... it neither can nor ought in any way to be extended to the salvation of souls.[7]

Indeed, Mill extended the importance of secular values beyond the sphere of "outward things" into the sphere of inner life by suggesting that the attempt "to form the mind and feelings" by an exclusively religious system of ethics such as Christian doctrine will only result in "a low, abject, servile type of character."[8]

The liberal quarantine of religion to the private realm and the curtailment of religious culture in the formation of ethical conduct, however, occludes the fact that liberal values are themselves shaped by a certain culture and religion. Mill himself linked the cultivation of individuality to a sanitized Greco-Christian tradition: "There is a Greek ideal of self-development, which the Platonic and Christian ideal of self-government blends with, but does not supersede ... It is not by wearing down into uniformity all that is individual in themselves, but by cultivating it and calling it forth, within the limits imposed by the rights and interests of others, that human beings become a noble and beautiful object of contemplation."[9] At the same time, he also rendered invisible the cultural-religious roots of liberalism by elevating its techniques of self-cultivation beyond mere custom, which he described as a form of despotism: "The despotism of custom is everywhere the standing hindrance to human advancement, being in increasing antagonism to that disposition to aim at something better than customary, which is called, according to the circumstances, the spirit of liberty, or that of progress or improvement."[10]

However, as Alexis de Tocqueville and Max Weber have pointed out in their different ways, liberal political institutions and economic systems grow out of and are sustained by Christian religious beliefs. Tocqueville is clearest on this point: "Religion, which among Americans, never mixes directly in the government of society, should therefore be considered as the first of their political institutions; for if it does not give them the taste for freedom, it singularly facilitates their use of it."[11]

In my view, one of the most important theoretical implications of globalization is that it leads us to question liberal political philosophy's axiomatic separation of liberalism from religion and culture. Globalization shows in the sharpest relief the fundamental compatibility and complicity of liberalism with religion and culture in two related ways.

First, economic globalization under the current dispensation of neoliberalism is suffused by a religious aura. The global dissemination of the ascetic techniques at the heart of economic liberalism through global economic institutions, corporate practices and the managerial discourse of business schools leads to what one might call after the Frankfurt School a religion of instrumentality. The magical inverted world of capitalist accumulation is sustained in our global era by a new religion of business management science and technological innovation that continually re-enchants the world with its promises of exponentially increasing efficiency, creative productivity and perfect control of an increasingly miniaturized and systematized world. The acceleration of the post-Cold War displacement of Europe as the traditional center for higher learning by the U.S. university system and the ascendancy of the U.S. as a center for business-oriented advanced technological research as a result of the high tech boom in the Silicon valley, is an index of this new religiosity. Notwithstanding the intensification of cultural reassertions outside the Western world, there are many Asian cities that desire to be the new Silicon valley and major center for biotechnological research. China, the *San Francisco Chronicle* reports, "is using the biotech contract research industry – in which companies take on projects for foreign clients – as a springboard to develop the expertise and technical prowess that will help Chinese companies compete internationally. The goal is to build a world-class biotechnology sector that develops a steady stream of proprietary products for the global market."[12] As I write this piece, the Center for Research on Chinese and American Strategic Cooperation, a part of the Institute of Management, Innovation, and Organization housed in the business school at my home institution, the University of California at Berkeley, is hosting a group of judges, policymakers and enterprise executives from China for a new training program on innovation and intellectual property rights.[13]

Second, and more importantly, the apparent incompatibility of liberal values with contemporary cultural and religious reassertions ought to be situated within the broader frame of the latter's fundamental compatibility with *economic* liberalism. Discussions of the undermining of liberalism by culture and religion have predominantly taken as their mesmerizing focus the rise of varieties of transnational Islamic movements, "fundamentalist" or otherwise, and their impact on political regimes outside the North Atlantic and on multicultural politics in the North. If we turn, however, to the second major example of cultural reassertion that Huntington discusses, namely, China, Greater China, and Confucian East Asia, then the complicity between liberalism and religious culture is patent. Now, in terms of the history of ideas, Huntington's use of Chinese culture as an example of what is inimical to liberal values is not fortuitous. Mill had pointed to China as exemplary of stagnation under the yoke of custom:

> We have a warning example in China – a nation of much talent, and, in some respects, even wisdom .... [T]hey have become stationary – have remained so for thousands of years; and if they are ever to be farther improved, it must be by foreigners .... [U]nless individuality shall be able successfully to assert itself against this yoke, Europe, notwithstanding its noble antecedents and its professed Christianity, will tend to become another China.[14]

Although Huntington's emphasis on the resurgence of a secular Confucian culture and the affirmation of Asian values overturns the characterization of Chinese culture as stagnating, he maintains the fundamental opposition between liberal values and Chinese culture.

In fact, the values and technologies of economic liberalism have been crucial in rearticulating Chinese culture in contemporary transnationalism, sometimes with the explicit sanction of the socialist mainland Chinese state. The neo-Confucian modernity that is regarded as the basis of the 1990s East Asian economic miracle is often characterized by its ideologues as *guanxi* or networks/connections capitalism (a form of capitalism underwritten by a Confucian humanism and that implies a degree of communitarianism) that is superior to Western capitalism because it can alleviate the atomistic individualism and instrumental rationality of Western liberalism.[15] But this purportedly Confucian culture in fact draws on the mercantile practices of the Chinese diaspora in East and Southeast Asia. This trading class had a low status in the Confucian mainland and its mercantile culture has more in common with the economic liberal values of all entrepreneurial trading diasporic communities in former European colonies in Asia.[16] In the colonial era, this trading class acted as buffer between the colonial powers and indigenous peoples. The younger generations of this class received a colonial education and the liberal values they learned were crucial in negotiations for formal decolonization.[17]

What we have witnessed with the rise of East Asian capitalism is the spectacular reconstellation of Chinese culture by liberal values and technologies disseminated through business practices and colonial education, initially by the strengthening of ties between the Southeast Asian Chinese diaspora and their ancestral hometowns as sites of foreign investment through Overseas Chinese Voluntary Associations, and later, by the accelerated economic modernization of mainland China with the inflow of global capital, especially in the aftermath of the handover of the former British colony of Hong Kong to the PRC.[18] The mainland wants to model parts of itself, especially the coastal cities of South China, after diasporic communities and external Chinese cities such as Hong Kong and Singapore. In his famous visit to South China in January 1992, Deng Xiaoping had called for the construction of a few new Hong Kongs. After 1992, overseas Chinese investment, which had earlier been concentrated in the South China Economic Periphery, expanded into the interior provinces of Hubei and Sichuan and the northeast beyond Beijing.[19]

This is no simple reassertion of a monolithic Confucian Chinese culture that undermines Western liberalism. To speak of Asian values as such is to posit mythical ties that bind together the many heterogeneous cultures and religions of Asia. Indeed, the very idea of a revitalized Confucian Chinese culture as the ethos of a superior path of economic development is a hegemonic construct that obscures the immense poverty and growing social divisions that are created in the mainland as a result of hyperdevelopment. Fruit Chan's recent film, *Durian, Durian* (2000), a portrayal of a Chinese woman who returns to the mainland from her sojourn abroad as a sex-worker, offers a biting parody of this myth of a monolithic Chinese cultural reassertion. The migrant sex-worker is intimately linked to the opening up of the mainland to the technologies and values of economic liberalism as a result of globalization. It is not only that economic development and the porosity of the border between the mainland and Hong Kong has increased the flow of migrant sex-workers because young Chinese women who are adversely affected by modern development resort to prostitution to improve their standard of living. More strikingly, the migrant sex-worker embodies many of the traits and characteristics of the old diasporic merchant subject as well as the values of the new Chinese transnational entrepreneurial subject that are celebrated as virtues and ideals in the PRC at the level of both state and society. But the superficiality of transnational Chinese ethnic fraternity is exposed by the fact that throughout her time in Hong Kong, Xiao Yan, the protagonist, is repeatedly subjected to insulting slurs from Hong Kong locals because she is from the mainland. Hence, when a client with a body covered with tattoos of a dragon tells her that all Chinese are descendants of the dragon, the statement rings with hollowness.

Globalization has also engendered varieties of spiritual-religious forms of cultural reassertion in the Chinese region that are compatible with economic and political liberalism. I am referring here to the rise of popular spiritual cults and communities at the local and transnational level that draw on and alchemize techniques and rituals from Daoism and Buddhism with sophisticated technologies of communication and organization.

The relation between these groups and the mainland state is complex. On the one hand, they can be seen as atavistic insofar as they come into conflict with the state's imperatives for economic modernization. On the other hand, however, they can also be understood as embodying in a non-self-conscious manner liberal political values if they are seen as an emerging civil society seeking autonomy from the totalitarian communist state that actively persecutes them. Hence, the *Falungong* has caught the attention of the international media as a religious movement engaged in a struggle for religious freedom and human rights against a secular socialist state.[20] Here, it is a secular communist state that shows religious intolerance and a religious movement that is aligned with liberal values. But other cults such as the Three in One, which syncretizes Confucianism, Buddhism and Daoism, cannot be explained in the recognizably political terms of civil society activism because they are resolutely local in origin even though they may open up new spaces for community by forming alliances with other villages with the financial help of transnational capital from overseas Chinese groups in Southeast Asia.[21]

Outside the mainland, another less noticeable but no less widespread community, the *Heqidao*, uses the discourse of electromagnetic audio technologies of transmission, reception, and recording to understand the "traditional" Chinese Daoist concept of *qi* (energy) as the source of spiritual well-being.[22] Unlike the *Falungong*, the *Heqidao* does not engage in organized public protest against government policies. "*Qigong* and *fengshui* techniques are blended with new technologies – music speakers and microphones, for example – but the Taoist idea of returning to the innocent and primordial state is re-articulated with the Romantic notion of a 'second harmony' together with Freudian theory of 'talking cure.'[23] The *Heqidao* is especially popular with middle-class professionals in Taiwan, especially engineers and telecommunications workers and businessmen. It is also extremely popular among the recent Chinese diaspora of middle-class origins. Like many other Chinese organizations associated with alternative techniques of healing, such as Buddhist organizations, it has a complex and globalized corporate organizational structure and has established TV networks, CD-circulation channels, websites, and email lists. It provides a form of spiritual refuge for those "who have rejected the unsafe or uncertain environments of their home countries while finding themselves caught in another set of losses – loss of jobs, networks, language command, prestige and privileges, above all, of a familiar world picture."[24]

These various Chinese cases of alchemical mixings of liberalism, culture, and religion indicate that the question of the crisis of liberalism and/as secularism needs to be reposed. The fundamental incompatibility of liberal values with those of culture and religion need to be reformulated beyond the rigid conceptual opposition inherited from its historical site of origin: the political thought of the European Enlightenment. The European Enlightenment bequeathed to academic research its problematic of religious freedom and tolerance, a problematic that is played out in the demarcation of boundaries between state and civil society, the public and the private realms. Globalization, however, is not so much a structure or a system that extends these stable topographies but a dynamic field where different forces such as liberalism, culture, and religion can come into conflict but also draw on each other for sustenance depending on how they find themselves aligned. Hence, instead of speaking of a monolithic Western liberalism that is opposed to an equally monolithic Chinese cultural reassertion (or Islamic "fundamentalism"), one might speak of the cultures and religions of liberalism, the cultures and religions that are formed from the spread of various forms of liberalism, and learn to track these different forms as they arise out of shifting alignments and their various turns.

One might then account for the crisis of liberalism in the current global conjuncture by distinguishing between liberalism as a political doctrine or philosophy with ideals and values based on the sovereignty of the individual and the various technologies of economic liberalism and neoliberalism.[25] These technologies historically made political liberalism possible and successful in the North Atlantic at the same time that they undermined its universal institutionalization because of their inherently competitive, exploitative, and unequal character. The crisis of liberalism in the North Atlantic as a result of more extreme forms of cultural and religious reassertion is then not a matter of the inherent antinomy between liberalism as such and culture and religion. It is merely the logical outcome of the effects of economic liberalism beyond the North Atlantic and the proliferation of new cultures and religions of liberalism.

Chapter 15

National Identity Versus Cosmopolitan Identity

*Montserrat Guibernau**

C osmopolitanism includes a set of values and principles based on the premise that, as members of humanity, all persons are in a fundamental sense equal and free and deserve equal political treatment regardless of their origin.[1]

I understand current accounts of cosmopolitanism to be closely related to the image of the world as a single interconnected place where an unparalleled degree of visibility brought about by the technological revolutions of the late twentieth century has provided exceptional awareness of political, cultural, linguistic, religious, economic and other forms of difference. Increased interaction – economic, political, cultural and social – strengthens the case for cosmopolitanism as the ethics of the global age.

Cosmopolitan values have already been accepted and included in some constitutions and international agreements. There is a big gap, however, between the theoretical vow to cosmopolitan principles and their practical implementation. At present, not a single institution is recognized by all humans as capable of enforcing compliance with cosmopolitan principles and having sufficient power, legitimacy and means to punish those transgressing them.

It should not escape our analysis that theories of cosmopolitanism originated in the West and that it is within the West that they find most of their supporters. Hitherto, we should be aware that in the developing world many

* **Montserrat Guibernau** is Professor of Politics, Queen Mary University of London. Her research focuses on the study of nationalism and ethnicity in the West with a particular emphasis on the study of Western nations without states. Guibernau takes a comparative approach to the study of national identity, nationalism, governance in multinational democracies, globalisation and citizenship in the European Union.

regard cosmopolitanism as a new Western strategy in its long-term quest to dominate the rest of the globe. But suspicion of cosmopolitanism is not confined to the developing world, quite the opposite, many Western working class and lower middle class people regard it as a luxury item at the disposal of an elite who can afford to defend and enjoy it while the vast majority continues either ignorant or indifferent.

This essay focuses on the cultural dimension of cosmopolitanism. In so doing, it establishes a clear-cut distinction between global and cosmopolitan culture. Crucially, it argues that cosmopolitan culture does not consist of an unqualified celebration of hybridity and difference. Instead, its components ought to respect cosmopolitan values.

The essay argues that national identity's proven capacity to generate solidarity bonds and a sense of community among fellow-nationals would be unmatched by the rise of an eventual cosmopolitan identity. In a similar manner, the mobilizing force of national identity, which involves love and loyalty to the nation, is unlikely to be equalled by the collective sentiment of belonging to humanity. To conclude, the essay advocates that the quest for a cosmopolitan identity – so far restricted to an elite – is best understood as an attitude in favour of freedom and equality among human beings which should, in turn, contribute to adding a new moral dimension to national identity.

COSMOPOLITANISM: A MULTI-LEVEL THEORY

Cosmopolitanism operates at various levels and acquires a different meaning according to whether we refer to legal, political, economic and cultural issues.

Legal cosmopolitanism is primarily concerned with global justice and the implementation of human rights. It challenges the almost exclusive capacity of the nation-state to act as the ultimate arbitrator of what should or should not be regarded as an infringement of human rights within its territory.

Political cosmopolitanism. Globalization has contributed to the generation of novel political spaces where interaction among a wide range of political actors including national, international, transnational and supranational actors, as well as other organizations and institutions, takes place. In my view, the emergence of these novel 'global political spaces' can either favour the expansion of cosmopolitan principles or, quite the opposite, utilize its unprecedented influence to promote authoritarian and neo-fascist doctrines as well as novel fundamentalisms hostile to global justice and the defence of human rights. It is not at all clear whether we are moving towards a freer and more equal world or, quite the reverse, we are to be confronted with new forms of tyranny.

For instance, the perception of terrorism as an ever-present threat – real, potential or imagined – could be employed to curtail civil liberties, expand surveillance mechanisms and limit the free movement of people. Populist authoritarian political parties capitalizing on anti-immigrant sentiments across the Western world could occupy new global political spaces.

Economic cosmopolitanism consists of applying cosmopolitan principles to trade and labour relations throughout the world. Complying with cosmopolitanism would automatically entail the end of political and economic doctrines based on the exploitation of 'others' regardless of how these are to be defined. It is to be expected that a full commitment to cosmopolitanism would signal the end of doctrines based on making profit out of taking advantage of people. Consequently, I envisage a forceful resistance to its implementation.

Cultural cosmopolitanism. I argue that a clear-cut distinction needs to be drawn between three main concepts: global culture, cosmopolitan culture and cultural cosmopolitanism. By 'global culture' I refer to a worldwide culture formed by a mixture of elements originating from a wide range of traditions. Currently, a single global culture does not exist despite the fact that a very specific and limited number of cultural elements have become almost global in scope. At present, the world is composed of a rich variety of cultures most of them based, created and promoted by particular nations. So far, the most efficient creator and disseminator of a homogenizing culture and language among a territorially circumscribed and diverse population has been the nation state.

By 'cosmopolitan culture', I refer to a culture, which, in addition to being global in scope, ought to be committed to the idea that all persons are in a fundamental sense equal and free. It is precisely the compliance with cosmopolitan values that should ultimately determine whether a particular item of a specific culture might be considered as a component of a cosmopolitan culture or not.

A cosmopolitan culture could be defined as a hybrid culture destined to overcome ethnocentrism and ready to emphasize those cultural traits capable of uniting human beings rather than separating them. Such a culture would be fluid, dynamic and open to change. It would add a thin layer of identity – containing a strong moral outlook – on peoples' national and local identities. Undoubtedly, the eventual emergence of a cosmopolitan culture raises significant issues concerning who should act as its creator, who should fund its dissemination and decide on its content.

I define 'cultural cosmopolitanism' as the endeavour towards the construction of a world culture based on ideas of equality and freedom. A novel type of culture global in scope and moving beyond the traditional remit of the nation, but also beyond emerging supranational cultures such as the now incipient European culture promoted by the EU.

In my view, the construction of a cosmopolitan culture is a highly complex moral enterprise, which should be based upon the following principles.

(1) The *principle of egalitarian individualism* assumes that all humans are free and equal beings; however, when applied to culture I do not understand it to mean that all cultures are equal, at least not if we were to adopt a cosmopolitan outlook according to which a distinction should be established between those principles that comply with cosmopolitan values and those which do not.

A cosmopolitan culture should exclude those values, principles and social practices present in some national and other types of culture, which deny the equal worth and dignity of all human beings. It should reject all aspects of particular cultures tolerating, defending and promoting discrimination and inequality on grounds of gender, age, health, race, religious faith, social status and other mechanisms utilized to exclude people and curtail their freedom.

(2) The *principle of reciprocal recognition* assumes that individuals can only be free and equal if they recognize each other as such. It is not for an external Leviathan, constitution or law to impose cosmopolitanism since, to exist, it requires the active engagement of all individuals without exception.

Yet we could appeal to consent, collective decision-making and agency as principles requiring freedom and equality among all humans. Dialogic democracy should act as the mechanism by means of which agreements and decisions could be reached.

(3) The *principle of impartial moral reasoning* assumes that all humans should be able to transcend their national and local cultures in order to attain a plain field free from prejudices and stereotypes within which they could engage in the free and unrestricted use of reason. It is incorrect to state that a cosmopolitan culture celebrates difference, diversity and hybridity without further qualifying such an assumption. In my view, diversity, difference and hybridity can only be deemed as components of an eventual cosmopolitan culture if and only if they respect cosmopolitan values. There are numerous examples of a wide variety of cultural elements which contribute to an unqualified celebration of diversity and hybridity within an already incipient global culture; however, many of them would never make it into a truly cosmopolitan culture if this was to ever emerge and be true to its name.

ON COSMOPOLITAN IDENTITY[2]

There are at least two main interpretations of what having a cosmopolitan identity means. First, it is commonly employed to refer to somebody who is 'sophisticated or urbane', a person who 'has lived and traveled in many countries, especially one who is free of national prejudices'.[3] Second, from an ideological perspective, I define cosmopolitan identity as the collective sentiment of belonging to humanity and being committed to the idea that all humans are free and equal. Various forms of cosmopolitan identity, restricted to a selected elite, have existed since ancient times. In its modern form, cosmopolitan identity is intrinsically bound up with the intensification and expansion of globalization processes allowing us, for the first time in history, to have a reasonably accurate idea of the composition, numbers and features of humanity. Previous images of the world were founded on limited awareness of other cultures and civilizations and resulted in partial accounts of human diversity entirely mediated by the circumscribed knowledge of various peoples who sought to describe the world according to their own cultural parameters.

By definition, a cosmopolitan identity is fluid, dynamic and a prerogative of a selected elite. Today's cosmopolitans belong to the middle and upper classes, tend to speak English[4] as a mother tongue or as a *lingua franca*, enjoy sufficient resources to take advantage of the goods and lifestyles associated with post-industrial societies and feel comfortable using the continuously emerging new ranges of sophisticated information technology and communications goods bombarding the market. Cosmopolitans transcend the limits of their national and local communities and enjoy travelling a world that, for them, has truly become a single place.

In my view, further to adopting a critical and constructive attitude towards existing national cultures – one's own as well as those of others – a truly cosmopolitan identity should engage in an active struggle against those ideologies, value systems and social practices impeding the fulfilment of human freedom and equality. The desire to transcend ethnocentrism, while achieving a radical transformation of the social can never materialize if cosmopolitan identity is made to fit the outlook of a single culture.

A cosmopolitan identity should emerge out of dialogue, exchange, understanding and the reciprocal respect for each other's cultural practices while taking into account the specific temporal and geographical social *milieu* within which they have been constructed.

In what follows I compare national and cosmopolitan identity by focusing on five dimensions: psychological, cultural, historical, territorial and political.

Psychological dimension

National identity fosters closeness, empathy and solidarity among fellow nationals. By emphasizing what is unique about a specific nation, it singles it out from the rest and generates a sentimental attachment to it. But, does awareness of being a member of humanity foster sentiments of solidarity and closeness among human beings? I argue that, up to a point, usually a theoretical point, yes; however in practice, it is incredibly hard to sustain an emotional attachment to such a vast number of people.

To identify with somebody we need to speak their language, understand their culture and, above all, we need the sensitivity to know how it would feel to be in their place. We also need the capacity to suffer and rejoice with the other. I argue that most people are not inclined to identify with those deemed too different, remote or alien, nonetheless, an entirely different matter concerns whether people should, in spite of all differences, be able to share an attitude in favour of the recognition and promotion of respect, dignity, equality and freedom for all.

Relations among people, in particular among strangers, do not tend to be based on cosmopolitan principles. Indeed, the contrary seems to be the norm. To illustrate this, let's just consider the incredible amount of violence present in human relations – personal and collective – that presumably would not exist if we were to truly identify with the other.

A raw test assessing the degree of mutual identification among people could consist of analysing whether people are able to inflict pain and use violence against those they identify with. It is my concern that only by emphasizing the alien condition of the other, individuals are capable of inflicting pain and suffering upon other human beings.

There are numerous examples – war, conflict, crime, repression, torture – in which individuals, pursuing their own private interest or just for the sake of it, ignore the human condition of others, degrading them and turning them into strangers.

People can sympathize and, in a superficial manner, identify with strangers whenever their humanity – limited to those traits they can relate to – is brought to the fore. For example we can, up to a point, feel for – that is identify with in some unspecified manner – the hunger, suffering, illnesses and deprivation endured by others when they are made visible to us, but the enormous amount of avoidable suffering which continues to exist, not only miles away from us but also within our own societies, shows that identification with strangers is light and often remains associated with the belief that people should take responsibility for their own lives and that we cannot aspire to resolve humanity's problems simply because these are huge and far too many.

Does cosmopolitan identity require the weakening and even the renunciation of national identity? In my view, cosmopolitan identity urges a critical attitude towards non-cosmopolitan principles present within national cultures as well as the commitment to change them. This does not imply the renunciation to national identity, nor does it denote the outright condemnation of a particular culture but preparedness to change it from within.

Cultural dimension

The realization of a cosmopolitan identity would be superimposed onto national and other forms of identity. In this regard, it should be best described as an attitude contributing to the cosmopolitanization of national and ethnic cultures.

A sense of common nationhood acts in tension with deep societal cleavages preventing fellow citizens from identifying each other as members of the same nation. National cohesion can only be attained if differences among citizens are upheld within certain limits, and it seems to me that a similar point including the whole of humanity should be made regarding a cosmopolitan culture and identity. I argue that in so far as humanity remains fractured by deep social, political and economic cleavages, such as those currently in place, it would be impossible to envisage the rise of a cosmopolitan culture, let alone a shared cosmopolitan identity beyond the remit of a privileged elite.

Historical dimension

Antiquity acts as a source of legitimacy for national cultures eager to remind their members that the nation pre-existed their very existence and will transcend their own life span. The collective memory shared by the national community emphasizes continuity over time and strengthens its unity. The selective use of history – including joyous as well as painful events – constitutes the backdrop against which intellectuals engage in the creation of a shared history, one usually based on a myth of common origin and a sense of mission including a common project for the future.

In contrast, the collective history of humanity is based upon the immemorial division of its peoples. Until the present, conquest, war and conflict have kept people apart and have contributed to the emergence of distinct national identities. Opposition to the other has proven key to fostering particular identities – individual as well as collective.

The construction of a cosmopolitan identity would require emphasizing those attributes that unite humanity above those that separate it. The worldwide expansion of some shared rights as well as access to sufficient resources for all to live with dignity are indispensable for a cosmopolitan identity to emerge.

Territorial dimension

Within a cosmopolitan culture, the sentimental attachment to the nation's territory should be complemented by an attachment to the whole planet. Probably the cosmopolitan principle, which has gained greatest prominence worldwide in the last few years, is the concern for the preservation of the environment. The reasons behind it are only partially to be found on altruistic grounds since, for most peoples and their governments, the preservation of the environment becomes a priority in so far as its continuous degradation poses a direct threat to themselves and to their successors.

A cosmopolitan identity would establish a radically different relationship with territory, which would have no resemblance with that of national identity. Such a relationship would be founded on the 'lifting out' of cultural experiences from their traditional anchoring.[5] It is envisaged that a cosmopolitan culture will disembed some cultural practices from the territories – spaces – within which they have emerged and portray them as shared by all.

Political dimension

The nation is a political community willing to decide upon its future, be it as an independent nation-state, an autonomous entity, a member of a federation, a province or a region. The terminology is subject to various nuances according to each particular case. Those sharing a national identity regard themselves as forming a *demos* with the capacity to reach and express a common will and act upon it. As previously stated, nations may or may not have a state of their own.

In contrast, the human community has never regarded itself as a single *demos* or acted as one. The eventual rise of a cosmopolitan identity would change this. By emphasizing the significance of sharing the human condition, humanity as a whole would be able to express itself as a single *demos*.

A cosmopolitan identity would call for a shared language to further communication and understanding among world citizens. Even if English is spoken by large sections of the world's population, it is still far from being a *lingua franca* at global level. In my view, it is impossible to generate a shared sense of identity among people who do not understand each other.

It is expected that a cosmopolitan identity would, in time, contribute to the constitution of cosmopolitan institutions with legislative, executive and judicial powers; a move burdened with issues concerning how to adapt the value systems of particular national cultures to the requirements of cosmopolitan principles.

Sharing a national identity facilitates mutual understanding, trust and solidarity among fellow nationals and, in so doing, it contributes to the unfolding and consolidation of democratic citizenship. It is difficult to envisage how such a function might be carried out at a cosmopolitan level. In addition, we should bear in mind that democracy evolves within societies endowed with a distinct culture and value system.

In my view, cosmopolitanism and the quest for a cosmopolitan identity are best understood as representing an attitude in favour of further equality, respect and freedom among human beings which should progressively permeate our national cultures by transcending ethnocentrism and widening our cultural horizon. Being a cosmopolitan involves adopting a critical attitude towards those elements of particular cultures – national and other – which do not respect cosmopolitan principles as well as the commitment to transform them.

Chapter 16

Cultural Diversity, Cosmopolitan Principles and the Limits of Sovereignty

*David Held**

Thinking about the future of humankind on the basis of the early years of the tweny-first century does not give grounds for optimism. From 9/11 to the 2006 war in the Middle East, terrorism, conflict, territorial struggle and the clash of identities appear to define the moment. The wars in Afghanistan, Iraq, Israel/Lebanon and elsewhere suggest that political violence is an irreducible feature of our age. Perversely, globalization seems to have dramatized the significance of differences between peoples; far from the globalization of communications easing understanding and the translation of ideas, it seems to have highlighted what it is that people do not have in common and find dislikeable about each other. Moreover, the contemporary drivers of political nationalism – self-determination, secure borders, geo-political and geo-economic advantage – place an emphasis on the pursuit of the national interest above concerns with what it is that humans might have in common.

Yet, it is easy to overstate the moment and exaggerate from one set of historical experiences. While each of the elements mentioned poses a challenge to a rules based global order, it is a profound mistake to forget that the twentieth

* **David Held** is Graham Wallas Professor in Political Science in the Department of Government at the London School of Economics and Political Science. A co-director of the Centre for the Study of Global Governance, he has published widely on topics related to globalisation, democracy and modern social theory.

century established a series of cosmopolitan steps towards the delimitation of the nature and form of political community, sovereignty and 'reasons of state'. These steps were laid down after the First and Second World Wars which brought humanity to the edge of the abyss – not once but twice. At a time as difficult as the start of the twenty-first century, it is important to recall why these steps were built and remind oneself of their significance.

From the foundation of the UN system to the EU, from changes to the laws of war to the entrenchment of human rights, from the emergence of international environmental regimes to the establishment of the International Criminal Court, people have sought to reframe human activity and embed it in a formal system of law, rights and responsibilities. Many of these developments were initiated against the background of formidable threats to humankind – above all, Nazism, fascism and Stalinism. Those involved in them affirmed the importance of universal principles, human rights and the rule of law in the face of strong temptations to simply put up the shutters and defend the position of only some countries and nations. They rejected the view of national and moral particularists that belonging to a given community limits and determines the moral worth of individuals and the nature of their freedom, and they defended the irreducible moral status of each and every person. At the centre of such thinking is the cosmopolitan view that human well-being is not defined by geographical or cultural locations, that national or ethnic or gendered boundaries should not determine the limits of rights or responsibilities for the satisfaction of basic human needs, and that all human beings require equal moral respect and concern. The principles of equal respect, equal concern and the priority of the vital needs of all human beings are not principles for some remote utopia; for they are at the centre of significant post-Second World War legal and political developments.

What does 'cosmopolitan' mean in this context?[1] In the first instance, cosmopolitanism refers to those basic values which set down standards or boundaries which no agent, whether a representative of a global body, state or civil association, should be able to violate. Focused on the claims of each person as an individual, these values espouse the idea that human beings are in a fundamental sense equal, and that they deserve equal political treatment; that is, treatment based upon the equal care and consideration of their agency, irrespective of the community in which they were born or brought up. After over two hundred years of nationalism, sustained nation-state formation and seemingly endless conflicts over territory and resources, such values could be thought of as out of place. But such values are already enshrined in the law of war, human rights law, the statute of the International Criminal Court, among many other international rules and legal arrangements.

Second, cosmopolitanism can be taken to refer to those forms of political regulation and law-making which create powers, rights and constraints which go beyond the claims of nation-states and which have far-reaching consequences, in principle, for the nature and form of political power. These regulatory forms can be found in the domain between national and international law and regulation – the space between domestic law which regulates the relations between a state and its citizens, and traditional international law which applies primarily to states and interstate relations. This space is already filled by a host of legal regulation, from the legal instruments of the EU and the international human rights regime as a global framework for promoting rights, to the diverse agreements of the arms control system and environmental regimes. Cosmopolitanism is not made up of political ideals for another age, but embedded in rule systems and institutions which have already altered state sovereignty in distinct ways.

Yet, the precise sense in which these developments constitute a form of 'cosmopolitanism' remains to be clarified, especially given that the ideas of cosmopolitanism have a long and complex history. For my purposes here, cosmopolitanism can be taken as the moral and political outlook which builds upon the strengths of the post-1945 multilateral order, particularly its commitment to universal standards, human rights and democratic values, and which seeks to specify general principles upon which all could act. These are principles which can be universally shared, and can form the basis for the protection and nurturing of each person's equal interest in the determination of the forces and institutions which govern their lives.

Cosmopolitan values can be expressed formally, and in the interests of brevity, in terms of a set of principles.[2] Eight principles are paramount. They are the principles of: (1) equal worth and dignity; (2) active agency; (3) personal responsibility and accountability; (4) consent; (5) collective decision-making about public matters through voting procedures; (6) inclusiveness and subsidiarity; (7) avoidance of serious harm; and (8) sustainability. While eight principles may seem like a daunting number, they are interrelated and together form the basis of a compelling political orientation – an orientation which helps illuminate what it is that humankind has in common.

The eight principles can best be thought of as falling into three clusters. The first cluster (principles 1–3) set down the fundamental organizational features of the cosmopolitan moral universe. Its crux is that each person is subject of equal moral concern; that each person is capable of acting autonomously with respect to the range of choices before them; and that, in deciding how to act or which institutions to create, the claims of each person affected should be taken equally into account. Personal responsibility means in this context that actors and agents have to be aware of, and accountable for, the consequences of their actions, direct or indirect, intended or unintended, which may substantially restrict and delimit the choices of others. The second cluster (principles 4–6) form the basis of translating individually initiated activity, or privately determined activities more broadly, into collectively agreed or collectively sanctioned frameworks of action or regulatory regimes. Public power can be conceived as legitimate to the degree to which principles 4, 5 and 6 are upheld. The final principles (7 and 8) lay down a framework for prioritizing urgent need and resource conservation. By distinguishing vital from non-vital needs, principle 7 creates an unambiguous starting point and guiding orientation for public decisions. While this 'prioritizing commitment' does not, of course, create a decision procedure to resolve all clashes of priority in politics, it clearly creates a moral framework for focusing public policy on those who are most vulnerable. By contrast, principle 8 seeks to set down a prudential orientation to help ensure that public policy is consistent with global ecological balances and that it does not destroy irreplaceable and non-substitutable resources.

It could be objected at this point that, given the plurality of interpretive standpoints in the contemporary world (social, cultural, religious and so on), it is unwise to construct a political outlook which depends upon overarching principles. For it is doubtful, the objection could continue, that a bridge can be built between 'the many particular wills' and 'the general will'.[3] In a world marked by a diversity of value orientations, on what grounds, if any, can we suppose that all groups or parties could be argumentatively convinced about fundamentally ethical and political principles?

It is important to stress that cosmopolitanism does not deny the reality and ethical relevance of living in a world of diverse values and identities – how could it? It does not assume that unanimity is attainable on all practical-political questions. The elaboration of cosmopolitan principles is not an exercise in seeking a general and universal understanding on a wide spectrum of issues concerning the broad conditions of life or diverse ethical matters (for example, abortion, the conditions for genetic research and public goods provision). This is not how a modern cosmopolitan project should be understood. Rather, at stake is a more restrictive exercise aimed at reflecting on the moral status of persons, the conditions of agency and collective decision-making. It is important to emphasize that this exercise is constructed on the assumption that ground rules for communication, dialogue and dispute settlement are not only desirable but also essential – precisely because all people are of equal moral value and their views on a wide range of moral-political questions will conflict. The principles of cosmopolitanism are the conditions of taking cultural diversity seriously and of building a democratic culture to mediate clashes of the cultural good. They are, in short, about the conditions of just difference and democratic dialogue. The aim of modern cosmopolitanism is the conceptualization and generation of the necessary background conditions for a 'common' or 'basic' structure of individual action and social activity.[4]

Contemporary cosmopolitans, it should be acknowledged, are divided about the demands that cosmopolitanism lays upon the individual and, accordingly, upon the appropriate framing of the necessary background conditions for a 'common' structure of individual action and social activity. Whether cosmopolitanism is an overriding frame of reference (trumping all other moral positions) – strong cosmopolitanism – or a distinctive subset of considerations (specifying that there are some substantive global rules, norms and principles of justice which ought to be balanced with, and take account of, those derived from individual societies or other human groupings) – weak cosmopolitanism – is not a question which will be focused on here.[5] However, some comment is in order if the rationale and standing of the eight principles are to be satisfactorily illuminated.

I take cosmopolitanism ultimately to denote the ethical and political space occupied by the eight principles outlined above. Cosmopolitanism lays down the universal or regulative principles which delimit and govern the range of diversity and difference that ought to be found in public life. It discloses the proper basis or framework for the pursuit of argument, discussion and negotiation about particular spheres of value, spheres in which local, national and regional affiliations will inevitably be weighed. In some respects, this is a form of strong cosmopolitanism. However, it should not be concluded from this that the meaning of the eight principles can simply be specified once and for all. For while cosmopolitanism affirms principles which are universal in their scope, it recognizes, in addition, that the precise meaning of these is always fleshed out in situated discussions; in other words, that there is an inescapable hermeneutic complexity in moral and political affairs which will affect how the eight principles are actually interpreted, and the weight granted to special ties and other practical-political issues. This cosmopolitan point-of-view builds on principles that all could reasonably assent to, while recognizing the irreducible plurality of forms of life.[6] Thus, on the one hand, the position upholds certain basic egalitarian ideas – those which emphasize equal worth, equal respect, equal consideration and so on – and, on the other, it acknowledges that the elucidation of their meaning cannot be pursued independently of an ongoing dialogue in public life. Hence, there can be no adequate institutionalization of equal rights and duties without a corresponding institutionalization of national and transnational forms of public debate, democratic participation and accountability.[7] The institutionalization of regulative cosmopolitan principles requires the entrenchment of democratic public realms.

A cosmopolitan perspective of this kind shares a particular commitment with weak cosmopolitanism in so far as it acknowledges a plurality of value sources and a diversity of moral conceptions of the good; it recognizes, accordingly, different spheres of ethical reasoning linked to everyday attempts to resolve matters concerning modes of living and social organization. As such, it seeks to express ethical neutrality with regard to many life questions. But ethical neutrality of this sort should not be confused with political neutrality and its core requirements.[8] The point has been succinctly stated by one commentator: 'a commitment to ethical neutrality entails a particular type of political arrangement, one which, for one, allows for the pursuit of different private conceptions of the good.'[9] Only polities that acknowledge the equal status of all persons, that seek neutrality or impartiality with respect to personal ends, hopes and aspirations, and that pursue the public justification of social, economic and political arrangements can ensure a basic or common structure of political action which allows individuals to pursue their projects – both individual and collective – as free and equal agents. Such a structure is inconsistent with, and, if applied systematically, would need to filter out, those ends and goods, whether public or private, which would erode or undermine the structure itself. For value pluralism and social pluralism to flourish, political associations must be structured or organized in one general way – that is, according to the constituting, legitimizing and prioritizing principles specified above. Arguments can be had about the exact specification of these; that is, about how these notions are properly formulated. But the eight principles themselves constitute guiding notions or regulative ideals for a polity geared to autonomy, dialogue and tolerance.

These principles are not just Western principles. Certain of their elements originated in the West; that is, in the struggle for a democratic culture and a distinctive conception of the person as a citizen who is, in principle, 'free and equal' in a manner comprehensible to everyone. But their validity extends much further. For these principles are the foundation of a fair, humane and decent society, of whatever religion or cultural tradition. To paraphrase the legal theorist Bruce Ackerman, there is no nation without a woman who yearns for equal rights, no society without a man who denies the need for deference, and no developing country without a person who does not wish for the minimum means of subsistence so that they may go about their everyday lives.[10] Such principles are building blocks for articulating and entrenching the equal liberty of all human beings, wherever they were born or brought up. They are the basis of underwriting the autonomy of others, not of obliterating it. Their concern is with the irreducible moral status of each and every person – the acknowledgement of which links directly to the possibility of self-determination and the capacity to make independent choices.

It has to be acknowledged that there is now a fundamental fissure in the Muslim world between those who want to uphold universal standards, including the standards of democracy and human rights, and reform their societies, dislodging the deep connection between religion, culture and politics, and those who are threatened by this and wish to retain and/or restore power on behalf of those who represent 'fundamentalist' ideals. The political, economic and cultural challenges posed by the globalization of (for want of a better label) 'modernity' now face the counterforce of the globalization of radical Islam. This poses many important questions, but one in particular should be stressed; that is, how far and to what extent Islam – and, of course, parts of the resurgent fundamentalist West (for instance, the Christian right in the USA) – have the capacity to confront their own ideologies, double standards and limitations.

It would be a mistake to think that this is simply an outsider's challenge to Islam. Islam, like the other great world religions, has incorporated a diverse body of thought and practice. In addition, it has contributed, and accommodated itself, to ideas of religious tolerance, secular political power and human rights. It is particularly in the contemporary period that radical Islamic movements have turned their back on these important historical developments and sought to deny Islam's contribution both to the Enlightenment and the formulation of universal ethical codes. There are many good reasons for doubting the often expressed Western belief that thoughts about justice and democracy have flourished only in the West.[11] Islam is not a unitary or explanatory category.[12] Hence, the call for cosmopolitan principles speaks to a vital strain within Islam that affirms the importance of autonomy, rights and justice.

The cosmopolitan principles set out above lay down some of the universal or organizing principles which delimit and govern the range of diversity and difference that ought to be found in public life. And they disclose the proper framework for the pursuit of argument, discussion and negotiation about particular spheres of value, spheres in which local, national and regional affiliations will inevitably be weighed. These are principles for an era in which political communities and states matter, but not only and exclusively. In a world where the trajectories of each and every country are tightly entwined, the partiality, one-sidedness and limitedness of 'reasons of state' need to be recognized. States are hugely important vehicles to aid the delivery of effective public regulation, equal liberty and social justice, but they should not be thought of as ontologically privileged. They can be judged by how far they deliver these public goods and how far they fail; for the history of states is, of course, marked not just by phases of corruption and bad leadership but also by the most brutal episodes.

The same can be said about political agents and forces operating in civil society. They are by no means necessarily noble or wise, and their wisdom and nobility depend on recognizing necessary limits on their action, limits which mark out the legitimate spaces for others to pursue their vital needs and interests. Actors in civil society, like states, need to be bound by a rules based order which articulates and entrenches the eight cosmopolitan principles. Only such an order can underwrite a political system which upholds the equal moral standing of all human beings, and their entitlement to equal liberty and to forms of governance founded on deliberation and consent. Here are the clues needed to build a politically robust and ethically sound conception of the proper basis of political community, and of the relations among communities in a global age. We need to build on the cosmopolitan steps of the twentieth century and deepen the institutional hold of this agenda.

PART IV

Soft Power and the Question of 'Americanisation'

INTRODUCTION

This section examines the extent and nature of American 'soft power', its connections with forms of market development, and the possibility that a 'fear of cultural loss' is driving both the proliferation of contemporary cultural differences and escalations in geopolitical and social conflict. Many, of course, have proposed that cultural conflicts are inevitable given the increasing global enmeshment of different civilisational transitions and the symbolic confrontations that inevitably arise in this process. The authors in this section offer an assessment of American 'soft power' through a number of different lenses, and in so doing suggest new ways of thinking about the relationships between cultural representation, dominance and future engagements in the context of both US hegemony and processes of globalisation.

The original creator of the term 'soft power', **Joseph Nye Jr**, offers a thorough reassessment of his concept in light of recent cultural changes related to globalisation, US foreign policy, and the cultural changes that have accompanied these. Nye argues that, for a variety of reasons not the least of which is the recent US intervention in Iraq, the reach of American soft power has suffered a general decline. Yet, he notes that it has not slumped as far as many depict and, at the same time, it possesses a capacity for recovery. Moreover, suggesting 'globalisation is not Americanisation', he argues that even symbols and cultural products that are interpreted as cultural exports of the US are interpreted differently in different places and social contexts, and that so-called forces of cultural homogenisation are not a real and sustained threat to diverse local cultures which are always dynamically changing, adaptive and fluid.

Reflecting on the discrepancy between cultural attitudes towards US power and the core values that it shares with many other nations, **Ann-Marie Slaughter** and **Thomas Hale** approach the issue of American soft power by addressing the ironies and tensions between perceptions of US nationalism and its deeper historical elements. Noting that supports for America's behaviour internationally 'may be at a historically low ebb', Slaughter and Hale argue that behind the resurgent 'anti-Americanism' of late there is a great and sad irony since the values of American nationalism properly understood have a deeply cosmopolitan dimension. Recovering this understanding, they argue, is vital for rebuilding America's influence and impact on the world.

Engaging with the theme of soft power through the 'global reign' of the Hollywood film industry, **Janet Wasko** assesses the US film industry's position in international markets and its capacity for hegemony. Wasko notes that historically, Hollywood has not only enjoyed the ability to be culturally adaptive in remarkable ways, but also used its political and economic strengths to dominate film markets around the world. Despite a series of structural advantages, Wasko explores a number of factors which threaten US dominance today. In this regard, resistance to perceived US interference, problems associated with piracy, the growth of co-production, the prospects for robust anti-trust enforcement and new competition in the global film market by both Europe and India all combine to make the continued strength of Hollywood's global reign questionable. Wasko concludes that, 'just like the US government, Hollywood companies are not infallible', and that ultimately the strength of Hollywood – and thus an important element in spreading US culture around the world – is intimately tied up with the prospects for US geo-political power in the future.

Paul Gilroy proposes a number of ways of thinking about the intersection of US power and race. Gilroy contends that, irrespective of the mix between the use of US 'hard' and 'soft' forms of power, qualitative changes have occurred in the way US power is conceived and exercised. To understand this qualitative shift demands that we invoke a more elaborate understanding of the ways in which the 'info-war' is projecting race and ethnicity in new geo-political patterns. Gilroy argues that the new form of war that the US is practicing requires the wholesale integration of struggles over information, language and symbols into the conflict itself – and that this signifies that hard and soft power are effectively fused. For Gilroy, Condoleezza Rice serves as an embodiment of the US struggle to extend political rights to its racial and ethnic minorities, providing an official face of US diversity united across racial lines by a patriotic commitment to the advancement of US national interests. Further, Gilroy argues that Rice adds something distinctive to the political visibility of the US in the world – her celebrity is deployed whither to convey that racism has been dealt with, 'or to raise unhelpful and unanswerable questions about the shifting importance of racial authenticity.'

The final piece in this section is a trenchant critical assessment of Nye's thesis by **Michael Cox** and **Adam Quinn**. They explore the current trends in European anti-Americanism in its diverse variants, and argue that these may well leave a long-lasting impact which survives the passing of the war in Iraq. In their words '[t]he present ill feeling towards the United States may well leave a footprint which it is hard to erase'. They suggest that the culture of anti-Americanism needs to be challenged in public discourse, and they call for moderates in the United States and Europe to focus on their core common values in order to ensure that a rule-based multilateral order can survive to face the great global challenges of our time.

Chapter 17

Culture, Soft Power, and 'Americanization'

Joseph S. Nye, Jr[*]

In 1989 when I was writing *Bound to Lead*,[1] the conventional wisdom was that the United States was in decline. As I tried to understand why the declinists were wrong, I totaled up American military and economic power and realized that something was still missing: the enormous capacity of the U.S. to get what it wanted by attraction rather than through coercion. This attractive, or 'soft,' power stemmed from American culture, values, and policies that were broadly inclusive and seen as legitimate in the eyes of others. Today polls show that American soft power has diminished around the world. According to the polls, the most important reason was the Bush administration's foreign policy strategies, particularly the invasion of Iraq. Attraction to American values and culture slumped much less. That could be good news for a future recovery of American soft power, since policies can change relatively quickly while culture and values change more slowly. But even if a new administration pursues policies that are more inclusive and legitimate in the eyes of others, a residual anti-Americanism will remain. It will be based on resentment of America's size, association of the U.S. with disruptive globalization, and local fears about loss of cultural autonomy.[2]

[*] **Joseph S. Nye Jr** is University Distinguished Service Professor, and the Sultan of Oman Professor of International Relations at Harvard University. He has served as Assistant Secretary of Defence for International Security Affairs, Chair of the National Intelligence Council, and Deputy Under Secretary of State for Security Assistance, Science and Technology. This essay draws upon his books, *The Paradox of American Power* (Oxford University Press, 2002) and *Soft Power: The Means to Success in World Politics* (Public Affairs, 2004).

GLOBALIZATION AS AMERICANIZATION

The idea that globalization equals Americanization is common, but simplistic. It is true that the United States is a giant in the contemporary phase of globalization. As Hubert Vedrine has written,

> the United States is a very big fish that swims easily and rules supreme in the waters of globalization. Americans get great benefits from this for a large number of reasons: because of their economic size; because globalization takes place in their language; because it is organized along neo-liberal economic principles; because they impose their legal, accounting, and technical practices; and because they're advocates of individualism.[3]

It is understandable that those who resent American power and popular culture use nationalism to fight it. Jose Bové, a French sheep farmer (who incidentally spent the early years of his life in Berkeley, California) became a French folkloric hero and earned global press coverage by protecting 'culinary sovereignty' through destroying a McDonald's restaurant. No one forces the French public to enter the golden arches, but Bové's success with the media spoke to the cultural ambivalence toward things American long before the Iraq war.

Several dimensions of globalization are indeed dominated today by activities based in Wall Street, Silicon Valley, and Hollywood, but globalization is not synonymous with Americanization. The intercontinental spread of Christianity preceded by many centuries Hollywood's discovery of how to market films about the Bible, and the global spread of Islam is not 'made in USA.' The English language which is the modern equivalent of Latin was originally spread by Britain, not the United States. Ties between French, Spanish and Portuguese speaking countries have nothing to do with the United States, nor do transnational relations among Asian diasporas, nor the contemporary spread of AIDS or avian flu, nor European banks lending to emerging markets in Latin America. The most popular sports team in the world is not American: it is Manchester United. Three of the leading 'American' music labels have British, German, and Japanese owners. Some of the most popular video-games come from Japan and Britain. The rise of reality programming that enlivened or debased the standards of television entertainment in the past decade spread from Europe to the United States, not vice versa.

As Anthony Giddens observed, 'globalization is not just the dominance of the West over the rest; it affects the United States as it does other countries'.[4] Or in the words of Singapore's Kishore Mahbubani, 'the West will increasingly absorb good minds from other cultures. And as it does so, the West will undergo a major transformation: it will become within itself a microcosm of the new interdependent world with many thriving cultures and ideas.'[5] Globalization is not intrinsically American, even if much of its current content is heavily influenced by what happens in the United States.

Several distinctive qualities of the United States make it uniquely adapted as a center of globalization. American culture is produced by and geared toward a multi-ethnic society whose demographics are constantly altered by immigration. America has always had a syncretic culture, borrowing freely from a variety of traditions and continuously open to the rest of the world. And European concerns over American influence are not new. A number of books were published on the subject a century ago – for example, a British author, W.T. Stead wrote about *The Americanization of the World* in 1902. The United States is also a great laboratory for cultural experimentation, the largest marketplace to test whether a given film or song resonates with one sub-population or another, or perhaps with people in general. Ideas flow into the United States freely, and flow out with equal ease – often in commercialized form, backed by entrepreneurs drawing on deep pools of capital and talent. A Pizza Hut in Asia looks American though the food, of course, is originally Italian. There seems to be an affinity between opportunities for globalization, on the one hand, and these characteristics of American society.

American culture does not always flow into other societies unchanged, nor does it always have political effects. The ideas and information that enter global networks are 'downloaded' in the context of national politics and local cultures which act as selective filters and modifiers of what arrives. McDonald's menus are different in China, and American movies are dubbed in varying Chinese accents to reflect Chinese perceptions of the message being delivered.[6] Political institutions are often more resistant to transnational transmission than popular culture. China has emphatically not adopted American political institutions, and Chinese students today are quite nationalistic in reaction to the United States at the same time that they seek visas to study there. For many countries, Canadian constitutional practices, with their greater emphasis on duties, or German laws, restrictive of racially charged speech, are more congenial than the first amendment absolutism of the United States.[7]

Globalization today is America-centric, in that much of the information revolution comes from the United States, and a large part of the content of global information networks is currently created in the United States and enhances American 'soft power.' Former French Culture Minister Jack Lang warned that soft power 'moved mostly in one direction because Americans were so closed-minded and provincial, if not grossly ignorant of other cultures.'[8] But Lang misses the openness of American society which accepts and recycles culture from the rest of the world. U.S.-made standards are sometimes hard to avoid, as in the rules governing the internet itself. But other U.S. standards and practices – from pounds and feet (rather than the metric system) to capital punishment or the right to bear arms – have encountered puzzlement or even outright hostility. American feminism attracts some and repels others. Hollywood films that show women working outside the home and divorcing their husbands often repel rather than attract conservative Muslims, and in a country like Iran they attract teenagers and repel the ruling Mullahs at the same time. Soft power does not accrue to the United States in all areas of life, nor is the United States the only country to possess it. Many observers in Asia, for example, report an increase in Chinese and Indian soft power. Globalization is more than just Americanization.

Conspiracy theorists describe the world as a cobweb with the U.S. as the spider in the middle. But there are many types of networks in globalization, and a hub and spokes model may blind us to changes that are taking place in their architecture. Network theorists argue that central players gain power most when there are 'structural holes' – gaps in communications – among other participants. When the spokes cannot communicate with each other without going through the hub, the central position of the hub provides power. When the spokes can communicate and coordinate directly with each other, the hub becomes less powerful. The growth of the internet provides these inexpensive alternative connections that fill the gaps.[9] Indeed Jihadist terrorists have proven quite adept at using the internet against American military power.

As the architecture of global networks evolves from a hub and spokes model to a widely distributed form like the internet, the structural holes shrink, and the structural power of the central state is reduced. It is true, for now, that Americans are central to the internet and comprise more than a third of all internet users at the beginning of the twenty-first century. English is the most prevalent language on the internet today, but at some point, Chinese internet users are likely to outnumber American users. Chinese websites will be read primarily by ethnic Chinese nationals and expatriates, and this will not dethrone English as the web's lingua franca, but it will increase Chinese power in Asia by allowing Beijing 'to shape a Chinese political culture that stretches well beyond its physical boundaries.'[10] And China will not be alone. With the inevitable spread of technological capabilities, more distributed network architectures will evolve. At some time in the future when there are a billion internet users in Asia and 250 million in the United States, more websites, capital, entrepreneurs, and advertisers will be attracted to the Asian market. And both China and India have begun to refer to the importance of increasing their soft power.

The United States now seems to 'bestride the world like a colossus.' Looking more closely, we see that American dominance varies across realms and that many relationships of interdependence go both ways. Large states like the United States – or to a lesser extent, China – have more freedom than do small states, but they are rarely exempt from the effects of globalization. And states are not alone: organizations, groups and even individuals are becoming players. For better and worse, technology is putting capabilities within the reach of individuals that were solely the preserve of government in the past.[11] Falling costs are increasing the thickness and complexity of global networks of interdependence. The United States promotes and benefits from economic globalization. But over the longer term, as capabilities spread, we can expect globalization itself to spread economic capabilities and thus reduce the extent of American dominance.

GLOBALIZATION AND LOCAL CULTURES

Local culture and local politics also set significant limits on the extent to which globalization enhances American power. Contrary to conventional wisdom, globalization is not homogenizing the cultures of the world. Although they are related, globalization and modernization are not the same. People sometimes attribute changes to globalization that are caused in large part simply by modernization.[12] The modernity of the industrial revolution transformed British society and culture in the nineteenth century. The global spread of industrialization and the development of alternative centers of industrial power eventually undercut Britain's relative position. And while the modernity of the new industrial centers altered their local cultures so that in some ways they looked more like Britain than before, the cause was modernization, not Anglicization. Moreover, while modernity produced some common traits such as urbanization and factories, the residual local cultures were by no means erased. Convergence toward similar institutions to deal with similar problems is not surprising, but it does not lead to homogeneity.[13] There were some similarities in the industrial societies of Britain, Germany, America and Japan in the first half of the twentieth century, but there were also important differences. When China, India and Brazil complete their current process of industrialization, we should not expect them to look like replicas of Japan, Germany or the United States.

Similarly, though the United States is widely perceived as being at the forefront of the information revolution, and that results in many similarities in social and cultural habits (such as television viewing or internet use) that are attributed to Americanization, correlation is not causation. If one entertains a thought experiment of a country introducing computers and communications at a rapid rate in a world in which the United States did not exist, one would expect major social and cultural changes to occur from the modernization (or as some say, post-modernity). Of course since the United States exists and is at the forefront of the information revolution, there is a current degree of Americanization, but it is likely to diminish over the course of the century as technology spreads and local cultures modernize in their own ways.

Evidence of historical proof that globalization does not necessarily mean homogenization can be seen in the case of Japan, a country that deliberately isolated itself from an earlier wave of globalization carried by seventeenth-century European seafarers. In the middle of the nineteenth century it became the first Asian country to embrace globalization, and to borrow successfully from the world without losing its uniqueness. During the Meiji Restoration Japan searched broadly for tools and innovations that would allow it to become a major power rather than a victim of Western imperialism. It sent young people to the West for education. Its delegations scoured the world for ideas in science, technology and industry. In the political realm, Meiji reformers were well aware of Anglo-American ideas and institutions, but deliberately turned to German models because they were deemed more suitable to a country with an emperor.

The lesson that Japan has to teach the rest of the world is not simply that an Asian country can compete in military and economic power, but that after a century and a half of globalization, it is possible to adapt while preserving a unique culture. Of course, there are American influences in contemporary Japan. Thousands of Japanese youth are co-opting the music, dress and style of urban black America. But some of the groups dress up like Samurai warriors on stage. As one claims, 'we're trying to make a whole new culture and mix the music.'[14] One can applaud or deplore or simply be amused by any particular cultural transfers, but one should not doubt the persistence of Japan's cultural uniqueness.

The image of American homogenization also reflects a mistakenly static view of culture. Few cultures are static, and efforts to portray them as unchanging often reflect conservative political strategies rather than descriptions of reality, often as male-dominated elites resist modern roles for women. The Peruvian writer Mario Vargas Llosa put it well in saying that arguments in favor of cultural identity and against globalization 'betray a stagnant attitude towards culture that is not borne out by historical fact. Do we know of any cultures that have remained unchanged through time? To find any of them one has to travel to the small, primitive, magico-religious communities made up of people ... who due to their primitive condition, become progressively more vulnerable to exploitation and extermination.'[15] Vibrant cultures are constantly changing and borrowing from other cultures.

Finally, there is some evidence that globalization and the information revolution may reinforce rather than reduce cultural diversity. In one British view, 'globalization is the reason for the revival of local culture in different parts of the world ... Globalization not only pulls upwards, but also pushes downwards, creating new pressures for local autonomy.'[16] Some French commentators express fear that in a world of internet global marketing, there will no longer be room for a culture that cherishes some 250 different types of cheese. But on the contrary, the internet allows dispersed customers to come together in a way that encourages niche markets, including hundreds of sites dedicated only to cheese. The internet also allows people to establish a more diverse set of political communities. The use of the Welsh language in Britain and Gaelic in Ireland is greater today than fifty years ago.[17] Britain, Belgium and Spain, among others in Europe, have devolved more power to local regions. The global information age may strengthen rather than weaken many local cultures.

Transnational capitalism and corporations are changing poor countries, but not homogenizing them. In the early stages of investment, a multinational company, with its access to the global resources of finance, technology and markets holds the high cards and often gets the best of the bargain with the poor country. With time, as the poor country develops skilled personnel, learns new technologies, and opens its own channels to global finance and markets, it may successfully renegotiate the bargain and capture more of the benefits. When the multinational oil companies first went into the Persian Gulf, they claimed the lion's share of the gains from the oil; today the local governments do. Of course there has been some change in Saudi Arabia as engineers and financiers have been trained abroad, incomes have risen, and some degree of urbanization has occurred, but as we have become increasingly aware, after sixty years of transnational investment, Saudi culture certainly does not look like that of the United States!

Skeptics might argue that modern transnational corporations will escape the fate that befell the giant oil companies because many are virtual companies that design products and market them but farm out manufacturing to dozens of suppliers in poor countries. The big companies play small suppliers against each other, seeking ever lower labor costs. But the technology of cheap communications also allows NGOs to conduct campaigns of 'naming and shaming' that threaten their market brands in rich countries, such that multinationals become vulnerable as well.

CONCLUSION

Economic and social globalization are not producing cultural homogeneity. The rest of the world will not someday look just like the United States. American culture is very prominent at this stage in global history, and it contributes to America's attractive or soft power in many, but not all, areas. At the same time, immigrants, ideas, and external events are changing American culture. In the past, this has enhanced American soft power. Today, American soft power is at a lower ebb than at any time since the Vietnam war. While Woodrow Wilson's narrative of 'making the world safe for democracy' may have enhanced soft power, George W. Bush's coercive policy of 'making democracy to make the world safe' has had the opposite effect. For the United States to regain soft power, it will have to realize that democracy promotion is best done by attraction: being the shining city on the hill. That will require not only a narrative and commitment to democratic values at home, but also an inclusion of John F. Kennedy's vision of 'making the world safe for diversity,' not just the export of American democracy.

As globalization spreads technical capabilities, and information technology allows broader participation in global communications, American economic and cultural preponderance is likely to diminish over the course of the century. This in turn has mixed results for American soft power. A little less dominance may mean a little less anxiety about Americanization, fewer complaints about American arrogance, and a little less intensity in the anti-American backlash. In any case, the political reactions to globalization will be far more diverse than a unified reaction against American cultural hegemony. The next time you hear someone claim that globalization is simply Americanization and the homogenization of cultures, tell them to calm down and read more history.

Chapter 18

Calling All Patriots:
The Cosmopolitan Appeal of Americanism

Anne-Marie Slaughter* and Thomas Hale#

On April 28, 2004 the CBS news program *60 Minutes II* broadcast pictures of American soldiers beating and mocking bound Iraqi prisoners, stacking them into pyramids like naked human bricks, humiliating them sexually, and setting dogs on them. In one of the most grotesque images, U.S. Army Pfc. Lynndie England flashes the "thumbs up" symbol over a pile of naked prisoners, a gesture that, thanks to the proliferation of American popular culture, was instantly understood by horrified audiences across the globe. Equally universal were the shock and outrage the pictures generated, though in the United States these feelings were joined by a third emotion – shame. Echoing the sentiments of many Americans, one of us wrote at the time, "Coming through Copenhagen Airport, with hideous pictures from Abu Ghraib staring out at me from every publication, I hesitated to show my passport. I felt tainted and ashamed."[1]

Those pictures – posted over and over on many internet sites – exemplify the ways in which the use of American "hard power" – coercive power – in Iraq and elsewhere is undermining American "soft power" – persuasive power. In Joseph Nye's now classic formulation, soft power is a country's ability to attract others to its goals and ways and make them want what it wants. American soft power is ebbing by many measures, beginning with the country's global popularity. The 2006 Pew Global Attitudes Survey shows a continuing decline in people who hold

* **Anne-Marie Slaughter**, Dean of the Woodrow Wilson School of Public and International Affairs at Princeton University, is the author, most recently, of *The Idea that Is America: Keeping Faith with our Values in a Dangerous World*.
# **Thomas Nathan Hale** is Special Assistant to the Dean at the Woodrow Wilson School, Princeton University.

a favorable opinion of the United States: 23 percent in Spain, 37 in Germany, 39 in France, and only 56 in the United Kingdom. Outside Europe the United States faces similar discontent, earning a favorable ranking from only 43 percent of Russians, 30 percent of Indonesians and Egyptians, 27 percent of Pakistanis, 15 percent of Jordanians, and an amazing 12 percent of Turks.[2]

These oft-quoted statistics, however, mask and muddle several different strains of what is generally lumped together as "anti-Americanism," each of which has quite different sources and quite different implications. First is a hate fueled by love: love of the ideals America proclaims and hate of American failure to practice them. Theo Sommer, former editor of the German newsweekly *Die Zeit*, has stated, "Beneath every hater of America is a disappointed lover of America."[3] The problem, for this group, are specific American policies – in the Middle East, on the treatment of detainees, in the embrace of unilateralism – that go against the principles for which American purports to stand.

Second, however, is a growing dislike – even loathing – of certain American values themselves. Not America's political values, but its actual or perceived cultural values – materialism, commodification of virtually everything that can be commodified, obsession with sex and appearance, tolerance of vast inequality, lack of social solidarity, and spiritual emptiness.

Third is a more general perception that globalization equals Americanization and that Americanization equals homogenization. In this optic, anti-Americanism is synonymous with defense of local, regional, and national culture. This resistance is often explicitly nationalist, striking at the very core of American soft power. It is impossible for the United States to convince other countries to want what it wants if American values and American culture are seen through the lens of clashing nationalisms.

Behind these trends is a great and sad irony. American nationalism, properly understood, has a deeply cosmopolitan dimension, both at home and abroad. Recovering this understanding of American nationalism – or, as most Americans would recognize it, patriotism – is vital for rebuilding American soft power. Equally important, it is vital for America's ability to work with other nations to promote a better life for all the world's citizens.

THE WAR ON TERROR AS A WAR FOR FREEDOM: A CODE OF DEEPENING DISTRUST

Since the September 11 attacks, the Bush Administration has sent the world two deeply contradictory messages about the United States. On the one hand,

President Bush offered even traditional U.S. allies a stark choice: "You are either with us or against us." This stance precluded dialogue and met even well-meant criticism with hostility. The United State's legitimate need to take all necessary steps to defend itself from attack intersected with a pre-existing belief in parts of Washington that the United States should be able to do whatever it wanted without regard for global opinion, international organizations, or treaty obligations. The 2003 National Security Strategy described what this policy meant in practice, positing the right of the United States to invade any country posing a severe threat to U.S. security or supportive of terrorism as a preventive measure.

This unilateralism extended to disregard for international institutions and international law. The Geneva Conventions, the Convention against Torture, and other international safeguards of human rights were subordinated to what the Administration saw as a need to detain, rendition, and at times "coercively interrogate" the people it deemed "enemy combatants." These policies have also run contrary to domestic law, perhaps none so clearly as the government's secret decision to wiretap the phones of U.S. citizens without warrants, a tactic explicitly outlawed by the Foreign Intelligence Surveillance Act of 1978.

The Administration has often rationalized these policies by claiming that the changed circumstances of the new war place unprecedented responsibilities on the United States and particularly the President to protect the American people, thus expanding the powers of both. The legal validity of such claims is slowly being tested by the U.S. court system, and the general tenor of the decisions handed down thus far has been a mix of judicial deference to executive authority in dangerous times and skepticism of presidential overreach. The recent landmark decision in *Hamadan v. Rumsfeld* indicated that the courts' patience with such arguments is wearing thin. Still, the Administration's defense of many of these policies depends less on sound legal footing and more on the siege mentality that has permeated U.S. society since September 11, 2001, an inward-looking, nationalist mindset that breeds arrogance.

On the other hand, the years since the September 11 attacks have also been marked by especially fervent pronouncements of America's commitment to democracy, freedom, and other lofty values. Immediately after September 11, President Bush declared, "What is at stake is not just America's freedom. This is the world's fight. This is civilization's fight. This is the fight of all who believe in progress and pluralism, tolerance and freedom."[4] Though made in universal language, such rhetoric rings peculiarly American. It is difficult to imagine the head of any other state describing a terrorist attack on a financial center and a military headquarters as an "assault on freedom," or labeling the terrorists "enemies of freedom." Certainly no other country would vent its frustration at a critical ally by replacing that country's name with the word "freedom," as in "freedom toast" and "freedom fries."

More recently, the Administration has chosen to emphasize the instrumental side of U.S. values, as in the following passage from the 2006 U.S. National Security Strategy:

> Championing freedom advances our interests because the survival of liberty at home increasingly depends on the success of liberty abroad. Governments that honor their citizens' dignity and desire for freedom tend to uphold responsible conduct toward other nations, while governments that brutalize their people also threaten the peace and stability of other nations. Because democracies are the most responsible members of the international system, promoting democracy is the most effective long-term measure for strengthening international stability; reducing regional conflicts; countering terrorism and terror-supporting extremism; and extending peace and prosperity.[5]

In this vision, the United States is not engaged in a bitterly partisan war to the death in which its judgment cannot be questioned, but rather, assuming the mantle of "democracy in chief" within a larger community of democracies, the U.S. tries to promote the kind of responsible and accountable domestic politics in all nations that will in turn advance global security.

When these two strands come together, the resulting hypocrisy feeds cynicism, mistrust, and worse. In the view of millions around the world, "liberty" becomes code for U.S. domination. "Democracy" becomes code for a government friendly to the United States. The "rule of law" becomes code for a U.S. unfettered by any constraints. The "war on terror" becomes code for "a war on Islam." "Human rights" becomes a blind for imperialist intervention.

This code destroys American soft power from within. Everything America does has two meanings – a proclaimed meaning and a received meaning. The received meaning makes a mockery of the proclaimed meaning, in ways that will limit the effect even of specific policy reversals, such as closing the detention facility at the Guantanamo Bay Naval base. A broader shift is needed, a period of renewal, revival, and a broad reclaiming of the meaning of American power.

FROM NATIONALISM TO PATRIOTISM

Americans generally believe in their country more than the inhabitants of other developed nations. Nearly 80 percent of Americans hold a favorable view of their country, compared with 65 percent of Germans or 68 percent of French.[6] This unabashed patriotism puts off many in the other 20-odd percent, as well as many Europeans, who see it, along with American religiosity, as a dangerous throw-back to the twentieth century. (It should be noted that both of these characteristics place most Americans closer to most of the world's people, who continue to attach great importance to national boundaries and religious beliefs, than to increasingly post-national and secular Europeans. Ninety-four percent of Chinese hold a favorable opinion of China, for example.[7])

As any survey of American public monuments, folk-songs, and even Hollywood films will reveal, Americans' pride in their country stands in large part on what Americans think the country represents, a series of principles laid out by Thomas Jefferson in the American Declaration of Independence as "self evident" truths:

> that all men are created equal, that they are endowed by their Creator with certain unalienable Rights, that among these are Life, Liberty and the pursuit of Happiness. – That to secure these rights, Governments are instituted among Men, deriving their just powers from the consent of the governed.

America's critics often take umbrage at the United States' claim to these universal values; after all, who elected America the guardian of democracy? But one of the things Americans most celebrate about "American" values is their universality. "*All* men are created equal"; these truths are not only self-evident in the middle swath of the North American continent, but to people all over the world.

As described in the previous section, Americans' commitment to universal rights can make the nation arrogant in a "we are more freedom-loving than you" sense, a flaw that can in turn blind Americans to situations in which American actions in fact run contrary to American values. But this commitment can also be a cosmopolitan bridge to the world.

In an essay entitled "From Nationalism to Patriotism: Reclaiming the American Creed," the Reverend Forrest Church, senior minister of All Souls Unitarian Church in Manhattan and son of the late Idaho Senator Frank Church, wrote: "If all people are created equal and are endowed by the Creator with certain inalienable rights," then " 'all people' represents more than merely the people of the United States. American patriotism demands a high level of moral engagement. In this respect, American isolationism is an oxymoron."[8] So is American nationalism. As Reverend Church has also pointed out,

> In 1816, Stephan Decatur proposed the ultimate toast to nationalism: "Our country, right or wrong!" American patriotism refutes this

sentiment by emending it. Speaking against the extension of "Manifest Destiny" into the Philippines in 1899, Senator Carl Schurz of Missouri said, "Our country, right or wrong. When right, to be kept right; when wrong, to be put right." What we need today are a few more patriots.[9]

In this view, true American patriotism rejects nationalism altogether. Americans stand for a universal, cosmopolitan vision of the rights of all humankind. This understanding of American values is grounded not in hubris but in a vision of common humanity.

PUTTING THE CREED INTO THE DEED

According to British observer G. K. Chesterton, "The United States is the only country in the world that is founded on a creed."[10] But pride in the creed alone is easily susceptible to the corruption of complacency, hubris, and even narcissism. The American Transcendentalist poet Ralph Waldo Emerson put the matter this way:

> United States! the ages plead,—
> Present and Past in under-song,—
> Go put your creed into your deed,
> Nor speak with double tongue.[11]

Emerson's words were written exactly eighty-one years after America had proclaimed itself independent of Britain by asserting that all men are created equal, on the eve of the American Civil War. The country was bitterly divided over the issue of slavery, and abolitionists like Emerson stridently invoked the principles of the Founding to combat the human bondage they considered to be America's original sin.

It was a common pattern. When the founders of the American republic set quill to paper the words came out right – "all men are created equal," "life, liberty, and the pursuit of happiness," "inalienable rights" – but the policy lagged far behind. When the U.S. Constitution came into force in 1789 only landed white men could vote. Women had few rights, and Native Americans were routinely uprooted or killed to make room for European settlers. And, of course, millions of Africans were enslaved as farm laborers and domestic servants. Since these inauspicious beginnings, the United States has indulged in such unsavory practices as nativist anti-immigrant campaigns, imperialist adventures in Latin America and the Pacific, racial segregation, the mass internment of Japanese during World War II, anti-communist witch hunts, the support of brutal regimes in the Third World, and other policies that were, for lack of a better word, decidedly un-American. Today Abu Ghraib and Guantanamo Bay can be added to this shameful list.

And so America has had a constant stream of Emersons. Throughout the nation's history, Americans have exploited the high-minded principles caught up in the country's sense of itself to effect change. The lesson of American history is that the American creed – above all our faith that the creed defines America itself – has repeatedly been a catalyst for progressive change.

Perhaps none have invoked the American creed more eloquently than civil rights leader Martin Luther King Jr., who in 1963 likened the process to a financial promise:

> It is obvious today that America has defaulted on this promissory note insofar as her citizens of color are concerned. Instead of honoring this sacred obligation, America has given the Negro people a bad check, a check that has come back marked "insufficient funds."
>
> But we refuse to believe that the bank of justice is bankrupt. We refuse to believe that there are insufficient funds in the great vaults of opportunity of this nation. And so we've come to cash this check, a check that will give us upon demand the riches of freedom and security of justice.[12]

That King was making this case 187 years after Jefferson had written, "All men are created equal" demonstrates the ongoing nature of the cause. There has been progress – consider the gains in, for example, equality, made since the 1960s – but the magnitude of our continuing challenges suggests that the perfection of liberty is an eternal task. Furthermore, it is a task that continually requires new generations of Americans – from the Founders, to suffragist Susan B. Anthony, to King – to stand up to those who would distort American principles. This distance between American ideals and American reality and the nation's constant struggle to close that gap are the defining characteristics of American political life.

FROM PATRIOTISM TO COSMOPOLITANISM: THE REAL CITY ON THE HILL

Under American-led globalization, this dynamic of American patriotism – that is, the critical patriotism of holding the American government to its word – has extended far beyond America's shores. We often think about American soft power through the famous metaphor coined by John Winthrop, the first governor of the Massachusetts Bay Colony: America as a "city on a hill," a shining example of democracy for the world. Americans usually consider this phrase the first statement of America's role as special guarantor and champion of democracy; foreigners often see it as the first expression of American arrogance. But consider the rest of Winthrop's oft-cited, yet seldom read speech:

> ... wee must Consider that wee shall be as a Citty upon a Hill, the eies of all people are uppon us; soe that if wee shall deale falsely with our god in this worke wee have undertaken and soe cause him to withdrawe his present help from us, wee shall be made a story and a byword through the world, wee shall open the mouthes of enemies to speake evill of the wayes of god and all professours for Gods sake; wee shall shame the faces of many of gods worthy servants, and cause theire prayers to be turned into Cursses upon us till wee be consumed out of the good land whether wee are going ...[13]

The "Citty upon a Hill" may be a beacon to the world, but the world is watching to see just how well its inhabitants keep their word. Today, in an age of unparalleled interconnectedness, this scrutiny has grown closer, revealing far more than orthographical errors.

As the world's sole superpower, the United States' actions bear heavily on many people's lives around the world. Understandably, foreigners affected by U.S. actions have started to hold the American government to account, just as generations of enslaved, or disenfranchised, or marginalized Americans have done before them. When in March 2003 thousands of people marched in opposition to the Iraq war in London, Paris, Buenos Aires, and Jerusalem, they were joined by Americans in New York, San Francisco, Atlanta, and Detroit. All were calling on the United States government to recognize their opposition.

Many Americans call such criticism "anti-Americanism," and point to it as evidence of declining U.S. soft power. In fact, nothing could be more American than holding the government to account for failing to live up to American – universal – principles. American flags were burnt in Berkeley – with the Supreme Court's Constitutional blessing – before they were burnt in the West Bank.

We must understand the supposed deterioration of American soft power through this prism. Certainly the Bush Administration's policies have generated much ill will against the American government and hampered its efforts to convince other nations to join with the U.S. on certain projects – rebuilding Iraq, for example. But in doing so the Administration has also provoked a large swath of critics who are not afraid to stand up for American principles, and even to confront the world's most powerful country in their name.

Neo-conservatives are fond of saying that "freedom is not free," it must be fought for. While reasonable (and less than reasonable) people can disagree about exactly what this idea means in practice, the underlying truth – liberty must be struggled for – drives American history. The declaration of lofty values and the fight to live up to them has always been an essential part of living in a democracy. As the world becomes increasingly interconnected, in part through U.S. hegemony, it is natural for this struggle to go global. That global political struggles increasingly resemble American history is strong evidence that soft U.S. influence remains potent, though perhaps not in the way the White House's office of public diplomacy would like. However, all those who believe in the universal values America holds dear but at times violates can take heart that, at least in this regard, the world has grown a little more American.

WHEN AMERICA STUMBLES, THE WORLD SUFFERS

To regain its credibility abroad the United States must realize just how much global politics resemble American politics. It must take seriously its insistence that American values are universal values, principles that apply to American conduct abroad no less than to domestic policy. It must understand that other people around the world – agreeing with America on universal values – will expect America to live up to those ideals and will oppose America when it does not. It must, essentially, remember another part of Winthrop's misappropriated speech, his commandment "to doe Justly, to love mercy, to walke humbly with our God."

The stakes in the domestic and global struggle for America to be, in the words of Texas's first black congresswoman Barbara Jordan, "an America that is as good as its promise," are very high. When the Bush Administration speaks of democracy and then pours aid into oppressive governments, when it proclaims justice and then renditions detainees to countries where they may face torture, when it eulogizes the rule of law and then brushes off any restraints on its own power, it risks tying the universal principles it would spread around the world to the policies the world finds repugnant.

As Emerson knew, the costs of speaking "with double tongue" can be high. Thomas Carothers has recently described how illiberal forces from Belarus, to Russia, to China, to Zimbabwe, to Venezuela have been cracking down on domestic pro-democracy groups in the name of resisting U.S. imperialism.[14] When in April 2006 the U.S. announced it was increasing aid to pro-democracy groups in Iran, Iranian democrats reacted with concern. Radio Free Europe reported outspoken student leader Abdolleh Momeni as saying "The only result of financial aid would be to inflame sensitivities, put civil society activists under threat, and give the regime an excuse to suppress opponents and opposition members."[15] America's touch has become poisonous to those who share U.S. goals.

Worse still, the weakening of U.S. soft power may damage more than merely American interests. By tying the goal of democracy promotion to unilateralism, preventive war, the flouting of international law, and arrogance, the Bush Administration may have tarnished the coin of democracy more generally. At times it seems that with friends like the United States, democracy has no need for enemies. And yet competitors exist, ranging from Islamic fundamentalism, to the so-called "Asian model" of Singapore or China, to the populism of Castro's Cuba or Chavez's Venezuela, to the increasingly "law and order" mentality of Putin's Russia. Democrats in these countries and liberals around the world fear that democracy's self-appointed champion may have actually hurt their cause.

Of course, democracy is not just America's to win or lose. The many countries that share values with America can and should do more to remind the world – including Americans – of their universality. Still, what America says and does about democracy matters a great deal. This unavoidable consequence of America's power and weight in the world means that America's critics abroad have a stake in being as constructive as possible. Understanding the cycles of American history and the dynamic of progressive change created when the gap between American behavior and American values grows too great should encourage those critics not only to criticize, but also to call for positive change.

CONCLUSION

Support for America's behavior around the world may well be at a historically low ebb. Yet support for America's values remains strong. Those values are not distinctively American. They are the heritage of the Enlightenment, of political philosophers who thought that they were reasoning on behalf of all humankind. They found early political expression in the Declaration of Independence and the French Declaration of the Rights of Man and have since been endorsed by nearly every government on the face of the planet in the Universal Declaration of Human Rights.

American history offers cause for hope. America's slow but steady – though never complete – history of striving to realize its highest principles suggests that the current injustices of American power will also be righted by critical patriots, together with – in a global age – critical cosmopolitans. If so, then America's soft power will grow again, fueled not only by the promise of American values but by the demonstration that America can be held to its promise. As Secretary of State Condoleezza Rice said in a speech to the Southern Baptist Convention annual meeting in Greensboro, North Carolina, "America will lead the cause of freedom in our world, not because we think ourselves perfect. To the contrary, we cherish democracy and champion its ideals because we know ourselves to be imperfect ... [w]ith a long history of failures and false starts that testify to our own fallibility."[16]

Of course, even if America succeeds once again in putting its creed into its deed, much of American culture will remain materialistic, scantily clad women (and men) will grind and bump on American music videos, and the American brand of capitalism will continue to champion self-reliance over solidarity, at least by European standards. At the same time, Europe – through the EU and through the underlying cultural and political traditions that define European democracy and European capitalism – will provide another illustration of how universal rights can be realized, as will the other members of the global family of liberal democracies. America may never again enjoy the unique soft power position that it did during much of the Cold War. But soft power is not zero-sum. And the proliferation of different models of achieving "ordered liberty," in George Washington's phrase, through the free choices of free people, will empower us all.

Chapter 19

Can Hollywood Still Rule the World?

*Janet Wasko**

The title of a recent Christian Science Monitor article posed an interesting question: "In 2,000 Years, Will the World Remember Disney or Plato?" Of course, the story provided no answer to the question, but did explore the U.S. contribution to global culture, observing: "As the unrivaled global superpower, America exports its culture on an unprecedented scale. From music to media, film to fast food, language to literature and sport, the American idea is spreading inexorably, not unlike the influence of empires that preceded it. The difference is that today's technology flings culture to every corner of the globe with blinding speed".[1]

While Hollywood films are not the only example of the global influence of U.S. culture, they represent a common target of cultural imperialism debates. In fact, there has been much more attention to this issue during the last few years because of debates about globalization, but also due to the continuing expansion and domination of Hollywood in global film and video markets.

Even film industry representatives draw attention to and usually celebrate Hollywood's global reign. For instance, while accepting a Global Vision Award from the World Affairs Council earlier this year, filmmaker George Lucas remarked that the United States is a provincial country that has invaded the

* **Janet Wasko** is the Knight Chair for Communication Research at the University of Oregon. This essay is based on her book, *How Hollywood Works* (Sage, 2003). Her other books include *Understanding Disney: The Manufacture of Fantasy* (Polity Press/Blackwell, 2001), and *Hollywood in the Information Age: Beyond the Silver Screen* (Polity Press, 1994). She is editor of *A Companion to Television* (Blackwell, 2005) and *Dazzled by Disney? The Global Disney Audience Project* (Leicester University Press/Continuum, 2001); as well as other volumes on the political economy of communication and democratic media.

world by way of Hollywood. "As long as there has been a talking Hollywood," Lucas explained, "Hollywood has had a huge impact on the rest of the world."[2]

While the character of such impact is certainly debatable and continues to be scrutinized by cultural analysts, it is important to understand that Hollywood films have not necessarily dominated global markets based on aesthetic or cultural allure alone. This chapter briefly examines the various factors that have contributed to Hollywood's global domination and then considers various developments that ultimately may challenge Tinseltown's global dominion.

It is indisputable that Hollywood currently dominates global markets for motion pictures, both at the box office and in other distribution formats. While there are various ways of estimating such strength, it is generally agreed that the major U.S. studios currently control anywhere from 75 to 80 percent of global film markets. The industry's trade association, the Motion Picture Association of America (MPAA), reports that U.S. films are shown in more than 150 countries worldwide. Further, the U.S. film industry provides the majority of prerecorded cassettes and DVDs seen throughout the world. Currently, Hollywood films are released to international cinemas from within a couple of days to as long as six months following domestic release, with distribution in home video formats and to television and cable markets following shortly thereafter.

George Lucas is correct in pointing out that the international distribution of U.S. films is not a new phenomenon, but dates back to even before the sound era began in the late 1920s and continued to gain strength over the following decades. A few developments have further reinforced Hollywood's global business since the 1980s. The ongoing deregulation or privatization of media operations have opened up new commercial channels and greatly expanded media markets. In addition, the development and proliferation of new technologies, such as satellite and cable television, VCRs and DVDs, continue to enhance the international market for entertainment products. However, other key factors are needed to explain why Hollywood rules, at least at the moment.

WHY HOLLYWOOD DOMINATES

While many sources have discussed Hollywood's international dominance, oftentimes the reasons for this global strength are either simplified or unstated. The following sections discuss the cultural, economic, historical, and political explanations, which all need to be considered before assessing the challenges to Hollywood's dominance.

Cultural factors

Hollywood's international success is often pinned to the superiority of the American film industry (higher budgets, better talent, or other reasons), or it is claimed that Hollywood films have universal appeal. Some scholars have offered more elaborate explanations, arguing that American films represent a kind of "narrative transparency."[3]

This kind of argument is even offered by economists who use the concept of "cultural discount" – the notion that because of language and cultural specificity, a film (or other product) may not be popular outside its own country. Thus, because of their "universal appeal" and the widespread use of English around the world, U.S. films have a small cultural discount in foreign markets, prompting one media economist to conclude that Hollywood films represent "a new universal art form."[4]

Economic factors

But the content and style of American films cannot be the only explanation for Hollywood's global success. It is essential to look at some of the economic explanations for part of the explanation for Hollywood's international dominance.

Home market advantage. The U.S. has a tremendous advantage in that its home market for motion pictures has developed as the largest in the world. Currently, there are around 37,000 screens in the U.S. and American moviegoers with high per capita income are claimed to account for 44 percent of the global box office. Indeed, the widespread domestic release of studio movies and the advertising power behind them still builds a strong market for films in foreign territories.

While some in the film industry argue that U.S. films depend on international markets to make a profit, it also could be argued that with such a large domestic market, profits can be gained through distribution to other countries where only incremental expenses are encountered. The concept of "infinite exportability" has been applied here, indicating that the highest costs are incurred in production and, thus, exporting, which requires only minimal additional costs, becomes quite profitable.

Economies of scale. Similar to other industries, large corporations in the film industry have advantages that smaller companies don't have, including access to talent for high-concept and blockbuster films backed by hefty promotion that is geared toward specific countries and regions. Many Hollywood films these days are deliberately created for international markets. In other words, the supposed "universal" appeal of Hollywood products, if it actually exists, is not unplanned or adventitious, as creative personnel in Hollywood continue to be urged to "think globally." Furthermore, the ability to launch huge blockbuster films with mega-stars is possible for the Hollywood majors, who often aim for a global audience with action-adventure films that have little "cultural discount."

International distribution system. U.S. film distributors have been globally savvy for many years as Hollywood has developed an extensive international system for distributing its own films and those of other countries. To get a motion picture booked into cinemas around the globe, the most advantageous strategy is to arrange distribution with a major U.S. distributor. Even though the cost may be higher than independent distribution, Hollywood's experience and resources are extensive.

In addition, Hollywood has operated historically in foreign markets through distribution cartels, which market U.S. films as well as other countries' products. The primary example is United International Pictures (UIP), representing Paramount, Universal, MGM/UA, but other distribution arrangements between the Hollywood majors exist as well. Alliances between Hollywood studios to distribute films abroad maintain the studios' dominance of foreign markets.

Diversification and vertical integration of the film business. It is important to note that the major studios are part of highly diversified, entertainment conglomerates. Not only are Hollywood films distributed internationally, but products associated with those films (i.e. merchandise, video games, etc.) are marketed globally as well. Ownership of other media outlets means that Hollywood products are promoted and linked with products across the media landscape, that is, on television shows, in magazines, newspapers, etc.

Historical factors

While these economic factors are fundamental, a historical perspective is also essential to understand how Hollywood supremacy evolved.

Hollywood's initial commercial orientation. While most histories of Hollywood reveal the strong commercial orientation in the evolution of the film in the U.S., this point is sometimes overlooked when discussing the nature of Hollywood's international marketing strength. American film pioneers took advantage of early technological advances from Europe and realized that distribution and exhibition were central to making profits in the film business, as well as appreciating the importance of developing mass marketing and star power. Thus, while other countries may have been developing film as art or propaganda, motion pictures activities in the U.S. developed early and strongly as a profit-oriented, commodity-based industry from early in its history.

World wars. Often overlooked is the fact that Hollywood's dominance was developed and strongly reinforced by two major world wars. After WWI, and again after WWII, European industries were decimated, and U.S. products were plentiful. In addition, the U.S. government assured Hollywood continued advantages through arrangements after WWII, as documented in research by Thomas Guback and others.[5] In other words, the U.S. film industry benefited immeasurably from the historical circumstances that allowed it to continue producing and distributing films during these global conflicts, as well as being tied to a conquering nation that became a world economic and political power (and later, the dominant world superpower).

Political factors

Political factors are vital in explaining the international success of the U.S. film industry, and include Hollywood's own lobbying activities, as well as the support it receives from the U.S. government.

The MPAA & the Little State Department. The MPAA serves as an effective lobbying force for its members, which include the major film studios. Meanwhile, the Motion Picture Association (MPA) was formed (originally, the Motion Picture Export Association) as an international branch of the MPAA in 1945, "... to respond to the rising tide of protectionism resulting in barriers aimed at restricting the importation of American films. Since its early days, the MPA, often referred to now as 'a little State Department,' has expanded to cover a wide range of foreign activities falling in the diplomatic, economic, and political arenas."[6]

One indication of the significance of this organization is the prominence of its former head, Jack Valenti, who was handsomely rewarded for his various efforts on behalf of the U.S. motion picture industry and was the first lobbyist to cross the $1 million mark. The film industry works effectively through the MPAA to influence political decisions, but entertainment industry companies and personnel make regular political contributions to gain the support of government officials as well.

State support. Valenti once claimed that, "Our movies and TV programs are hospitably received by citizens around the world."[7] Perhaps. But it doesn't hurt to have a little help from friends in high places. The U.S. government has supported the film industry in various ways over the years, but especially in overcoming resistance to Hollywood exports in global markets.

Support for the film industry (and other American export industries) was especially boosted when the Webb-Pomerene Act was passed in 1918, allowing companies that must compete in the U.S. to collaborate in foreign markets. The Hollywood majors organized an export cartel that operated as the sole export agent for its members, working with the State Department and the Office of the U.S. Trade Representative to monitor trade barriers, etc.

In addition, the government also supports the U.S. film industry in international treaty negotiations, such as NAFTA, GATT, WTO, etc., as well as providing the clout to back up industry threats when countries don't cooperate by opening their markets, enforcing copyright, or other obstacles to trade.

CHALLENGES TO HOLLYWOOD'S REIGN

While the international strength of Hollywood is formidable, there still are challenges that may ultimately crack the U.S. film industry's dominance.

Resistance to U.S. dominance. Historically, there have been various ways that countries have attempted to resist Hollywood's dominance. To the dismay of the MPAA and the major Hollywood studios, these efforts continue. Forms of resistance include import quotas, tariffs, licensing, screen quotas, frozen earnings, and subsidies. In some countries, duties are added to theater tickets, or foreign distributors encounter local ownership requirements. Screen and airtime restrictions also prevent American movies from appearing on television in some countries.

In addition, subsidies for domestic film industries are funded through taxation of foreign movie revenues. While admissions taxes are a common means of subsidizing domestic film production, licensing fees, tax rebates, loans and grants are other ways that nations fund their film subsidies.

Only a few specific examples are import quotas imposed in China, ticket taxes of 100 percent in India, a special distribution tax of 20 percent added for pornographic and violent films in Hungary, a 25 percent municipality tax on receipts from foreign films in Turkey, and a 10 percent tax on American distributors who do not market Australian films in Australia.

These various forms of resistance have been aimed at U.S. films in markets around the world for many, many years. Even though some have been successful, Hollywood's overall domination has still continued.

Piracy problems. One of the most difficult problems that the U.S. industry faces is piracy, or the unauthorized use of copyrighted material. The MPAA estimates that the U.S. motion picture industry loses more than $3 billion annually in potential worldwide revenue due to piracy, a figure that does not account for internet piracy losses, which are currently difficult to estimate.

The MPAA established an anti-piracy program in the U.S. in 1976 and continues to fight piracy globally in various ways. But despite all of these activities, different types of piracy inevitably develop with the ongoing introduction of new technology. Recently, the major U.S. distributors have shifted to near simultaneous foreign release dates to combat film piracy. However, it is likely that the problem will continue to be a thorn in the side of Hollywood for years to come.

Growth of co-productions/runaway production. For various reasons, the number of co-productions by Hollywood companies has been increasing, leading as well to issues related to "runaway production." Incentives for indigenous films, cheaper labor costs, etc., have led to more co-productions and more production in countries other than the U.S. Indeed, some industry insiders note that the majority of today's Hollywood films are produced somewhere outside Los Angeles.

International anti-trust enforcement. Hollywood's notorious anticompetitive tendencies have been challenged in some markets recently, specifically by the European Union and Korea, and may face similar challenges in the future. The more dominant the transnational entertainment corporations become, the more attention they bring to their market power and the more likely it is that more countries will actually enforce anti-trust laws in the future.

New formations and competition. Meanwhile, new forms of competition may ultimately undermine Hollywood's global strength, as an increasing number of films are being produced around the world. What Hollywood calls "local product" may ultimately challenge U.S. domination in a number of different areas, although only two examples will be mentioned here.

In Europe, where American movies continue to pack in audiences overseas, local films have had some domestic and international success in recent years. Though reliance on state support has resulted in many European productions playing to a narrow market, European Union funding of co-productions and distribution, plus box-office-driven policies for awarding subsidies, have given filmmakers the freedom to seek a wider audience. Growing competition in the television industry, channel proliferation, digital television and continuing deregulation of broadcasting markets also have tended to increase co-production activity.

In other parts of the world, film industries that have been relatively provincial are beginning to pay attention to global film marketing. India is a prime example. The Indian film industries include not only "Bollywood" (based in

Mumbai and producing Hindi-language films), but also Tamil, Telegu, Malayalam, Kannada, and Bengali language film industries.

There are various indications that Indian film, especially Bollywood, is aiming to increase global film revenues. Revenues from India's film industry are growing rapidly, and expected to reach over $3 billion by 2010. In addition, India's government has been encouraging the industry by improving access to bank finance and reforming taxation laws to encourage exports. Indian films are distributed to markets in Europe, North America, and Africa, as well as some of the Gulf states.

Other national film industries may also threaten to put chinks in Hollywood's global armor. As geographer Allen J. Scott pointed out a few years ago:

> If the history of other formerly triumphant industrial juggernauts – from Manchester to Detroit – is any guide, the continued leadership of Hollywood is by no means automatically assured. In spite of Hollywood's acquired competitive advantages, it cannot be ultimately free from economic threats emanating from elsewhere.[8]

Only a few of the challenges to Hollywood's dominance have been referred to here, but other questions are looming:

Will the growing anti-Americanism ideology around the world ultimately have an impact on the export of American culture? Or in other words, can Hollywood films still attract global audiences that increasingly reject America and its way of life?

What about China's stringent policies on film and television imports? Will the Chinese government be able to protect and build its own film industry and prevent Hollywood from conquering the huge and lucrative Chinese market?

What about the increasing number of Hispanic films that attract a growing Hispanic population in the U.S., as well as in Spanish-speaking regions? Hollywood seems to be gradually moving into these markets, but it remains to be seen how successful these efforts will be.

Along the same lines, will Hollywood take advantage of more local film production and take steps to produce and distribute more films that appeal to "local" audiences? There is already evidence of this trend with what could be called the "Asianization" of American cinema, as outlined recently by a number of film scholars.[9]

And what about the internet? How will the online distribution of films – Hollywood productions, as well as others – affect Tinseltown's grip on global cinema markets?

THE FUTURE?

The issue of Hollywood's global dominance is relevant in considering the cultural transformations that may occur in the future. Indeed, whether or not film prevails as a significant cultural entity may be open to discussion. At least, at this point in time, it is possible to recognize that Hollywood's dominance continues to influence the development of indigenous film around the world, as well as siphoning capital away from local economies. Whether or not Hollywood films (and other American cultural products) have cultural or ideological effects or dominate global culture also are significant questions that continue to be raised by cultural analysts (see Nye and Tomlinson's essays in this volume). Perhaps the analysis could be enhanced by understanding that Hollywood's dominance has been sustained not only because of cultural or ideological dynamics, but also economic, political and historical factors.

Historically, Hollywood has displayed considerable ability to adapt and use its economic and political strengths to dominate film markets around the world. However, it cannot be assumed that Hollywood will persevere. Neither can it be assumed that the U.S. will necessarily continue to play a dominant role in globalization, generally. Indeed, just like the U.S. government, Hollywood companies are not infallible. The Hollywood-style of filmmaking may ultimately catch up with some of these transnational conglomerates, despite their attempts to minimize the supposed riskiness of the film business and to overcome various forms of resistance and competition around the world.

Thus, there are still many open questions that may influence whether or not Hollywood's domination can be sustained. While it is difficult to predict at this point, the answers to these questions also will undoubtedly have something to do with whether the U.S. can sustain its dominant global position, and thus influence whether Disney or Plato will be remembered in 2,000 years.

Chapter 20

Race, Rice and the Info-war

Paul Gilroy*

The last few years have witnessed the reach of African American culture being extended. In popular form, it has become influential in supplying the soundtrack and the stylistic signatures of globalisation. For many outside the US, the culture that they know and enjoy as American derives from black America. Others receive and enjoy the cultural offshoots of black life without even knowing their origins.

The significance of this pattern has been altered by the consolidation of hip hop as the lingua franca of global youth culture and by the appearance of Condoleezza Rice at the helm of the US ship of state. The visibility and celebrity of prominent minority Republicans does more than help to hold the party's electoral bloc together. Outside the US, it communicates the country's openness and promise as well as suggesting that the old racial hierarchies born from slavery are no longer intrinsic to its political order and may even be becoming less relevant to contemporary inequalities.

These recent changes have prompted questions about the character, shape and provenance of American culture. By no means everybody is content to see the nation represented on the world stage by its disreputable and sometimes profane black vernacular. That concern has fed new anxieties that have been expressed about the ebbing of a "core culture"[1] which could anchor national identity as the country completes a large transition towards new circumstances in which its whites will have to adjust to the new experience of being a minority. There is a sense that the de-centring of that core culture by multiculturalism

* **Paul Gilroy** is the first holder of the Anthony Giddens Professorship in Social Theory at the London School of Economics and Political Science. His intellectual background is multi-disciplinary and he has extensive interests in literature, art, music and cultural history, as well as in social science. He is best known for his work on racism, nationalism and ethnicity and his original approach to the history of the African diaspora into the Western hemisphere.

has been damaging even if some official forms of diversity have added flexibility and global branding to corporate and economic power.

The evident diversity of those who died on 11 September 2001 may have helped to build the identification with and sympathy for the US which have now been squandered. Since then, the over-amplified rhetoric of civilisationism has taken hold of US geo-political pronouncements and the pursuit of an impossible invulnerability seems to determine many of the country's strategic choices. These developments have impacted upon the cultural conflicts that have been integral both to the exercise of US power and to the various forms of resistance against it.

Segregated dwelling remains a normal feature of social life regardless of region and conspicuous racial and ethnic variations in markets for goods and services are accepted as though they were inevitable results of natural difference.[2] At the same time, the US military now represents the nation's diversity and cultural plurality more comprehensively than any other institution. Recruitment shortfalls mean that collaborations with MTV and BET are routine and an engagement with black culture is now obligatory if communication with young viewers is to be credible. The poetic script which regulates presentation of information and policy by the government has been larded with doses of an eschatological Christian outlook but that reversion to WASP type is necessarily qualified in many areas of government practice by the prominence of minority cultures, tastes and habits.

A manichaean political theology that should be very familiar to analysts of colonial history is being articulated with a nationalism that is as pious as it is brittle, exceptionalist and belligerent. A sketchy and duplicitous anthropology solidifies mere cultural contrasts. The idea of race assists in culture's transformation into metaphysical difference that can, in turn, fuel and justify the tactical calculations of emboldened imperial statecraft. An unbridgeable division between friends and enemies has been conveniently projected as the centre of a combative stance which has decisively altered the pattern of cultural relationships between the US and the rest of the world. It is not clear how significant racial differences between blacks and whites are to be in this new conflict.

The fissures within civilisations are played down so that the inevitable clash between them can be presented as a common-sense explanation of current conflicts and an urgent stimulus for future adventures. This shift has militarised government and everyday life in many places and transformed understanding of the emergent cultural and political forms of globalisation. A revival of Christendom is being sought. The antique conflict between cross and crescent has returned in post-modern, cartoon form.

In these conditions the inescapable fate of the overdeveloped, "Western" countries has been regularly and repeatedly specified as an endless, or more recently, a long war in which culture itself is an element in the protracted conflict. This is to be waged against a constantly shifting group of targets: failed or recalcitrant states and non-state actors as well as ideas, ideologies, dispositions and various cultural pathologies that attend the wretched lives of barbarous and implicitly infra-human peoples.

It is important to appreciate what the global pollsters say about changes in the way that the US is seen from the outside.[3] The popular idea that individual success can be measured by the goal of becoming American or perhaps more realistically, by the prospect of migrating to the US, still retains widespread appeal; however the country has lost much of the unique allure invested in it by its economic and military pre-eminence and by its ebbing control of the "infotainment telesector".[4] That US dreamscape still represents the cornucopia of consumer culture, but the government is likely these days to be seen instead as decadent, bullying and unjust both in its dealings with its own citizens and in its apparently authoritarian attempts to direct world politics in its own interests. Problems arising from how these perspectives might be reconciled have created a new field of political and cultural conflicts.

The poll data cited above shows that the proportion of distrustful and negative views varies from country to country and can be highly contradictory in character. The critical judgements pronounced by the outside world represent one kind of problem for the US. A second set of difficulties arises from the gap that has appeared between the way in which the political projects of the Bush Administration sound and work inside the country and the ways in which they are heard and interpreted beyond its borders. That communicative gulf is another unanticipated effect of global convergence. It has been deepened by what appears to be an instance of the old imperial double standard in which the lives, habits and choices of US citizens are rated much more highly than those of others. Even inside the fortified homeland, citizenship is not what it was. Its residual protections are unevenly distributed and qualified by the de facto racial hierarchy even if it is residual. Emergency legislation has made revocation relatively easy. The tension between the hyperbolic pronouncements about freedom and democracy and the untidy reality of US society not only provides a framework through which these injustices are perceived but has also helped to nurture a global public sphere by transmitting internal dissent outwards to a global public whose resistance aspires to be as fluid and mobile as capital has itself become. The information technology that facilitates these global networks is still heavily concentrated in the overdeveloped countries and we must remember that a sizeable majority of people on the planet have never even heard a telephone dial tone. However, a nascent global immanence[5] conditions the larger setting in which the political dynamics of US culture is being recast and contested.

The manifestation of these new geo-political and geo-cultural arrangements has done more than simply alter the balance previously struck between so-called "hard" and "soft" forms of power. Qualitative changes have occurred in the way that power is conceived and exercised. This situation demands a new critical vocabulary and a more elaborate understanding of the dynamics of political culture transformed by the relentless tempo of the info-war which is projecting race and ethnicity in novel geo-political patterns.

When asked to account for the fact that the US has become widely disliked and distrusted as a result of its recent attempts to improve and reorganise the world by violence, the primary architects of this situation seem disinterested or indifferent. They may be unable or reluctant to calculate the consequences likely to follow from spurning so much sympathy. They argue that this long or endless war is a wholly new type of conflict. Its novelty is identified not only in the protean nature of the shadowy enemies against whom flexible, hi-tech and often privatised violence is to be directed but also in a new relationship between information and violence. Some aspects of this decisive change had been foreshadowed in the writings of twentieth-century analysts of propaganda, truth, media and government such as Freud, Orwell and Edward Bernays.[6] Today, military initiatives are no longer conceptualised as punctuated, complemented and facilitated by psychological operations, "psyops", that are essentially external to them. The tempo and character of this new variety of war – and the secure forms of social life that correspond to it – require the wholesale integration of struggles over information, language and symbols with the prosecution of the conflict. These conditions also require that hard and soft varieties of power are effectively fused. Securitocracy requires that each takes on characteristics and tactical significance associated with the other.

What Bernays identified long ago as the "engineering of consent" saturates the workings of the twenty-four-hour media environment. Any democratic potential inherent in increasing the flow of information is circumscribed by the role of governmental and media institutions in the systematic cultural production of ignorance. This process has been given the useful proper name "agnatology" by the historians Robert Proctor and Londa Schiebeinger.[7] These changes have been accelerated and rendered more elaborate by recent technological developments, but they are not reducible to the effects of technology alone. The partial and uneven dissemination of photographic archive of US prisoner abuse at Abu Ghraib can be used to illustrate many of the fundamental mechanisms involved; however digital photography is already an anachronistic vector in this contest of images, symbols and icons. The period since Major General Geoffrey Miller's epoch-making transfer to Iraq to secure the "gitmo-isation" of the US prison regime has been characterised by a quantum leap in video-blogging, uploading and self-documentation that has expanded immediate public access to the experiential and political detail of the info-war. The integrity of this free communicative space seems now to be essential to the morale of the occupying force. It seems that soldiers deprived of the right to communicate will be harder to control.

Digitisation breaks culture into easily reassembled, recombinant fragments that can be readily circulated and are not amenable to the rules of copyright. Issues of origin and ownership fade in the face of different post-proprietary claims based on utility and effect. Marine Corporal Joshua Belile was, for example, filmed and recorded singing "Hadji Girl" his supposedly humorous Iraq war ballad to an appreciative audience at the Al Asad airbase in March 2006.[8] Since then, anyone with access to a computer has been able to enjoy his performance of it on network sites like YouTube or Google video regardless of whether his employers, the US Marine Corps, found it to be inappropriate and contrary to the high standards expected of all Marines.

Exposure to raw cultural material of that sort does not guarantee a particular political result. It can signify different things to different constituencies, all of which are likely to employ the voguish language of cultural insiderism to invoke the precious shield of incorrigibility. The result is what can be called a culture of uploading that has de-centred the geo-politics of information and re-worked the patterns of distribution beyond the point where they can be effectively orchestrated by any national state. This helps to explain how, even in a "unipolar" world, what might be called the brand value and identity of the US appears to be openly at stake in the conduct of their long, global war. The historically unprecedented rate at which journalists have been killed on the battlefields of the Iraqi insurgency and the war on terror is another development which bears eloquent witness to these changed circumstances.[9]

Many dimensions of this new technological and cultural environment merit detailed investigation; however the questions of racial hierarchy and injustice that have loomed large within it are seldom addressed directly or recognised as an increasingly significant element in how political judgements of the US are to be formed and how its cultural power is understood. Those issues which did so much to compromise the democratic integrity of the US during the embittered era of civil rights struggle, have acquired a new meaning in the post-colonial world where representations of multiculture and diversity can acquire a high market value even if politicians and governments find it difficult to imagine, to appreciate and to manipulate. That disjunction results in the strange situation whereby the camps in Guantanamo Bay, like detention facilities run elsewhere by the US, can boast of feeding their detainees "culturally appropriate meals" while simultaneously using the very same knowledge of cultural differences to perpetrate specific forms of humiliation and abuse. James Yee, formerly US Military Imam in the Cuban base, has for example, described the desecration of religious texts and the use of culturally inappropriate gender behaviour as a recurrent part of the interrogation process.[10] Janis Karpinski, the Arabic-speaking former General in charge of the Abu Ghraib facility before Miller took over, claims with the greatest sincerity that reading the Koran "enhanced" her own spirituality.[11] These illustrations cannot be dismissed as the institutional residues of "politically correct" management culture. They provide small, valuable windows through which we can consider the contradictory, day to day functioning of the US racial technology embedded in the conduct of the long war against terror.

Even when they are triggered by problems that exceed her own specific areas of political responsibility, contemporary reflections on the question of racism and its relationship to rights, opportunity and democracy now arise under the symbolic umbrella conveniently provided by the pivotal, historic personality of the US Secretary of State Condoleezza Rice. Whatever their degree of professional competence, Condoleezza Rice and the torture-sanctioning Attorney General Alberto Gonzales, who serves a similar function among the Hispanic voters in the Republican electoral bloc, are timely embodiments of the US struggle to extend political rights to its racial and ethnic minorities. They supply smiling human ciphers for the national security strategy and present the official face of US diversity united across racial lines by a fundamental, patriotic commitment to the advancement of national interests.

It bears repetition that the polished aura of Rice's racialised humanity adds something distinctive to the political visibility of the US in the world. This epiphany can and perhaps should offer an immediate and vivid lesson about the irrelevance of race to the operations of government. However, her studied celebrity is usually deployed either to convey the contentious proposition that racism has been dealt with and equality of opportunity finally secured, or to raise unhelpful and unanswerable questions about the shifting importance of racial authenticity.[12]

The political debates over racism and ethnicity that have emerged in response to Rice's obvious power and presence have been evident in several interconnected contexts. Firstly, they have been raised by critical considerations of the legal and humanitarian conduct of the war on terror itself. Pertinent questions have been asked about the issue of US war crimes, about the routine practice of torture and the habitual use of extra-judicial detention all of which seem to bear the imprint of older forms of colonial warfare animated by orientalist, civilisationist and racialist conceptions of human hierarchy and history.[13] Secondly, considerations of the place of racial divisions in the functioning of the US polity became prominent after governmental responses to the flooding in New Orleans revealed continuing effects of segregation that appeared to be at odds with the promise of US society as a place where diversity and democratic solidarity were not in conflict and citizenship was not allocated in colour-coded forms. The same themes have also been debated at great intensity since the pursuit of rights and recognition by the country's substantial Latino/a minorities resulted in mass demonstrations of their centrality and value within the US economy. That development also prompted important reflections on the history and memory of the twentieth-century civil rights movement by African Americans at a moment when they are no longer their country's largest "non-white" group and have been struggling to come to terms with the fact that their distinctive cultural habits and styles have been more comprehensively mainstreamed than ever before. Finally, the global expansion of hip hop has had important and unanticipated effects. Numerous soldiers on the frontline of US military operations have opted to articulate both their disenchantment and their resignation in the form of rap performances which have often been edited together with their own video footage.

Rather than consume a ready-made soundtrack for their experience devised elsewhere and then sold back to them as a commodity – Beyoncé's 2005 hit "Soldier" is a good example of that corporate dynamic – they have acquired the digital tools not only to produce their own alternative musical accompaniment but to distribute it worldwide as well.[14] The same is of course true of their opponents the insurgents who have also uploaded videos of their own exploits: sometimes choreographed to a peculiarly inappropriate US heavy metal soundtrack.

This interfacing of militarised hip hop with endless war reveals something profound about the changing character of US society and the evolving shape of the country's new racial settlement. In Iraq, 23 per cent of troops on the ground are African American and the graffiti of Chicago's Latino gangs has been found sprayed on walls by soldiers who have apparently retained civilian affiliations they regard as more fundamental than their transient attachment to the Army.[15]

Under the aegis of the Hummer Corporation, these unlikely connections have been essential to the process of military recruitment for some time.[16] What is at issue now, is whether the US strong attachment to and persistent celebration of its distinctive conception of racial hierarchy will prove an obstacle to the continued export and circulation of its culture. Many people outside the US will not share the country's peculiar appetite for seeing its reality TV contestants divided into race-specific teams, or having DNA analysed according to the local rules of US phenomics in order to establish the probity of one's racial heritage. The question now is whether race retains the power to detonate the unstable reconciliation of hard and soft power. On the anniversary of the disaster in New Orleans, this looks possible whatever Dr Rice may suggest to the contrary.

Chapter 21

Hard Times for Soft Power?
America and the Atlantic Community

Michael Cox * *and Adam Quinn*#

I f soft power can be measured by how well a nation is liked and respected, then there has been a run on US reserves which may threaten not just the nation's present cash-flow, but its structural solvency well into the future. Switching the metaphor from the fiscal to the medical, America under the Bush Administration has been haemorrhaging its stock of international goodwill to such a frightening degree that it now finds itself in danger of being bled white. America may not be quite so alone as some have argued. In Europe in particular it still has friends. But it would be unwise to pass off the latest bout of anti-Americanism as being merely a transitory phenomenon that all great powers have to endure by virtue of their privileged position in the world. This time it is more serious; the gap more profound; the lack of solidarity greater. But how have we arrived at where we are today? What are its potential consequences? And is there anything Europeans – as opposed to Americans – can do to build real as opposed to shaky bridges across the Atlantic?

* **Michael Cox** is Professor of International Relations at the London School of Economics, Co-Director of its Cold War Studies Centre and Chair of the European Consortium for Political Research. The author and editor of several books on international relations, his most recent publication was an eight volume edited study entitled *Twentieth Century International Relations* (Sage, 2006).

\# **Adam Quinn** is Lecturer in International Relations at the Department of Politics and International Relations, University of Leicester. Recent publications include: 'The Deal: the balance of power, military strength and liberal internationalism in the Bush National Security Strategy', *International Studies Perspectives*, Feb 2008.

CLINTON TO BUSH

We should not romanticise the period before President Bush's inauguration as a golden age of transatlantic harmony. Before the 2000 election, with Bill Clinton still shining his now-legendary charisma upon the process of US diplomacy, there was already serious concern that the European perception of America was sliding into darker shades, nudged in part by such events as the Senate's rejection of the Comprehensive Test Ban Treaty and foot-dragging over Balkan commitments. Still, talk to most officials in Brussels today and the story they invariably tell is an interesting and indicative one. The 1990s were at times difficult, they agree, especially when it came to Bosnia. Indeed, during the early part of the decade, even the British and the Americans did not get on too well. Overall though, the period was a usefully experimental one which allowed NATO to expand without too much fuss being kicked up in Europe, and the process of European integration moving forward without raising too many fears in Washington. Moreover, though Clinton had more than his fair share of European critics, he was in the end viewed (and on the day of his departure from office even characterised by at least one senior European official as being) 'a true friend of Europe'. It is unlikely the same will be said of the current occupant of the White House when he makes that last long ride down Pennsylvania Avenue in January 2009.

The most recent data on the subject seems equally unequivocal: Bush's arrival, and the subsequent deluge of controversies – his early rejection of several treaties, going it alone in Afghanistan, declaring a War on Terror, and forcing the issue over Iraq – has brought about, in most parts of the world, a steep decline in regard for US policies, America's leading role in the world and increasingly for the American nation itself.[1] Europe, seat of America's most reliable allies, has been no exception. Some occasional mild fluctuation aside, it is a trend from which the US image in European eyes has shown no sign of recovering. Such reports having received persistent, widespread media coverage in Europe, it seems likely that this in itself has done something to make negative views of America settle in as part of the landscape in the collective European mind.[2]

Joseph Nye is no doubt correct to point out, elsewhere in this volume, that the equation drawn by fearful foreigners between the United States, globalisation and modernity is inaccurate and misleading. There is also a certain plausibility to his view that the inevitable future decline in America's relative power in the world will lessen the force of this equation and hence allow America's soft power – its ideological and cultural attractiveness – to recover somewhat.

Nevertheless, there is still cause for concern. For one thing, America's relative decline is a decades-long, maybe century-long prospect. Given the strength of anti-American sentiment even in some previously allied places, and the serious consequences America's loss of soft power has for the international order, such a long-range projection of improvement still leaves policymakers with plenty to worry about on a more human timescale. But beyond that, can we afford to be so sanguine about the long-term recovery of America's image? After all, we might just as plausibly speculate that the damage being done today, whether through specific policy snafus or the more generalised association of America with unwelcome international trends, could leave a legacy of suspicion and resentment of the United States that could substantially outlast the initial spurs themselves. As evidence that such is possible we need only consider the residual association in many Third World minds of European powers with imperialism and colonialism, many decades after the last major outpost of formal empire was cut loose.

Most of the points that Nye makes concerning America's relationship to globalisation – that it is a complex global phenomenon which cannot be equated with 'Americanisation' and which affects the US just as much as those to whom it relates – could likewise be made about the European relation to colonialism. The point is not that the US relationship to others through globalisation is similar to colonialism; that is a decidedly separate argument. The point here is merely that major global phenomena, such as the trends currently promoting anti-Americanism, can leave a sentimental impression which long survives the passing of the original basis for bad (or good) feeling. The present ill feeling towards the United States may well leave a footprint which is hard to erase.

Though there are some extremists in Europe, the vast majority of Europeans do not subscribe to the most outlandish brands of anti-Americanism widespread in certain other parts of the world. Nevertheless, a significant number of Europeans are today turning to a discourse which is notable for its underlying emotional aversion to the US, and its determination to reach the worst conclusions regarding both US policy and US society more generally, even if at the cost of intellectual consistency or fair presentation of the facts. Thus an eavesdropper on the various 'national conversations' of Europe often finds the discussion of America and Americans in terms of stereotypes and the ready attribution of malign intent. There is of course a more complex story to be told. Hence, those living in former communist countries are more inclined to be more sympathetic to the US and its views. Nor does Europe, in its mainstream culture at least, touch the lows of the Arab world in the generation and consumption of black propaganda mining these ideological seams. Only closed ears, however, could fail to recognise thematic similarities in much political comment falling comfortably within what is considered the acceptable spectrum of European political views. At its most brazen, the trend towards this sort of thinking can be seen in the widespread popularity of conspiratorial narratives concerning 9/11.[3] More insidious, however, is the more moderately intoned discourse of anti-Americanism which makes persistent assertions as to the ignorance, insularity, materialism, imperialism, violence, greed, disingenuousness and/or profound malevolence of the American nation and its government acceptable, indeed casual and predictable, currency at political meetings and dinner tables throughout Europe.

That such practices should have taken hold among the citizens of nations which were long America's closest allies is a sign of just how severely America's 'soft power' political and cultural appeal has contracted. None of the particular stances on Europe's part which have punctuated the recent years of diplomatic discord – opposition to the invasion of Iraq, irritation at the impact of US trade and culture on Europe, concern for the effect of American foreign fecklessness on environmental policy on future generations –intrinsically demand the stigmatising label of 'anti-American'. If presented the right way, these can all be quite sensible positions. But the way that such stances have been articulated, especially beyond the cautious circles of diplomacy – in the media and party politics – has nurtured the flourishing of an atmosphere of 'gut' suspicion of all which emanates from across the Atlantic. The consequences of this 'turn' in the mood of the forum within which foreign affairs is discussed in Europe merit discussion, as does the possibility of how those Europeans who regret anti-Americanism might best respond.

RECOVERING THAT COLD WAR SPIRIT?

Those inclined to look for structural factors explaining today's swell of disharmony often conclude that the end of the Cold War has much to answer for. During the half-century which followed the end of WWII, what differences there may have been between the United States and its European partners needed, ultimately, always to be managed in light of the undeniable dependency of Western Europe on American power to defend it against clear and present danger in the form of the Soviet Union. Both left and right in Europe – for their own differing reasons of anticapitalism and national pride – had serious qualms concerning America even in the years of greatest collaboration. International circumstances, however, made sure that such worries had to remain in check in the interests of fundamental security. In today's international arena, the threat, in the form of the Soviet Union, which once compelled

European allegiance, has evaporated. As a result, we find patterns of thought among European political leaders which are in their fundamentals not dissimilar to those of the Cold War period, but which operate in a context bereft of the same ultimate guarantee of restraint at the governmental level.

With the 'War on Terror' and the proclamation of a transformational strategy towards the Middle East, George W. Bush's presidency has painted a grand new canvas of international affairs to replace the fading paradigm of the Cold War. The reactions of Europeans to the new American grand strategy, on left and right, are broadly consistent with their former Cold War instincts. The left combines an ideological rejection of the American political and economic model with complaints, implicit or explicit, that the United States itself is acting in significant part as the cause of the defining problems of the world – extremism and terrorism – or at the very least that its actions are serving to exacerbate them. The mainstream right, on the other hand, accepts to a greater degree the righteousness of American goals and the overlap of values and interests between Europe and America, but nevertheless worries that by throwing blind support behind the United States their nation may become hostage to questionable US decision-making. Always by its very nature wedded to some level of nationalism, the European right especially resents the perception which arises from subscription to the American agenda that their nation and government may have become a thoroughly subordinate creature of an American president, its support invoked as evidence of multilateralism while any tentative criticisms are ignored utterly. For example, few charges have done more harm to the credibility, across the political spectrum, of Britain's Tony Blair than the persistent accusation that his world role had been reduced to that of George Bush's 'poodle'.

One might ask whether the threats posed by today's world – terrorism, extremism, weapons proliferation – might not serve as the same sort of external threat that the Soviets once did, promoting cooperation on the basis of passably common values and interests. However, it seems clear that Europeans have too many doubts about American prescriptions for addressing these problems, and do not feel a sufficiently sharp existential threat to cause them to suppress these for the sake of appearances. The suggestions of some cultural critiques notwithstanding, it is reasonable to note that Europeans and Americans are today as close in terms of values and interests as two separate continents can have any reasonable expectation of finding themselves. However it seems that without a pressing reason for Europeans to doubt their basic security, this will not provide the basis for the sort of self-denying coordination of policy to which the latter half of the twentieth century made us accustomed. This means that the instincts of 'lite anti-Americanism' – to talk in stereotypes, ascribe sinister global omnipotence to America and to seek defence against 'guilt by association' by minimising ties – will likely continue be a major part of the public discourse of European societies. The reasons why such talk has long been tempting still apply with full force, while the reasons it was once frowned upon no longer apply.

ATTITUDES HAVE CONSEQUENCES

If anti-American sentiment holds its present strength in Europe, the political consequences could be serious indeed. The first is the likely effect on the tone, not just of public discourse, but of political leaders. European politicians are increasingly forced to operate in an environment where anti-American positions are regarded as statements of common-sense wisdom, while statements of support for the US government are subject to prolonged hostile analysis. There are thus more straightforward political rewards to be reaped from pronouncements deriding American positions than from any effort to justify collaboration. There may of course be leaders, Nicolas Sarkozy now being one, who are capable of resisting such a trend in the popular sentiment of their nations and are disposed to do so. It would seem foolhardy, however, to predict that a general movement of public feeling in democracies will not tend to dictate a drift in the thinking of elected representatives towards compatible positions. Hence, one political consequence of rising public anti-Americanism will be increased difficulty for European leaders in sustaining a pro-American stance, or supporting policies which are associated in the public mind with the United States – especially those which involve the threat of military action of any sort – even if the leaders themselves might by their own instincts be disposed to favour such policies. In short, the political price of visible pro-Americanism has risen substantially, with predictable effects for the number of political actors willing to buy the product.

Secondly, if domestic political conditions make it more difficult for pro-American politicians, or at least pro-American policy positions, to succeed in Europe, then there will also be an effect on the alignment of the broader international community. The world has been used to seeing the United States and leading European nations collaborate closely on the serious issues of international affairs, often to the extent of viewing them as a cohesive Western bloc. While it seems unlikely that the new wave of anti-American sentiment in Europe could produce such an extreme effect as to drive Europe into the arms of any other partner in opposition to America, it does seem plausible that more energy will have to be devoted by the United States to shoring up support from Europe which in the past it has become accustomed to take for granted.

Thirdly, a related consequence of a drift towards resistance to following the 'American course' may be a certain forgetfulness regarding the degree to which European and US interests and values still coincide. Much has been written concerning the differences between Europe and the United States: America is a less statist, more individualistic and more religious society than European nations can claim for themselves.[4] Nevertheless, there are rudimentary principles to which the two adhere with a steadiness which cannot be found so readily in other places. For all their disagreements over the War on Terror and the invasion of Iraq, Americans and Europeans have far more uniting them with one another than with the proclaimers of Islamist *jihad* or Stalinist relics like North Korea's Kim Jong-Il. Even more acceptable prospective partners such as China or Russia seem on due analysis to be many moons away from having the basis of commonality with either side required to supplant the transatlantic bond.

Their periodic gestures of spectacular lethal nihilism notwithstanding, it still seems highly unlikely that the enemies of the Western social model have the ability to destroy it, though they can certainly visit harm upon its citizens. Still, the throwing of rhetorical stones and the inculcation of a self-conscious 'values gap' between the two continents which provide the supporting pillars of the West cannot but weaken it. As suggested above, it seems plausible that a more pressingly existential sense of threat to Europe would more likely reinvigorate than destroy the Euro-American partnership. For now, however, in as much as European and American solidarity may be said to aid the defence of their common interests and values, European anti-Americanism (and its reciprocal counterpart in American sentiment) threaten to take eyes off the ball when it comes to pursuing what should be both sides' highest priority: the uncompromising defence of their shared way of life.

Fourthly, there is a very real risk that the movement of mainstream political discourse towards anti-Americanism may give comfort to anti-democratic forces in European societies. Within those societies, there will always be a certain amount of extremism, which, in the case of the subject of interest here, is characterised by a powerful hatred of America and subscription to outlandish conspiracy theories concerning American deeds and their context. We are all by now at least partially familiar, through the analysis of terrorist attacks, successful and foiled, in the United Kingdom, with the processes by which citizens can be led to draw radical religious and political conclusions as a result of exposure to propaganda blaming the United States for a global 'crusade' against Islam. It would be inaccurate and unfair to hold those who posit more moderate criticisms of the United States responsible for the words and actions of extremists, and we certainly would not seek to do so. However, in the same way that the Iraq war can be observed to have provoked an upsurge in terrorist intent without that statement in any sense suggesting that the former justifies the latter, so it may be justly argued that the culture of intellectual hostility towards United States foreign policy which has taken root among the general population of Europe has made fighting the 'war on terrorism' more difficult.

Fifth and finally, a sad consequence of anti-Americanism's rise may be the entrenchment of an unedifying mental laziness, likely to enervate the intellectual content of the European debate about international affairs, even as high passions continue to flow. It would no doubt be to romanticise the process of foreign policy-making in democracies to suggest that what emerges is usually the product of dialectics of flawless reason on the part of the general public. Nevertheless, it is to be hoped that, at least on matters of the greatest importance, the public does engage to some degree, and the greater the sophistication and rationality of its analysis the better for the political process. If, however, back-to-front reasoning, which assumes the worst concerning agendas associated with America, continues to be a feature of European debates; if crass generalisations concerning American culture and politics retain their grip over the European public mindset; if the government of the United States continues to be ascribed a malevolence and omnipotence detached from any balanced reading of the facts; then the result can only be to infantilise and stunt the public discussion of international affairs in Europe. Only by eschewing easy intellectual shortcuts which assume generalised good or ill to lie at the root of American policy; only by embracing the reality that the United States is far from all-powerful, and thus far from all-responsible for the world's problems; only by accepting that despite lacking omnipotence the US nevertheless has a shot at achieving at least some important, positive things through the application of its substantial power and is disposed to attempt to do so, in a way which may infringe on the claimed prerogatives of others; only in these ways can those who seek to offer critique of US policy hope to emerge from their analysis with useful, productive conclusions. The best way to achieve the spread of such an approach to the subject is by demanding fairness and consistency from America's critics in Europe.

MODERATES OF EUROPE UNITE

In lamenting the likely effects of a visceral anti-Americanism, i.e. one founded more in emotion than in thought through political analysis, we should not seek to encourage in its place a simple-minded pro-Americanism, which would be equally a vice. Mature policy debate requires that Europeans, as individuals and also collectively, think critically about the actions of the United States and the direction in which it intends to nudge international society through the exercise of its unprecedented power. However, it would be healthy for the forum of European political debate if the practitioners of emotional and often inconsistent anti-Americanism were put under more pressure to justify themselves. It is simply too easy at the moment for European thinkers to disavow anti-Americanism ('it is Bush we oppose not the United States') while still churning out a hotchpotch of inconsistent or half-baked criticisms of all that America actually does. Through our tolerance of this, the respectable appearance of reasoned argument is lent to what in reality amounts to the rationalisation of an emotionally-founded desire to castigate the United States come what may.

Those who criticise the United States should thus be challenged to explain their own position with precision: that is, the values to which they subscribe, the goals they would wish to see pursued in international society, and, beyond the level of generalities, the policies which they would see the US and Europe pursue to advance them. Such obligatory thinking through might force a great many casual anti-Americans to accept that there is considerably more overlap than they presently avow between their own values and those of the United States, and that the actions of the US government, while at times ill judged, are, except in the rarest cases, at worst well-intentioned but counterproductive efforts to achieve goals not so very far from those of their European critics. If such an acceptance were possible, the mainstream of European discourse might be moved away from a fruitless attribution of malevolence, idiocy and cultural degeneracy to the United States; few Europeans could retain such positions if made to think about them harder than they are presently obliged to do. Ideally it would move towards a more productive discussion of what, in detail, Europeans think they ought to be doing, in cooperation with the United States, to advance their largely shared macro-level ambitions for world reform.

Moderate critics of specific policies of the United States in Europe often resent talk of anti-Americanism, imagining themselves to be lumped in with a supposedly prejudiced and ignorant mass. Sometimes this is a fair reaction to what amounts to a pro-American broadside seeking to undermine all critics by labelling all criticism as a manifestation of anti-Americanism. In truth, however, those who possess broadly Atlanticist instincts based on the common values and interests of Europe and the United States – but who reserve the right to disagree publicly with American policies when they see fit – should consider the fight against anti-Americanism, properly conceived, their own. For in a social environment where casual anti-Americanism has become the norm in the national conversation, it is all too easy for moderates to have their cautious criticisms seized upon as the basis for a far less respectable enterprise of blanket condemnation of America and its works.

Wise moderates should disassociate themselves from the whatever-the-weather anti-Americanists just as firmly as they would from the excesses of the pro-American fringe. The threats to liberal democratic nations today do not seem strong enough to truly endanger their continued prosperous existence. However, in a world of advancing technology, shifting power balance and newly emergent threats, it would be enlightened for Europeans and Americans to secure the foundations of their partnership in defence of their core shared values. Then, and only then, might it be ready for challenges yet to come.

PART V

Interpretive Communities

INTRODUCTION

How do different groups reflect and think about themselves amidst the manifold changes associated with globalisation? This section takes a regional perspective on the nature and form of changing interpretive communities, and in so doing offers a number of contrasting case studies on the relationship between the cultural interpretation of local groups and wider socio-economic transformations. The case studies are from six different areas of the world: Afghanistan and Pakistan, China, Ghana, India, South Africa and the European Union. **Akbar Ahmed** begins by offering an incisive critique of Thomas Friedman's argument that 'The World is Flat' by emphasising how the culture, custom, and ideas of the past are often highly prized as marks of identity within many communities. It is widely acknowledged that the relationship between religion and identity is once again taking on a geopolitical character. But how can we understand the processes of identity and will formation within locally nested communities and its relation to contemporary political struggles? Using the example of tribalism within Islam and the case of local reactions to the 'War on Terror' in Afghanistan, Ahmed illustrates how culturally inherited notions of honour and dignity inform present groups' behaviour and, importantly, their expectations and judgements about others. Ahmed offers the more general observation that social scientists need to advise policymakers and agenda setters how to deal with a world which is not flat so that the complexities and historicity of locally situated – and locally resilient – cultures and transitions can be better grasped.

Mayfair Yang describes the relationship between religious revival and economic development in the city of Wenzhou in southeastern China. Yang argues that the apparent rise of popular religiosity has deep historical and institutional roots which can be traced back to the late imperial Chinese commercial culture. The popular religiosity Yang depicts strengthens local identities and cultural practices and at the same time drives aspects of capitalist development while placing limits upon them.

Kwame Anthony Appiah focuses on Ghana and considers the relationship between globalisation, cultural homogeneity and the preservation/continuity of local cultures. He differentiates between the preservation of culture – which he regards as laudable – and the preservation of cultures, which he regards with suspicion because it assumes that they are in need of protection. In addition, Appiah then touches on the issue of threats from dominant cultural forces. He suggests that 'cultural imperialism' is a non sequitur, arguing powerfully that different cultures will always interpret the same cultural artefact differently. The assertion that 'cultural imperialism' serves to structure the consciousness of those in peripheral geographies is not only deeply condescending but empirically untrue. Appiah praises the hybrid exchange of 'cultural contamination' and notes that even the most famous global cultural commodities are subject by people to their own sense of meaning and use in different parts of the world.

Kriti Kapila engages with the claim that globalisation has led to cultural homogenisation by exploring a powerful counter-example inducing identity politics and cultural classification in India. Kapila traces the different ways in which different cultural groups have been classified in India historically, and examines these in relation to the emerging bioscientific classification of different groups. Kapila's thesis is that assertions derived from identity politics – of cultural difference, claims for group-differentiated rights, and demands for equal respect – are paramount and important but one should not forget that these forms of self-identification have emerged in a complex interplay of politics, knowledge regimes and states practices.

Archbishop **Njongonkulu Ndungane** describes the cultural transformations within post-apartheid South Africa and illustrates how new identities are overtaking the old. He focuses on the underlying principles of restorative justice which has informed this development and offers some thoughts on how the South African experience could assist in a wider breadth of disputes. The challenges that South Africa faced in trying to create a new society, Njongonkulu Ndungane argues, were enormous in that they 'had no respectable past on which to draw, no fertile historic soil in which to plant and nurture a new future.' Despite this momentous challenge, the actual experience of the South Africa case offers important insights into how cultures literally at war with each other may engage in dialogue together and begin to address their shared pasts.

James Tully takes on the subject of cultural integration through an examination of different practices of democratic integration in the European Union. Tully argues that the dominant approaches to cultural integration gives little role for the active engagement of diverse citizens and immigrants in establishing the conditions and norms of integration, 'yet culturally diverse Europeans are creating a new diversity-savvy solidarity across cultural differences.' Noting that the dominant form of democratic integration within the European Union is inherently undemocratic given its elite-driven, non-participatory character, Tully calls for a European integration that turns more to the active participation of its citizens for guidance.

Chapter 22

The World Is Not Flat*

*Akbar S. Ahmed***

[...]

Thomas Friedman, in his influential book *The World is Flat* (2005), gushes with excitement – not unlike "stout Cortez," in the poem by Keats, who believing he is the first European to "discover" the Pacific Ocean, stares at it "with a wild surmise" – because he believes he has "discovered" a new world through the lens of globalization and it is "flat."[1] Friedman's use of the term "connected" to describe the new world means the lowering of trade and political barriers and the exponential technical advances of the digital revolution which make it possible for large numbers of people to be connected across the planet. To him globalization is simply put "Americanization" with all that the term implies from McDonald's to political ideas of democracy.[2] Although he shows greater nuance recently his essential position is the same. Friedman's optimism also contains an implicit message: if you resist, you will be trampled on and soon flattened. You have been warned: globalization cannot – indeed must not – be resisted.

The world as seen from the point of view of a traditional society like Islam is not flat but still diverse with valleys, ravines, and mountains. Culture, custom, and ideas of the past are highly prized as marks of identity. Notions of honor and dignity inherited from forefathers characterize behavior itself and define how people judge each other. This is perhaps best exemplified by those who are able to maintain and perpetuate tradition – the tribal peoples of Islam.

The tribes of Islam are not marginal or isolated communities living on the verge of extinction. They are large and powerful and many have the defining

---

* The ideas and material in this chapter are expanded in his forthcoming book *Reining in a Runaway World* which is based on an intensive field trip to the Muslim world in 2006 for the Brookings Institution, Pew Forum and American University in Washington DC.

** Professor **Akbar Ahmed** is the Ibn Khaldun Chair of Islamic Studies at American University, Washington DC. He was High Commissioner for Pakistan in the UK and held the posts of Political Agent in South Waziristan Agency and Commissioner Sibi Division which included the Bugti Agency.

characteristics of a fully developed nation – language, territory, common culture, a shared history, and a sense of identity. They have one advantage over the modern nation state and that is that all members of the tribe can trace descent from one common ancestor whose name is given to the tribe itself and therefore members have no doubts regarding their loyalties. The Yusufzai, for example, one of the most aristocratic tribes among the Pukhtuns, are descended from a common ancestor Yusuf. In Pukhto, the language of the Pukhtuns, *zoi* or *zai* means son or sons of: thus anyone claiming to be Yusufzai can legitimately trace his ancestry to Yusuf himself.

These Muslim tribes have countries, provinces, and districts named after them. Saudi Arabia is named after the tribe of Saud. Afghanistan means, literally, the land of the Afghan (another name for Pukhtun), as *stan* means "land of." Thus Uzbekistan is the land of the Uzbeks; Baluchistan, in Pakistan, is the province of the Baluch. North and South Waziristan Agencies, also in Pakistan, are the district or agencies of the Wazir much to the chagrin of the other powerful tribe, the Mahsud, who live in the south. The Bugti agency in Baluchistan is named after the Bugti tribe.

The tribes – whether Muslim or non-Muslim – which are spread across Africa and Asia all now face the juggernaut of globalization. It is a zero-sum situation. Globalization demands submission to a universal culture imported from across the seas; tribalism insists on maintenance of indigenous custom and culture. Globalization assumes the dissolution of boundaries; tribalism defines itself on the basis of boundaries. The inherent conflict between two ways of looking at the world is dramatically illustrated by what is currently happening in Iraq, Afghanistan, Pakistan, and Somalia, countries which contain large and important Muslim tribes. Tribes no longer exist in quite the same nomadic way as they did only a few generations ago when they could preserve their customs by crossing international borders and thereby remaining isolated from mainstream society. On the other hand, it is interesting how tribal behavior marks even those societies considered modern. The Muslims in Malaysia and Indonesia display a tribal sense of cohesion which is heightened when confronting the large and influential Chinese populations living in these Muslim nations. The religion, language, culture, and rites of passage of the Muslim and Chinese communities are different. These differences have created bitter tensions which can erupt into violence in both societies. In Malaysia the ethnic Chinese were seen as successful capitalists and their wealth was envied. In Indonesia, they were seen as successful communists and their political influence was envied. Both the Muslim Malays and Indonesians felt that their identity was under threat by immigrants in their own homeland. Thus their violent reaction, which has cost thousands of lives, was almost tribal and ignored the Islamic values of justice and compassion.[3]

A Mahsud elder in Waziristan told Evelyn Howell, the British Political Agent in charge of the area, a century ago "that a civilization must be judged by the kind of man it produces." The elder argued that it was better to leave the tribe alone so that they could "be men like our fathers before us – that is men of honor and tradition." The two were discussing the prospective merits of their respective cultures and the Mahsud criticized British reforms "which have wrought such havoc in British India." Howell after much reflection agreed.[4]

Friedman is not as self-reflective as Howell. He is more confident about the merits of the world civilization that he represents, yet it may be a salutary lesson for him to recall that only a few decades after the conversation, the British Empire – on which the sun never set – disappeared from Waziristan leaving behind a few deserted forts and some half-remembered traditions carried on by Pakistani political officers.

Waziristan's refusal to be "flattened" by globalization was tested when the American media reported bin Laden was hiding here.[5] The media frenzy and speculation brought unwelcome publicity to an area zealous about its own privacy. In the spring of 2004, American troops launched "Operation Mountain Storm" along the Afghan-Pakistan frontier to look for bin Laden and the remnants of the Taliban. Under direct and immense pressure from the United States, President Pervez Musharraf of Pakistan sent large numbers of Pakistani troops into Waziristan for the first time in the history of the country. The generals sitting in Rawalpindi, and heady with the knowledge that they now possessed the latest weapons given by the Americans to fight "terrorists," felt that the subjugation of Waziristan would be an easy task. President Musharraf appeared on American television and identified a "high-value target." There was speculation that bin Laden or his second-in-command, al-Zawahiri, would be captured soon. The media was agog with excitement.

Neither the Americans nor the city-dwelling Pakistanis like Musharraf and his generals appeared to have done their homework. In their own area, with its high mountains and isolated valleys, these tribes of Waziristan are virtually invincible. Acting upon orders from the United States to find and kill terrorists, Musharraf lost several hundred soldiers and the tribes complained of the indiscriminate killing of women and children as the American-supplied gunships bombarded their settlements. Musharraf then scaled down military activity, negotiated with the tribes, and when talks broke down sent in the army again. The cycle was repeated all over again. Tribal councils were now called and elders consulted. Many lives and the destruction of much property would have been saved if this had been done in the first place.

Because the foreign policy of the U.S. is now being conducted on the assumption that the world is flat it is assumed that societies abroad will succumb nudged by the persuasive powers of the deadly "daisy cutter" or the seductive charms of the almighty dollar. An application of either, or both, and any community would be supine. Not so, we discover in Waziristan. Popular British novelists like John Masters who knew the Wazir and the Mahsud tribes had called them "physically the hardest people on earth" (*Bugles and a Tiger*, 1965: 161). In 1920 they decimated an entire British brigade killing 400 men, including 28 British, and 15 Indian officers. In the following years, there were more British and Indian troops in Waziristan than in the rest of the subcontinent. This was the area that Musharraf with his Karachi background hoped to casually enter and conquer.

In an interview in March 2006 Musharraf told me he admired Napoleon but it seemed he had not learned lessons from Napoleon's military failures. Even Napoleon could not fight successfully on two fronts. With his Waziristan front fully occupying him in the hunt for bin Laden, Musharraf now sent in the army to pacify the Bugti tribe in Baluchistan. Like the Wazir and the Mahsud among the Pukhtun, the Bugti is renowned among the Baluch for its martial character and tribal sense of honor. Musharraf had landed himself in a dilemma which even the British during colonial times would have taken care to avoid: although they were foreigners, they knew that taking on these powerful tribes simultaneously would spell disaster. Musharraf now confronted the fiercest tribes in South Asia diverting time and energy from the war on terror.

This was not the first time that Pakistan had attempted a military solution to force its will on Baluchistan and Waziristan. Zulfiqar Ali Bhutto, prime minister in the 1970s, had sent in the army into both areas. The difference in the situation then and now was that people understood that while Bhutto had attempted to maneuver his own political party into power, Musharraf was only doing the bidding of the Americans. In that sense, contemporary developments taking place in the region are directly linked to a wider and more international situation.

As a direct result of the fighting in Waziristan – and as Pakistanis poured in troops under American pressure – the tribes of Waziristan did two things, one of which went against their own tradition: they began to unite under one platform in order to resist the invading army which was typical tribal strategy and, secondly, they allowed leadership to fall into the hands of religious leaders who were allied to the Taliban which challenged their own elders. Both developments were of significance and would have ramifications for the politics of globalization and its post-9/11 chapter. This is precisely how the Taliban emerged early in the 1990s in Afghanistan. As local tribal leadership collapsed and to check the anarchy, people first looked to and then welcomed the Taliban. It was only later that the disillusionment set in. We can see similar reactions setting in wherever Islamic movements have taken over, including Iran.

A similar mood that encouraged young Afghans to support the Taliban in the 1990s has now settled in over the young men of Waziristan. The Taliban on both sides of the border had already expressed their attitude to globalization by banning TV and the pop culture of the West. To them, their identity as Muslims and upholding their traditions mattered more than joining the world order. When pressure was brought to bear on the Taliban to hand over bin Laden after 9/11, the response of the Taliban was couched in tribal terms: the code of honor does not permit the surrendering of a guest. Even international experts like former U.S. Secretary of State Madeline Albright who have had dealings with this part of the world in the past did not understand the significance of this code of behavior: "The Taliban leaders didn't say no; instead they offered a menu of lame excuses. They argued that [to turn in bin Laden] would violate cultural etiquette to mistreat the beneficiary of their hospitality and that bin Laden was a hero to Afghans because of his 1980s anti-Soviet role. 'We will be overthrown if we give him to you,' they said. 'Our people will assume we took money from you or the Saudis.' "[6]

While the Taliban's obdurate attitude would cost them dearly and they would be bombed out of Kabul, sympathy for them among ordinary people soon began to grow. Pukhtun tribes on the Pakistani side of the border formed their own Taliban organizations which eventually emerged to dominate Waziristan. My former student from American University, Nick Schmidle, traveled to the Pukhtun areas of Pakistan in February, 2006, and wrote about the rise of Taliban power in Waziristan.[7] He described a DVD distributed widely by the Taliban in which they hang five alleged criminals from a water tower. He reports that the DVD shows "the five men's bodies go limp, they are lowered, decapitated and then re-strung, upside-down and headless, from the scaffold." Many of the tribesmen in these areas are still trying to look for justice from the Pakistani authorities, but are getting very few results. [...]

The religious leaders in Waziristan imposed a strict Islamic order on a society so far dominated by tribal custom. Where the Taliban had failed in Kabul, they now succeeded in Waziristan. Ideas of fighting for Islam against the West are now fused with tribal notions of revenge. One man from the area explained that the fighters "are all local people who are seeking revenge for their homes being destroyed and their families being killed" (Schmidle 2006). Another said that "Every death will be avenged. This blood is not as cheap as some think it is. One dead creates hundreds of avengers."

By early 2006, they were confident enough for their leader Haji Omar to give a face-to-face interview with the BBC from Wana in which he said: "We will not stop our jihad against the Americans. We are not even willing to discuss anything with the Americans. We just want them out." Haji Omar did not blame the Pakistanis entirely: "We understand that Pakistan attacks us only under American pressure." Haji Omar's interview in Wana tells us how influential the Taliban are in Waziristan because this is the headquarters not only of the political agent from the Pakistani government but of the South Waziristan Scouts, the paramilitary forces that maintains law and order in the area. For the leader of a group declared a terrorist organization by the Pakistan government to be holding press conferences in an Agency headquarters reveals the extent of his confidence and influence.

The Taliban had emerged from the debris of the long and debilitating Soviet occupation.[8] There was anarchy in the land. Tribal warlords had established spheres of influence and many of them imposed an uneasy truce based on brute power in their area. Looting, pillaging, and raping were common. Poppy crops became the number one harvest of the farmers. The final breaking point for this conservative tribal society came when a warlord "married" a young boy in Kandahar in a public ceremony which defied all Islamic and local customs. Religious scholars were incensed and, joined by young enthusiastic supporters, mounted a campaign to cleanse society of its social ills. They called themselves "Taliban" from the word *talib*, or student, because many were students of the madrassahs or religious schools. The Taliban were seen as the good guys, coming to restore order and justice. Their first acts were to ban gambling and alcohol. They also imposed a rigid implementation of Islamic law which affected women especially in the cities. Starting from their base in Kandahar in the early 1990s, and supported by Pakistan, they rapidly moved north to occupy most of Afghanistan. The main opposition to the Taliban came from what was called the Northern Alliance composed of tribes living in the north such as the Tajiks and backed by Russia and India.

After their defeat and removal from Kabul the Taliban faced an onslaught on their reputation from the Western media. They were now depicted as the personification of medieval barbarism. The fact of the matter is that today, years after the removal of the Taliban, and the installment of the American-backed government of Hamid Karzai, Afghan society is still run on the principles familiar to us from the time of the Taliban. Western commentators not understanding Afghan culture and custom assumed that the removal of the Taliban would usher in a new era of Westernization. While women undoubtedly have a much better chance of being educated and even finding jobs, the old customs and traditions are very much in place.

Simply removing one political group in a society does not eradicate centuries of culture and custom. Take the example of Mr. Shinwari, the Chief Justice of Afghanistan. He attacked the introduction of television as a harbinger of moral corruption: "as a responsible official I cannot allow cable TV in any part of Afghanistan" (BBC, January 21, 2003). Justifying his statement, Shinwari said "People who filed complaints to the Supreme Court said they were airing half-naked singers and obscene scenes from movies." However, the general sympathy for the government in Kabul today means that few in the Western media appear to be minding the new government's rhetoric or behavior. Today, because of the unsatisfactory handling of law and order and the failture to create political stability, the Taliban have re-emerged in the Pukhtun areas of Afghanistan along the borders with Pakistan and their values are once again dominant in the land.

Afghanistan and Pakistan show us the deadly tensions in traditional societies caught up in the whirlwind that for them is globalization. Tribal, national, and international compulsions intersect through local societies and appear to be tearing them apart. We can point to many other societies across the world which find themselves in a similar predicament.

We have argued that the world is not flat. By assuming its flatness and conducting foreign policy on that assumption the U.S. along with its allies in the West has encouraged conditions that are destabilizing traditional societies. The turmoil not only along the border areas of Afghanistan and Pakistan but also within Iraq can be seen in this context. The emphasis on using brute military force alternating with transparent attempts at buying over local support has created widespread cynicism and resistance. The reaction to what is seen as an invasion of the West translates into violence in the context of locally understood notions of honor and revenge. A cycle of violence is thus created which feeds on itself and we see widespread murder and mayhem which negate the beneficial effects of globalization.

We need to discover a new paradigm to deal with a world that is not flat. We need to listen more to the sociologists and anthropologists and their talk of culture and tradition and less to the analysts who have convinced us that the world can be flattened by modern technology. Once we appreciate the resilience of local culture in societies and acknowledge their integrity and difference we will be well on our way to resolving the problems engendered by globalization. The present mismatch of ideas and societies may then be overcome. But this will not happen unless Western presidents and prime ministers, and their advisors, those who set the agenda for and dominate our world, understand that the world is not flat. This perhaps will be the great test for the social scientists concerned about our world in the twenty-first century.

Chapter 23

Ritual Economy and Rural Capitalism with Chinese Characteristics

*Mayfair Mei-hui Yang**

In this chapter, I would like to discuss an intriguing linkage between the current rural economic development of Wenzhou, Zhejiang Province, on the southeastern coast of China, with Chinese popular religiosity. Once this linkage is made, we can see that what has been taking place in this area of coastal China is not merely another penetration of capitalism, but the hybrid reconstruction of a ritual economy whose genealogy can be traced back to the late imperial Chinese commercial culture of the common people. This ritual economy involves not only the profit motive and material production based on the household unit, but also heavy investment in the cosmic ledger of merits, the sacred world of the gods and ancestors, and the Underworld of ghosts, demons, and the dreaded courts and officials of Hell.

In discussions of globalization, global capitalism, and Americanization,

* **Mayfair Mei-hui Yang** is currently Director of Asian Studies, University of Sydney, Australia. She is the author of *Gifts, Favors, and Banquets: the Art of Social Relationships in China* (University of Minnesota Press, 1994), which won an American Ethnological Society prize; the editor of *Spaces of Their Own: Women's Public Sphere in Transnational China* (Cornell University Press, 1999), and *Chinese Religiosities: Afflictions of Modernity & State Formation* (forthcoming); and articles in such journals as *Current Anthropology, Annales, Cultural Anthropology, Public Culture, Journal of Asian Studies* and *Comparative Studies in Society & History*. She has produced two documentaries: *Through Chinese Women's Eyes* (distributed by Women Make Movies) and *Public and Private Realms in Rural Wenzhou, China*. She is currently at work on a new book: *Re-enchanting Modernity Sovereignty, Ritual Economy, and Indigenous Civil Order in Coastal China*.

three issues are often absent from the conversation: the question of alternative capitalisms, the power of historical traditions and practices, and the religious and ritual dimensions of economy. Let me first expand briefly on each of these three themes, for they will inform my discussion of post-Mao rural economic development and religious revival in Wenzhou.[1]

First, on the question of alternative capitalisms, the critical political economists J.K. Gibson-Graham (two authors with one name) have pointed out the problems inherent in simplistic and uniform models of Western capitalist penetration of the globe, and have called for greater attention to the diversity of cultural and institutional constructions of capitalism around the world.[2] Thus, we may have entered into an era of global capitalism, but *not* into a single model of capitalism. In other words, capitalism does not simply plow down whatever was there before, but creatively combines with older forms and produces new configurations of capitalism, and even mobilizes older cultural resources as new forms of counter-capitalist practice.[3] After all, in *The Grundisse*, Marx himself recognized that modern capitalism had absorbed older pre-capitalist modes of production and economy into its body, although he did not go on to assign much agency to these older modes, nor did he elaborate on structural tensions between older and newer economic forms.[4] What I seek to highlight here is that, beneath the much-publicized multi-billion-dollar contracts between Chinese state corporations and foreign firms, there is another less visible, but more indigenous sector of the dynamic Chinese economy, as seen in the rapid rural economic development in parts of China's southeastern coast, where production and commerce are embedded in a ritual economy.

Second, the importance of a longer historical perspective in thinking about globalization are underscored by path-breaking revisionist economic historians such as Janet Abu-Lughod, Andre Gunder Frank, Kenneth Pomeranz, and R. Bin Wong, who have shown us that in the five centuries before modern European global domination, a commercial globalization was already underway in long-distance and maritime trade among Arab, Persian, Chinese, South, and Southeast Asian merchants.[5] The Europeans were latecomers who merely appropriated and expanded an already existing lucrative global trade network that stretched from the Middle East, around India, and through Southeast Asia, to China, an empire that was from at least the eleventh through seventeenth centuries, a global maritime power whose handicraft industry exports (silk, laquerware, porcelain) were much in demand. Although subsequent centuries saw the decline and increasing impoverishment of China, and the take-off of European industrial, military, and commercial might, the seeds and cultural *habitus* of Chinese entrepreneurial and commercial culture were not destroyed.[6] First laid down in the great commercial and urban revolutions of the Song Dynasty (960–1279 CE), and fitfully allowed to sprout by ambivalent imperial court policies in the Ming (1368–1644 CE) and Qing (1644–1911) Dynasties, these seeds lay dormant in the modern period of the nineteenth and twentieth centuries, through famines, wars, semi-colonialism by the West, revolutions, and state collectivization. The astounding explosive growth in Chinese economic production and trade since the 1980s, especially in southeastern Chinese coastal cultures, attests to the enduring potency of these seeds of the Chinese historical and cultural *habitus* of commercial and maritime culture.

Third, Max Weber's thesis on capitalism as an outgrowth of the Protestant ethic's focus on doing good works in this world as a way to reveal their divine destiny, has alerted scholars to the imbrication of economic practices with forms of religiosity.[7] However, given the prominent and vociferous attention to Weber for several decades, actual detailed empirical studies of economy and non-Western religious traditions have been quite sparse, and virtually none of them have entered into the realm of theoretical discussion. It is curious that there are so few studies of this nature, or that they have not garnered more theoretical interest, since just looking at a few major religious traditions, we know that they must harbor as yet not fully understood major economic implications. For example, Buddhist teachings of reincarnation and *karma*, the law of causality as the link between this life and the next, is translated in popular practice as the concern for merit-making, doing good deeds in this life, to off-set one's demerits for a propitious next life. The often complex accounting system of accumulating and recording merits and demerits must have some implications or offshoots in temporal economic practices. Similarly, the prophet Mohammed was himself a merchant, one of the Five Pillars of Islam is charitable donations, and the religious system he founded has a long history of mercantile civilization, yet there are few English-language studies to chart this relationship between religious doctrine and economy.

The "economic miracle" of the "Four Asian Tigers" (Hong Kong, Taiwan, Singapore, South Korea), and later of China, has been attributed to "the Confucian ethic," since these economies share a Confucian cultural legacy that supposedly encourages a strong work ethic.[8] I would like to contest this thesis of the Confucian ethic and suggest that we must look to Chinese popular religion instead. In the writings left by Confucius and Mencius, there is a distinct anti-profit and anti-merchant slant. Furthermore, Confucianism's main institutional home was the imperial state and its bureaucracies and academies, where it exerted the power of state orthodoxy. Since the Ming Dynasty, the late imperial state, aided by Neo-Confucian thought (*daoxue* or *Song-Ming lixue*), entered into periods of intense anti-commercial policies, including the "maritime prohibitions" (*haijin*) that closed the entire eastern coastal waters to private merchant trade with foreigners and the tightening of sumptuary laws against social mobility.[9] Another problem with the "Confucian ethic" thesis is that it essentializes China into a monolithic unchanging culture and cannot account for China's diversity of languages and regional cultures, and differences today in the ability of local populations to adapt to market economy and capitalist globalization. Historically, it was and is the maritime commercial cultures of the southeastern coast that have been the most economically dynamic in late imperial times, while north China and the interior have been less developed. Furthermore, the entrepreneurial spirit has emerged more often from non-official families than from the elite Confucian gentry or scholar-official class who prized educational and political capital over economic capital.

RURAL WENZHOU TEMPLES AND RITUALS: THE CIRCULATION OF MONEY BETWEEN RURAL INDUSTRY AND COSMIC-DIVINE WORLDS

When one speaks of "privatization" (*siyouhua*) in China's economic reform era of the past three decades, the "Wenzhou Model" (*wenzhou moshi*) of rural development, based on small household industries, joint-stock firms, and restless entrepreneurial expansion across the whole area of China looms large. Even before the official promulgation of the economic reforms of the Third Plenum of the Eleventh Party Congress in 1978, many parts of rural Wenzhou had already quietly and secretly de-collectivized agriculture. In the space of two decades, with virtually no state, foreign, or overseas Chinese investment, the Wenzhou area transformed itself from a geographically isolated and impoverished area where electricity was only brought to rural areas in the 1960s and bicycles in the 1970s, to an economically dynamic, prosperous, and rapidly industrializing and urbanizing region. Between 1978 and 1994, Wenzhou's GDP increased from 132,200,000 yuan to 2,967,800,000 yuan, an increase of 4.5 times, with an annual growth rate of 15.4 percent.[10] Wenzhou manufactured goods (shoes, medical needles, pipes and valves, porcelain tiles, paper goods, etc.) are shipped not only to all areas of China, but also exported to countries around the world. Rural incomes in Wenzhou shot up from an average personal annual income of 113.5 yuan in 1978, which was 15 percent *below* the national average, to 2,000 yuan in 1994, which was 63.9 percent *higher* than the national average (Zhang 1998:1032).

When I first visited rural Wenzhou in 1991, rice paddies and water buffalos stretched to the horizon, and chickens and pigs ran underfoot in villages and towns. Although most families no longer pursued agriculture, but had moved on to running their small factories, they were still embedded in traditional peasant culture, celebrating only lunar calendar festivals and engaging in exchanges of bridewealth and dowry for marriages. The frenetic, purposive, and cheerful way that the local people went about their various businesses, and the fast-paced rural-to-urban transition occurring all around, reminded me of my childhood in Taiwan in the early 1960s. On each of my trips to Wenzhou in the 1990s, I was presented with new signs of economic development. By 2001, not only the water buffalos had been replaced by "iron buffalos" or tractors, but many of the rice paddies and old water transport canals had been buried under concrete pavements and new roads. Villagers and townspeople made urgent business calls across the country on their mobile phones and had switched from VCD to fully digitized DVD players. To my further shock, some wealthy rural families had purchased not just motorcycles, but new cars, others had just returned from family trips to Southeast Asia, and many families kept bank accounts in U.S. or other foreign currencies. Not all the economic developments were salutary, however, since air and water pollution were becoming more serious, due to the factory exhaust and refuse, and official corruption was on people's minds.

What really intrigued me about this area was the distinctive revival of traditional culture and popular religion alongside the economic development, a fact rarely examined or even mentioned by Chinese scholarship on the "Wenzhou Model" of development. Despite official restrictions on the expansion of popular religion, and a long, still ongoing twentieth-century history of radical state secularism,[11] this religious revival in Wenzhou not only kept pace with economic growth and prosperity, but often seemed to drive it. Each time I returned to Wenzhou, I found new deity temples and lineage ancestor halls built or restored and the local people emboldened further to expand their religious rituals, festivals, and ritual processions.[12] Each village had more than one deity temple dedicated to one or more of the multitude of gods and goddesses in the popular Chinese pantheon. Temples gathered together local worshipers on the birthdays of their tutelary gods and other festivals to hold rituals and share a collective banquet. Most townships or county seats had reclaimed their City God temple, which had been appropriated by the state and turned into offices or storehouses in the Maoist era. A new Buddhist temple in Jinshan County was being built in 2004, with a huge five-story-high wooden statue of Guanyin, the most important Chinese Buddhist deity, going up inside. I talked with the village leader, who told me of his efforts in scouring the Buddhist centers of the country for models upon which to base his village's temple, and for a reputable Buddhist priest to head the temple, and of his ambitious plans to rebuild the Buddhist monastery and seminary that once flourished there in the Song Dynasty. Lineages had resumed their ritual sacrifices to ancestors and competed with each other to collect the most elaborate genealogies, build the biggest and costliest ancestor hall, or put on the most impressive sacrificial ritual. Families also competed with each other in the collective wealth of all family members, as expressed through the scale of the funeral rituals and feasts they could provide for their dead. Christian churches are also part of this religious revival, and many churches dot the countryside here.

All of these religious resurgences of course require money, which comes from the willing, sometimes eager donations of ordinary people, especially the wealthy, who have stronger obligations to give. Besides building and restoring their religious sites, and paying for ritual expenditures, temple associations, lineage organizations, and churches all serve as conduits for charitable donations and social welfare: they gather money from the rich and distribute it to the poor and needy (widows, orphans, disaster victims) in local communities, and finance efforts for the public good, such as building schools, roads, and bridges. Religious sites all make public their annual lists of donors or special fund-raising event records, and the amounts that they donated are written on paper and plastered on temple walls or carved into permanent stone steles reminiscent of imperial times. These public records further spur on the will to be generous. Thus, a significant proportion of the wealth generated from industrial production and commerce is diverted into non-productive uses, such as community welfare and construction that increase one's merit accumulation, or investments in the divine world.

In addition to donations to temples, lineages, and churches, and the expenditures on a plethora of different lifecycle and religious rituals, there is another type of ritual expenditure that is part of the ritual economy of rural Wenzhou and should be counted as part of its economic growth. This is the expenditure by local people on the services of ritual experts: geomantic masters are hired to select the most propitious sites for tombs and new houses; diviners using tortoise shells and the sixty-four hexagrams of the ancient *Book of Changes* (*Yi Jing*)[13] are employed to tell fortunes or to calculate the most propitious dates for lowering a coffin into the ground, getting married, or opening a new business; and Daoist and Buddhist monks and nuns are paid to perform a range of different rituals for the community and its individual families. New temples, ancestor halls, and churches have also spurred the growth of a skilled artisan-craftsman occupational group: wood carvers (of deity statues), temple mural painters, coffin-makers, traditional architecture masters, religious scripture and lineage genealogy printers, and others who cater to religious and ritual needs. These artisans are not averse to technological innovations. I talked with one young printer of genealogies who in the early 1980s learned how to carve individual Chinese characters out of wood and ran a wood-block printing press (Song Dynasty technology) to serve lineage organizations in the area. He said genealogies are always printed with Song Dynasty-style characters (*Songti*), to commemorate the scholar-official Ou Yangxiu of the Song, who promoted genealogies for the common people, not just the aristocracy. In the year 2000, he switched to computer desktop printing and uses the Chinese software program's Song-style font for his Chinese characters. In the space of twenty years, he had leaped from an eleventh- to a twenty-first-century technology.[14]

It is not clear when the practice of burning paper spirit money for the gods and ancestors started, but certainly Chinese popular religion underwent expansion and innovation in the commercial revolution of the Song Dynasty (960–1279 CE), which witnessed the invention of both paper money used in trade, and wood-block printing. Today in Chinese popular religious practice, spirit money is one important medium of communication and exchange between the temporal and divine worlds. In rural Wenzhou, important occasions for burning spirit money are such rituals as funerals, ancestor sacrifices, birthday festivals for deities, and the Ghost Festival (*Zhongyuan pudu*) in the seventh lunar month. These money offerings to gods, ghosts, and ancestors ensure their blessings on the living. In funerals, the most important lifecycle ritual, money is burned for the use of the deceased in the Underworld, where the soul is taken after death to stand judgement before each court of the Ten Kings of Hell. Although the burning of spirit money produces only a symbolic loss of wealth, the idea is significant: wealth can be made by families, but not all of it should be consumed or kept in material form. One must invest or divert part of one's wealth to other divine worlds for one's future good fortune, one's family and descendants, and one's larger community.

It is evident to me that if the Chinese state, whether the central government or party, or the local Wenzhou municipal or county officials, did not restrict the expansion of popular religion so much, due to their internalization of nineteenth-century Western and Christian condemnations of "backward superstitions," religious and ritual development in rural Wenzhou would be even stronger and more able to exert beneficial social transformations. Religious revival is engaged in rebuilding an ethical system damaged by decades of "class struggle" (in which individuals, families, and groups were pitted against and betrayed each other in loyalty to the state) and by increasing popular cynicism toward Communist Party ideals and homilies. The homage to deities and ancestors in community rituals also bolster an important element, prominent in late imperial China, but virtually eroded in the course of twentieth-century nationalism: local identities. The gods, goddesses, and ancestors are icons of local identity, autonomy, local initiative and self-organization, building blocks of an indigenous rural Chinese civil society, while the rituals and festivals put on for them gather and celebrate local communities, thus counterbalancing the hegemonic and monolithic nationalism disseminated by public schools and the state media.

Finally, Chinese popular religion and its aforementioned signs of revival can be seen as an indigenous response to the perennial problem of capitalism: the unbridled and socially destructive profit-motive. Given China's long history of commercialization, capitalism is not entirely new. As China today joins the world of global capitalism, some of its rural coastal regional cultures, such as rural Wenzhou, have drawn upon imperial China's petty entrepreneurial and commercial cultural legacy, where the market economy was embedded in and also checked by cultural institutions such as the family, lineage organizations, temple associations, Daoist and Buddhist institutions, and community ethics. Unlike the urban areas, they have not embraced the (Western) version of capitalism that is much more disembedded from the traditional encumbrances of kinship and family obligations and religious commitments to the divine world.[15] In the indigenous capitalism that we find in places like Wenzhou, the capitalist drive for accumulation of wealth is tempered by the religious and kinship ethics of generosity and social rivalries of giving away wealth. The significance of the "Wenzhou Model" of economic development lies not in its economic success, but in its ability to show Chinese state policymakers that – just as the West modernized without having to wipe out "superstitious" Christianity, which also has an ethos of generosity and charity[16] – economic development in China, especially in rural cultures, cannot do without religious inspiration. Whereas in many other places in China, a century of radical state secularization swept away the religious impulses that could both drive the money-making ethos of capitalism as well as counter its destruction of the social fabric, rural Wenzhou's capitalism has managed to preserve or reinvent a distinctive anti-capitalist component. Here, the emphasis is not just on material investment, but also on investments into the non-productive realms of community welfare, ritual consumption, and conversion of material wealth into the currency of transcendent divine worlds. In rural Wenzhou, the local culture exerts pressure on capitalism to conform with the outlines of an ancient ritual economy, where rituals must be financed and performed, the gods must receive offerings, and wealth must be diverted from this temporary world to other more powerful and lasting realms of the cosmos.

Chapter 24

Cosmopolitan Contamination*

*Kwame Anthony Appiah***

GLOBAL VILLAGES

People who complain about the homogeneity produced by globalization often fail to notice that globalization is, equally, a threat to homogeneity. You can see this as clearly in Kumasi as anywhere. The capital of Asante is accessible to you, whoever you are – emotionally, intellectually, and of, course, physically. It is integrated into the global markets. None of this makes it Western, or American, or British. It is still Kumasi. What it isn't, just because it's a city, is homogenous. English, German, Chinese, Syrian, Lebanese, Burkinabe, Ivorian, Nigerian, Indian: I can find you families of each description. I can find you Asante people, whose ancestors have lived in this town for centuries, but also Hausa households that have been around for centuries too. There are people there for all regions, speaking all the scores of languages of Ghana as well. And while people in Kumasi come from a wider variety of places than they did a hundred or two hundred years ago, even then there were already people from all over the

* This piece is extracted from Kwame Anthony Appiah, 'Cosmopolitan Contamination' in *Cosmopolitanism: Ethics in a World of Strangers*, London: Penguin (2006), pp. 101–113.

** **Kwame Anthony Appiah** is Laurance S. Rockefeller University Professor of Philosophy and the University Center for Human Values at Princeton University. His work focuses on philosophy of mind and language, African and African-American intellectual history, and political philosophy. Among his books are *Assertion and Conditionals* (Cambridge University Press, 1985), *For Truth in Semantics* (Blackwell, 1986), *In My Father's House: Africa in the Philosophy of Culture* (Oxford University Press, 1992), *Color Conscious: The Political Morality of Race* (with Amy Gutmann; Princeton University Press, 1996), *Thinking It Through: An Introduction to Contemporary Philosophy* (Oxford University Press, 2003), *The Ethics of Identity* (Princeton University Press, 2004), and most recently *Cosmopolitanism: Ethics in a World of Strangers* (Penguin and Norton, 2006).

place coming and going. I don't know who was the first Asante to make the pilgrimage to Mecca, but his trip would have followed trade routes that are far older than the kingdom. Gold-salt, kola, nuts, and, alas, slaves have connected my hometown to the world for a very long time. And trade means travellers. If by globalization you have in mind something new and recent, the ethnic eclecticism of Kumasi is not the result of it.

But if you go outside Kumasi, only a little way – twenty miles, say, in the right direction – and if you drive off the main road down one of the many pot-holed side roads of red laterite, you can arrive pretty soon in villages that are fairly homogenous. The people have mostly been to Kumasi and seen the big, polyglot, diverse world of the city. Here, though, where they live, there is one everyday language (aside from the English in the government schools), a few Asante families, and an agrarian way of life that is based on some old crops, like yam, and some new ones, like cocoa, which arrived in the late nineteenth century as a commercial product for export. They may or may not have electricity (this close to Kumasi, they probably do). When people talk of the homogeneity produced by globalization, what they are talking about is this: the villagers will have radios; you will be able to get a discussion going about the World Cup in soccer, Muhammad Ali, Mike Tyson, and hip hop; and you will probably be able to find a bottle of Guinness or Coca-Cola (as well as Star or Club, Ghana's own delicious lagers). Then again, the language on the radio won't be a world language, the soccer teams they know best will be Ghanaian, and what can you tell about someone's soul from the fact that she drinks Coca-Cola? These villages are connected with more places than they were a couple of centuries ago. Their homogeneity, though, is still the local kind.

In the era of globalization – in Asante as in New Jersey – people make pockets of homogeneity. Are all these pockets of homogeneity less distinctive than they were a century ago? Well, yes, but mostly in good ways. More of them have access to medicines that work. More of them have access to clean drinking water. More of them have schools. Where, as is still too common, they don't have these things, this is not something to celebrate but to deplore. And whatever loss of difference there has been, they are constantly inventing new forms of difference: new hairstyles, new slang, even, from time to time, new religions. No one could say that the world's villages are – or are about to become – anything like the same.

So why do people in these places sometimes feel that their identity is threatened? Because of the world. Their world is changing, and some of them don't like it. The pull of the global economy – witness those cocoa trees whose chocolate is eaten all around the world – created some of the life they now live. If the economy changes – if coca prices collapse again as they did in the early

1990s – they may have to find new crops or new forms of livelihood. That is unsettling for some people (just as it is exciting for others). Missionaries came a while ago, so many of these villagers will be Christian, even if they also have kept some of the rites from earlier days. But new Pentecostal messengers are challenging the churches they know and condemning the old rites as idolatrous. Again, some like it; some don't.

Above all, relationships are changing. [...] Cosmopolitans think human variety matters because people are entitled to the options they need to shape their lives in partnership with others. What John Stuart Mill said more than a century ago in *On Liberty* about diversity within a society serves just as well as an argument for variety across the globe:

> If it were only that people have diversities of taste, that is reason enough for not attempting to shape them all after one model. But different persons also require different conditions for their spiritual development; and can no more exist healthily in the same moral, that all the variety of plants can exist in the same physical, atmosphere and climate. The same things which are helps to one person towards the cultivation of his higher nature, and hindrances to another ... Unless there is a corresponding diversity in their modes of life, they neither obtain their fair share of happiness, nor grow up to the mental, moral and aesthetic stature of which their nature is capable.[1]

If we want to preserve a wide range of human conditions because it allows free people the best chance to make their own lives, there is no place for the enforcement of diversity by trapping people within a kind of difference they long to escape. There simply is no decent way to sustain those communities of difference that will not survive without the free allegiance of their members.

DON'T EVER CHANGE

Even if you grant that people shouldn't be forced into sustaining authentic cultural practices, you might suppose that a cosmopolitan should side with those who are busy around the world "preserving culture." It's one thing to provide people with help to sustain arts they want to sustain. I am all for festivals of Welsh bards in Llandudno funded by the Welsh Arts Council, if there are people who want to recite and people who care to listen. I am delighted with the Ghana National Cultural Centre in Kumasi, where you can go and learn traditional Akan dancing and drumming, especially since its classes are spirited and overflowing. Restore the deteriorating film stock of early Hollywood movies;

continue the preservation of Old Norse and early Chinese and Ethiopian man-uscripts; record, transcribe, and analyze the oral narratives of Malay and Maasai and Maori: all these are a valuable part of our human heritage. But pre-serving *culture* – in the sense of cultural artefacts, broadly conceived – is differ-ent from preserving *cultures*. And the preservers of cultures are busy trying to ensure that the Huli of Papua New Guinea or, for that matter, Sikhs in Toronto or Hmong in New Orleans keep their "authentic" ways. What makes a cultural expression authentic, though? Are we to stop the importation of baseball caps into Vietnam, so that the Zao will continue with their colourful red head-dresses? Why not ask the Zao? Shouldn't the choice be theirs?

"They *have* no real choice," the cultural preservationists may say. "We have dumped cheap Western clothes into their markets; and they can no longer afford the silk they used to wear. If they had what they really wanted, they'd still be dressed traditionally." Notice that this is no longer an argument about authentic-ity. The claim is that they can't afford to do something that they'd really like to do, something that is expressive of an identity they care about and want to sustain. This is a genuine problem, one that afflicts people in many communities: they're too poor to live the life they want to lead. If that's true, it's an argument for trying to see whether we can help them get richer. But if they do get richer and they still run around in T-shirts, so much the worse, I say, for authenticity.

[...]

THE TROUBLE WITH "CULTURAL IMPERIALISM"

Cultural preservationists often make their case by invoking the evil of "cultural imperialism." And its victims aren't necessarily the formerly colonized "natives." In fact, the French have a penchant for talking of "cultural imperialism" to make the point that French people like to watch American movies and visit English-language sites on the internet. (*Évidemment*, the American taste for French movies is something to be encouraged.) This is surely very odd. No army, no threat of sanctions, no political sabre rattling, imposes Hollywood on the French.

There is a genuine issue here, I think, but it is not imperialism. France's movie industry requires government subsidy. Part of the reason, no doubt, is just that Americans have the advantage of speaking a language with many more speakers than France (though this can't be the whole explanation, since the British film industry seems to require subsidy, too). Still, whatever the reason, the French would like to have a significant number of films rooted deeply in French life, which they watch alongside all those American movies. Since the resulting films are often wonderful, in subsidizing them for themselves, they have also enriched the treasury of cosmopolitan cultural experience. So far, I think, so good.

What would justify genuine concern would be an attempt by the United States through the World Trade Organization, say, to have these cultur- ally motivated subsidies banned. Even in the United States, most of us believe it is perfectly proper to subsidize programs on public television. We grant tax- exempt status to our opera and ballet companies; cities and states subsidize sports stadiums. It is an empirical question, not one to be settled by appeal or to a free-market ideology, how much of the public culture the citizens of a demo- cratic nation want can be produced solely by the market.

But to concede this much is not to accept what the theorists of cultural imperialism want. In broad strokes, their underlying picture is this. There is a world system of capitalism. It has a center and a periphery. At the center – in Europe and the United States – is a set of multinational corpora- tions. Some of these are in the media business. The products they sell around the world promote the interests of capitalism in general. They encourage con- sumption not just of films, television, and magazines, but of the other non- media products of multinational capitalism. Herbert Schiller, a leading critic of "media/cultural imperialism" has claimed that it is "the imagery and cultural perspectives of the ruling sector in the centre that shape and structure con- sciousness throughout the system at large."[2]

People who believe this story have been taking the pitches of magazine and television company executives selling advertising space for a description of reality. The evidence doesn't bear it out. As it happens, researchers actually went out into the world and explored the responses to the hit television series *Dallas* in Holland and among Israeli Arabs, Moroccan Jewish immigrants, kib- butzniks, and new Russian immigrants to Israel. They have examined the actual content of the television media – whose penetration of everyday life far exceeds that of film – in Australia, Brazil, Canada, India, and Mexico. They have looked at how American popular culture was taken up by the artists of Sophiatown, in South Africa. They have discussed *Days of Our Lives* and *The Bold and the Beautiful* with Zulu college students from traditional backgrounds.[3]

And they have found two things, which you might already have guessed. The first is that, if there is a local product – as there is in France, but also in Australia, Brazil, Canada, India, Mexico, and South Africa – many people prefer it, espe- cially when it comes to television. For more than a decade in Ghana, the one program you could discuss with almost anyone was a local soap opera in Twi called *Osofo Dadzie*, a light-hearted program with a serious message, each episode, about the problems of contemporary everyday life. We know, do we not, how the Mexicans love their *telenovelas*? (Indeed, people know it even in Ghana, where they are shown in crudely dubbed English versions too.) The academic research confirms that people tend to prefer television programming that's close to their own culture.[4] (The Hollywood blockbuster has a special status around the world; but here, as American movie critics regularly complain, the nature of the product – heavy on the action sequences, light on clever badinage – is partly determined by what works in Bangkok and Berlin. From the point of view of the cultural-imperialism theorists, this is a case in which the empire has struck back.)

The second observation that the research supports is that how people respond to these American products depends on their existing cultural context. When the media scholar Larry Strelitz spoke to those students from KwaZulu-Natal, he found that they were anything but passive vessels. One of them, Sipho, reported both that he was a "very, very strong Zulu man" and that he had drawn lessons from watching the American soap opera *Days of Our Lives* – "especially relationship-wise." It fortified his view that "if a guy can tell a woman that he loves her she should be able to do the same." What's more, after watching the show, Sipho "realized that I should be allowed to speak to my father. He should be my friend rather than just my father ..." One doubts that that was the intended message of multinational capitalism's ruling sector.

But Sipho's response also confirmed what has been discovered over and over again. Cultural consumers are not dupes. They can resist. So he also said:

> In terms of our culture, a girl is expected to enter into relationships when she is about 20. In the Western culture, the girl can be exposed to a relationship as early as 15 or 16. That one we shouldn't adopt in our culture. Another thing we shouldn't adopt from the Western culture has to do with the way they treat elderly people. I wouldn't like my family to be sent into an old-age home.[5]

The "old-age homes" in American soap operas may be safe places, full of kindly people. That doesn't sell the idea to Sipho. Dutch viewers of *Dallas* saw not the pleasures of conspicuous consumption among the super-rich – the message that theorists of "cultural imperialism" find in every episode – but a reminder that money and power don't protect you from tragedy. Israeli Arabs saw a program that confirmed that women abused by their husbands should return to their fathers. Mexican *telenovelas* remind Ghanaian women that, where sex is at issue, men are not to be trusted. If the *telenovelas* tried to tell them otherwise, they wouldn't believe it.

Talk of cultural imperialism structuring the consciousnesses of those in the periphery treats Sipho and people like him as *tabulae rasae* on which global capitalism's moving finger writes its message, leaving behind another homogenized consumer as it moves on. It is deeply condescending. And it isn't true.

IN PRAISE OF CONTAMINATION

Behind much of the grumbling about the cultural effects of globalization is an image of how the world used to be – an image that is both unrealistic and unappealing. Our guide to what is wrong here might as well be another African. Publius Terentius Afer, whom we know as Terence, was born a slave in Carthage in North Africa, and taken to Rome in the late second century AD. Before long, his plays were widely admired among the city's literary elite; witty, elegant works that are, with Plautus' earlier, less cultivated works, essentially all we have of Roman comedy. Terence's own mode of writing – his free incorporation of earlier Greek plays into a single Latin drama – was known to Roman littérateurs as "contamination." It's a suggestive term. When people speak for an ideal of cultural purity, sustaining the authentic culture of the Asante or the American family farm, I find myself drawn to *contamination* as the name for the counter-ideal. Terence had a notably firm grasp on the range of human variety: "So many men, so many opinions" was an observation of his. And it's in his comedy *The Self-Tormentor* that you'll find what has proved something like the golden rule of cosmopolitanism: *Homo sum: humani nil a me alienum puto.* "I am human: nothing human is alien to me." The context is illuminating. The play's main character, a busybody farmer named Chremes, is told by his overworked neighbor to mind his own affairs; the *homo hum* credo is his breezy rejoinder. It isn't meant to be an ordinance from on high; it's just the case for gossip.

Then again, gossip – the fascination people have for the small doings of *other* people – shares a taproot with literature. Certainly the ideal of contamination has no more eloquent exponent than Salman Rushdie, who has insisted that the novel that occasioned his fatwa "celebrates hybridity, impurity, intermingling, the transformation that comes of new and unexpected combinations of human beings, cultures, ideas, politics, movies, songs. It rejoices in mongrelisation and fears the absolutism of the Pure. Mélange, hotchpotch, a bit of this and a bit of that is how newness enters the world. It is the great possibility that mass migration gives the world, and I have tried to embrace it."[6] But it didn't take modern mass migration to create this great possibility. The early Cynics and Stoics took their contamination from the places they were born to the Greek cities where they taught. Many were strangers in those places; cosmopolitanism was invented by contaminators whose migration was solitary. And the migrations that have contaminated the larger world were not all modern. Alexander's empire molded both the states and the sculpture of Egypt and North India; first the Mongols and then the Mughals shaped great swathes of Asia; the Bantu migrations populated half the African continent. Islamic states stretch from Morocco to Indonesia; Christianity reached Africa, Europe, and Asia within a few centuries of the death of Jesus of Nazareth; Buddhism long ago migrated from India into much of East and Southeast Asia. Jews and people whose ancestors came from many parts of China have long lived in vast diasporas. The traders of the Silk Road changed the style of elite dress in Italy; someone brought Chinese pottery for burial in fifteenth-century Swahili graves. I have heard it said that the bagpipes started out in Egypt and came to Scotland with the Roman infantry. None of this is modern.

No doubt, there can be an easy and spurious utopianism of "mixture," and there is of "purity." And yet the larger human truth is on the side of Terence's contamination. We do not need, have never needed, settled community, a homogenous system of values, in order to have a good home. Cultural purity is an oxymoron. The odds are that, culturally speaking, you already live a cosmopolitan life, enriched by literature, art, and film that come from many places, and that contains influences from many more. And the marks of cosmopolitanism in that Asante village – soccer, Muhammad Ali, hip hop – entered their lives, as they entered yours, not as work but as pleasure. There are some Western products and vendors that appeal to people in the rest of the world *because* they're seen as Western, as modern: McDonald's, Levis. But even here, cultural significance isn't just something that corporate headquarters get to decree. People wear Levis on every continent. In some places they are informal wear; in others they're dressy. You can get Coca-Cola on every continent, too. In Kumasi you will get it at funerals. Not, in my experience, in the west of England, where hot milky Indian tea is favored. The point is that people in each place make their own uses even of the most famous global commodities.

A tenable cosmopolitanism tempers a respect for difference with a respect for actual human beings – and with a sentiment best captured in the credo, once comic, now commonplace, penned by that former slave from North Africa. Few remember what Chremes says next, but it's as important as the sentence everyone quotes: "Either I want to find out for myself or I want to advise you: think what you like. If you're right, I'll do what you do. If you're wrong, I'll set you straight."

Chapter 25

On Global Measures of Culture:

A View From India

Kriti Kapila*

Belying erstwhile anxieties that globalisation would herald the advent of a hegemonic and universal monoculture, transformations in the cultural sphere have taken almost an opposite direction in recent years. Assertions of cultural difference, claims for rights based in one's culture, and demands for equal respect for all cultures are but some of the forms identity politics have taken. None of these is particularly new in all but one respect and that is the ways in which local movements have forged solidarities around the world, giving birth to new categories of social and self-identification ranging from claims to indigeneity to pan-religious subjectivities. In this piece, I discuss the emergence of how global axes for social and self-identification have had particular salience in contemporary Indian social movements where these processes of 'dynamic nominalism' have made for new forms of self-identification and political agency.[1] In particular, I wish to discuss the emergence of indigeneity as category of self and social identification in recent years, with the protagonists aligning themselves and their conditions with struggles in places as different from theirs as Latin America. However, I argue that these forms of self-identification have emerged in a complex interplay of

* **Kriti Kapila** is a British Academy postdoctoral fellow at the Department of Social Anthropology, University of Cambridge. She is currently working on the politics of recognition and indigeneity in contemporary India. Her publications include, *Globalisation at Work: Livelihoods and Imagination in Contemporary India*, Kriti Kapila and Akhil Gupta (eds) (forthcoming), Duke University Press.

politics, knowledge regimes and state practices. In the case of the politics of indigeneity in particular, the links between culture, developments in research on human genetics and neoliberal economic policies of the state cannot be ignored.

What makes cultures distinct from one another, how they transform over time, and how new cultural morphologies come about are questions that have been the mainstay of anthropology traditionally. But these are not academic questions alone, because they are also faced by states and their policy-makers, especially when culture itself becomes the basis for a politics of difference and is seen to be the source of social (in)justice and (mis)recognition. While the older, bounded ideas of culture may have been jettisoned from scholarship – and for good reason – in the world at large, it is precisely this bounded and boundary-making idea of culture that has made a come-back in public life.[2] Such a situation poses particular problems, both for anthropologists, and for states and policy-makers. Nowhere is this contradictory process more pressing than in the case of affirmative action. Cultural politics is often aimed at making claims for recognition based on an expansion of group-based rights deriving from the state. These claims and the state-response to such claims are to a great extent an outcome of modern governmental techniques of classification embedded within a statistical imagination.[3] The interlocking of governmental classification, knowledge regimes and cultural politics of identity have had a particular significance in contemporary India. This is not just because of the evident diversity of Indian society – in a quasi-official study conducted in the early 1990s, there were at least 4000 caste and over 400 tribal groups in India[4] – but more importantly because the Indian state runs the largest affirmative action programme in the world, both in terms of the total number of people and the percentage of its population involved. 'Anekta mein Ekta' or 'Unity in Diversity' is the most well-known of state slogans in India signalling its emphasis on its unique brand of multiculturalism and the carefully constructed pluralist self-image of the postcolonial Indian state.

In order to provide an objective basis on which to run its affirmative action programme, the government of India relies on a series of procedures and institutions that bring together academic research, public policy and cultural politics. The interface between these different forms of knowledge and their attendant practices has over time produced both new facts and new fictions concerning Indian society, but what is even more interesting is how global morphologies of 'culture' have come to influence these processes of knowledge production.

REDISTRIBUTIVE JUSTICE AND THE POLITICS OF IDENTITY: A SHORT HISTORY

In their present form, the two morphological categories of caste and tribe – now part of commonsensical and official worldviews in India – are themselves the product of a long history of enumeration in India.[5] In 1931 the British colonial government tabled the report of the last full-blown census it was ever to conduct in India. Compiled by J. H. Hutton, the Cambridge anthropologist, the report was a collection of statistical and ethnographic information on the peoples of India. In 1945, the Constituent Assembly of the newly Independent State of India used the 1931 census as the basis for its programme of redistributive justice.[6] The names and the criteria of classification of the groups to be targeted were contained in Hutton's ethnographic notes appended to the census. Hutton's definition of what constituted castes and tribes emerged from and remain within an older anthropological understanding of culture itself. At the time, culture in the colonies was conceptualised in terms of discrete groups living in bounded spaces. The measure of culture inherent in the colonial censuses was premised on a meta-discourse on civilisational progress. Types of belief-systems, the forms of economic and symbolic exchange, marriage and kinship systems, and the primary occupation of the groups in question were each measured and hierarchically assessed against an abstract, if often unstated, metropolitan equivalent. Culture was thus understood in essentialist and reified terms.

The 1931 census report did not invent the categories of 'caste' or for that matter 'tribe'. Nor was this the first time these two categories were used for enumerating the population in the colony. All censuses conducted in British India, right from the first census of 1871 were caste and religion-based,[7] and by the first quarter of the twentieth century these categories had already made permanent a grid of understanding of Indian sociality that enumerated and classified the peoples of India into tribes, caste and religions. Successive censuses came to bestow a greater ontological force on these sociological categories than was ever ascribed to them by local practices and understandings. My interest in invoking this vignette is to prompt a discussion about how cultures begin to assume a particular morphology at particular moments and how this morphology in turn is shaped by and through the knowledge practices of the state.

One of the key principles underlying the modern state of Independent India, as it emerged in the Constituent Assembly debates between 1946 and 1949, was the idea of redistributive justice as guaranteed by the Constitution. All citizens of India are deemed equal under the Constitution and Article 15 maintains that 'the state shall not discriminate against any citizen on grounds only of religion, race, caste, sex, place of birth or any of them'. Against, and alongside this principle of equity for all, the Constitution provided for special treatment of those thought to suffer from exploitation or discrimination. These latter principles of redistributive justice were applied to what became known as the Scheduled Castes and Scheduled Tribes. The explicit aim was to engage in the 'uplifting' of those groups who were poor and 'backward' whether as a result of ritual discrimination or economic deprivation.

Article 342 of the Constitution allows for special provision for the educational and economic development of the Scheduled Castes and Scheduled Tribes, and for reserved jobs for them in Central and State governments, as well as reserved seats in Parliament and provincial Legislative Assemblies. The Constitution enshrined a basic difference in its understanding of the potential for progress and modernity with regard to the categories of caste and tribe. Scheduled Castes were defined by the link between ritual status and economic deprivation and it was thought that positive discrimination could speedily result in their integration into a modern state founded on equality between all citizens.[8] Scheduled Tribes, however, were defined primarily in respect of their tribal origin, their distinctive and primitive way of life, their remote location and their 'general backwardness in all respects'. Thus, the definition of Scheduled Tribe contained an inherent contradiction and one which arose from the problem of culture. While Scheduled Tribes were to be developed, they were also to be protected as autochthones or *adivasi.*[9]

It is notable that though Article 342 was meant to be in force for the first ten years after independence, it has not only yet to be repealed, but over the intervening period of nearly sixty years, the range of the population covered under this article has increased greatly. Not only have a number of communities in India reinvented caste and group histories in order to be reclassified within this schedule, but also as a result of the acceptance of the Mandal Commission Report in 1990, there has emerged another category of citizens, known as Other Backward Classes. This category of citizens is also eligible for state redistributive and affirmative action. In brief, as a consequence today, a total of 50 per cent of all government jobs, places in state-run educational institutions and welfare schemes must be reserved for people belonging to Scheduled Castes, Scheduled Tribe and Other Backward Classes, and India's programme of redistributive justice covers more than half of the population. Keeping in mind a population of a billion plus citizens, this is affirmative action on a mammoth scale.

In order to run this programme 'scientifically', the state seeks advice and help from two of its own research bodies – the Anthropological Survey of India

(AnSI) and the Registrar General of India (RGI). The former is an institution of colonial vintage and conducts a wide-range of anthropological research sometimes with a direct policy focus. The latter is the office responsible, among other things, for conducting the decennial census. Both bodies have professional anthropologists on their permanent staff for conducting field and secondary research. Any claim for a revision of status by a group is made as a recommendation by the provincial government to the Registrar General's office, which may or may not seek direct help from the AnSI for the verification of the veracity of the claim and a decision as to whether a particular group should be deemed a 'tribe', or part of a 'caste' etc.

The RGI office mainly conducts socio-cultural and/or ethnographic research to complement its mainstay – the statistical census exercise. The AnSI, however, has historically held the view that physical (or biological) anthropology is of equal significance to socio-cultural understandings of humankind (Singh 2002). Thus, over the years, it has collected anthropometric and other data, including blood-sampling and other physiological indices (notably height and weight) for various ethnic groups. Such studies may and do form crucial 'evidence' in the event of a claim of a revision of status by a group. While the anthropological research carried out by the RGI and the AnSI is conducted along different vectors, the two bodies operate within a shared notion of culture and a broad range of agreement about what constitute the markers of cultural difference.

The 1990s saw a surge in the number of fresh claims for constitutional reclassification presented to the RGI, even if most of them were ultimately unsuccessful. The growth in these claims to avail better chances for redistributive justice was in great part in response to the adoption of neoliberal economic policies by the state. While a percentage of the population have obviously benefited from policies of economic globalisation,[10] for a vast majority of people, the structural readjustment of the economy has led to greater immiseration, increased levels of indebtedness and insecurity.[11] The retreat of the state from the social and economic sector has prompted a surge in caste and group-based identity politics aimed at gaining greater political representation and enhanced welfare from the state. According to Partha Chatterjee, there is an inevitability in the rise of such politics 'emerging out of the developmental policies of the government aimed at specific population groups' (Chatterjee 2004: 40). More groups have petitioned respective federal governments for constitutional reclassification in recent years than in the preceding five decades, while others have lobbied with the state to increase the purview of affirmative action to include the private sector. As a result, the Indian state has been forced into the recognition of ever more evolved forms of cultural difference in order to remain true to its politics and policies of redistribution.

INDI(E)-GENE

The 1990s was a critical decade for identity politics and the processes of identification in India in another way as well. Away from the world of official categorisation and enumeration, a new axis has been identified for coalescing and claiming cultural identity. At the first International Convention of the UN Working Group on Indigenous Affairs held in Geneva in 1994, a number of caste and tribe groups in India joined the global platform and demanded that they be considered as indigenous as opposed to a tribal or a caste group.[12] The number of such groups has steadily increased in the following decade and this development has given rise to a public as well as academic debate on whether or not the term indigenous has any purchase for particular social formations in India.[13]

At the same time, in the wake of the decoding of the Human Genome, scientists and (physical) anthropologists working in various state research bodies in India have been working on the historical genetics of the Indian population. At present, under the aegis of the Department of Biotechnology of the Government of India, scientists and researchers based in universities and state research bodies are engaged in conducting research that is aimed at uncovering the historical migrations and emergence of caste and tribal groups.[14] While the findings are at a preliminary stage, they are ultimately aimed at bringing to light the 'original' inhabitants of India.

In such an identity politics a global discourse on indigeneity can be seen to make for local subjectivities, as well as provide the impetus for research on historical genetics. If the colonial enumerative exercises were an adumbration on the idea of civilisational progress, then research into historical genetics aimed at understanding the origins and the original are elaborations of a pre-occupation with the idea of migration, itself seen to be the hallmark of globalisation and globalised culture. Potentially, the research on historical genetics of the Indian population, is set to sit alongside the ethnographic research produced as evidence for constitutional reclassification. Given its ostensibly superior scientific basis, it is not inconceivable that facts collected under this rubric may well trump their sociologically based counterparts.

On the face of it, it would appear that historical genetics moves within an understanding of culture more in sync with the more sophisticated accounts produced by latter-day anthropologists, where culture is seen as diffuse, mutable and fluid, and the fixity between territory, people and culture characteristic of bounded notions of culture is challenged, if not cast aside altogether. It thus seems that in official understandings of culture in India, essentialist definitions may be being superseded. But on closer examination, one can discern that here is not just the political history of migration but one that is presented as the *natural* history of culture. Culture is in one's genes, quite literally. In this understanding of indigeneity and historical genetics, a complete interiorisation of culture seems to have taken place, such that one can access the genotype from the phenotype. Thus, at the turn of a new century, yet another recalibration of the morphology of Indian society seems to be taking place, where caste/tribe are to be superimposed on notions of the original and the migrant. The emancipatory potential of the discourse of indigeneity lies in enabling groups to move out of oppressive hierarchies of ritual rank and civilisational progress. At the same time, in the absence of unambiguous datelines in the calculus of indigenous and outsider, the potential, if not inevitable appropriation of such a formulation by exclusionary forms of political instrumentality cannot be discounted.[15]

CONCLUSION

The categories through which social identities are expressed, claimed and recognised are by no means 'natural'. But more than that, these categories themselves are a result of the interplay between a number of processes – regimes of documentation, conventions of description, techniques of government and the politics of difference. Cultures transform in their figurations in this complex interplay. Caste and tribe may have been naturalised as morphological units of Indian society, but today these units are being understood alongside and within a global discourse on movement and migration.

This is not to say that ideas of the origin and the original have not played a role in identity politics in India until recently. In fact they have been thrown up from time to time, especially in the context of understanding religious affiliation of various groups and its relationship to political power. But what is unique about the recent emphasis on uncovering the origins of groups is the relation they bear not so much to developments within India but to wider struggles and solidarities. The language of indigeneity facilitates the scaling up of local struggles on the one hand, and bringing in new interlocutors and arbiters into the debate on the other. For example, groups demanding recognition as indigenous (as opposed to a tribe or a caste group) address not only the Indian state, but equally the United Nations Working Group on Indigenous Affairs, and in doing so seek parity and solidarity with indigenous people of the Americas and Oceania. At the same time, the discourse on indigeneity in India will indeed be aided by (with variable degrees of critical judgement) the scientific research on the sources of indigeneity. Research on the historical migrations and the 'original' homes of different population groups in India on the other hand are part of the phenomenon described by Rabinow as bio-sociality.[16] Such a biologicalisation of identity, Rabinow argues in the context of health and identity, is different from older biological categories, such as gender, age and arguably race, and genes are understood to be inherently manipulable and re-formulable (Rabinow 1999: 13). But the impetus behind the research in historical genetics is exactly for the opposite reasons. Genes are being decoded in order to uncover the origins of culture, an attempt to scientifically locate culture in something that apparently cannot be manipulated or reformulated according to the demands of politics.

Not too long ago Oprah Winfrey proclaimed she was Zulu, having had her mitochondrial DNA traced in one of the burgeoning commercial laboratories undertaking such quests on behalf of the identity-anxious. Despite Ms Winfrey's popularity in South Africa and among Zulu television audiences, the Zulu community were not entirely pleased to hear this. Local historians believe that there is little evidence that the tribe had any connection with the African slave trade, and the Zulu leader Prince Buthelezi promptly issued a statement saying that Ms Winfrey was 'sadly mistaken'. Once again showing how slippery is the terrain (or assemblage if you like) made of identity, culture, origins and evidence.

Chapter 26

Culture, Reconciliation and Community Building:
Lessons from South Africa

*The Most Reverend Njongonkulu Ndungane**

W hen did apartheid end? When did the building of the new South Africa, a 'home for all South Africans', get beyond the foundations and truly begin to take shape? Was it with the 1990 un-banning of liberation movements, or with Nelson Mandela's release from jail a fortnight later? Or was it with the first democratic elections in May 1994? Certainly from the early nineties, our heads knew that the past was behind us. But it can take a little longer to convince the heart.

For many of us that moment came with the 1995 Rugby World Cup Final when South Africa defeated New Zealand. Those of us who loved the game but who for our whole lives had always supported the Springboks' opponents, no matter who they might be, now found ourselves cheering for the men in green and gold.

Within apartheid's social engineering, rugby had held an iconic position, a potent symbol of Afrikaner identity. The Ellis Park stadium was one of its chief shrines. Yet when President Nelson Mandela appeared in the stands for the final, wearing the same No. 6 jersey as our captain, he melted many hearts. Last year, ten years on, he was there again, for a match against Australia, and when he walked out onto the pitch to greet the players, the stands erupted as South Africans of every complexion united in chanting his clan name, 'Madiba!

* **Winston Hugh Njongonkulu Ndungane** is the Anglican Archbishop of Cape Town, South Africa. He has been deeply involved in campaigns to abolish debt, combat poverty, and tackle HIV/AIDS. He speaks widely on these issues as well as on the rebuilding of the new South Africa and theological questions. In 2005 he was the only civil society panelist at the World Trade Organisation's tenth anniversary Symposium.

Madiba!' Had anyone doubted it, it was confirmation that the transformation of our society was irreversible.

When I consider the creation of new forms of social identity, my perspectives are inevitably, and indelibly, shaped by my experience of apartheid and the subsequent peaceful transition to democracy. I live now in a vibrant and optimistic society which aspires to celebrate together our diverse heritage, upholding these rights through our progressive and widely acclaimed constitution.

I also approach the subject in the full expectation of our potential for human flourishing through a unity expressed in creative diversity. This is a fundamental tenet of my Christian faith, and I have found plentiful evidence of what might be achieved, in rich and varied ways, within the life of Southern Africa and beyond.

SOUTH AFRICA – THE CONFLICTS OF THE PAST

For us, creating a new society has been a very different challenge to that faced, for example, by countries such as Poland after the collapse of communism. As a single integrated nation, we had no respectable past on which to draw, no fertile historic soil in which to plant and nurture a new future.

Inter-cultural and inter-racial conflict has a long and deeply entrenched history in Southern Africa. It is worth recounting some of this in order not only to see how remarkable our current situation is, but also to grasp how even the most recalcitrant of situations can find unimaginable redemption.

The seventeenth-century colonialist settlers spreading north and east from the Cape found themselves on a collision course with the varied populations, including my ancestors, who were already living, not always peacefully, across the subcontinent.

To cut a long story short, the colonisers got the upper hand. British and Afrikaners agreed on an Act of Union, which totally excluded the black majority. A delegation of African and Coloured politicians swiftly set off to London, unable to believe that Crown or Government would accede to such injustice. But they failed to find support, the draft Act was passed by the British Parliament, and a single state of South Africa was established in 1910. In response, in 1912 the South African Native National Congress, the forerunner of the African National Congress, was founded.

Thereafter, various laws increasingly enshrined racial discrimination, until the nationalist election victory in 1948 led to the comprehensive systematisation of apartheid – under which more than fifteen different racial categories were distinguished.

The extent and vicious severity of this discrimination is hard to imagine for those who did not experience its atrocities. Not surprisingly, it was widely predicted that the collapse of apartheid would bring a bloodbath of retribution.

That carnage did not ensue is nothing short of miraculous. Furthermore, the impetus for peaceful change came from the oppressed. From early in the struggle, the liberation movements were committed to a non-racial South Africa that had an equal place for everyone. For decades before we achieved it, this was discussed and debated among the politically 'conscientised', who were predominantly those discriminated against. We believed that this, for which we yearned, was a living and achievable hope.

This desire was famously expressed by Nelson Mandela at his 1960 trial, when he said 'I have fought against white domination, and I have fought against black domination. I have cherished the ideal of a democratic and free society in which all persons live together in harmony and with equal opportunities. It is an ideal I hope to live for ... But if needs be, it is an ideal for which I am prepared to die.' Twenty-six years in prison did not change his view.

His perspective was widely shared, not least among those who experienced similar incarceration. Though Robben Island was an indescribable hell-hole, it also became a beacon of hope for overcoming adversity. I spent three years there as a political activist. It was my 'university of the world' in which I majored in humanities. Though separated in society, prisoners of every complexion rubbed shoulders together – even with those whose evidence had helped convict us – and we found our common humanity. The sadistic brutality of many white warders also opened our eyes to see they were merely human like us, and certainly not the near-angelic higher beings that propaganda presented. We emerged from these inhospitable conditions renewed in our belief in freedom and justice for all, committed to a life of service, and convinced that lasting peace could only come through reconciliation and forgiveness.

RESTORATIVE JUSTICE

This was the path we chose to tread when political change finally came. This spirit underlay the Truth and Reconciliation Commission, which moved us so far forward in our building of a new nation. There has been extensive analysis of its strengths – and its weaknesses – which I shall not repeat here.

However, I should like to dwell a little on the underlying principles of 'restorative justice' which strongly influenced its approach, and which I see as having immense potential to assist in a wider breadth of disputes. It is increasingly employed in the secular world, for example in some areas of crime. As a Christian, I also have to say that I find this stance profoundly 'gospel shaped' – breaking into negative cycles with redemptive hope, the possibility that God can and does work for good in every circumstance of life, no matter how desperate, if we are prepared to let him (as St Paul wrote in his letter to the Romans). It is a way of not just dealing with wrong-doing but making it the stepping stone to something better. The situation itself becomes the very crucible in which new beginnings are forged.

To be more specific: restorative justice is a systematic response to conflict or wrongdoing, that emphasises healing the wounds of all parties concerned – whether offended against, or offending, since all are damaged by division – while also pursuing whatever makes for greater wholeness in whatever is the wider community. This may range from nations and ethnic communities to colleagues within an office setting, or even members of a family. It is a process that upholds the need for justice, and which expects those who have caused injury to take steps to repair it. (In more serious cases, it may run in parallel with other judicial processes.)

Yet this happens as an intrinsic part of genuine deep encounter between the concerned parties. All sides must be willing to engage openly and honestly, and be prepared to contribute appropriately to help bring resolution, in ways that may only emerge as this holistic process unfolds. The desired outcome is that everyone involved will become contributing members of a community that grows and shapes itself to minimise the possibility of similar harmful actions finding fertile ground in the future.

The South African experience shows something of what can be achieved. When political change came, sworn enemies had to overcome bloodshed, even murder, and work together under democracy. The Truth and Reconciliation Commission provided an arena where some of that hard, hard work could be done. Of course, there is still far more to be done – but the ball was set rolling. The ideals and processes of the TRC have found continuing life in other spheres, and we must ensure that they are kept alive at the heart of our private and public consciousness.

It may well take another generation or more to heal some of the wounds of the past (to say nothing of tackling the persisting economic injustices and inequalities). We are certainly not at a point where we can 'draw a line' and forget the past, as some suggest. That is not to say that we dwell in the past, but, as the saying goes, we certainly need to know where we have come from, in order to know where we are headed, and what route to pursue towards our desired destination. We cannot afford to forget the lessons of the past, painful though they often still are at every human level.

A CONSTITUTION FOR A RICHLY PLURALIST SOCIETY

Another vital tool in the building of our new nation and new national identity is South Africa's constitution. Promulgated in 1996, after two years of extensive consultation, it explicitly states it is intended to 'heal the divisions of the past and establish a society based on democratic values, social justice and fundamental human rights; and lay the foundations for a democratic and open society ...'

It outlaws unfair discrimination on any grounds, 'including race, gender, sex, pregnancy, marital status, ethnic or social origin, colour, sexual orientation, age, disability, religion, conscience, belief, culture, language and birth.' Commitment to a unity expressed in diversity is demonstrated in the constitution's promotion of eleven official languages, three endangered indigenous languages and sign language; and the safeguarding of all other community languages (with eight examples cited), together with Arabic, Hebrew, Sanskrit and 'any other languages used for religious purposes'. Likewise, there is a guaranteed role for traditional leaders, and for traditional, community and religious laws, insofar as they are compatible with wider provisions of the constitution.

This last point is crucial. Through evolving case law, the Constitutional Court is addressing how apparent incompatibilities should be addressed. For example it has ruled that all daughters, of whatever community, faith or tradition, have equal inheritance rights, so that the property of a man without sons should not pass instead to the nearest male relative. In this case, broader constitutional provisions are overriding. But in many other areas traditional practices are upheld within the courts of the land.

The Constitution's implementation is proving productive to the development of a richly pluralist society. Our aim is not to be a Westernised liberal democracy – we want to draw on the best of that tradition, but not its worst. Nor are we attempting merely to recapture earlier cultures of this region. We can do without the patriarchies of the past, for example, though we endorse and encourage a fuller integration of the principles of ubuntu into today's society.

The main philosophy of this important African concept is captured in the phrase 'I am, because we belong together.' The values of ubuntu are to live and care for others, to act kindly to one another; being kind, just, fair, compassionate, trustworthy, honest; assisting those in need; and upholding good morals. All are virtues that not just South Africa, but the whole world needs. All are virtues that cannot be practised alone. They respect individuality, but each individual must also respect others and the whole. All strengthen the fabric of society and build up the common life.

MORALITY AND DIVERSITY

It is noteworthy that the constitutional provision for diverse community, cultural, linguistic and religious expression does not confine these to the private realm, but ensures a full place within the public arena. This contrasts with the widespread assumption that seems to dominate in many liberal democracies – that within the public sphere, there exists some shared, normative, secular, stance that all players should adopt, with faith perspectives having relevance only on narrowly circumscribed faith-related issues. But there is no Archimedean socio-political fixed neutral place where we can stand, for every starting point comes laden with its own ideological baggage and unacknowledged assumptions. To pretend to this sort of secular objectivity also leaves us dangerously susceptible to dominance by market forces rather than human realities and needs.

Public affirmation of diversity allows for a far broader, more textured, debate on the goals of society – the appropriate flourishing of each individual, as part of the wider human family, in harmony with creation. It offers possibilities of constructive dialogue around moral issues, without any community feeling under threat or in competition. The strengths of traditions offer checks against unfettered relativism, and the blind imperatives of unbridled economics. Those of us who believe in the revelation of a God who is absolute, can in turn stand firm in our faith, while acknowledging that finite human comprehension is always challenged to fuller understanding and expression, and is best explored in the dialogues of the whole human family.

South Africa also has an obligation to share what we have experienced more widely. In the past 'The Voice of South Africa' was used to broadcast propaganda across the continent. Now we transmit both radio and television, committed to contributing to the African Renaissance, both through sharing our own good news, and through producing extensive balanced African news coverage, that does not endlessly portray us as a place of famine, war, instability and irredeemable poverty.

THE ECONOMIC DIMENSION

Instabilities and potential for conflict thrive where individuals and communities are prevented from prospering appropriately – whether through denial of self-expression, or of resources. In South Africa, there is a strong statistical link between poverty and crime which cuts across all other differences. Tensions between communities are generally linked to competition over power and access to economic means.

This is one of our hardest challenges. On a macro-economic level, South Africa sidestepped the economic disintegration that some predicted, and is enjoying unprecedented sustained growth. However, that disguises lasting economic disparities within the population. Though black people now constitute the majority of the richest 10 per cent of the population, the black community remains overwhelmingly the poorest sector, and, according to some indicators, the gulf is widening. We cannot afford to let this persist. We cannot create new inequalities in place of the old. Yet, amazingly, opinion polls continue to show that the most optimistic sector of society is generally the most disadvantaged. This gives me continuing confidence.

I am nonetheless convinced that persistent, systemic, economic injustice is the greatest threat to global human well-being, stability and security. Injustice readily turns difference into division. Equitable societies and international systems can promote healthy and productive diversity. South Africans know this. Globally we know this. But we are not so good at putting our money where our mouth is.

On my own continent, I am spearheading the African Monitor initiative, which aims to catalyse and harness civil society voices across our continent in support of the implementation of promises made for Africa's development during 2005, whether by donors or by our own nations. From the private sector to the faith communities, we must all throw our weight behind overcoming the injustices of poverty, and in support of equitable and sustainable prosperity for all.

On a global scale, if the international community really did guarantee the provisions of the Universal Declaration on Human Rights (notably Article 25) for example, constructive debate over global resources and economic competition would be conducted in quite a different atmosphere. Now over fifty years old, the UDHR has become an intrinsic part of international customary law, and as such all international and multilateral bodies, and all their member states and organisations, are bound by its provisions, whatever their particular institutional objectives. Yet we discuss issues such as debt and trade as if human rights were irrelevant – whereas the outcomes of these talks are a real matter of life and death for too many people. Collaboration against such threats as HIV/AIDS would be far more automatic, and require far less justification in the face of narrow competitive self-interest, if we acted in the conviction that human beings are considerably more than economic entities. We must learn to measure success in quality of life, not just quantities of dollars.

CHRISTIANITY IN SUPPORT OF DIVERSITY

Christianity offers important insights. Human diversity is part of our intrinsic self-understanding as created in the image of God who is the mystery called Trinity, three-in-one and one-in-three – Father, Son and Holy Spirit in one Godhead. They are diverse, distinct, in person, character and function. But they are united in substance and purpose, collaborative and complementary, the whole greater than the sum of the parts.

This is a model for human interaction: none superior to another, reciprocal rather than hierarchical; none acting independently or at another's expense, but always with mutual awareness and in relation; none dominating another's particular role or characteristics or responsibilities; all are always open to one another, honest and vulnerable, complemented not diminished in their common life.

This is our understanding of what it means to live as fully human – as individuals, yet in families, in communities, in nations, and in relation to the whole of creation. Created diversity allows for creative diversity and rich mutual engagement. Pluralism is an opportunity not a threat. This applies not just to faith and culture, ethnicity and nationality, but to differences in personality and character, generation and gender, circumstance and experience. It is far too easy to allow even such trivialities as accent or fashion sense to blind us to what we share in our intrinsic humanity.

We must allow our eyes to be opened to the redemptive potential that is offered when we live as humanity was meant to live.

As William Temple, Archbishop of Canterbury at the end of the Second World War, pointed out, there is no aspect of human activity which is outside God's concern and purposes, and therefore Christians are 'bound to interfere' in the world of politics, as anywhere else. It is the particular responsibility of the Church to place before humanity a vision of what society could be.

CONCLUSION

I am writing this when our cricket team has just defeated New Zealand in a test series. The 'player of the series' in this traditionally white-dominated sport was black bowler Makhaya Ntini. Not only that, but he was also recently voted sportsman of the year by the black community – overwhelmingly followers of football in the days of segregated sports. A potent example that new identities are indeed inexorably overtaking the old.

Against all expectation, we overcame vast differences, even violent conflict, to go forward with commitment to a thriving, open, diverse society with room for everyone in their own unique particularity, within communities of their own choosing. Now we are determinedly proceeding with the long hard journey of transformation – a transformation that touches heart and head, private and public life, and every area of politics and economics.

During a recent visit to South Africa, Kofi Annan described our country as, almost uniquely, having managed to turn a bitter experience into a bright future. Yet surely, with South Africa something of a global microcosm in our diversity and plurality, we should be an example that others can follow with confidence.

If we can achieve all we have done, with the odds of the past so heavily stacked against us, then surely no one on this planet need live without hope in the face of culture-clash and conflict.

BIBLIOGRAPHY

de Gruchy, John W. (2002) *Reconciliation: Restoring Justice.* Cape Town: David Philip.

Krog, Antje (2003) *A Change of Tongue.* Johannesburg: Random House.

Meiring, Piet (1999) *Chronicle of the Truth Commission.* Vanderbijlpark: Carpe Diem.

Ndungane, Njongonkulu (2003) *A World with a Human Face.* Cape Town: David Philip.

Terreblanche, Sampie (2002) *A History of Inequality in South Africa 1652–2002.* Scottsville: University of Natal Press.

Tutu, Desmond (1999) *No Future Without Forgiveness.* London: Rider, Random House.

www.africanmonitor.org

www.polity.org.za/html/govdocs/constitution

www.restorativejustice.org

Chapter 27

Cultural Diversity and Integration in the European Union*

*James Tully***

[...]

THREE APPROACHES TO DEMOCRATIC INTEGRATION

The general definition of '*democratic* integration' is that the individual and collective members who are integrated into the European Union must have an effective democratic say over the norms of integration to which they are subject. The norms of integration must be 'open' to the democratic negotiation of those who are subject to them. Those who are subject to them must be 'free' to enter into these negotiations, in the sense of actually being able and encouraged to participate, either directly or indirectly through trusted representatives who are held accountable in turn by practices of democratic negotiation by those they claim to represent. We can put this by saying that the legitimacy and effectiveness of norms of integration rest on their grounding in two ongoing types of 'practices': (1) of interpreting and following the norms differently in practice

* A longer version of this piece appears in *Critical Review of Social and Political Philosophy* Volume 10(1).
** **James Tully** is the Distinguished Professor of Political Science, Law, Indigenous Governance and Philosophy at the University of Victoria, Canada. He is Fellow of the Royal Society of Canada and a Fellow of the Trudeau Foundation. He is the author or editor of eight books and many articles in the field of contemporary political and legal philosophy (or theory) and its history, and in Canadian political and legal philosophy.

without challenging them directly; and (2) of questioning, challenging, agreeing and disagreeing, negotiating modifications and transformations or reaffirming the existing norms, implementing and experimenting with a modified regime of integration norms, acting in accordance with it, and testing it in turn. These two practices comprise the traditional meaning of 'democracy' – rule by and of the people – and the traditional meaning of 'democratic citizenship' or 'democratic freedom' – that citizens have a participatory say in and over the laws to which they are subject – as applied to rules of integration.

Although this general definition of democracy is widely shared, there are three very different approaches to integration that claim to follow from it. The first approach is democratic in the most attenuated of senses and should be called anti-democratic. This is the approach that bypasses the democratic condition and imposes integration regimes on immigrants and other diverse members without their say, on the grounds that technical elites know best about culture, economics and foreign policy, complex modern systems integrate members 'behind their backs', the situation is too volatile and dissonant for democratic procedures, immigrants are subjects but not yet citizens so they do not have a say, the demos comes after integration, and so on. I think most Europeans would agree that this anti-democratic approach is both illegitimate (democratic deficit) and ineffective (it fails to cultivate attachment to norms through participation and elicits disintegrative responses over its imposed integration policies). Yet this is the paramount form of integration today. Moreover, the propaganda around terrorism, security, and the clash of civilizations strengthens this anti-democratic approach and the reactions its policies cause are then used to justify its extension.[1] According to the European Monitoring Centre on Racism and Xenophobia the prevailing forms of integration increase discrimination and segregation. And in this atmosphere of ignorance and fear the interior ministers of the six largest member-states (France, Italy, Germany, Poland, Spain and Britain) meet privately to devise even more offensive citizenship tests, integration contracts and other policies of coercive assimilation. This approach is clearly part of the problem rather than a solution.[2]

The second and third approaches both claim to be opposed to the anti-democratic approach and to embody the democratic ideal. Yet they are very different. I will call the second a 'low intensity' or 'restricted' democratic approach and the third an 'open-ended' or 'non-restricted' democratic approach. The open-ended approach is the one that is overlooked and which I recommend. I think that the central question today in Europe and elsewhere is which of these three orientations to integration is to prevail in the twenty-first century.[3]

The major differences between the restricted and non-restricted approaches can be seen clearly by comparing them across four aspects of democratic negotiation of integration regimes.

The restricted approach is 'restricted' in that it places limits on all four aspects of democratic negotiation:

1. The democratic negotiation of norms of integration takes place only in what we might call the official institutions of the public sphere. Additionally, usually official representatives of the people subject to the norm in question partake in the negotiations.

2. Democratic negotiation takes place within a set of pre-established procedures, and having a say within them usually consists in saying YES or NO to a proposed norm developed elsewhere (as for example in the vote on the constitution).

3. The general outline of what a norm of integration must look like at the end of the negotiations is given at the beginning. It is usually given as beyond question by some grand narrative of global processes of modernization, good governance, democratization, human rights, or civilization.

4. The discursive practices of norm negotiation are seen as a discrete step in a larger process of norm generation that comes to an end. Democratic negotiation is one phase in the development of acceptable and final norms of integration.

The open-ended or non-restricted orientation to democratic integration opposes this restricted model on all four limits that it places on democratic negotiation:

1. The democratic negotiation of norms of integration takes place not only in the official fora of the traditional public sphere, but also *wherever* individuals, groups, nations or civilizations in the EU come up against a norm of integration they find unjust and a site of disputation emerges. What makes a norm of integration 'democratic' on this view is precisely that those subject to it have the right to call it into question here and now, to present reasons for interpreting it in different ways, or, if necessary, for changing it; and to enter into democratic negotiations over being able to act differently under it or, if this is not possible, to negotiate its amendment or transformation. Additionally, it is not only the official representatives of constituencies who have a right to enter into the multiplicity of public spheres, but, in principle, every member represented by an official spokesperson who is affected by the norm in question. The democratic principle of *audi alteram partem* – always listen to the other side – is applied all the way down so everyone who speaks for another is held accountable.

2. Since the procedures of negotiation are themselves just another set of norms of integration, they cannot be set beforehand and placed beyond question by some dubious argument or another about their meta-democratic status. They too must be open to different interpretations, to question and modification by those subject to them in the course of the negotiations. This is often the main dispute. It is also not sufficient that those subject to a norm be constrained simply to take a YES/NO position on a proposed norm that has been drafted elsewhere and handed down from on high. The formulation of the norm and the interpretation of its various meanings and ways of acting in accord with it must pass through democratic negotiations of the culturally diverse subjects who are subject to it.

3. The general form that the norm of integration must take cannot be imposed beforehand by an appeal to allegedly universal, necessary, or self-evident processes of modernization, democratization, juridicalization or Europeanization, for, in many cases, it is precisely these framing discourses that are being called into the space of questions and challenged in the deeply diverse Europe of today. There are alternative ways of living modernity and a multiplicity of cultures and civilizations *of* Europe today that need to be acknowledged and accommodated if Europe is to be democratically and effectively integrated. We know from recent experience that attempts to integrate undemocratically, through the imposition of partial, assimilative and inflexible integrative regimes, only leads to the worst kinds of reaction on both sides.

4. Finally, the dialogues or, rather, *multilogues*, of negotiating the terms of integration are not some discrete step towards a final end-point. They are ongoing, open-ended and non-final constituents of a democratic way of life.

On the open-ended view, a multicultural, multinational, and multicivilizational association is not held together by some definitive set of public institutions of discussion, procedures of negotiation, shared narratives, or final norms of integration on which all must agree and which set the limits to democratic negotiation. While the restricted approach allows for inclusion in democratic negotiations over norms of integration, in contrast to the anti-democratic exclusionary approach, it places four assimilative limits on democratic negotiation precisely where disagreement is most likely to irrupt in diverse societies, and thus displaces rather than faces the urgent conflicts over integration today. Rather, the answer is found in the contrasting and quotidian democratic attitude that none of these four features is ever beyond question or the subject of unconditional agreement. What holds the diverse members together and generates bonds of belonging to the community as a whole across ongoing differences and disagreements is that the prevailing institutions, procedures and norms of integration are always open to free and democratic negotiation and experimentation with alternatives by those subject to them.

Finally, the term 'democratic negotiation' comprises two distinct practices of negotiation involved in integration (as noted in the first paragraph). The first involves the activities of challenging a prevailing norm of recognition and integration, calling it into question, entering into negotiations, and, if successful, modifying the prevailing norm, and implementing and experimenting with the modified norm. This form of democratic negotiation, at least in its more public and official instances, has received the lion's share of attention by researchers of deliberative and agonistic democracy.

The second form of democratic negotiation occurs where diverse members share the same norm of integration yet act differently in accord with it. They interpret and practice norm-following in a variety of different ways, yet all can be seen, from their diverse cultural, national, civilizational or creative perspectives, to be acting in accord with the norms of integration they share with others. We might call this diversity of *practices within* a field of shared rules diversity of 'ethical substance' or 'democratic *ethos*'. This distinct form of diverse integration under shared norms has received less attention and it is often overlooked altogether. The vast landscape of the diversity of human practices within the shared rules of any complex association is overlooked because of the dominant yet nevertheless false view that norms are applied and followed in only one right way: that is, a rule determines rule-following behaviour. On this false view of rule following (rules as rails), if members want to change anything or act differently they have to change the rules of the game, and so theory, research, policy and political practice tend to focus exclusively on the rules and procedures, thereby disregarding diverse practices of rule following.[4] Yet, as Antje Wiener shows in her empirical and theoretical study, aptly titled *The Invisible Constitution*, diverse members of the European Union negotiate the shared rules and procedures (the visible constitution) through their culturally, nationally and improvisationally different *practices* of rule-following on a day-to-day basis (the invisible constitution).[5]

[...]

THREE EXAMPLES

Let us briefly apply these three approaches to three deeply intertwined and contested fields of integration in the European Union (or any other culturally diverse society): cultural, economic, and foreign policy integration.[6] In each field integration is presently based on the anti-democratic approach or a watered-down version of the second approach, and it fails. The reason is that both approaches overlook and override actual practices of integration that exist in the daily lifeworlds of Europeans and which only the third approach can recognize and connect effectively to policy communities.

First, 'cultural integration' comprises culturally diverse citizens and minorities (multiculturalism), the member states with their diverse national cultures (multinationalism), and the diverse civilizations of individuals, minorities and majorities (multicivilizationalism). The two dominant approaches give virtually no role for the active engagement of the diverse citizens and immigrants in working up the conditions and norms of integration, yet culturally diverse Europeans are creating a new diversity-savvy solidarity across cultural differences in daily practice that Paul Gilroy calls 'conviviality'.[7] While it is precisely this conviviality that makes daily life so livable in Europe today (despite the cultural problems), it is only an integration approach of the open-ended kind that can recognize these successful practices and link them to policy making.

Second, in the overlapping field of economic integration the situation is similar. Citizens are offered two models of economic integration and very little say over their formulation: the dominant neoliberal model or a social democratic alternative. Yet, again, on the ground citizens engage in a host of alternative forms of economic integration both within Europe and between Europeans and non-Europeans: fair trade rather than free trade, cooperatives rather than corporations, aid to local economic democracy rather than aid tied to Westernization, sustainable development and consumption, deep ecology, intermediate technology, Diaspora economics, and so on. Only the open-ended democratic approach could link these alternative modernities to the official debates over economic integration.

Third, in the field of foreign policy, citizens are offered two models: continuation of the post-World War II subordination to the imperial foreign policy of the United States and United Kingdom or a more multilateral and law-based European imperialism.[8] Yet, as the massive protests against the current wars illustrate, millions of Europeans are engaged in and deeply committed to alternative relationships with non-Europeans: building relationships with non-European countries based on non-violence and democratic negotiation rather than war and force. An open-ended approach to foreign policy would bring these long-standing European alternative traditions of non-violence, democratic partnerships and mutual aid into a genuinely democratic foreign policy.

[...]

CONCLUSION: LINKING COMMUNITIES

I have proposed a more democratic and open-ended approach to cultural, economic and foreign policy integration. I have also suggested that this approach already exists to some extent in the daily practices of democratic negotiation and conviviality among millions of Europeans and non-Europeans within the fields of the dominant norms of integration. These practical arts of democratic integration and 'acting otherwise' are often overlooked, but they could be an actual source of legitimate and effective integration if they were given prominence in the official policies of integration.

The central problem is one of overlooking and overriding these sources of democratic integration. James Scott diagnoses this type of problem as 'seeing like a state': overlooking the multiplicity of existing practical arts of interaction and integration of diverse citizens, involving non-theoretical embodied *savoir faire*, by seeing them as an unorganized field that needs to be organized in accordance with a master plan of abstract rules and procedures.[9] This type of 'seeing' is not restricted to states and large entities like the European Union. It also informs 'seeing like a corporation', where the activities of citizens are seen as inchoate patterns of production and consumption open to organization under a system of contract and commodification rules.[10] Unfortunately, the main tendency of the European Union at present seems to be a combination of these abstract rationalities – legal juridification, governmental planification and corporate commodification – across all three areas of integration.

If this diagnosis is correct, then the task for researchers is, first, to study the practices of cultural, economic and foreign policy integration that exist beneath the paramount way of looking at and organizing citizen activities, and, second, to link these practices to official policies of integration by means of democratic negotiation fora, in which citizens, policy-makers and researchers can work together and learn from each other without the subordination inherent in the restricted models. The traditional forum for linking citizen practices with policy makers has been the political party, but, as Peter Mair argues, political parties are failing at this task, not only in the European Parliament, but more generally.[11] One explanation for this might be the thesis advanced by Manuel Castells. He argues that over the last thirty years societies and their institutions have undergone a transformation in their form of organization that he calls networkization. The dominant 'social morphology' of almost all organizations now, from multinational firms, military-industrial complexes, European Union and global governance to the smallest volunteer organization is the network form.[12] If this is correct, then one of the reasons for the crises of political parties may be that, while citizens' grass-roots democratic practices of integration have made the transition to networkization, parties have not. The task then is twofold: (1) to networkize European political parties so they can mediate more effectively between citizens and policy makers; but, more importantly, (2) to invent new types of democratic networks of negotiation that are tailor-made to mediate in an open-ended democratic way in the network age.[13]

I think we need to turn to the everyday practices of democratic integration for guidance here as well, for there are already creative experiments in such mediating networks in the practices I referred to across the three areas of integration. Furthermore, one of the most promising research methods in Europe today can be used to study existing networks from the critical perspective of open-ended democracy, namely the actor-network approach of Bruno Latour and his colleagues, and related approaches.[14] Actor-network research shows that most of the existing networks that link citizens with policy makers are composed of unequal relationships of hegemonic actors who set the conditions of negotiations and subalterns who are constrained to comply.[15] Notwithstanding, research also shows that the multi-layered networks of communication, power and law are not closed structures of domination. Rather, they are, to varying degrees, open to the negotiation and modification, and even occasional transformation, of the subaltern actors who are subject to them yet also actors in them.[16] So, here again there are good reasons for applying the open-ended approach and some modest grounds for hope.

A European Union that had the courage and humility to turn to the practical wisdom of its sovereign citizens for guidance in this critically reflexive and experimental way would be a new and democratic Europe. It would not be a union that brought its demos into being at the end of the day but one that brought itself into a conversation of reciprocal elucidation and co-articulation with the demoi who have been there since daybreak. This conversation *is* the democratic relation between the people and their governors.[17]

PART VI

Markets, Corporations and Ethics

INTRODUCTION

Markets and corporations are both movers of cultural change and organisations with an interest in cultural adaptation. Corporations play a major role in the process of cultural transformation described in this book. They do not just react to economic activity, they also take part in the shaping of socio-cultural practices that affect it. The issue of culture and cultural heterogeneity has been subsumed within many corporate business strategies, and corporations have to be capable of cultural change.

Beginning this section, **Jeffrey Sturchio** offers his company's insights into cultural innovation and the role of business in one area of cultural practice, the pursuit of healthcare in the developing world. For Sturchio, corporations must engage with other stakeholders to play a role in addressing public health challenges, contributing where they have unique expertise and resources. He argues that public/private partnerships (PPPs) are a cultural innovation which offers an important mechanism which really works to harness the complementary resources and expertise of the public and private sectors to achieve health goals. To make use of this cultural innovation, Sturchio argues that societies 'have begun to forge a new culture, based not on the idea that companies and governments are natural antagonists, but rather on the conviction that there are important opportunities to achieve social good through cooperation and collaboration'. Reflecting on what Merck has learned, Sturchio offers six lessons in its engagements with various cultures around the world in its public-private partnerships.

Yusuf Hamied, also from the pharmaceutical industry, offers a scathing critique of the global patent regime, arguing for the urgency of international reform. The colossal power of the large multinational pharmaceutical MNCs, he argues, have usurped the newly developing international intellectual property regimes and in so doing have forged new contradictions between the health interests of the developing world and the economic interests of pharmaceutical companies. In making his critique, Hamied outlines the historical importance within India of pharmaceutical self-sufficiency and also outlines the moral imperative for national autonomy over the definition of public health problems and solutions. Hamied offers a number of potential solutions for addressing the current crisis in global pharmaceutical distribution.

Georgina Born explores the mechanisms by which corporations seek to control and mediate the future. Born argues that the deployment of social scientific expertise has become crucial to the manner in which corporations construct the future through the use of economics, sociology, social psychology and ethnography. After charting the spread of these practices in information technology corporations, Born highlights a number of insights from the literature on performativity, and builds from this to elucidate the mechanisms through which corporations construct their futures. Focusing on the media and IT industries, she identifies two such mechanisms. The first is through the now ubiquitous use of market forecasting, whereby consumer behaviour and market developments are speculated upon, examined and calculated. Born argues that this creates a 'theatre of abstractions' whereby collective imaginings of the future are forecast. The second mechanism is the use of market research that utilises the insights of social psychology, sociology and ethnography. It is here that the social and cultural elements of consumption activity, which are excluded in economists' calculations, re-enter the calculative frame. Born's contention is that this integration of the future may signify a qualitative shift in capitalism – one which raises questions about the instrumentalising of culture for profit – but which simultaneously may result in significant shifts in corporate orientation and their relations with consumers.

Contemporary discussions of the globalisation process often invoke deeply entrenched thinking about the supposed 'threats' posed from less economically developed countries to both business practice and the fate of social welfare. In his essay, **Will Hutton** addresses and contextualises these fears, which he argues can be discounted in light of the reality of economic processes which highlight the beneficial developments of globalisation. Making particular reference to China, Hutton argues that rather than less developed countries representing a threat to the West's privileges, the more real concern is that less developed countries will become cast as low-knowledge subcontractors to the knowledge-rich developed world in a new and more subtle form of colonialism. A more nuanced and institutionally rich understanding of the nature of modern economies forces us to rethink not only the challenges and opportunities of globalisation, but also the discourse of competition between the developed 'West' and the less economically developed nations.

Exploring the prospects of diversity or homogenisation in institutional design amidst the focus of globalisation, **Howard Davies** focuses his attention on the financial sector, and asks to what extent the manifold pressures of international capital markets so much a part of globalisation have led to a convergence of financial systems. In Davies' account, while there has been considerable convergence along an Anglo-Saxon model, there is still considerable diversity in the governance of financial systems worldwide – a diversity that is as much driven by institutional path dependence as it is by the particularity of national governance cultures. In his own words, 'we are not seeing the appearance of Wall Street clones in Asia'.

Davies focuses on the cultural and political particularities in countries like China and Italy to explain non-convergence to a single financial governance standard. While these variations may be obvious enough, Davies also explores the reasons for the divergence in governance norms in two financial centres that are often described as most similar: New York/USA and London/UK. Even within this pair, he contends, there are significant and notable differences – such as different cultures of governmental oversight, different corporate management cultures, and a different culture of critique embedded within the financial press of the two countries. Based on this notion of cultural heterogeneity in the broad institutional sense, Davies offers some reflections on the coming financial governance issues expected to emerge in India and China.

Chapter 28

Business and Global Health in an Era of Globalization:

Reflections on Public/Private Partnerships as a Cultural Innovation

*Jeffrey L. Sturchio** *

Globalization seems a lot like the weather at times: we all talk about it, but what can we do to change it? The facts of globalization are undeniable. The internet and mobile telecommunications have an increasing impact on the extent and pace of communications. Media networks bring events in Bangkok into living rooms and offices in Berlin and Boston and Bujumbura simultaneously. Trade barriers are coming down around the world. It's trite, but nonetheless true, to observe that as the world has become a smaller place, the opportunities for interaction and innovation with people half a world away have become a reality for many. Thomas Friedman writes of a small firm in the U.S. Midwest making insulated concrete building forms that used an imported machine from Korea to improve the usual process, found a customer in Kuwait to buy the new device, and provided them with an instruction brochure in Arabic produced by a local ad agency owned by the Winnebago Indian tribe in Nebraska. Friedman quotes an apt statement by

* **Dr Jeffrey L. Sturchio** is Vice President, Corporate Responsibility, Merck & Co., Inc., in Whitehouse Station, New Jersey, USA, where he leads initiatives in global health partnerships, corporate philanthropy and corporate responsibility reporting. He is responsible for the development, co-ordination and implementation of a range of health policy and communications initiatives for the region. He has been centrally involved in Merck's efforts to help improve HIV/AIDS care and treatment in the developing world and serves on the ACHAP Board in Botswana. He is also a member of the private sector delegation to the Board of the Global Fund to Fight AIDS, TB and Malaria, and Vice-Chair of the Corporate Council on Africa.

Nandan Nilekani, CEO of Infosys, which underscores the implications of this new culture of globalization: "That society which has the least resistance to the uninterrupted flow of ideas, diversity, concepts and competitive signals wins. And the society that has the efficiencies to translate whatever can be done quickly – from idea to market – also wins."[1] Of course, there is more to understanding the nature and impact of globalization than seeing its undoubted effects on modern commerce and the global economy. But this is inevitably where much of the debate has centered in recent years, together with investigation of the political ramifications of the "new world order."[2]

We have yet to see as intense an exploration of the changing relationships between culture and globalization. As a former academic (trained in the history and sociology of science and technology) who has spent nearly twenty years working for multinational corporations, I'm keenly aware of the ways in which cultural traditions are mediated by institutional contexts and political and economic trends. Given this background (there can't be many corporate executives who read Mary Douglas, Clifford Geertz, and Bruno Latour in graduate school!), I have a fairly eclectic view of "cultural innovation" as posed in the title of this essay. With that in mind, I offer some initial observations on globalization, cultural innovation and the role of business in one area of cultural practice, namely health and healthcare.

GLOBALIZATION AND HEALTH

In this age of globalization and growing insecurity, health is everybody's business. The world faces continuing threats of war, poverty, environmental degradation, and disease. And with the impact of global transportation and communications networks, a SARS outbreak in China can reverberate rapidly from Canada to Cairo. As Gro Harlem Brundtland, former Director-General of the World Health Organization, has observed, "in an interconnected and interdependent world, bacteria and viruses travel almost as fast as e-mail messages and money flows." So public health, like economics and defense before it, has now become an area of foreign policy focus.[3]

This is not just a concern for social scientists and politicians. Whether and how the world's poor gain access to the benefits of globalization will be a key factor in defining the political, business, and economic climate for societies and for companies such as Merck in coming years.

Just as transnational challenges affect private citizens and governments in a variety of ways – some obvious, others less so – corporations too must wrestle with the uncertainties of this new world, with new challenges, new actors, new governance mechanisms, and new institutions.[4] Businesses need to engage with other stakeholders to play a role in addressing these challenges, contributing where they have unique expertise and resources.

Merck's global engagement as a research-based pharmaceutical company logically has health at its core. The private sector – multinationals as well as local companies working in developing countries and emerging markets – has a vital role to play in helping to scale up and strengthen the provision of healthcare products and services. We discover and develop new medicines and vaccines – and these medicines must also benefit the people of poor nations.

THE ROLE OF PUBLIC/PRIVATE PARTNERSHIPS

As with any other multinational enterprise, companies like Merck can also make contributions to health and development by building robust public/private partnerships to address the challenges that face developing countries. Working together, we can achieve more than any single organization or country can do on its own. Yet all too often public officials and others in civil society have neglected the resources and expertise that private sector companies can bring to bear in helping to find sustainable solutions to healthcare crises like HIV/AIDS.

Public/private partnerships (PPPs) are a cultural innovation that offers an important mechanism that really works to harness the complementary resources and expertise of the public and private sectors to achieve health goals.[5] Michael Reich has offered a helpful working definition that clarifies what we mean by public/private partnership: (1) a collaboration between "at least one private for-profit organization with at least one not-for-profit organization"; (2) a "joint sharing of efforts and of benefits" among the core partners; and (3) a commitment to the "creation of social value (improved health), especially for disadvantaged populations."[6] PPPs can help to ensure that we can contribute to collective learning in addressing global health challenges more effectively. And because good health leads to wealth, which in turn leads to growth and economic productivity, communities are then better equipped to deal with other challenges like poverty and social inequality.

To make use of this institutional innovation, societies have begun to forge a new culture, based not on the idea that companies and governments are natural antagonists, but rather on the conviction that there are important opportunities to achieve social good through cooperation and collaboration. As William H. Foege has written:

> The marketplace is not the answer to all questions facing society. Likewise, the public sector cannot solve all social problems. But the combination of public and private efforts, when harnessed together, in an effort to achieve a clear and shared health objective, provides a powerful force that exceeds the sum of its separate efforts.[7]

On both the private and public sides of healthcare issues, attitudes have changed in recent years – largely, I believe, for the better.

MERCK'S APPROACH TO PUBLIC/PRIVATE PARTNERSHIPS IN HEALTH

Responding to global health challenges such as HIV/AIDS is not an option, but rather a strategic and humanitarian necessity: as former Merck Chairman Raymond V. Gilmartin has observed, "... for every global company, understanding and responding effectively to the tangle of economic, environmental and security problems that surround health are keys to future growth."[8] Indeed, as the global community is coming to understand, successful outcomes in the fight against HIV/AIDS in developing countries will depend on robust multisectoral responses. We are helping to respond to the pressing social needs of HIV/AIDS and other diseases in ways that reinforce the efforts of governments and civil society.

Merck's partnership approach is founded upon the belief that pharmaceutical companies have an obligation to offer assistance when social, political, and economic conditions make it impossible for patients to receive lifesaving therapies for diseases such as HIV/AIDS, and that Merck and others should help remove the barriers that stand between patients and the therapies they need. Indeed, we believe that "improving global health is one of the single most important contributions we can make to economic development around the world." This commitment to social responsibility is central to the company's view of corporate citizenship – going beyond philanthropy to contribute in substantive and sustainable ways to adding broader social, economic, and environmental value.[9]

But while pharmaceutical companies have a critical role to play in improving public health and facilitating access to medicines, we cannot do it alone. Other stakeholders need to be involved in strengthening health system infrastructure, developing human resource capacity and providing sustainable financing. Given the daunting challenges we face in global health, especially in developing countries, governments and other agencies involved in international assistance will make progress more quickly if they involve as many stakeholders as possible who have skills and resources to contribute to effective solutions.

In this respect, the private sector is often overlooked, yet companies (both multinationals active in developing countries, and the national business sectors as well) are actively contributing to health and to development in ways that go beyond their obvious roles, by fostering economic growth and productivity and complementing the efforts of donors, other sectors of civil society and developing countries themselves.[10] In fact, engaging the private sector more fully, drawing on their specific areas of competence and their practical approach to addressing challenges, can be an important element of a successful strategy to deliver better results for public health and development. PPPs focused on addressing public health problems in a sustainable manner offer an important mechanism to contribute even more, by pooling resources and by enhancing collective learning.

Much of Merck's own work in the developing world is in building successful, practical, field-based PPPs, covering many aspects of health care.[11] For example, in 1987 Merck launched the first large-scale, comprehensive global health initiative of its kind, the MECTIZAN Donation Program (MDP), to donate the drug MECTIZAN (ivermectin) to treat onchocerciasis, or river blindness, in countries where the disease was endemic. Through a unique, multisectoral partnership, involving the WHO, the World Bank, and UNICEF, as well as ministries of health, non-governmental development organizations and local communities, Merck has donated more than 1.8 billion tablets of MECTIZAN, with more than 530 million treatments administered since 1987, and the program currently reaches more than 60 million people in Africa, Latin America and the Middle East (Yemen) each year.[12] Another ambitious and innovative public/private partnership in which Merck participates is the African Comprehensive HIV/AIDS Partnership in Botswana, a collaboration among the Government of Botswana, the Bill & Melinda Gates Foundation, and Merck. This particular PPP was designed to help Botswana transform its approach to the HIV epidemic across the spectrum of prevention, care, treatment, and support.[13] Based on these experiences at Merck, it is clear that fostering PPPs among pharmaceutical firms and others, and promoting best practices in such collaborations, will in the long run be the most efficient means of realizing our common goal: measurable improvements in public health and health infrastructure in the developing world.

LESSONS LEARNED

Our experiences with PPPs have shown us that fighting the AIDS pandemic and eliminating river blindness as a public health problem require robust and creative partnerships, embracing all stakeholders with resources and expertise to contribute. Kofi Annan once observed that the world faces an increasing number of "problems without passports," which will require all of our efforts to solve. Given these challenges, it is important to find common ground in defining and working together on sustainable solutions. Even if Merck develops great products for the developing world, without the right health system infrastructure or trained doctors and nurses to deliver care and treatment, those medicines and vaccines can't do their jobs. With our knowledge base as a profit-making organization, there are ways in which we can apply our skills within public/private partnerships – working together with governments, other companies (both local and multinational), NGOs, and affected communities – to help developing countries achieve tangible results themselves. Such partnerships require careful planning, flexibility, and an openness to try new approaches, since they require bridging very different cultural environments. But traditional thinking no longer suffices – a generation of assistance to many developing nations has so far failed to meet the health goals of donors or recipients. There is growing awareness that the problems faced by developing countries are so daunting, and the financial resources required so substantial, that new ways of working are essential.

In a borderless world, the unexamined categorical distinction between the public and private sectors needs reassessment. Corporations, governments, and NGOs alike are beginning to recognize that a continued narrow focus on each institution's internal goals will not enable us to meet global needs. Based upon our experiences, we have learned six major lessons that have made a difference in the success of our partnerships. These lessons embody practical advice for donors and developing countries aiming to increase access to basic services, such as health, in developing countries.

1. *High-level political commitment and engagement are critical.* Without political will on the part of national leadership, success is unlikely. This is clear from global experience with the HIV epidemic: the countries that have made significant progress – Botswana, Brazil, Senegal, Thailand, Uganda – could count on the unequivocal commitment of senior political leaders.

2. *Partnerships have a key role to play in marshaling the necessary resources and expertise.* It is tempting – and sounds efficient – to try to go it alone. But our

experience with the Merck MECTIZAN Donation Program for preventing river blindness shows that it is critical to work closely with NGOs that were already delivering care to remote villages and with government health officials to ensure that the program was effectively integrated with the national health system. We have learned similar lessons in Botswana, where the multisectoral approach coordinated by the government has mobilized community groups and other sectors of civil society to help in the fight against HIV/AIDS. These experiences have made it clear that involving more partners, bringing local ownership and complementary expertise, makes success more likely.

3. *Programs must be country-led to succeed for the long term.* Our collaboration in Botswana, for example, is fully integrated with the government's HIV/AIDS strategy, and includes regular reviews of all relevant public- and private-sector partners. Success is based on common objectives, mutual respect, clear shared targets and agreed metrics to monitor progress, with transparency for all stakeholders involved. Working in this way builds trust and confidence among the partners. But it's important to note that the agenda is Botswana's, not Merck's – this is fundamental to sustainable success. National cultures embedded in multinational organizations must give way to a more global culture embedded in cooperative endeavors.

4. *Building local capacity is also a critical element.* When we began some of our partnerships, we thought that the major challenges would relate to money and access to medicines. But in fact, public officials were more concerned with training physicians and nurses with the skills to treat and care for patients; with building hospitals, treatment centers and diagnostic facilities; with educating teachers and their students about healthy behaviors; and, in the case of HIV/AIDS, with finding the means to care for AIDS orphans. Investing in human resource capacity and health infrastructure were the main building blocks of success, not just money and medicines.

5. *A comprehensive approach is needed to make real headway against HIV/AIDS.* In the case of Botswana, the government's Masa antiretroviral treatment program, now one of the largest in Africa, is just one part of the complex mosaic of programs and interventions across the spectrum of prevention, care, treatment, and support. Without the availability of treatment, people are reluctant to go for testing. And there also is concern with stigma and discrimination against HIV-positive people, which makes the policy of routine testing pioneered by Botswana in 2004 all the more important. By routinizing HIV within the public health arena, citizens feel empowered to get tested, knowing that treatment and other post-test services are available to them. And as more and

more people know their status, the social stigma associated with HIV diminishes. And local, national, and international cultures are changing as these programs progress.

6. *Persistence pays off.* In establishing the government's ARV treatment program in Botswana, there was a relatively long period of uptake as the treatment centers were built and patients began to enroll in the program. But by being patient and remaining focused on working out the kinks in the system, the Masa program soon began to grow exponentially, and now adds some 2000 patients a month. Without the long-term focus and commitment to persevere – and the willingness to change in significant ways – Botswana would not have been able to make the progress it has achieved so far.

Taken together, these six elements provide a proven prescription for success in global health programs. Programs that bring complementary resources and expertise together as noted above, drawing on the ingenuity and commitment of all who have something to contribute, will lead to robust results. Progress is possible, with the right level of political commitment, the right policies, and the right partners – including the private sector.

THE POWER OF PARTNERSHIPS

Let me close by coming back to the theme of partnership. In another context, Secretary-General Annan has said, "No company and no government can take on the challenge of AIDS alone. What is needed is a new approach to public health – combining all available resources, public and private, and using all opportunities, local and global."[14]

By working in this spirit – finding new approaches that work, building trust through cooperative action, embracing cultural differences and community values to find common ground, and harnessing the expertise and commitment of the private sector and other constituencies in civil society – together we can create innovative solutions to such global challenges as HIV/AIDS, environmental crisis, poverty, and social inequality. New cultural configurations continue to emerge as we make progress in the fight against HIV/AIDS and other global health challenges, and public/private partnerships have played a vital and positive role in these transformations. We all have a stake in seeing that these transformations and the cooperative culture sustaining them grow in the years ahead.

Chapter 29

Pharmaceuticals, Healthcare and Anomalies of the Patent System

*Yusuf Hamied**

The very foundation of Cipla, in 1935, Mumbai, more than a decade before India gained independence from Britain, was no ordinary event. Cipla's founder, Dr K.A. Hamied was a man ahead of his times and combined several progressive elements in his personality. He was a scientist with a PhD in Chemistry from the University of Berlin, a nationalist and patriot who was closely involved with the Indian Freedom Movement and its leaders, an educationist, secularist, modernist, an enlightened politician and, above all, a humanitarian. Cipla was set up to fulfil his vision of establishing a chemical laboratory for research and manufacture of drugs and chemicals in India.

Today, Cipla, with gross sales of US$ 825 million for the year ended 31 March 2007, is among the largest pharmaceutical companies in India and produces a wide range of active pharmaceutical ingredients and their formulations to combat asthma, cardiac ailments, malaria, cancer, TB and many other ailments. Its products are available in 170 countries and are internationally approved by virtually all regulatory authorities.

In a globalised world, any debate on the issue of healthcare, particularly for the poor in the developing world, is linked to the policies followed by big pharmaceutical companies which control nearly all access to life-saving drugs. The

* **Yusuf K. Hamied** is the Chairman and Managing Director of Cipla, a leading Indian pharmaceutical company which produces generic drugs for India and the developing world. Also an elected fellow of Christ's College, Cambridge, Dr Hamied has led a global fight against HIV and AIDS for many years. Cipla has been committed to fighting HIV/AIDS worldwide by providing affordable antiretrovirals to countries in Africa, Asia and Latin America.

world has to consider the manner in which the current patent system marginalises humanitarian issues implicit to healthcare delivery for the poor and search for a better alternative to it. For, the globalisation of healthcare should not imply that we have the means of treating the sick and needy but we are at liberty to make the terrible choice between profits and lives.

THE CREATION OF ARTIFICIAL BARRIERS

Today, nobody can doubt that the much vilified generics drug industry has mastered the challenges of science and manufacturing and has provided safe and effective medicines to all. Nevertheless, a generic drugs producer, such as Cipla particularly from the Third World, is routinely castigated as a copycat and condemned for engaging in so-called piracy. What is overlooked is that this industry has made affordable drugs available to the nations of the South, home to over three billion people, most of whom are poor and trying to cope with an ever worsening disease burden with little or no help from their governments.

As the world and its poorest communities are faced with an exploding disease burden and shrinking public health provisions, artificial barriers created by a combine of corporate greed and political interest helped along by growing apathy from the international community have kept drugs out of reach of those who need them most. It is also forgotten in this context that generic competition has been necessary and effective and has been one of the most powerful tools that policy makers possess to lower drug prices in a sustainable way. Lessons can be learned from Brazil where the price of HIV/AIDS drugs fell by 82 per cent over five years as a result of generic competition, while the prices of drugs that had no generic competitors remained stable.

CREATING OBSTACLES FOR GENERICS DRUGS PRODUCERS

Consider for instance, the actions of the big pharmaceutical giants and the First World's response to the global AIDS pandemic. Not only has there been apathy in the face of devastation and human loss, generic drug producers have faced severe roadblocks at every step when they have tried to offer affordable and safe drugs to HIV/AIDS patients in some of the most poverty stricken regions of our planet.

It has been six years since the first offer from a generic company for a combined formulation HIV/AIDS treatment at vastly reduced prices was made public. In September 2000, at the European Union, Cipla offered its Triomune formulation to the international community at US$ 600 per patient per year when a similar treatment from the MNCs was priced above US$ 10,000 per year. Cipla also offered ARV drug production technology, totally free, to any Third World government which wanted to produce its own drugs against AIDS. Subsequently, an offer to supply Nevirapine, totally free, which prevents the transmission of HIV from mother to child was also made worldwide.

This was followed by an even bolder humanitarian offer. In February 2001, Cipla announced a drastic price reduction for its leading first-line therapy drug cocktail Triomune. The price of AIDs treatment now dropped to under US$ 1 per patient per day and the patient was only required to take two pills a day, rather than the six or more required in other regimes. In mid-2001, it was alleged that Cipla was not approved by the World Health Organisation (WHO). In a relatively short span of time, approvals for anti-retroviral drugs as well as for drugs meant for combating the opportunistic diseases that arise out of HIV/AIDS, were qualified by WHO which audited and physically inspected the company factories where they were produced. A longer approval process reflective of the thoroughness of the approval system, was followed before Cipla received approval for Triomune in December 2003 on World AIDS Day. Despite this, The Global Fund, the major source of AIDS funding for the poor, prohibited the use of generics – which were approved by the WHO as safe and effective and recommended as first-line treatment for the disease.

The biggest disappointment to generics drugs producers, NGOs and those working in the field of healthcare has been the failed promise of the State of the Union address in January 2003 by US President George W. Bush. This is what he said on that occasion:

> On the continent of Africa, nearly 30 million people, including 3 million children have AIDS. There are countries in Africa where one third of the population carry the infection, and 4 million require immediate treatment. Only 50,000 people are receiving the medicines they need. In an age of miraculous medicines no person should hear: "You've got AIDS. We can't help you. Go home and die." AIDS can be prevented. Anti-retroviral drugs can extend life for many years. And the cost of those drugs has dropped from US$ 12,000 to US$ 300, which places a tremendous possibility within our grasp. Seldom has history offered a greater opportunity to do so much for so many.

He went on to commit US$ 15 billion from PEPFAR (the President's Emergency Plan for AIDS relief) over the next five years to help stem the AIDS pandemic.

Three years later this promise has been left unfulfilled. The multinationals began to protest soon after President Bush made that commitment and today, as before, they are blocking the supply of affordable quality drugs. Meanwhile 8000 people continue to succumb to HIV/AIDS each day in Africa alone and the pandemic rages stronger than ever. Over 45 million are afflicted already and by some estimates this number will escalate to 75 million worldwide by 2015 of which unfortunately nearly half will be in India alone. A refusal to recognise the magnitude of the problem and simultaneously to create barriers to obstruct drugs to these patients must rank as one of the most shameful episodes of modern civilisation.

HOW PATENTS CREATE MONOPOLIES IN THE GUISE OF FREE TRADE

Exorbitant pricing is a by-product of the notion of exclusivity claimed by the large pharmaceutical MNCs and granted to them by governments and regulators through the mechanism of patents. Patents are the very lifeblood of the pharmaceutical industry. When manufacturers are assured that their drugs will not be copied, they are naturally in a position to price them in a unilateral way and negotiate for higher prices with public health authorities and governments irrespective of any public health crisis. This gross injustice is ironically enough being dispensed by the votaries of free trade who are dependent on patents to grant them monopolies. These in turn translate into the excessive profits earned by the large pharmaceutical MNCs.

THE DANGERS OF IMPOSING A UNIFORM PATENT REGIME FOR ALL COUNTRIES

Until recently, every country had widely divergent national patent laws. This was sensible because it was based on the fact that every sovereign country had the right to decide on and prioritise issues of national significance on the basis of the requirements of its people. WTO and TRIPS (Trade Related Intellectual Property Rights), which has sought to establish a uniform patent regime the world over, has also in effect usurped the rights of people in sovereign countries to have a say in the formulation of public policies which will affect them irreversibly in the future. The idea of there being a standard and homogenous patent regime for all countries is tantamount to saying that the healthcare capabilities, priorities and infrastructure of the American people are at par with those of countries in Sub-Saharan Africa. This "one size fits all" patent system will definitely hamper efforts to protect public health interests of middle and low income individuals in the developed world as well as the developing world.

PATENTS AND THE QUESTION OF SOVEREIGNTY

The truth is that at various stages of technological development the requirements of a nation are bound to differ. It is no coincidence that at various points the industrialised and developed countries themselves had flexible patent rights. For instance, the German Patent Law of 1877 provided only process patents for chemical products. Product patents on chemical products in Germany only came into force as late as 1967. Pharmaceutical substances were not patentable in France until 1967 and in Canada until 1988. In Switzerland, product patents for medical and chemical substances were granted only in 1978 and in Spain they became patentable only in 1992.

In India, the British introduced a patent system in 1856. In 1911, they enforced the Indian Patents and Designs Act of 1911 to make the Indian market subservient to British industry. British patent holders made millions exploiting Indian markets through high priced exports to the country. Inevitably such exploitation entered the field of drugs as well. In 1961, the US Senate Committee headed by Senator Kefauver stated in its findings that "in drugs generally, India ranks amongst the highest priced nations of the world".[1]

THE CREED OF SELF RELIANCE

During the late 1930s and early 1940s, as the world went through another terrible war, millions of Indians had to face the prospect of being denied lifesaving drugs when supplies from the West dried up. It was at this juncture that Mahatma Gandhi visited Cipla in 1939 and urged it to produce medicines to aid not just the British war effort, but also with a view to overcoming shortages in the long-term interest of the nation. A desire to serve national interest and the determination to be self-reliant, has thus been a part of Cipla's ethos from the beginning.

However, like many other indigenous pharmaceutical companies at the time, Cipla too was unable in the 1950s and 60s to manufacture any drug in the country because of the prevailing system of product patents. The Indian consumer was denied the use of several lifesaving drugs which were being launched internationally. Beecham introduced the semi-synthetic penicillin, ampicillin in Europe in the early 60s. The originators were unwilling to market this drug in India except on terms and conditions which were totally unacceptable. This was also the case with the cardiac drug, propranolol, introduced by ICI internationally in the mid 60s.

THE INDIAN PATENT ACT 1972

Soon after in 1961, a group of like-minded Indian pharmaceutical companies formed the Indian Drug Manufacturers' Association (IDMA) in order to lobby with the government to change its patent laws. Ten years later and after a spate of intense deliberations which went right up to Parliament, the Indian Patent Act 1970 was passed in 1972. The Act held that in the two vital areas of health and food, there could be no patent on end products, only on production processes and that too for a period of seven years only. This change proved very fortuitous – for the industry and for innumerable low and middle income Indians who now had access to safe and affordable medicines in all disease categories. Three decades later, 85 per cent of the Indian pharma market of US $6 billion and virtually all exports are controlled by indigenous companies. This change in the patent regime led to a sharp reduction in prices as well.

In a country with a permanent health crisis this is very crucial indeed. The truth about India's disease burden makes for very grim reading. The country is estimated to have 80 million cardiac patients, 80 million afflicted with mental illness, 60 million diabetics, 50 million asthmatics, 50 million Hepatitis B cases and one in three Indians is a latent carrier of TB. Given these facts, the patent regime should have been devised so that the utmost priority was granted to securing the people's rights of access to affordable and quality healthcare without monopoly.

However, India's recent amendment of the Indian Patents Act 1972 in compliance with WTO patent laws and TRIPS, came into effect from 1 January, 2005 and shows complete disregard for its healthcare priorities. Indigenous companies will now no longer be able to produce or export affordable medicines. Moreover, most new drugs will now be out of reach of most Indians and poor people worldwide. Generics companies will now no longer be in a position to perform the humanitarian role that they have so far. In addition, the supply of affordable new medicines will dry up in due course as well.

Moreover, despite the amended Act being TRIPS compliant, MNCs have pressed for the inclusion of even more stringent clauses with a view to disallowing any room for manoeuvre that may have been left for generics drug producers. Thus quite apart from TRIPS, considerable effort has been spent on lobbying for measures such as data exclusivity and free trade agreements or differential pricing which will only succeed in creating more non-patent barriers for generic drug producers in the years to come.

By insisting on maintaining that key scientific and medical data pertaining to the discovery of a new chemical entity remains exclusive even after the end of the patent period, MNCs seek to further reinforce their monopolistic grip over the healthcare sector. Similarly, by advocating a differential pricing structure which entails low prices for countries with no patent laws and high prices for countries covered by patent laws, MNCs are only perpetuating their existing monopoly status in large parts of the world while simultaneously preventing generics producers from finding markets for their products.

CREATING CONDITIONS FOR GOOD CORPORATE BEHAVIOUR

How can the world ensure that humanitarian principles are not violated even as corporations, created and fashioned by the socio-legal environment provided to them, continue to grow and expand their business? The repercussions of allowing monopolistic and unregulated behaviour – which is what patents in their current manifestation do – are too serious to be left to the good intentions of the industry. Governments, alliances of right thinking people and civil society organisations like Public Citizen in the United States for instance, need to come together and examine at each juncture if public interest is being violated by the vested interests of the large pharmaceutical MNCs and their agencies.

We need to enquire into the several malpractices that the pharmaceutical sector has been implicated in time and time again. Marcia Angell, in her book *The Truth about the Drug Companies* has highlighted a number of important criticisms in this regard.[2]

THE MYTH OF THE HIGH COSTS OF R&D

However, the MNCs would like us all to believe that a call for reform in their functioning will undermine the industry and its ability to offer the healthcare solutions of the future. The world will then be plunged into a more unimaginable health crisis than any it has known before.

Facts need to be placed in the public domain. The costs of R&D are often touted as the justification for the pricing. The truth is that at least a third of all major drugs marketed by pharmaceutical companies are now licensed from universities and small bio tech firms and these tend to be the more innovative ones. In addition, many pharmaceutical companies have actually enjoyed tax-payers funded public health programmes to do the bulk of the intensive scientific work and many have simply licensed them from smaller research firms.

In the US, this is a result of the Bahy-Dole Act which enabled universities and small businesses to patent discoveries emanating from research sponsored by the NIH (National Institutes of Health), the major distributors of tax dollars, and then to grant exclusive licenses to drug companies. As Angell points out, the most startling fact about 2002 is that the combined profits that year for the top ten pharmaceutical companies in the Fortune 500 (US$ 35.9 billion) was more than the profits for all the other 490 businesses put together. Besides, quoting information from the industry's own disclosures to the SEC (Securities and Exchanges Commission) and to stockholders, she reveals that money spend on marketing and administration was higher than the spend on R&D by at least two and a half times.

MOBILISING THE INTERNATIONAL COMMUNITY

At the international level, the influence of the large pharmaceutical MNCs is considerable and in several well documented cases actually overrides the aspirations of smaller and less developed countries. The clout of this cartel can be seen in the manner in which governments, international trade treaties and regulators are often subverted and co-opted to further the expansion of this industry in its present form. The WHO for example, has collaborated with the large pharmaceutical MNCs by encouraging overly restrictive intellectual property policies in return for unsustainable and limited donations.

Yet international bodies such as the WHO are still in a unique position to argue the case for health reform at an international level. Health related non-governmental and consumer organisations certainly have a supportive role to play as well, but the WHO is the only intergovernmental organisation with a formal mandate to protect and advance health internationally. While the WHO's authority in this area has suffered in the last few decades, part of the WHO's strategies in this area should be to clearly and unambiguously put health first and provide much needed leadership in promoting access to essential drugs. This will compel the large pharmaceutical MNCs to adopt a more responsive and genuinely humane approach with regard to addressing issues of equity and access to their products, particularly in the less developed countries.

ENFORCING EQUITY PRICING

The WTO Agreement on TRIPS ratifies the worldwide implementation of a free trade economy. Its enforcement with regard to the pharmaceutical sector raises several concerns for a world already besieged by poverty and an exploding disease burden.

Essential drugs are the foundation for nearly every public health programme aimed at reducing morbidity and mortality in the developing world. Important health programmes that rely on essential drugs include child survival programmes, antenatal care and treatment of respiratory pathogens and control of tuberculosis and malaria.

While the US$ 406 billion drug industry researches, develops, markets and prices medicines for the industrialised world, there is no mechanism to make newer medicines affordable to developing countries. Newer drugs which are usually under patent and more expensive than those off patent are expected to become even more expensive with the implementation of the WTO Agreement on TRIPS. The ability of generics producers to provide the same medicines to its own people and the poor in other countries as well will be severely hampered by the change in patent regimes worldwide.

HOW TO SURVIVE THE WTO

It would be rational to assume that given the current trajectory of international trade and investment regimes, the MNCs will be further emboldened to charge higher prices in the future. Several strategies need to be combined for equity pricing. Countries can counter rising drug prices by building TRIPS-compliant safeguards into their national laws including compulsory licensing, parallel importation and measures to accelerate the introduction of generics.

Governments can reduce prices by granting compulsory licenses for the production or importation of lower priced generics of patented products. Using parallel importation, they can also buy patented products at the lowest price offered on the world market by the patent holder. Global procurement and distribution can also help lower drug prices by guaranteeing high demand and reliable payment for large quantities of drugs – bulk purchasing will also make it easier to negotiate lower prices. UN agencies like UNICEF have considerable experience in the global procurement of medicines. A system of patent exception for globally procured medicines would also offer some hope to the poor.

The indisputable fact is that TRIPS threatens public health in developing countries by giving patents on medicines for a period of twenty years. Coupled with the growing political and economic clout of the large pharmaceutical MNCs, this may well prove to be disastrous. However, the world can do a lot to ensure that such an industry which has enjoyed so many special privileges is finally made accountable to broader publics than just its shareholders. We owe it to the poor and the diseased and to our own hopes of leaving behind a better world for future generations.

Chapter 30

Future Making:
Corporate Performativity and the Temporal Politics of Markets

*Georgina Born**

W̶e often hear it proclaimed that the global economy is in the midst of epochal transformations. Analyses of these shifts frequently resort to grand claims about the economy's laws of operation, attributing a totalising, retrospective omniscience to corporate capitalism, as though its forms of knowing and acting were unitary and rational, largely untroubled by doubt or risk.[1] Alternatively, the capitalist economy is portrayed as unstable and contingent, a 'project ... permanently "under construction" ... [one that is] always engaged in experiment [and a] constantly mutating formation'.[2] Rather than choose between these characterisations, in what follows I draw on a decade of ethnographic fieldwork inside the media and information technology industries in Britain and the USA, centred on international and national corporations and companies which – in their rapid development and interconnectedness, and in their enabling role in relation to financial, industrial and wider cultural processes – represent cutting-edge modalities of contemporary capitalism.[3] In particular, I highlight two performative or protentive mechanisms or techniques that are in widespread use in the media and IT industries in their efforts to tame chronic uncertainties by making the future knowable and predictable. The two mechanisms are market forecasting and market

* **Georgina Born** is Professor of Sociology, Anthropology and Music at the University of Cambridge, Honorary Professor of Anthropology at University College London, and a Fellow of the Center for Cultural Sociology, Yale University. She gave evidence on the Government Green Paper on the review of the BBC's Charter to the House of Lords Select Committee, and has been policy advisor to the National Endowment for Science, Technology and the Arts.

research. Both have been features of corporate capitalism for decades; both have grown in prominence since the late 1980s, burgeoning into substantial industries. Both amount to cultural or knowledge practices that play an increasingly formative role in the global 'informational economy'.[4] I take the concept of performativity from J. L. Austin's exposition of the illocutionary power of language, the capacity of speech acts to bring about that which they state.[5] By analogy, I point to the power that such knowledge practices have to act in the world, bringing into being the very conditions that they purport merely to name or describe.

For individual companies the future may be highly unpredictable. But this does not mean that it is unmanageable, or that firms do not seek to shape the future. The mechanisms by which the future is controlled are varied. They include the cultivation of privileged relations with governments in order to influence regulation, or lobbying for industry standards that block out competitors. Sometimes they entail patents or intellectual property rights, laying claim to potential spaces of activity and knowledge which rivals cannot occupy. Increasingly they occur through the creation of brands. However, I want to argue that the deployment of social scientific expertise has become critical to the way that firms construct the future, powerfully influencing the dynamics of new and evolving markets. Put to work in the service of forecasting or market research, economics, sociology, social psychology and ethnography do not simply describe the world: they help to bring the future into being. I chart the intensification and proliferation of these practices as they are inserted ever more closely into the kernel of media and IT corporations.

In their performativity, these mechanisms evidence distinctive kinds of temporal politics. By temporal politics I point to the importance of attending to the constructions of cultural-historical time characteristic of different social spaces, constructs that form part of the calculative agency of actors. As Peter Osborne observes, such constructs involve 'a distinctive way of temporalising "history" – through which the three dimensions of phenomenological time (past, present and future) are linked together within the dynamic unity of a single historical view. Associated with such temporalisations are both particular historical epistemologies, and particular orientations towards practice ... particular interventions in the politics of time'.[6] Osborne alludes to the Husserlian model of time-consciousness, which addresses the perspectival constructions of past, present and future as they continually alter in cognitive time. Central to this dynamic experience of time is the existence of retentions – memories or traces of the past – and protentions – projections or anticipations; thus, the future is experienced as a protention of possible eventualities – a construct of the present – just as the past is experienced through a retention of previous events – also a present construct. In the following I point to the politics of protention or anticipation in commercial fields in which corporations utilise particular technologies as they engage in struggles with both commercial competitors and consumers to control the projection of what will come to be, and thence what will come to be, thereby rendering the result of those struggles, paradoxically, both natural or inevitable, and 'innovative'.

Two of my themes – performativity and temporality in capitalist markets – have recently been addressed by other writers (although in relation to finance). The two themes are related, as Donald Mackenzie points out addressing the performativity of money. Money has a future-orientation, he says, in that 'a piece of paper treated as money today will also be treated as money tomorrow', a self-validating inference loop, as he calls it, which is revealed as such only in precarious times of hyperinflation or economic collapse.[7] Both Mackenzie and Nigel Thrift write also of the performative nature of capitalism. As a rule, Thrift says, capitalism is performative. Summarising what he calls a 'Latourian-cum-Deleuzian notion of political economy as composed of a series of modulations', and noting the irony that such an account 'increasingly resembles capitalism's description of itself',[8] he stresses capitalist firms' inherent uncertainty about the future, whether caused by energy crises, economic downturns or consumer activism, and the way the future 'unfolds as a virtuality'. His idea of capitalism's performativity, then, takes this general form. Notably, he does not specify the mechanisms that lie at the core of the virtual unfolding of the future.

Here we encounter, then, a problem: the potential over-extension or banalisation of performativity in these accounts: money is performative, capitalism is performative, and so on. Certainly, both entities are self-reinforcing; they depend on authorities that translate the statement or protention 'X' into the reality 'X'. But analytically, the *future-orientation* of these uses of 'performativity' is weak since these writers do not fill out the processes by which the protention accrues the authority or power that enables it to bring about the real. This is where an Austinian account of performativity, with its focus on the illocutionary effectivity of discourse, must give way to anthropological analysis, one that probes precisely how, and if, that effectivity is achieved.

In his list of the causes of uncertainty in today's markets, Thrift does not mention the most continuous challenge facing corporations producing both material and non-material goods, a challenge at the heart of their drive to control the future and so their evolution: the need to plan and strategise the future in terms of conceiving and developing the next generation of products – which comes down to the question, what goods or services shall we produce next? This depends in turn on another question: what direction is this market going in? And, therefore, how shall we intervene in and re-configure this market? In the intensely competitive and fast-moving media and IT sectors, firms constantly face the need to analyse the markets in which they operate, and their direction-ality, the better to imagine where to place themselves and their products within them. These are processes to which Don Slater draws attention in theorising the role of marketing in framing competition, as well as the double movement of stabilisation and destabilisation by which markets evolve.[9]

Also close to my concerns is the debate between Michel Callon and Daniel Miller over the ways in which economics is implicated in the workings of markets: that is, economics as performative. For Callon, economic theory actively participates in making economic realities.[10] The diverse forms of economics format markets through framing what will and will not count as relevant in economic calculation, in this way rendering certain features 'externalities' or outside the frame: 'Externality and framing describe the ways in which "insides" and "outsides" emerge, and change'.[11] In response, Miller criticises Callon for missing the ways in which calculative practices invariably remain socially embedded, arguing that Callon reifies economic calculation and is in this sense complicit with market ideology.[12] As we'll see, I endorse Callon's position by showing how specific modes of social scientific expertise enter into the projection and constitution of markets, including strong processes of framing and of the creation of externalities.

Later revisions to Callon by Andrew Barry and Slater stress the contested, politicised nature of such framings.[13] I suggest, however, that the degree of instability or contestation is an empirical matter that will vary across different sectors and epochs. In my material corporate strategists, when planning what to do next, unquestionably deal in economic and sociological abstractions; while there is always a politics, there may be little contestation, but rather a con-sensus on the framings entailed and the efficacy of the projections based on those framings. Both Miller and Callon elide distinct phases in the construction of markets: the phase of strategic planning, and the transactional moments of sales and of what Callon calls 'qualification'.[14] In different ways both risk forc-ing complexity to conform to theoretical end-points; instead we should disag-gregate and de-reify corporate capitalism by attending to its differentiation, including both its abstracting and re-embedding imperatives, and its proten-tions and the contingency of their effects. Such an analytics acknowledges that not only the 'cultural' and 'knowledge' practices engaged in by corporations, but their 'economic' practices as well, must be grasped as fully cultural.

This orientation is evident in recent anthropological studies which uncover theological or utopian dimensions of corporate capitalism. Thus Hirokazu Miyazaki probes the experience of 'temporal incongruities' among Japanese arbitrage traders in the 1990s as they effectively foresaw their own obsolescence. He attributes to arbitrage a utopian vision 'of efficient markets in the form of correct prices'.[15] Bill Maurer, on the other hand, identifies a repressed theological unconscious in the mathematics of financial derivatives. He draws an analogy between the 'fetishization of equilibrium in economics' and the fetishisation of the normal distribution curve in probability theory. Both entail a faith in the possibility of prediction and explanation of reality: 'Equilibrium is theology', he says.[16] If these writers risk exoticising the knowledge forms of finance capital, Mackenzie takes the opposite tack. From an account of the role of stochastic mathematics in the development of arbitrage, he argues that finance theory 'is among high modernity's most sophisticated mathematical products'.[17] Mackenzie equates finance theory's performativity with its rationality, as though the rigour was necessary for the performativity. In my material, in contrast, the performativity of the social sciences is not predicated on their rigour; but nor do I want to valorise as moral or theological what are thoroughly disenchanted forms of expertise.

Let us turn to the two mechanisms: first, the use of market forecasting, now ubiquitous in the media and IT industries. Here, on the basis of analyses usually of existing North American markets and consumer behaviour, forecasters derive speculative models that purport to predict the future unfolding of, say, British digital television markets or global markets in audio-visual content for mobiles. The economists' projections willfully obscure their origins in particular cultural and geo-political conditions; the data are de-cultured, universalised through abstraction, and in interpretation, their specificity is ignored. There is collusion in their universalisation; after all, corporations require such models: they cannot proceed without planning their future on the basis of some kind of oracular knowledge.

The forecasts are commissioned by firms or regulators from consultancies (e.g. KPMG, McKinsey, Price Waterhouse Coopers) for private use or presentation at industry and policy events. At these events, corporate actors throw challenges and probe the models' reasoning; the politics of the industry flare up as competing parties air conflicting interpretations. In due course, strategists are charged with using the projections as a basis to design market interventions and medium- or long-term strategies; plans are made and acted upon.

Forecasting is, then, a theatre of abstractions in which are conceived and enacted 'collective' imaginings of the future. Technological and economic speculations derived from very specific conditions become concretised in corporate and regulatory strategies and, thereby, practically universalised. In this way the projections *become protentions* – translated into the collective calculations and strategies of corporations, regulators and governments, which in turn powerfully form how markets develop. Forecasting can fail, but it always constructs and acts. It is a sturdy performative mechanism: at best it achieves a taming of uncertainty and a temporary closure for these industries.

An example is provided by the emerging field of digital television which is increasingly convergent with other media (the internet, mobile communications). Recently I examined how, through the use of forecasting, the BBC and Britain's other public broadcaster, Channel 4, were developing strategies for their entry into digital media. The broadcasters' projections of future markets were remarkably different. While the BBC saw new media as a means to expand its public service activities, C4's projections were driven by the search for new revenues, unencumbered by public service aims. C4's core assumption, based on American data and presented as self-evident (despite being contentious), was that pay media will become the consumption norm in Britain. C4's projection entailed, then, a *will to redefine consumption.* In short, where the BBC anticipated a continuation of non-commercial media, C4 projected a future only of pay media, precisely the conditions which justified and reinforced its ongoing commercial direction.[18] In both broadcasters the market projections were folded into institutional strategies, becoming the basis for their new media practices. In this way the projections emanate out to condition wider media markets and the media culture, altering the relative positioning of competitors, restructuring the field, delimiting the alternatives available to consumers, opening up some possibilities and closing down others. The gulf between the BBC's and C4's forecasts points to the veneer of scientificity in these economics applications, as well as the lack of any necessary unity and the political nature of such projections: to *forecasting as a political art.*

The second mechanism is the use of market research with the aim of folding consumption back into production, thereby appearing to reduce uncertainty by bringing full circle the unruly circuit of production-consumption. Here, through the labours of social psychology, sociology or ethnography, sciences that can capture and image dispersed consumption practices, the 'social' and 'cultural' excluded by the economists can be made to re-enter the calculative frame. Callon calls this the 'economy of qualities', in which a range of experts mediate between the world of objects and the world of consumers, effecting a 'distributed cognition' that takes as its object the attachment of consumers to products.[19] In the past in the media industries this was accomplished via ratings, sales graphs or product trials. But rather than increased abstraction, for a decade the tendency has been to offer ever more embedded accounts of consumption, initially through focus groups, and increasingly, in the case of corporations like the BBC, Intel and Microsoft, through ethnography.

In the BBC market research has escalated since the 1990s. There is a telling duality in the use of research: it plays a key part in the centralised planning of schedules – ironically, techniques at the heart of commercial media; yet research is also seen as a means of boosting public accountability by enabling the BBC to understand how its consumers (or 'tribes') are well- or under-served, their desires fulfilled or ignored. In this sense research is understood as a *technology for cultural democracy*, forcing a narcissistic organisation to look outside itself and attend to consumer experiences.[20] Similarly, the drive to introduce ethnography in the IT industry, with early forays in the 1980s by Xerox, Hewlett Packard and Apple, is portrayed both as a mundane means of delivering products attuned to users, and as an experimental way of construing a newly ethical capitalism. Such a capitalism conceives of itself as concerned with the entire lifeworld of consumers and with augmenting its responsiveness to diverse cultural worlds that have hitherto been occluded from the corporate culture and imagination, and that in some diffuse way should in future be taken into account. In this view, incorporating the 'social' and 'cultural' will fuel innovation. Intel is at the forefront of these new uses of ethnography; the claim is that we are witnessing a shift to a responsive capitalism – what might be called 'Intel capitalism'.

The question immediately arises: is this an embedding – an attempt to replace virtual consumers in corporate imaginations with a portrait of real people gaming on mobiles and toiling at laptops? Or is it a *simulation* of such an embedding? The history of these techniques is suggestive. For much of the last twenty years, by 'ethnography' the IT firms actually meant ethnomethodology; and ethnomethodology generated micro-sociologies of technologies in use, analyses that fed neatly into improving human-computer-interface design. Anthropological ethnography was rare, but has been championed in recent years by leading figures in HCI (among them Intel researchers) who argue on intellectual and ethical grounds for a rejection of instrumental ethnography and for granting it epistemological autonomy – a proposal that meets vocal resistance from some ethnomethodologists (among them influential Microsoft researchers). There is, then, both *an autonomy and a politics* to the evolving knowledge practices, in which demands for greater subtlety, naturalism or verisimilitude, as well as ethical concerns over the reification of findings, can fuel revisions in the knowledge techniques.

In reality, the practice of corporate ethnography departs from anthropological norms, and the resulting analyses can be reductive. Yet in comparison with focus groups, this ethnography *can* offer far richer insight into diverse lives. Moreover it acts as a disciplinary force within the corporations, requiring commitment to non-immediate, less reductive conceptualisations, to supporting travelling researchers who go out – as a corporate prosthesis – to witness other lives. The externalities or disavowal can be shocking, as when corporate ethnographers researching the space of public libraries in American cities, a space colonised by homeless people, were irritated and found it impossible to conceive of the homeless as anything other than anomalous, a human detritus blocking their proper object of study. Yet if the knowledge is less reductive, and if the corporation encompasses research arms that go out to connect tenuously with the 'local' and 'everyday', does this mean that the corporate telos is necessarily less reductive? From one perspective, whatever the cultural knowledge obtained, culture is the object of instrumental calculation: corralling tastes, administering demand. At issue is a 'specific instrumentalising of culture in order to profit'.[21] From another, the subtleties and embeddedness proffered by ethnography might, even given this telos, have unintended effects and result in significant shifts in corporate orientation, in design and production, so as to construe relations with and between consumers differently.[22]

It is a commonplace that capitalism is engaged in continual processes of transformation. As Tim Mitchell observes, 'Capitalism ... has no singular essence. It survives parasitically ... drawing its energies from the chemistry of others, its force from other fields ... They are presented as something exterior to capitalism, yet these outsides are at the same time vital to capitalism.'[23] New subjects and objects are drawn in, new agencies discovered, new manoeuvres adopted, transforming the relations between what is inside and outside, calculable and disavowed. What is striking about contemporary capitalism is not that it contains utopian elements, or virtual moments, but that it involves the deployment by corporations of systematic techniques to conceptualise and protend the future: to bring the future into the present, delimit it and close it down. The mechanisms that I have outlined amount to *technologies for producing teleology*. Contrary to the critics of Marx, we might say, it's the capitalists who have become teleologists. If these mechanisms channel the development of capitalism in ways that are not fully predictable, this does not mean that it is entirely contingent or endlessly inventive. On the contrary: if we look closely, the tropes, mores and meta-strategies at work in corporate capitalism remain patterned and perceptible.

Chapter 31

Globalisation and Threats to the West

*Will Hutton**

Mention globalisation and a curious mist descends that prevents straight thinking. It is now a given on both left and right that billions of low paid workers are going to take away Western jobs and make European welfare and taxation levels unaffordable luxuries. The only options are trade protection or accepting a Darwinian low tax, low welfare fight to the finish – equipped with whatever education and training we can get. We must all accept our fate.

The problem is this nexus of givens is wrong. Globalisation and trade have greatly enlarged the global economic cake and our economic options rather than narrowed them. The problem is too much of the world is an excluded onlooker, largely because the rules of the game are massively and unfairly tilted in the West's favour. Both need to change rather than globalization stop. It is alarmist, intellectually mistaken and plain counterproductive to blame foreigners for our problems when they are not.

Even China, portrayed as the Big New Threatening Thing, has not managed to change the rules of the game. Close to 60 per cent of its exports, nearly all its high tech exports and more than half its patents come from foreign companies. In essence it is a sub-contractor to the West, boosting the profits of our multinationals and the real incomes of our consumers.

* **Will Hutton** is the chief executive of the Work Foundation, an independent, not for dividend research-based consultancy in Britain. He began his career as a stockbroker and investment analyst, before working in TV, radio and print journalism as a producer, reporter and columnist. He has written several books on economics and society, such as *The World We're In* (Abacus, 2002) (launched in the US as *A Declaration of Interdependence*), *The State We're In* (Vintage, 1996), *The State to Come* (Vintage, 1997), *The Stakeholding Society* (Polity, 1999), and *On The Edge* (ed. with Anthony Giddens) (Jonathan Cape, 2000). His latest book on China and the West is entitled *The Writing on the Wall: China and the West in the 21st Century* (Little Brown, 2007).

China has not a single brand in the world's top hundred despite the projection it will become the world's largest exporter in 2008. It has only one company in the top 300 ranked by R and D spending. Two-thirds of the goods confiscated by the US Customs as counterfeit are Chinese imports. It is the fourth largest economy in the world but has only 20 organisations, ranked by revenue, in the Forbes top 500. Ranked by profit and extent of their overseas operations it has virtually none. Buying Rover, and shipping some of the plant back to China, was portrayed as an act of strength; in fact it is an act of economic desperation. By lending $200 billion a year to finance the US trade deficit, China underpins the international dominance of the dollar. In the upper echelons of the communist party and the state council there is an anguished debate about why so many manufactured goods are made "in China", and not "by China", and why indigenous innovation is so disastrous. In 1995 China set a target of having 50 companies in the world's top 500 multinationals by 2010. It will be lucky to have any.

Sub-contractors tend to have a limited impact on their contractors' employment. So it proves with China. The most hawkish, protectionist think tank in the United States is the Economic Policy Institute. It believes Chinese imports have cost the US cumulatively 2.24 million lost jobs between 1989 and 2005 – but the overall job churn over the same period exceeded 400 million. The impact of off-shoring, which attracts so much political venom from the American left, is even smaller. The National Bureau of Labor Survey of Mass Lay-offs identified 884,000 job losses in 2005 of which 12,030 went overseas – two-thirds of the total to China and Mexico. In Britain it is a similar story. According to the European Restructuring Monitor in the 40 months between April 2003 to July 2006 we lost 390,000 jobs. Only 19,000 went abroad. The UK Trade Union Confederation set up a unit to monitor off-shoring four years ago; it has had to close because there has been so little to monitor.

The reason is simple. Manufacturing assembly represents only a minority of the value in any good – there is invention, design, financing, marketing, transporting, warehousing, advertising – and even then wage costs are not decisive. A Chinese worker may earn 4 per cent of the wage of an American or British worker, but he or she is only 4 per cent as productive. Consultants McKinsey, for example, estimate that only one-fourth of Indian engineers and one-tenth of Chinese engineers are genuinely equipped to work in multinational companies. In a separate survey of Californian companies, they estimated the savings from off-shoring to China range from 13 per cent in a textiles company to a tiny 0.6 per cent for high-tech companies. Cheap labour is not everything.

Western companies can still compete successfully against low wage Asians, as a massive survey of 500 multinationals by MIT's Suzanne Berger has confirmed – documented in "How We Compete".[1] Western companies tend to be organised better and tend to be embedded in better institutional networks. According to Berger and her associates strategies for minimising costs are essentially short-termist and self-defeating. Even a company like Dell, which has embraced the outsourcing philosophy very aggressively, is careful to make sure that it retains the ability to customise its equipment with local in-house productive capacity – and its marketing and distribution services are kept very close to its markets. Other electronic companies, like Texas Instruments, pursue a more mixed strategy, keenly aware that they may need to overhaul any stage in the production and distribution process and if they contract it out they risk losing control of the ability to be responsive.

Product cycles are shortening dramatically. It required six years to take a car from concept to production in 1990; now it requires only two years. This phenomenon is general. One study found that the time it took to launch new products or make substantial product improvements fell from an average of 35.5 months in 1990 to about 23 months in 1995. Firms that outsource too much production too far away from their markets are putting all their eggs in one basket; that is, low wages become the sole determinant of competitiveness. Such firms risk being outcompeted by firms closer to home who can better exploit new technologies and new patterns of demand.

In the face of these challenges many firms choose to remain integrated. Sony and Toshiba in Japan; Samsung in Korea (Samsung is Asia's largest chip and mobile phone maker); and the clothes manufacturer Zara in Spain are hugely successful companies that have built their performance around keeping part or all of their production in-house and sourcing most of the balance locally. Half of Zara's products come from trusted, local suppliers located in and around its base in La Coruna. When Ford built its flexible factory in Chicago it insisted on having its suppliers physically close to its new plant. The well-known clusters of high-tech firms in California and Boston in the United States and in Cambridge in Britain are testimony that cluster effects trump low-wage costs.

In low-tech textiles in Italy small-firm clusters outcompete their rivals despite higher Italian wage costs. Benetton, Safilo, Max Mara, Luxottica, Geox, Tie Rack and Ermenegildo Zegna, for example, are all globally recognised companies whose production base is still firmly anchored in Italy; they form a critical mass of producers with design genius whose collective output and profitability supports trade fairs, design schools, training and information about foreign markets – all of which feeds back into the productivity of the firms. In fact, despite their high wages they are short of labour; and in Modena, the centre of the Italian garment industry, the Chinese have bought into 200 of the 3,200 garment businesses in order to learn. Low wages, it turns out, far from being trump cards in the economics of today's business are only a small part of the story.

Nor is globalisation tearing down the welfare state. Since 1980, according to the University of California's Peter Lindert, social transfers (which he defines as assistance to the poor, the unemployed and pensions for the elderly together with spending on health and public housing) have continued to rise in the industrialised world. He can find no evidence that this trend, or the taxation to finance it, has had any deleterious effect on economic growth rates or been adversely affected by globalisation. Indeed there is some evidence that high social spending is good for growth. The critics of social spending make three errors, Lindert argues. First, they bundle it up with all government spending so that their statistical tests are not targeted enough on what they claim is the significant variable – the relationship between social spending and growth. Second, they assume that governments design and finance welfare states to create disincentives, and that taxation itself is a disincentive. Third, they assume that there can be nothing economically positive about social spending. Lindert demonstrates that they are wrong on all three counts.

First, he separates out social spending from government spending to test the correlation between it and growth; he finds no negative correlation. Second, he shows that countries with high social spending go to great lengths to design the structure of their spending and its financing to avoid disincentives. Indeed, paradoxically countries with a very tight-fisted approach to social spending – countries that use means-testing and withdraw benefits aggressively as recipients' circumstances improve – create more disincentives than countries with more generous systems. Nor do countries with high social spending, notably the Nordic states, finance it with confiscatory taxes on capital or high incomes. They look for broad-based sources of funding such as income tax, social insurance and sales taxes. And they are careful to keep their system economically rational; they encourage unemployed workers to search for work in return for unemployment benefits and they raise the eligibility age for pensions as life expectancy lengthens.

Third and most important, social spending, rather than being a ball and chain on the economy, has positive economic feedbacks. It enables a steady growth in consumption from the poor, and it has a strong counter-cyclical stabilising influence during recessions. It can also have an amazing effect on employment participation rates and skill levels. Denmark's universal childcare system, for example, produces two economic wins. It allows young mothers to re-enter the labour market quickly, but it also ensures that young children from low income homes have the kind of emotional, social and intellectual engagement that supports the development of their cognitive skills at a crucial age. All the Nordic countries, with similarly high levels of social spending, report high employment participation rates for both men and women, high levels of educational attainment and a general readiness – because their living standards are ensured – to take risks, retrain and change jobs. The Nordic economies are thus win-win. They enjoy all the benefits of a market-based system of incentives for their dynamic, high-productivity private sectors; and they also enjoy the benefits of high social spending which makes it easier rather than harder for workers to accept the sometimes high cost of economic change.

The most salient fact about today's Western economies is less globalisation, which in any case can only impact on those sectors which trade internationally and which are sensitive to low wages – probably no more than 10 per cent of GDP – and more the general level of affluence that rising productivity and rising property prices have brought. Western consumers are moving up Maslow's hierarchy of needs – away from the simple satisfaction of basic wants and towards wanting their psychological, experiential and emotional needs met, what Maslow calls self-actualisation. They are "apex consumers", a trend that is discernable across the income distribution and in all Western economies. And with the new technologies companies are capable of being much more responsive to these demands – but as described above they need to be close rather than distant from their markets.

This has led to the phenomenon of the Knowledge Economy, now well established in most Western societies and growing fast. Harvard Business School's Shoshana Zuboff and her husband James Maxmin have mapped this new geography of demand in their book "The Support Economy".[2] Contemporary consumers, they say, now want psychological self-determination. Today, requiting core material needs is no longer sufficient for happiness – material consumption is recognised as an inadequate route to well-being. Consumers want their own voice and feel the need for sanctuary. Rewards, argue Zuboff and Maxmin, will fall to those businesses that create value not just from efficiently combining material inputs into outputs, but helping consumers navigate their way through complex choices, and from finding answers to consumers' questions about attaining psychological well-being.

The choices created by affluence are stunning. From running shoes to soft drinks, television channels to magazines, the range of new goods and services is growing at a mind-boggling rate. This multiplicity of choice reflects both today's flexible capacity to produce such customised products and the sophistication of demand in richer societies. But it also reflects the deeper psychological and emotional needs identified by Zuboff and Maxmin. Ronald Inglehart makes a complementary point when he argues that economic growth and physical security have freed affluent societies from necessity, allowing the emergence of post-material values. The new values emphasise autonomy and heterogeneity over tradition and conformity: "Post-modern values bring declining confidence in religious, political and even scientific authority; they also bring a growing mass desire for participation and self-expression ... today, the spiritual emphasis among mass publics is turning from security to significance; from a search for reassurance in the face of existential insecurity to a search for the significance of life."[3] This is reflected in the quest for spirituality and happiness; but also in the quest for goods and services that exactly meet the specifications of particular consumers.

The knowledge economy is the economic response. Soft knowledge is becoming as crucial as hard knowledge in the chain of creating value. By hard knowledge I mean the specific scientific, technological and skill inputs into a particular good or service; hard knowledge, for example, is needed to build a new chip or jet engine, devise a distinctive marketing campaign or invent a new financing vehicle. Soft knowledge refers to the bundle of less tangible production inputs involving leadership, communication, emotional intelligence, the disposition to innovate and the creation of social capital that harnesses hard knowledge and permits its effective embodiment in goods and services and – crucially – its customisation. Their interaction and combination is the heart of the knowledge economy. While some definitions focus narrowly on technology and science, my own extends the conception from high-tech manufacturing to creative industries like advertising and web design, from investment banking to the world of psychoanalysis – and also includes education and health care. On this definition, for example, some 41 per cent of the United Kingdom labour force is now employed in knowledge-based occupations and the proportion is rising rapidly.[4]

Ironically the West feels that its position is precarious when in many respects its advantages in terms of institutions and processes that take decades or even centuries to build are ever more marked. These are essential to the infrastructure that supports the knowledge economy and the creation of hard and soft knowledge. As long as the West recognises and nurtures this asset, its economic strength is guaranteed. There should also be a reality check, especially in the United States. The fear of job insecurity and the reality of mounting inequality should be placed in the context of an American economy with one of the highest employment participation rates in the world. The United States is the pre-eminent world economic power. Its technological leadership in many frontier sectors ranging from ICT to biotechnology is years ahead of its competitors. The strength and depth of its universities are unparalleled. American researchers rank top in terms of papers published and the rate at which those papers are cited by others.[5] American productivity growth is beginning to accelerate again, albeit from a low base. In many respects this is a success story against which the rest of the world benchmarks itself. Even Britain, whose exports of knowledge-based services have trebled between 1995 and 2005[6] and whose universities are second only to the United States, has reason for confidence if it can develop its own Enlightenment soft infrastructure more aggressively.

For the less developed countries it seems a magic circle that is ever harder to break into; if even China is no more than a sub-contractor to the West's knowledge economy, what chance have they to break the Western armlock on the process? And yet the west is hysterically convinced it is the loser – the reason for both the collapse in the Doha round of trade talks and no less than twenty anti-China trade bills in Congress.

The argument is false everywhere you look. Higher inequality is not because of low wage competition driving wages to the bottom or ever higher rewards to the skilled. The relationships are remarkably stable. What has changed is the new super-rich. Ian Dew-Becker and Robert Gordon of Northwestern University show that in the US what has lifted the incomes of the top 10 per cent of the income distribution is the outlandish growth of incomes of the 99.99th percentile – up by 497 per cent between 1979 and 2002 – and not higher incomes more generally. It is the same story in Britain. Twenty years ago the average CEO of a FTSE 100 company earned 25 times the average worker; today the multiple is close to 120 times.

Globalisation is not to blame. In both Britain and America a new business culture has developed in which the share price has become the be all and end all of company activity. Everything is consecrated to raising it, and under the desperately weak and unreformed corporate governance arrangements in the United States and Britain, in effect CEOs have written their own pay deals.

And to deliver the higher share price, they have embarked on the world's biggest ever takeover boom. In hard cash the cumulative value of deals in the US between 1995 and 2005 was over $9 trillion, with $4 trillion between 1998 and 2001 alone. In Britain over the last three years there has been a no less astonishing £500 billion worth of deals. These are the chief driver of job loss, down-sizing and redundancy – and typically for negligible real productivity gains. The Enlightenment obstacles to this in both countries – regulation, a sense of long term ownership, media scrutiny, competition rules, strong trade unions and a belief in equality – have been progressively weakened. Western capitalism is losing its embedded checks and balances, its morality and ultimately its legitimacy.

The more accurate fear in today's world is the concern of less developed countries that they will be cast as low-knowledge subcontractors to the knowledge-rich developed world in a new and more subtle form of colonialism. For middle-income, less developed countries like Mexico or Thailand the problem is particularly acute. They neither have the low wage advantage of China nor a sufficiently sophisticated infrastructure to develop a Western style knowledge economy, and caught between a rock and a hard place their relative per capita incomes have been stagnating.[7] Indeed the Chinese are not immune to this anxiety.

The less developed world needs to develop its own soft Enlightenment infrastructure; and we need to nurture and protect our own rather than throwing it to the wolves because allegedly globalisation makes it too expensive. Talk of more than a billion new cheap wage workers joining the world labour market is alarmist and silly; they will have no more impact on Western living standards than they did forty or fifty years ago. This is a world, remember, in which firms within Canada are twenty times more likely to trade with each other in Canada than with the US – so very similar to themselves. There is a similar story within the EU.

The big point remains. An open global system is of proven universal benefit. The West has to be brave enough to believe in it, demonstrate the advantages, live by the same rules which need to be fairer to the less advantaged and to practice what it preaches. Most importantly the West needs to keep its markets open. What is made can be unmade. If nobody defends globalisation it will cease to be. We need to recapture the argument about globalisation from those who use it to serve their own interests – and to do so fast. The costs of closure would be devastating.

Chapter 32

Cultural Transformations:
Financial Markets and Corporate Governance

*Howard Davies**

T he dotcom boom and bust at the end of the twentieth century, and the accounting scandals on Wall Street tarnished the image of North Atlantic capital markets. Yet they continue their advance around the globe. Can we expect to see Wall Street clones in Shanghai, Mumbai and elsewhere, or will new models be developed?

Most conventional definitions of economic globalisation are founded on the four great freedoms: the free movement of goods, services, labour and capital.[1] Except in the particular circumstances of the European Union, these freedoms are by no means absolute, and even in Europe countries still impose barriers in the way of free movement of people. But of the four, the freedom of capital movement is the easiest to promote, and the hardest to resist.

In a world in which international capital markets are increasingly intertwined, the nationality of capital is often hard to establish. The scale of foreign exchange trading and of cross-border capital flows has escalated dramatically in recent years. In some developing countries, the majority of the banking system is now foreign owned. And while a few countries, North Korea and Cuba among them, continue to resist the temptations of global capital markets, almost all others are linked to them in various ways. Unless a government chooses an extreme autarchic model, it cannot ignore the impact of those markets. Even apparently rigid convertibility and capital controls are no longer fully effective. Countries which seek to insulate themselves can often find that an offshore market in their financial assets has been established, outside their control.

* **Howard Davies** has been the Director of the London School of Economics since 2003. From 1997 to 2003 he was the first Chairman of the Financial Services Authority, Britain's single regulator for the whole financial sector.

This is by no means a bad thing. Global capital markets can provide a helpful discipline on profligate governments. Also, domestic financial reform is often impeded by vested interests and corrupt relationships between the government and financial institutions. And failure to reform the financial sector can be very costly. A recent World Bank report maintains that 'there is now a solid body of research strongly suggesting that improvements in financial arrangements precede and contribute to economic performance. In other words, the widespread desire to see an effectively functioning financial system is warranted by its clear quantifiable link to growth, macro-economic stability, and poverty reduction.'[2] The World Bank's argument is based on analysis which shows that developing countries with relatively deep financial markets in 1960 subsequently grew far faster than those with relatively shallow ones.

A recent paper by a former chief economist of the IMF and others[3] offers a more nuanced assessment, noting that premature opening of the capital account can make a country vulnerable to sudden outflows of funds. But the authors nonetheless conclude that 'financial globalization appears to have the potential to play a catalytic role in generating an array of collateral benefits that may help boost long-run growth'.

But how do we define an 'effectively functioning financial system'? What do we mean by 'improvements in financial arrangements?' These seemingly neutral formulations are typically heavily laden with political and cultural baggage. They conventionally assume that what the French call the 'Anglo-Saxon' model of free and flexible money and capital markets is the 'end of history' in terms of financial development. How far is that assumption justified, and how wise is it to recommend the same end point to all countries in all circumstances? Are there cultural factors which might make it imprudent for a country to adopt the practices of Wall Street and Lombard Street?

A simplified taxonomy of financial systems identifies four distinct models, although transitional arrangements can sometimes leave countries poised uncomfortably between them.

Model 1 we might describe as full state control of the financial system, as practiced in the Soviet Union in the past, in China until the early 1980s, and still today in North Korea. In these cases, while there may be entities described as 'banks' the functions of financial intermediation are carried out by the state, and the state ultimately determines the return on savings and the allocation of capital. There is no role for independent regulation. The massive inefficiencies of these systems, and the huge economic costs involved, are so well understood that there are no examples of countries wishing to move back to such a model, once they have escaped from it.

Model 2 typically preserves some elements of model 1, while injecting some market disciplines. So there are still a number of countries, India being one example, where a lively capital market, with active private shareholders, co-exists with a largely state-run banking system, which allocates capital according to a complex mix of economic and developmental criteria. In these models the roles of financial regulators are sometimes complex and ambiguous. However apparently independent the regulatory body may be, it is inevitably con-strained in its actions when dealing with banks whose sole shareholder is the government on which it also depends for its budget. In recent years most coun-tries operating variants of model 2 have tended to move in the direction of injecting more market disciplines and private capital into their systems, the most dramatic recent example being that of China.

While model 2 might be thought of as an essentially state-run system with elements of market discipline injected into it, *Model 3* is the other way round. Inevitably, there are many sub-variants. One example can be found in Germany where, while the major commercial banks are in private hands, until recently more than half the deposits of the banking system were in entities either owned by regional governments, or by cooperatives protected from competition by statute. And while the stock exchange is now relatively large, controlling blocks of shares in many major German cooperations are tightly held in banks and insurance companies with complex cross-holding structures and interlinked board memberships, reducing the free play of market forces quite considerably. In Japan, similarly, the state-run post office savings bank is huge and the government has explicitly guaranteed the security of private banks in times of economic difficulty, preventing or slowing the restructuring which would otherwise have occurred. There are pressures, both from the mar-kets and, in the case of Europe, from the European Commission, to reduce or remove these state interventions, but they are often strongly supported by vested interests and by public and political opinion. It seems highly likely, therefore, that these hybrid plants will continue to have a place in the flora of the global financial markets.

In *Model 4* we reach the nirvana of the so-called 'Anglo-Saxon' arrange-ments. The principal characteristics of this model are:

- a banking sector exclusively, or almost exclusively owned by private share-holders, with the banks typically held by a large number of shareholders, with no single controlling interest
- large and actively traded equity and bond markets, which are typically larger in total capital value than the assets of the banking system, supported

by efficient clearing and settlement systems, and reinforced by active derivatives markets

- a corporate governance model which gives high priority to the rights of minority shareholders, in which most corporate assets are widely held, and where boards are dominated by independent directors charged with acting in shareholders interests
- open borders with few restrictions on flows of capital, and floating exchange rates a robust system of independent external audit, and powerful independent regulators, whether one as in the UK, or several as in the US, with strong powers over those who transgress the rules.

This is an alluring combination, and there is considerable evidence to suggest that it is the construction which is most likely to promote optimal decisions on capital allocation, allowing as it does the free interplay between different economic actors with different perceptions and sources of information. The availability of diverse funding sources tends to reduce the overall cost of capital for companies, and the variety of investment opportunities open to large and small investors facilitates risk diversification and allows even small investors to achieve significant capital growth.

There is, of course, a dark side. There are plenty of examples of small investors being abused by unscrupulous intermediaries. There is considerable prima facie evidence of insider dealing, even in London and New York, and relatively fewer examples of successful prosecution. There are, in spite of all the corporate governance checks and balances, still opportunities for unscrupulous managers to enrich themselves at the expense of shareholders, and to evade controls. The spate of corporate scandals in the first two years of the twenty-first century, particularly in the United States, demonstrated the potential for abuse and provoked a significant ratcheting up in regulatory intensity through the Sarbanes-Oxley Act and other measures.[4]

In spite of these weaknesses and abuses, many other countries are now moving in this direction. Within the European Union regulatory reform is tending to require countries to converge on a European version of model 4. Italy has recently removed its controls on banking takeovers and Germany is opening up competition in its savings bank sector. Elsewhere, countries in Latin America have sold important parts of their banking systems to overseas interests, as have Turkey and some other Middle Eastern countries. China has embarked on the policy of floating its major banks on the Shanghai and Hong Kong stock exchanges, allowing foreign institutions to take significant equity stakes in the process. The Chinese are also beginning to dismantle controls on overseas participation in their equity market. In the regulatory arena, the international organisations such as the Basel Committee on Banking Supervision and the International Organisation of Securities Commissions (IOSCO) have been strengthening their regulatory standards and the IMF has embarked on a series of financial sector assessments, looking at the extent to which countries meet these international requirements.[5] That, in turn, is causing many people to adopt models of independent financial regulation which owe much to examples in the UK and Scandinavia, in particular. (The US financial regulatory system, with its multiplicity of agencies, is not typically a useful model for other countries.)

But this reading of events is too simplistic. While there is a general trend towards some of the elements of model 4, a closer reading of what is happening in individual countries shows that the outcomes of the changes under way are by no means straightforward. We are not seeing the appearance of Wall Street clones in Asia. It also shows that seeking to adopt elements of this model in environments where other aspects of the political and social culture are incompatible with them can have perverse consequences.

Three examples will help to illustrate this point.

Financial reform in China

In the third decade of their economic restructuring, the Chinese Government have embarked on a far reaching programme of financial reform.[6] The first step was to reorganise the previously monolithic People's Bank, separating out the 'big four' banks and giving them independent statutes and separate identities. The second step involved establishing three new regulatory commissions, for banking, securities and insurance, operating at arms length from both the People's Bank and the financial institutions which they oversee. The next step involved reforms to the equity markets, though they have yet to produce a major change in the performance of the Shanghai and Shenzhen markets, which remain sluggish. Most recently, the authorities have begun to float the major banks on first the Shanghai and then the Hong Kong exchanges. At the same time, foreign financial institutions such as Bank of America, HSBC and the Royal Bank of Scotland have taken significant, though still minority stakes in those banks and, at least in the case of Bank of America and HSBC, have begun what looks likely to become significant strategic partnerships in the longer term. Perhaps in response to these developments, the Chinese banks have adopted board structures which follow the broad lines of corporate governance practiced in the English speaking world, albeit with some particular Chinese features.

These have been remarkable changes, implemented in a very short period of time. But there remain major question marks about whether this reform package will in practice produce a more efficient financial market, operating along the lines of those in New York and London. In an environment in which the state continues to own a dominant stake in the major financial institutions, can the independent directors really perform the role set out for them in the 'Anglo-Saxon' model? Where the principal senior managers of the People's Bank, the regulators and the financial institutions themselves are all part of a single cadre of state functionaries, and are moved from one organisation to another with some regularity, is it possible to create the kind of institutional loyalties, and indeed to promote the kinds of cross-institutional tension on which the British and American models depend for their rigour and vitality? Where the great majority of the entities which issue equities and bonds are wholly state owned, can one expect a lively market to develop, with different sets of expectations of profitability and sustainability? What is the meaning of credit ratings in that environment?

There are no easy answers to these questions, and it seems likely that, for a considerable period at least, the Chinese market will be a 'shadow' form of model 4. The cultural changes needed to breathe life into the new structures created cannot be imposed by administrative fiat, and indeed some of them require political and constitutional changes which are not currently in prospect.

Financial reform in Italy

Within the European Union Italy has experienced more difficulty than other large member states in coming to terms with the implications of a single financial market. On the one hand, the traditions of the Bank of Italy – until very recently – were hostile to the idea that banks themselves might be subject to hostile or contested takeovers, or indeed that Italian banks should be owned by non-Italian shareholders. On the other, the market for corporate control in Italy is very different from that in London, with corporate assets typically traded in large shareholding blocks, and where minority shareholders own insignificant proportions of major Italian corporations. In these circumstances, the British corporate governance model is not obviously appropriate and it may be that different types of regulation are needed.

In 2006 the banking dimension of this conundrum came into sharp focus as the Governor of the Bank of Italy sought actively to prevent the takeover of an Italian bank by a Dutch predator, resulting in a major political and constitutional crisis, which was only resolved when some personal indiscretions made the Governor's position untenable. Even in the European Union, therefore, it is clear that there can be significant tension between the dictates of the model, and the cultural realities on the ground.

Trans-Atlantic differences

We should also note that there is no single 'Anglo-Saxon' model. The regulatory systems of the US and the UK are very different. That difference has been brought into sharp focus since the collapse of Enron, as the United States implemented a series of aggressive reforms. The Sarbanes-Oxley Act tightened up corporate governance and imposed greater discipline on the roles of independent directors on the one hand, and external auditors on the other. While small changes were made in the UK, following the Higgs review[7] of corporate governance, the UK regime remains significantly less intrusive than that in the US. One consequence has been a revival of overseas interest in listing on the London Stock Exchange, as American corporate governance requirements now seem to be excessively burdensome to many international companies.

Why did this change happen, and how did this difference open up between the two centres of free market capitalism?

One partial answer is that the most egregious corporate governance scandals of the turn of the century occurred in the United States. But there are other reasons, too. Politicians in the US have few illusions about the motivations of many of those who work on Wall Street. The first Chairman of the US Securities and Exchange Commission likened the clients he regulated to termites on a dung heap – language which would cause any Chairman of the UK Financial Services Authority to be driven out of town.[8] In the UK, politicians are much more cautious. They worry that tight regulation might cause the highly mobile financial firms who dominate the city of London to relocate to some more favourable jurisdiction. So ministers constantly talk of the need for a 'light touch', for market-sensitive regulation, and indeed media support for tough action by the regulator is conspicuous by its absence. Typically those prosecuted by the FSA or by the competition authorities are portrayed as martyrs, being pilloried by nit-picking bureaucrats who have little understanding of the creative forces of wealth-enhancing entrepreneurs. That is not the case in the US. There, the sight of a billionaire Chief Executive in handcuffs on his way to a Houston court room is greeted with near universal approbation, with the cheers led by the aggressively free-market *Wall Street Journal*.

The second major cultural difference between the US and the UK is in the area of corporate governance. While there are surface similarities between the two regimes – both have boards with independent Directors in a majority – US companies typically operate with a combined Chairman and Chief Executive, while in the UK it is now inconceivable to do so.

This is a very significant difference. And in spite of much evidence that single leaders are more inclined to act in a cavalier fashion (especially if they are allowed to remain in office for decades), majority opinion in the US remains supportive of this model of leadership. While there are growing concerns about huge pay packets for CEOs (memorably described by J. K. Galbraith as 'a warm personal gesture by the individual to himself'[9]) US cultural norms favour the cultivation of corporate 'heroes', who are lauded and revered for their success and wealth – until their feet of clay become impossible to ignore. The British are suspicious of success – the 'tall-poppy' syndrome is prevalent – which makes us more comfortable with a balance of power in the boardroom. Be the CEO never so mighty, there is always a shadowy chairman in the background to bring him low if necessary.

The scandals and excuses of free and unfettered capital markets at the end of the twentieth century clearly demonstrate that they are the least satisfactory means of organising finance and investment in a modern economy, except, that is, for all the other models previously tried. So in spite of the obvious risks, most countries with an ambition to participate in the global economy are adopting versions of the north Atlantic systems.

But capital markets do not exist in isolation. They are influenced by many political and cultural factors, as is evidenced by the striking differences between the practices in the two most closely linked financial centres, London and New York. We can therefore expect a wide range of different models of 'free financial markets' to emerge. In the jargon of this chapter, we will see models 4A to 4Z.

It is likely that in China, for example, the approach to enforcement will be robust. The Chinese are sensitive to criticisms of the corrupt nature of their business culture. Organisations like Transparency International continue to score them poorly on measures of business integrity. Also, the human rights culture in China is, shall we say, less well developed than in the West, making summary justice easier to deliver. There is also little consumer focus in the Chinese regulatory system, unlike in the UK and the US. Furthermore, in the absence of the inter-institutional tensions which characterise the British and American system, the Chinese are obliged to rely more on self-discipline within the state apparatus.

In India, by contrast, individual investors are likely to have a stronger voice, given the longer tradition of individual stock holding. The judiciary are also far more important and independent, and politicians take a lively interest in financial market issues, but focusing especially on the needs of rural development, and the availability of micro finance. India is already developing imaginative cooperative models in that area which go well beyond the local structures in most developed countries. In Russia, the recent assassination of the Head of banking supervision shows that the authorities have to tread very carefully in seeking to impose their will on what is still a 'cowboy' culture in the financial sector. Under President Putin, this is likely to result in more aggressive actions by the authorities, as a tit for tat response. And it is highly unlikely that regulators with the same degree of independence from the executive will be established in Russia in the near term. Cross-country and cross-cultural analyses of financial markets will be a rich field for financial analysts and political scientists in coming decades.

PART VII

The Production of New Desires and Subjectivities

INTRODUCTION

This section discusses how new forms of social identity, as well as new versions of 'older' identities are shaping and renewing relationships between communities, faiths and nationalities. It explores the lines of fracture and analyses the possible changes and transformations that are taking place in identity formation across communities and generations. This section begins with a discussion of the concept of Utopia. **Zygmunt Bauman** conducts a conceptual diagnosis of the concept in contemporary life, and argues that the contemporary moment is characterised by a historically significant cultural shift in the way we conceptualise progress and the search for betterment. Whereas Utopia used to be thought of in terms of a discourse of shared improvement, it now is seen as a venture of individual survival; it is not about rushing forward, but merely staying in the race, and progress is increasingly defined as avoiding being excluded. Bauman draws these thoughts out in an appealing metaphor of different historical periods and different conceptions of human agency.

The essays that follow all explore the changing nature of subjectivity and the understanding of self in the contemporary world and how ideas about the self are connected through ideas of choice and self-fashioning to group identities and identitarian politics. Approaching the issue of desire, subjectivity and cultural transformation from a psychoanalytic perspective, **Darian Leader** forces us to reflect on the possible consequences of a world where the self is seen as perpetually open to change, and asks a series of important critical questions in this regard. Leader asks whether or not an apparent pluralism of the self underpinned by a discourse of choice actually offers new possibilities for social transformation or not. He explores whether new forms of subjectivity based on ideas of autonomy and self determination have altered the ways in which we think about group identities.

Jacqueline Rose addresses the phenomenon of migration and displacement, and provokes us to think about the dilemma of 'subjectivity of the move' through a discussion of the concrete cultural tensions of Israelis and Palestinians. Given the incredible importance placed on the international movement of bodies Rose argues that not enough attention is paid to the accompanying (im)mobility of the mind. Rose entwines her psychoanalytic analysis with a narrative of a displaced Christian Croation turned new Israeli Jew and a narrative of a young French woman whose particular Jewish identity is formed and magnified by the anti-Semitism around her. What is made evident in Rose's analysis is that the reflective capacity of people to reflect on their experiences at a very local level can often have the power to shape larger social and economic transformations. At the same time, Rose's analysis highlights in a very meaningful way how subjectivity is itself subject to the larger geopolitical conflicts that riddle the world: 'nobody is ever playing the part only of themselves'.

Doreen Baingana offers a fictional narrative of a young Ugandan woman newly arrived in Los Angeles, trying to come to terms with her new cultural surroundings among ex-pat Ugandans and conflicting cultural messages. In Baingana's story the protagonist's personal experience of cultural displacement and integration is refracted through the politics of diasporic communities, race, class and individual and national aspirations. Her work demonstrates the complex processes of differentiation and identification that make up a sense of self and the multiple ways in which we construct a sense of belonging. Home is always nearer and farther than one imagines.

In coming to terms with the new emerging forms of power associated with cultural change, **Irit Rogoff** and **Florian Schneider** propose a notion of 'productive anticipation'. They argue that we need to look away from traditional centres of power as defining the questions that have to be asked with regard to political and cultural change. They alert us to focus instead on the new forms of participatory activism that have emerged with globalisation, and they point to the use of diverse cultural spaces which seek recognition, rather than trying to establish new institutional structures that will replace existing ones. Rogoff and Schneider propose an understanding of cultural practices in which culture serves to articulate and create points of access for engaging with, and defining, contemporary issues. They suggest an alternative language through which to engage with contemporary politics and cultural change, and in so doing endeavour to lay out the basis for further creative investigation in this area.

Renata Salecl focuses her attention on the relation between subjectivity and contemporary capitalism. She discusses how capitalist ideologies encourage individuals to think that everything in their lives is a matter of choice and that the possibilities for enjoyment are potentially limitless. This brings with it, says Salecl, a new host of social pathologies, such as the anxiety of being overcome by endless choice and of not being able to achieve an ideal result in every case, or the fact that human relationships increasingly start to mimic relationships between commodities. Salecl argues that Lacanian psychoanalysis gives us the appropriate tools with which to understand these phenomena in that the art of choosing can be seen as traumatic precisely because there is no authority (Big Other) to dictate the conditions of our choice or provide us with guarantees – and when we do create one for ourselves, this is itself a choice in itself, thus leading to the continuation of the choice-induced anxieties that characterise our contemporary condition in late capitalism. Salecl notes that with the lack of traditional authorities in today's world, the anxiety-ridden subject desperately searches for new authorities – which often themselves end up being commodities.

Addressing some of the same concerns as Salecl's essay on the challenges and paradoxes of subjectivity in times of choice, **Susie Orbach** takes the discussion of production of new desires and subjectivities in globalisation to the corporeal – to the level of the body. Orbach encourages us to think about the democratisation of beauty in late capitalism and the ways in which beauty offers 'an apparent entry point that girls and women use to establish identity and belonging.' Discussing beauty as a requirement of modernity, Orbach notes that as our globalised world gets smaller, this democratisation of beauty is exported globally as aspiration. While acknowledging the manifold contradictions and limitations of this phenomenon, Orbach nevertheless points out that it offers an entry point that girls and women use in order to craft identity and situate belonging.

Chapter 33

Living in Utopia*

Zygmunt Bauman**

Lives of even the happiest people among us (or, by common envy-tainted opinion of the un-happy, the luckiest) are anything but trouble-free. Not everything works in life as one would like it to work. Unpleasant and uncomfortable events abound: things and people keep causing us worries which we would not expect them, and certainly not wish them, to cause. But what makes such adversities particularly irksome, is that they tend to come unannounced. They hit us, as we say, 'as bolts out of the blue' – so we can't take precautions and avert the catastrophe, since no one would expect a thunderbolt from a cloudless sky. The suddenness of the blows, their irregularity, their nasty ability to appear from anywhere and at any moment, make them unpredictable, and us defenceless. As far as the dangers are eminently free-floating, freakish and frivolous, we are their sitting targets – we can do pretty little, if anything at all, to prevent them. Such hopelessness of ours is frightening. Uncertainty means fear. No wonder we dream time and again of a world with no accidents. A regular world. A predictable world. Nor a poker-faced world. Reliable, trusty world. A secure world.

'Utopia' is the name which we, courtesy of Sir Thomas More, commonly give to such dreams since the sixteenth century; since the time when the old and apparently timeless routines began to fall apart, old habits and conventions started to show their age and rituals their seediness, violence became rife (or so it seemed to people unaccustomed to unorthodox turns of events), the heretofore omnipotent powers found the emerging realities too unruly and unwieldy

* This essay is based on the Ralph Miliband lecture of 27 October 2005, delivered at the London School of Economics and Political Science, entitled: 'Melting Modernity: Living in Utopia'.

** **Zygmunt Bauman** is Emeritus Professor of Sociology at the University of Leeds and Emeritus Professor at the University of Warsaw. He is the author of over thirty books, translated into many languages – most recently *Liquid Fear* (Polity, 2006) and *Liquid Times: Living in an Age of Uncertainty* (Polity, 2006).

to be held in check and too intractable to be tamed in the old and apparently tested ways. Improvisation and experimentation fraught with risks and errors were fast becoming the order of the day.

Sir Thomas, to be sure, knew only too well that as much as it was a design for good life's setting, his blueprint for a world cleansed of insecurity and fear was but a dream: he called that blueprint 'utopia', hinting simultaneously on *two* Greek words: *eutopia*, that is 'good society', and *outopia*, which meant 'nowhere'. His numerous followers and imitators, however, were more resolute or less cautious. They lived in a world already confident, rightly or wrongly and for better or worse, that it had the sagacity needed to design a preferable, fear-free world, and the acumen required to lift the 'is' to the level of the 'should-be'. And so they had also the gumption to try both.

For the next few centuries, the modern world was to be an optimistic world; a world-living-towards-utopia. It was also to be a world believing that a society without utopia is not livable and therefore a life without utopia is not worth living. [...] Utopias played the role of the rabbit dummy – pursued, but never caught in dog races. Even more that that, progress was a continuous effort to run away from the utopias that failed; a movement away from 'not as good as expected', rather than from 'good' to 'better'. Realities declared to be the 'realizations' of utopias were invariably found to be ugly caricatures of dreams, rather than the things dreamt of. The overwhelming reason to 'set sail' again was the aversion felt to what *has been* done, rather than the attraction of what *may be* done yet ...

[...]

First and foremost, utopia is an image of another universe, different from the universe one knows or knows of. In addition, it anticipates a universe originated entirely by human wisdom and devotion – but the idea that human beings can replace the world-that-is with another and different world, entirely of their making, was almost wholly absent from human thought before the advent of modern times.

Grindingly monotonous self-reproduction of pre-modern forms of human life gave little occasion and even less encouragement to ruminate on alternative forms of human life on earth, except in the shape of apocalypses or the last judgment, both of them of divine provenance. To put human imagination at the drawing board on which first utopias were sketched, one needed the accelerating collapse of the human world's self-reproductive capacity.

To be born, the utopian dream needed two conditions. First, the overwhelming (even if diffuse and inarticulate) feeling that the world was not functioning properly and had to be attended to and overhauled to set it right.

Second, the confidence in human potency to rise to the task, belief that 'we, humans, can do it' – being armed as we are with reason able to discern what is wrong with the world and find out with what to replace its diseased parts, and with the strength to graft such designs on human reality: in short, the potency to force the world into a shape better fit to the satisfaction of human needs, whatever those needs already are or yet may become.

One can say that if pre-modern posture towards the world was akin to that of a gamekeeper, it was the gardener's attitude that could best serve as a metaphor for the modern world-view and practice.

The main task of a gamekeeper is to defend the land assigned to his war-denship from human interference, in order to defend and preserve, so to speak, its 'natural balance'; the gamekeeper's task is to promptly discover and disable the snares set by poachers and to keep alien, illegitimate hunters away from trespassing. His services rest on the belief that things are at their best when not tinkered with; that the world is a divine chain of being in which every creature has its rightful and useful place, even if human mental abilities are too limited to comprehend the wisdom, harmony and orderliness of God's design.

Not so the gardener; he assumes that there would be no order in the world at all, were it not for his constant attention and effort. Gardeners know better what kind of plants should, and what sort of plants should not grow on the plot entrusted to his care. He works out the desirable arrangement first in his head, and then sees to it that this image is engraved on the plot. He forces his pre-conceived design upon the plot by encouraging the growth of the right type of plants and uprooting and destroying all the others (now re-named 'weeds'), whose uninvited and unwanted presence disagrees with the overall harmony of the design.

It is the gardeners who tend to be the most ardent producers of utopias. It is on the gardeners' image of ideal harmony first blueprinted in their heads, that 'the gardens always land', prototyping the way in which humanity, to recall Oscar Wilde's postulate, should tend to land in the country called 'utopia'.

If however one hears today phrases like 'the demise of utopia', or 'the end of utopia', or 'the fading of utopian imagination', repeated often enough to take root and settle in common sense and so be taken for self-evident – it is because the gardener's posture is giving way nowadays to that of the *hunter*.

Unlike the two types that happened to prevail before his tenure started, the hunter could not care less of the overall 'balance of things' – whether 'natural', or designed and contrived. The sole task hunters pursue is another 'kill', big enough to fill their game-bags to capacity. Most certainly, they would not consider it to be their duty to make sure that the supply of game roaming in the forest will be replenished after the hunt. If the woods have been emptied of game due to the particularly successful hunt, hunters may move to another relatively unspoiled wilderness, still teeming with would-be hunting trophies. It may occur to them that sometime, in a distant and still undefined future, the planet could run out of undepleted forests. This is not, however, an immediate worry and certainly not *their* worry; it won't jeopardize the results of the present hunt, and so surely this is not a prospect which a single hunter or a single hunting association would feel obliged to ponder, let alone to do something about.

We are all hunters now, or told to be hunters and called/compelled to act like hunters, on the penalty of eviction from hunting, if not of relegation to the ranks of the game. No wonder then whenever we look around we are likely to see mostly other lonely hunters like us, or hunters hunting in packs which we also occasionally try to do. What we do and see is called 'individualization'. And we would need to try really hard to spot a gardener who contemplates a predesigned harmony beyond the fence of his private garden and then goes out to bring it about. We certainly won't find many gamekeepers with similarly vast interests and sincerely entertained ambitions (that being the prime reason for the people with 'ecological conscience' to be alarmed and trying their best to alert the rest of us).

It stands to reason that in a world populated mostly by hunters there is no room left for utopian musings; and that not many people would treat utopian blueprints seriously, were they offered them for consideration. And even if we knew how to make the world better and took making it better to heart, the truly puzzling question would be, who has sufficient resources and strong enough will to do it ...? Those and suchlike expectations used to be vested with the resourceful authorities of nation states – but as Jacques Attali recently observed in *La voie humaine*, 'nations lost influence on the course of affairs and have abandoned to the forces of globalization all means of orientation in the world's destination and of the defence against all varieties of fear'.[1] And the 'forces of globalization' are anything but notorious for their 'gamekeeping' or 'gardening' instincts or strategies; they favour hunting and hunters instead. Roget's Thesaurus, justly acclaimed for its faithful recording of the successive changes in verbal usages, has every right to list now the concept of the 'utopian' in close proximity to 'fanciful', 'fantastic', 'fictional', 'chimerical', 'air-built', 'impractical', 'unrealistic', 'unreasonable', or 'irrational'. And so perhaps we are indeed witnessing the end of utopia?

Progress, to cut the long story short, has moved from the discourse of shared *improvement* to that of the individual *survival*. Progress is thought about no longer in the context of an urge to rush ahead, but in connection with the desperate effort to stay in the race. We do not think of 'progress' when we work for a rise in stature, but when we worry about staving off the fall. 'Progress' appears in the context of the avoidance of being exluded. You listen attentively to the information that this coming year Brazil is 'the only winter sun destination *this* winter' mostly to know that you must avoid being seen where people of aspirations similar to yours were bound to have been seen *last* winter. Or you read that you must 'lose the ponchos' which were so much *en vogue* last year – since the time marches on and you are told now that when wearing a poncho 'you look like a camel'. Or you learn that donning pinstripe jackets and T-shirts, so much 'must do' in the last season, is over – simply because 'every nobody' does them now ... And so it goes. The time flows on, and the trick is to keep pace with the waves. If you don't wish to sink, keep surfing and that means changing your wardrobe, your furnishings, your wallpapers, your look, your habits – in short, yourself – as often as you can manage.

I don't need to add, since this should be obvious, that such new emphasis on the disposal of things – abandoning them, getting rid of them – rather than on their appropriation, suits well the logic of consumer-oriented economy. People sticking to yesterday's clothes, computers, mobiles, or cosmetics would spell disaster for an economy whose main concern and the condition *sine qua non* of its survival is a rapid and accelerating assignment of sold and purchased products to waste; and one in which the swift waste-disposal is the cutting-edge industry.

Increasingly, *escape* becomes now the name of the most popular game in town. Semantically, escape is the very opposite of utopia, but psychologically it is its sole available substitute: one would say – its new rendition, re-fashioned to the measure of our deregulated, individualized society of consumers. You can no longer seriously hope to make *the world* a better place to live, you can't even make really secure that better *place* in the world which you might have managed to cut out for yourself.

What is left to your concerns and efforts, is the fight against *losing*. Try at least to stay among the hunters, since the only alternative is to find yourself among the hunted. And the fight against losing is a task which to be properly performed will require your full, undivided attention, twenty-four hours a day and seven days a week vigilance, and above all keeping on the move – as fast as you can ...

Joseph Brodsky, the Russian-American philosopher-poet, vividly described the kind of life that has been set in motion and prompted by the compulsion to escape. The lot of the losers, of the poor, is violent rebellion or, more commonly, drug addiction: 'In general, a man shooting heroin into his vein does so largely for the same reason you buy a video' – Brodsky told the students of Dartmouth College in July 1989. As to the potential haves, which the Dartmouth College students aspire to become, you'll be bored with your work, your spouses, your lovers, the view from your window, the furniture or wallpaper in your room, your thoughts, yourselves. Accordingly, you'll try to devise ways of escape. Apart from the self-gratifying gadgets mentioned before, you may take up changing jobs, residence, company, country, climate, you may take up promiscuity, alcohol, travel, cooking lessons, drugs, psychoanalysis ...

In fact, you may lump all these together, and for a while that may work. Until the day, of course, when you wake up in your bedroom amid a new family and a different wallpaper, in a different state and climate, with a heap of bills from your travel agent and your shrink, yet with the same stale feeling toward the light of day pouring through your window ...[2]

Andrzej Stasiuk, an outstanding Polish novelist and particularly perceptive analyst of the contemporary human condition, suggests that 'the possibility of becoming someone else' is the present-day substitute for the now largely discarded and uncared-for salvation or redemption. Applying various techniques, we may change our bodies and re-shape them according to different patterns ... When browsing through glossy magazines, one gets the impression that they tell mostly one story – about the ways in which one can re-make one's personality, starting from diets, surroundings, homes, and up to rebuilding of psychical structure, often code-named a proposition to 'be yourself'.[3]

Sławomir Mrożek, a Polish writer of worldwide fame with a first-hand experience of many lands, agrees with Stasiuk's hypothesis: 'In old times, when feeling unhappy, we accused God, then the world's manager; we assumed that He did not run the business properly. So we fired Him and appointed ourselves the new directors.' 'But', as Mrożek, himself loathing clerics and everything clerical, finds out – business did not improve with the change of management. It has not – since once the dream and hope of a better life is focused fully on our own egos and reduced to tinkering with our own bodies or souls, 'there is no limit to our ambition and temptation to make that ego grow ever bigger, but first of all refuse to accept all limits' ... 'I was told: "invent yourself, invent your own life and manage it as you wish, in every single moment and from beginning to end". But am I able to rise to such a task? With no help, trials, fittings, errors and rehashings, and above all without doubts?' The pain caused by the unduly limited choice has been replaced, we may say, by no lesser a pain, though this time caused by the obligation to choose while having no trust in the choices made and no confidence that further choices will bring the target any closer. Mrożek compares the world we inhabit to a 'market-stall filled with fancy dresses and surrounded by crowds seeking their "selves" ... One can change dresses without end, so what a wondrous liberty the seekers enjoy .... Let's go on searching for our real selves, it's smashing fun – on condition that the real self will be never found. Because if it were, the fun would end ...'[4]

The dream of making uncertainty less daunting and happiness more permanent by changing one's ego, and of changing one's ego by changing its dresses, is the 'utopia' of hunters – the 'deregulated', 'privatized' and 'individualized' version of the old-style visions of good society, society hospitable to the humanity of its members. Hunting is a full-time task, it consumes a lot of attention and energy, it leaves time for little else; and so it averts attention from the infinity of the task and postpones *ad calendas graecas* the moment or reflection when the impossibility of the task ever to be fulfilled needs to be faced point blank. As Blaise Pascal centuries ago prophetically noted, what people want is 'being diverted from thinking of what they are ... by some novel and agreeable passion which keeps them busy, like gambling, hunting, some absorbing show ...' People want to escape the need to think of 'our unhappy condition' – and so 'we prefer the hunt to the capture'. 'The hare itself would not save us from thinking' about the formidable but intractable faults in our shared condition, 'but hunting it does so'.[5]

The snag is, though, that once tried, hunt turns into compulsion, addiction and obsession. Catching a hare is an anticlimax; it only makes more seductive the prospect of another hunt, as the hopes that accompanied the hunt are found to be the most delightful (the only delightful?) experience of the whole affair. Catching the hare presages the end to those hopes – unless another hunt is immediately planned and undertaken.

Is that the end of utopia? In one respect it is – in as far as the early modern utopias envisaged a point in which time will come to a stop; indeed, the end of time as *history*. There is no such point though in a hunter's life, no moment where one could say that the job has been done, the case open and shut, the mission accomplished – and so could look forward to the rest and enjoyment of the booty from now to eternity. In a society of hunters, a prospect of an end to hunting is not tempting, but frightening – since it may arrive only as a personal defeat. The horns will go on announcing the start of another adventure, the greyhounds' bark will go on resurrecting the sweet memory of past chases, the others around will go on hunting, there will be no end to universal excitement ... It's only me who will be stood aside, excluded and no longer wanted, barred from other people's joys, just a passive spectator on the other side of the fence, watching the party but forbidden or unable to join the revellers, enjoying the sights and sounds at best from a distance and by proxy. If a life of continuing and continuous hunting is another utopia, it is – contrary to the utopias of the past – a utopia of *no end*. A bizarre utopia indeed, if measured by orthodox standards; the original utopias promised temptingly the end to the toil – but the hunters' utopia encapsulates the dream of toil never ending.

Strange, unorthodox utopia it is – but utopia all the same, as it promises the same unattainable prize all utopias brandished, namely the ultimate and radical solution to human problems past, present and future, and the ultimate and radical cure for the sorrows and pains of human condition. It is unorthodox mainly for having moved the land of solutions and cures from the 'far away' into 'here and now'. Instead of living *towards* the utopia, hunters are offered a living *inside* the utopia.

For the gardeners, utopia was the end of the road – whereas for hunters it is the road itself. Gardeners visualized the end of the road as the vindication and the ultimate triumph of utopia. For the hunters, the end of the road would be the lived utopia's final, ignominious *defeat*. Adding insult to injury, it would also be a thoroughly *personal* defeat and proof of personal failure. Other hunters won't stop hunting, and non-participation in the hunt can only feel as ignominy of personal exclusion, and so (presumably) of personal inadequacy.

Utopia brought from the misty 'far away' into the tangible 'here and now', utopia *lived* rather than being *lived towards*, is immune to tests; for all practical intents and purposes, it is immortal. But its immortality has been achieved at the price of frailty and vulnerabity of all and each one of those enchanted and seduced to live it.

Unlike the utopias of yore, the hunters' utopia does not offer a meaning to life – whether genuine or fraudulent. It only helps to chase the question of life's meaning away from the mind of living. Having reshaped the course of life into an unending series of self-focused pursuits, each episode lived through as an overture to the next, it offers no occasion for reflection about the direction and the sense of its all. When (if) finally such an occasion comes, at the moment of falling out or being banned from the hunting life, it is usually too late for the reflection to bear on the way life, one's own life much as the life of others, is shaped, and so too late to oppose its present shape and effectively dispute its propriety.

Chapter 34

New Subjectivities?

*Darian Leader**

M any analysts have shared the enthusiasm of philosophers and social theorists in proclaiming the rise of new forms of subjectivity in the late twentieth and early twenty-first century. With the pluralisation of the self celebrated by postmodern thought and the unravelling of subjectivity into the supposedly myriad forms offered by technological and cultural change, it might seem as if this plasticity is the source of new possibilities for transformation. Other analysts, however, have had a less positive view: the self in flux is simply a surface form which conceals a return to the most entrenched essentialist positions and even, in fact, new fundamentalisms.

The lack of unity of the self is, of course, a feature of modernism as such. Whether it is through the structural changes to literary form in fiction or the decentred perspectives of Cubist art, identity is seen as fluid and changing rather than fixed and stable. TV shows today allow paupers to become princes, wives to swap husbands, and the body to become periodically reconfigured through surgical intervention. The self, in other words, is perpetually open to change, and the apparent abandonment of the anchoring points of fixed social roles is given a relentlessly positive gloss. Less bemoaned as a tragedy, this flexibility becomes a source of new and hopeful prospects of transcendence.

Such images of social change pose a number of questions. First of all, we can ask if the widely documented lack of subjective unity is really such a novelty or whether it is simply society's ways of responding to fragmentations that are new. Secondly, we can ask what the social effects are of a discourse that insists

---

* **Darian Leader** is a psychoanalyst and a founding member of the Centre for Freudian Analysis and Research in London. He is the author of several books including *Why do women write more letters than they post?* (Faber and Faber, 1997), *Freud's Footnotes*, (Faber and Faber, 2000), *Stealing the Mona Lisa* (Counterpoint, 2003) and, most recently, *Why do people get ill?* (Penguin, 2007). He has just completed a study of mourning, melancholia and depression to be published in Spring 2008.

on subjective plasticity. And thirdly, we can ask how these problems might affect the way in which we think about groups and communities.

Social historians have given many different accounts of the forging of new subjectivities, from the eighteenth-century split between public and private self to the nineteenth-century subject of constitution and character and the late twentieth-century individual construed as the site of autonomous self-determination, choice and self-realisation.[1] The motors for such shifts have been ascribed variously: religious, economic, legal and cultural. Without focusing on the history of these debates, it is clear that a division is always present in the way that subjectivity has been described: between reason and passion, between instinct and education, between individual and social will, and so on. Although it is a commonplace to claim that it is only today that we have come to experience the self as fragmented, the contemporary Western ideology of selfhood indicates precisely the opposite: that what is new is the idea that there could be a coherent, unified self concealed behind it. Through documenting the loss of this self, it is, in fact, made to exist.

Psychoanalysis, in contrast, has only rarely appealed to the image of a unified self. Fragmentation has been seen more often as both ubiquitous and structural. From Freud's Oedipal theory to Klein's notion of the paranoid-schizoid and depressive positions and Balint's idea of the basic fault, a fundamental lack of attunement between the human infant and the world it is born into is posited.[2] For Lacan, this is both physiological – the fact that infants are always born prematurely, unable to master their motor functions and at a biological level, unfinished – and linguistic, since the register of need is skewed by the demand for love present in linguistic exchange.[3] Our early demand for love, according to all the above thinkers, introduces an out-of-jointness into our relations with others and with the world around us. The attachments dear to psychologists and evolutionary biologists become then, as Slavoj Žižek points out, less primary instincts of the infant than defensive measures that respond to our basic out-of-jointness.[4]

The analytic thinkers listed above all believed that subjectivity is less a given than the result of a process. The process in question would involve the setting into place of certain basic significations: primarily those of prohibition and loss. The negative space created by these limits would in turn produce the subject, and classically this was understood to be made possible by the introduction of a third party: most obviously, the father and the paternal ideal. This intervention would provide a relay to the socio-symbolic universe where symbolic places are firmly inscribed and identity is apparently stable.

If we now turn to our first question – is the lack of unity new or society's response to it? – it could be argued that it is not that the self is any more or less fragmented, but that the relay mechanisms responsible for providing mediation and inscribing it in the socio-symbolic space have been undone. The traditional explanation for this set of problems is to see it as a consequence of the collapse of the nuclear family. But as social historians have questioned the very concept of the nuclear family, another alternative becomes clearer. It is less the loss of the patriarchal father that matters here than the loss of the separate strands of the paternal function. Rather than the implicit separation of the two functions of the father – to prohibit and to encourage – the imperative today is for the father to unite both of these functions in himself. Since this is a tall order, the insufficiency it generates will then invite appeals to mythical figures of the father to do just that. And hence all the new figures of paternity that popular culture never tires of conjuring up.

These figures inhabit a spectrum that moves seamlessly from the criminal to the righteous. The popularity of mafia gang bosses in movie franchises like *The Godfather* and TV series like *The Sopranos* shows how the last refuge of the law-governed family is to be found outside the law. Only here do fathers really exist. On the other hand, when protest groups like Fathers4Justice perform publicity stunts to draw attention to their cause, they adopt invariably the uniforms of superheroes like Spiderman or Batman. The irony here is that these supposed father figures are always in fact sons. In the comics and films that depict their transformation into superheroes, they are shown to be avenging trauma suffered by their parents: their position, however, is not that of adults, which is why they never marry or have children. Here again, the function of the father emerges as a beyond rather than a point that someone can actually occupy.

Social theorists have observed a further problem here. If the paternal relay is no longer effective at allowing a conduit to the socio-symbolic universe, surely, they point out, the socio-symbolic universe is no longer effective either. The symbolic order, itself, they say, is no longer the same.[5] Gone are the inherent vectors of trust and non-reflected commitment that allowed traditional forms of authority to function. The figures of the judge, the politician and the general, for example, are no longer trusted, so instead we turn to Others of the Other. The Opus Dei of the *Da Vinci Code* and all the conspiracy theories that flood the bookshops and the internet are testimony to this multiplication of Others. Any tragic or contingent event like the death of a public figure or an outburst of violence in a school or social institution will spawn countless such theories, despite the efforts of those traditionally assumed to arbitrate on their meaning. Beyond the contingency, someone must be in pulling the strings. The new decentred subject may have freed him or herself from traditional forms of authority but still seeks a new master to be subject to. If the symbolic order is being undone, as it were, 'from the inside', this does not lessen the call to the Other but, on the contrary, strengthens it.

We should still be cautious here in comparing today's devalued symbolic with the apparently robust symbolic of previous centuries. Any detailed study of a given historical period – say, the famous twelfth century with its rise of supposedly new forms of subjectivity – reveals problems which recall in many ways today's so-called 'crisis of investiture'. The symbolic has never been easily incorporated and the Other has never been without its Others. Today, just as before, there is an appetite for subjection, and the offers of free choice that fill the market-place quickly collapse in its shadow. A couple of years ago, I noticed that in the street adjacent to my office a new restaurant was being built. The street already had at least a dozen other restaurants, and I wondered how it would fare given the competitive market which had seen a couple of them close over the previous few months. Its advertising hoarding set out its agenda unambiguously: this restaurant would only serve one dish. Not a daily dish chosen by a chef, as we find in haute cuisine establishments, but just one dish all year round with no possibility of choice. When it finally opened, queues formed every evening stretching right round the block. Given the alternative between several restaurants with wide-ranging menus and hundreds of dishes, the public chose the one restaurant where, precisely, they would have their choice removed and pay handsomely for this privilege.

This appeal to what Slavoj Žižek has called new forms of subjection is echoed in many other phenomena. Much of the protest against the widening in use of surveillance technology like CCTV, phone tracking and computerised retail spending analysis is made in the name of the right to privacy. As authors of our own lives, we resist the intrusive gaze of the Other and its efforts to shape our habits and tastes. And yet beyond this surface protest, there is surely a far deeper anxiety lest this surveillance actually *not* take place. If being watched worries us, the possibility that we are *not* being watched is far more terrifying. The world depicted in *The Truman Show*, in which reality is a stage-managed TV show for the unsuspecting character played by Jim Carrey, is more dream than nightmare. The absence, rather than the presence, of the Other is a far greater risk for us. Those arguments that claim we are living more autonomously now in a society without any Other hardly do justice to these aspects of human subjectivity.

If we turn now to our second question – what effect does society's demand for plasticity have? – we could argue that it moves in the direction of consolidating subjective essentialism. The more that technological and cultural change open up pathways for the free choice of the individual and the more that basic human orientations are seen as an arena for a free process of selection, the more that the unconscious wish to have choice removed becomes powerful. Human life starts with an imbalance: we are helpless and dependent, and we always strive to recreate some form of this imbalance, particularly that inflected with our own, early libidinal choices. No social change can ever affect this early discordance. Yet the more that an emphasis is placed socially on the idea of free choice – backed up by an intrusively available technology – the more that we search for ways to make the Other visible in its discordance. We will do our best, in many cases, to demonstrate our inequality and to create scenarios in which someone or something else has power over us.

This imbalance is reflected in the implicit tension at play in modern ideologies of the self. As Nikolas Rose has observed, the modern decentred and nomadic self is also the self of autonomous choice and self-realisation. Regulatory practices today presuppose the self as an agent of choice and unified biography while at the same time a legion of philosophers and social theorists rob the self of exactly those qualities. The logic that lies beneath this confusion is that the self is actually a project to be realised rather than a point of internal consistency. As Rose has shown, the very capacities to shape our destinies in terms of the goals of self-determination, rational choice and autonomy are effectively rendered impossible by the same agencies that promote these goals.[6]

This deadlock opens up an important point of dialogue between psychoanalysis and social theory. The experience of impossibility is at the heart of analytic formulations of the self, and in particular, the notion of superego. Rather than the devilish figure inciting us to do bad things, the superego is conceptualised – at least in Lacanian psychoanalysis – as a structural consequence of the failure of the symbolic universe to unify itself. At the points where the symbolic universe is unable to negotiate its own origins or to generate any internal consistency, this structural flaw may then take on imaginary forms, to generate the figures of superego described by classical psychoanalysis. Since every society makes demands which cannot be fulfilled, principally through ideals and imperatives that are impossible to realise, these figures will appear in guises that may well vary from one place and time to another. At a structural level, their place is homologous, situated at the points where the symbolic fails to subsume or appropriate itself.

This suggests that although new subjectivities may conceal old ones, there may well be new figures of the superego, in the sense of new imaginary forms of the structural flaw at the heart of the symbolic world. Such figures can certainly be observed, and perhaps never more clearly, than in the field of education. Emotional intelligence classes now take place in many schools in Britain and even infant nurseries have stringent lists of government imperatives that must be completed each day, to produce well-adapted children with social skills who will pose little threat to society at a later date. Staff spend time intended to be with the children in filling out forms, in front of the gaze of the children themselves. These daily reports, designed to lower future risk, become the very instrument of future risk, as the children understand that they are less important than the Other that must be pleased and kept content at all costs. It is less a question of children being well-adapted here than of being well-adapted *for* the Other.

The vociferousness of these directives as to what a human being has to be is remarkable. Many earlier efforts in education were focused more on the idea that education had to suppress or abolish the unruly aspects of infancy and childhood. Today's vision, on the contrary, is less about governing than about allowing expression. It is not about suppressing the voice of the child, but allowing it to truly speak, yet this speaking is almost ventriloquised. It does not mean expressing the internal world of the child but *creating* this internal world through, for example, the language of emotional intelligence that is being taught. As several theorists have pointed out, subjective interiority is colonised and rendered external in today's ideologies of the self.[7]

We see this not only in education but also in the clinical field. Here it is increasingly a question of teaching a new language to the patient as if it were their own true tongue. Interiority is spirited away, as we see in the following definition of the self coming from two contemporary psychoanalysts: 'an authentic organic self image' with the self taken as 'a rational agent with understandable desires and predictable beliefs who will act to further his goals in the light of these beliefs'.[8] This definition could have been lifted word for word from a description of the self in an economics textbook. What we see clearly is how so many of the disciplines which aimed traditionally to explore the interior life are becoming vehicles for market ideologies, where humans are depicted as more or less rational agents determined to increase their stock of goods and access to services.

What seem to be new subjectivities, then, are those emptied out of everything that psychoanalysis put there. The interior becomes the exterior. This means, in effect, a return to mental hygiene, in which exterior deviances are corrected to conform to an ideal of observable normality. Modern mental health doesn't want to know that symptoms involve questions about existence, and therapists are called upon to make specific localised interventions to correct unadapted behaviours. One of the consequences of the paradox of the self explored by Rose – forced to be free by the agencies that prevent this freedom – is that the malaise generated by the inability to satisfy such imperatives turns therapists into the new experts supposed to heal the wound of insufficiency and impossibility. Yet the very framework of their intervention forms a part of the same set of imperatives.

There is a certain irony here in that the only organised and powerful bodies able to resist such trends are the traditional enemies of psychoanalysis: religious groups. We witness here two different versions of the violence of the Ideal, that vehicled by the ideologies of the self generated by market societies and that sanctioned by religion, although it seems clear that many areas of religious life are being reorganised along managerial lines. We could also observe how the violence involved in these visions of the self is disguised by the modern idea of community. Communities are often defined along symbolic lines, with key symbolic traits given priority as defining features. In addition, it is assumed that there is a shared form of enjoyment which binds the community together. Yet what we see in practice is that the notion of community is used precisely in order to cover over the divergence of both symbolic and libidinal anchoring points.

A curious parallel emerges here between cultural and sexual difference. It was widely hailed as progress when John Gray's book *Men are from Mars, Women are from Venus* became an international bestseller.[9] At last, it seemed, men were able to understand that women were different from them. But this covered over the terrifying fact that women were not only different from men but different from each other. In other words, that they were not only from Mars, but Mars, Venus, Pluto, Neptune ... In the same way, it could be observed that not only are Muslims different from Jews, but also different from each other.

A recognition of difference should, of course, encourage dialogue. Differences ought to be articulated and voiced, rather than stifled beneath rigid conceptions of community. But this recognition brings with it another threat. As Slavoj Žižek noticed, the ever-increasing specificity of difference claims serves ultimately to depoliticise social action. As each statement of diversity is reduced to a localised difference claim, these differences lose their value as *metaphors* for political antagonism itself. Instead of a difference claim mattering as a way of representing a more wholesale disagreement, it is treated precisely 'for what it is', thereby removing its symbolic value as a gesture of protest. And subjectivity, in the end, cannot be equated with a set of difference claims, however minimal. As Žižek points out, subjectivity in the analytic sense is simply the refusal of any form of interpellation. The forms of this interpellation will change over time and in different cultures – from the emphasis on moral duties to today's imperatives to be autonomous and self-determining – and the forms of refusal of these imperatives will also change – from Medieval Acedia to the nineteenth-century theatre of hysteria and today's so-called depressive illnesses. But the study of these forms should not obscure for us the difference between the self – construed as the locus of social imperatives and ideals – and the subject – defined as the point of refusal of all interpellation.

Chapter 35

Displacement in Zion: Modern Subjectivities on the Move*

*Jacqueline Rose***

One news item from the stream of disturbing news that pours daily out of Israel–Palestine that I came across a couple of years ago, has particular resonance for thinking about subjectivity in modern times. It was the story of Maayan Yaday and her husband who were hauling their packing cases into their new home in the tiny settlement of Nezer Hazani just as Ariel Sharon was making his announcement that he was planning to make Gaza 'Jew free'. Five years ago, Maadan Yaday had been Croatian and a Catholic, but with a fervour made all the more intense by Sharon's 'betrayal', she insisted that this was her land: Israel and not Palestine: 'Now I am a Jew,' she stated, 'I understand that this is our land.' What was so striking about this story was not however the somewhat surreal nature of that claim, but the misplaced energy with which she defended it. It was precisely *because* she had been Croatian and a Catholic that she understood the danger besetting the Jewish people, with

* This piece is an adaptation from Jacqueline Rose, 'Displacement in Zion' in Kate Tunstall, (ed), *Displacement, Asylum, Migration: Amnesty International Lectures* (Oxford University Press, 2005).

** **Jacqueline Rose** is Professor at the School of English and Drama at Queen Mary College, London. Her research focuses on modern subjectivity at the interface of literature, psychoanalysis and politics, as well as on the history and culture of South Africa and of Israel–Palestine. Her most recent publications are *The Question of Zion* (The Princeton University 2003 Christian Gauss seminars, Princeton University Press and Melbourne University Press, 2005), *On Not Being Able to Sleep – psychoanalysis in the modern world* (Chatto, 2003) and the novel *Albertine* (Chatto, 2001) based on her reading and teaching of the writing of Marcel Proust.

whom her identification was now total. 'In Croatia,' she explained, 'we gave up one piece of land, then they wanted another piece of land.' For 'they', read Muslims. From Croatia to Palestine, history was not so much repeating, as simply reproducing itself: 'The Muslims don't want to stop. They want our souls and they want our blood.'[1]

Although, as it turns out, Maayan Yaday had met her Israeli husband when she was working as a cocktail waitress on a cruise ship, she could still be categorised – and most certainly she sees herself – as a displaced person. 'I was seven years in that war in Croatia [...] But people here will not give up like the Croatians and just leave.' She sees herself, that is, as someone who has been forced, under pressure of intolerable political circumstances, to leave her home. That she so fully enters into a religious and historical identification with the land of her exile may, at first glance, seem to make her untypical. After all, one of the main, explicit or implicit, reproaches against refugees, asylum seekers and indeed most immigrants is that they are not, ethnically and culturally, one of us, that they do not *fit in* (unless they are one of the new Europeans to which Britain is far happier to open its doors). But Maayan Yaday is not alone, I would like to suggest, in her ability – we might call it a need – to transfer one unbearable historical identity into another. Remember that to choose to live in an Israeli settlement is to choose to place yourself more or less directly in a line of fire (it is also a fact that, from the 1930s, emigration to Israel has increased whenever the conflict has intensified).

In December 2003, Daniel Ben Simon of *Ha'aretz* newspaper, wrote a long feature on the rise of anti-Semitism in France and the breakdown of relations between Muslims and Jews. One schoolgirl in a Jewish high school located in a suburb of Seine-Saint-Denis, stated 'Because of the anti-Semitism, I feel I will always remain a Jew in the eyes of others so I want them to know I am proud to be a Jew and proud of Israel.' This is of course a very different case. This French schoolgirl is turning to her Jewish identity as a legitimate response to hatred. Unlike Maayan Yaday, she is, you might say, making a claim on her own past. There is nonetheless an irony here, as the week before Ben Simon had written an equally long feature on the increasingly isolated Muslim community of France (reading them one after the other, very naively I wanted all the people from each article to sit in a room with each other). But this young girl is not pondering what might be wrong with her own country. She is also, like although unlike Maadan Yaday, internally if not literally, on the move. Fear generates an identification – with somewhere else. It travels. And, in doing so, it becomes its own fortress. She wants 'them' to know that she is 'proud of Israel'.[2]

How much does this young French woman know about the nation of Israel? Does she know what the state is perpetrating against the Palestinians in the name of the Jewish people as she speaks? Does she know that 'ethnic transfer' is something now being openly discussed? Today there is a greater displacement and dispossession of Palestinians inside and out of the territories than at any time in Israel–Palestine since 1948. Inside Israel, there is rising unemployment and the economy is close to collapse. The country is in the middle of its worst crisis – in the words of David Grossman: 'more militant, nationalist and racist than ever before'.[3] According to Ben Simon at a meeting in northern France which I attended in 2004, before 2002 a crucial discussion was taking place inside Israel about the relationship between a secular and religious future for the country – or as he put it, between democracy and clerical fascism. Now it has simply stopped. There is no longer any consideration of what kind of a country Israel wants itself, or ought, to be. In response to the second *intifada*, Arabic has been downgraded on the school curriculum, if it is taught at all. And, according to Varda Shiffer, former chairperson of the Israeli Section of Amnesty International, in a discussion on anti-Semitism organised by the Jewish Forum for Justice and Human Rights in London in February 2004, there is – there can be – no discussion of racism. Since racism equals anti-Semitism, it is impossible for a racist to be a Jew.[4]

I would hazard the guess that the schoolgirl in France knows about the suicide bombings. But there was no allusion whatsoever to the conflict in her interview with Ben Simon. She was simply proud of Israel. It is not for me to judge her; indeed I have every sympathy with her predicament. French anti-Semitism is real. Between 2002 and 2004, 2,500 French Jews, double the rate preceding the anti-Semitic incidents, emigrated to Israel. My sense is that should she follow them, her pride in Israel, born on French soil out of fear and hatred, would, like a tiny cherished diamond in the soul, become her claim. And her view of the Palestinians would blend and blur with the colours of the Muslims of France.[5]

These two stories take us to the heart of the matter. In the analysis of the migration and displacement of peoples, we tend to be talking mainly about the physical movement of bodies across boundaries. In a paradox that may well be a defining feature of our age, these boundaries have become at once increasingly mobile or porous (more and more people on the move), and increasingly entrenched (more and more restrictions and policing of borders). To leap for a moment to a very different historic legacy – when Gillian Slovo spoke at the unveiling of the plaque to Ruth First and Joe Slovo in Camden, London, in 2003, she simply contrasted the welcome with which her parents had been greeted in

Britain as political exiles in the 1960s with Britain's policy on asylum seekers today. But in discussion of this dilemma of our times, not enough attention is paid, I want to argue, to the accompanying mobility and immobility of the mind.

What happens to a mind on the move? There is a common truism of what goes by the name of post-modern theory that because people today are caught in so many histories and places, likewise identities, miming the uncertainties of nations, people are dissolving and unravelling themselves. Both Maayan Yaday, and the French schoolgirl mentioned above, suggest that this is not the case. There is a baggage of the mind. When you move across a national boundary, you are just as likely to carry your enemies with you. Nothing, as psycho-analysis will testify, is ever simply left behind. We need to understand the peculiar relationship between the shifting sands of migration and the fortress of the soul. Whenever a door in the world is open, a closet of the heart can just as equally well close (the open door is of course at best a mixed blessing for any-one who feels they have been pushed). In a world of teaming diasporas, how, or perhaps we should be asking *why*, do identities – against the surface drift, as it were – so fiercely entrench themselves?

To answer, or rather ask, this question, I think we need Freud. Although 'displacement' as a term has a particular resonance for the migration of peoples, it is also a key term for psychoanalysis. Interestingly for the purposes of this discussion, when it first appears very early indeed in the work of Freud, it signals the mobility – not to say agility – of mental life. The mind has a remarkable capacity to move its psychic energies from one quantity to another: 'in mental functions something is to be distinguished', writes Freud, in 1894, 'which is capable of increase, diminution, displacement and discharge'[6] (note just how early: three years before *Studies on Hysteria* and close to a decade before he started writing *The Interpretation of Dreams*). It is as if at this point Freud was genuinely taken unawares – pleasantly surprised might be going too far – by the movements, *the creativity*, that the mind is capable of. It is the basic discovery of psychoanalysis that the mind cannot be held to one place. None of us are ever simply the child of the place where we are meant to be. Displacement gives, if you like, a more fluid, dynamic component to the idea of the uncon-scious which famously de-centres man from his own mental self-possession.

But as the idea of displacement progresses in Freud's thinking, it starts to change its hue. It battens down, as it were. It comes more and more to mean substitution. There is something you cannot bear to think about or remember, so you think about or remember something else. A young man recalls, with dis-arming and enchanting vividness, a lyrical moment from his childhood with a young girl in a bright yellow dress in a field. He does not want to remember that the visit to his young cousin was precipitated by the failure of his father's business.[7] I wake from a dream in terror at a burning house, because I do not want to notice the infant, ignored in the general conflagration, who has been abandoned by her mother in a nearby street in a pram. All this happens unconsciously – which is why it works so well. We are the past masters at getting rid of something un-masterable so that we can panic at the threat, which then becomes as inflexible as our own violent response to it. And from displacement to projection requires only one short step. Although I have come half way round the world, in flight from a country where I could never have even set eyes on you, yet you are the one – now, today – who will be answerable for my fear. Whole histories can hang on this turn. From the very beginning, the story of the founding of Israel is full of moments of just such historic displacement. For the early Jewish settlers in Palestine, in flight from the Russian pogroms at the end of the nineteenth century, the barely armed Arab marauders took on the features of mass city rioters buttressed if not incited by the full apparatus of the state.[8] When you move from one nation to another, whatever you find before your eyes, what, or rather who, do you see?

It is one of the tragedies of the Israel-Palestinian conflict that the Palestinians have become the inadvertent objects of a struggle that, while grounded in the possession of the land, at another level has nothing to do with them at all. A struggle which makes of them the symbolic substitutes, stand-ins, 'fall-guys' almost, for something else entirely. I have become convinced that in political conflicts of any obduracy, nobody is ever playing the part only of themselves. It goes without saying of course – although this too is often a consequence of such primordial, enduring, mostly unspoken displacements – that nobody is ever in the right place.

But if Israel–Palestine has a particular resonance in this context, it is because of the immense complexity with which it surrounds the issue not only of displacement but that of rights. Two displaced peoples – the Jewish people and the Palestinian people – the latter forced (800,000 of them) to leave their land so that the former can have a home (one displacement leads to another). Two peoples claiming the right to national self-determination, each one supporting that right with another one – the right of return – which definitively pulls the ground from under their antagonist's claim, saps the very foundations on which the first claim rests. The law of return stipulates that any Jew, but only any Jew, throughout the world, including one who was only a matter of months ago a Croatian and a Catholic, has the right to settle in Israel. The right of return of the Palestinians demands that the Palestinians have the right to re-enter a

land in which the majority of citizens believes that to allow this would demographically, as well as politically, destroy the nature of the state (although in fact
only 2 per cent of Israelis live on refugee land).[9] Add to this the fact that,
although the clash is between two peoples, the right to the land is justified on
radically discrepant grounds or histories – one biblical, going back 2000 years,
one based up to 1948 on a far more recently lived connection between the
native and her soil. In fact even that is a simplification – for the earliest Jewish
settlers in Palestine, the right to a state would emerge as much out of the up-
building of the land as out of the mists of time. They were careful to insist that
theirs too was a lived connection and that it was this, as much as biblical history,
which justified their claim. 'It was the service to the soil,' Chaim Weizmann,
first President of Israel, wrote, 'which determined the right in our favour.'[10]

'I belong here.' The statement is almost impossible to contest – grammati-
cally it consists of a shifter ('I'), a performative ('belong') and an indexical sign
('here'). It depends for its truth on the moment of utterance, even if it claims an
eternity of time. This is my land because this is where I see myself. Now and forever. We have entered the region of the heart. Between two claims for national
self-determination there cannot in fact be any arbitration at law. This is
Yeshayahu Leibowitz, the famous Israeli philosopher and dissident, in his 1976
article, 'Rights, Law and Reality':

> Fortunate is the people whose conception of its tie to its country is recog-
> nised by others, for should this connection be contested, no legal argu-
> ment could establish it [...] Considerations of historical "justice" are
> irrelevant. The conflict is not one of imaginary "rights". Nor is it a clash
> between "Justice and Justice" – since the legal (or moral) category of jus-
> tice does not apply.[11]

What, we might ask, does it in fact mean to say that nationhood is a 'right'? In
an Amnesty lecture in 2004, Bhikhu Parekh argued that some of the most important exchanges and responsibilities between individual subjects – of loving and
caring for example – cannot fall under the mantle of rights or only do so at the
gravest cost.[12] He was talking about individuals and the clash between the concept of rights and another very different vision of ethical or virtuous life. The
problem posed by Israel–Palestine is different. This is a situation where the idea
of rights can be seen tearing itself apart from the outside and from within.
Nationhood is not a right, it is a claim; agonistic, most likely to destroy another. Self-determination is a myth, because as a right it depends on the other's
recognition. The worst delusion of all perhaps is that of national selfhood. Not
just because no nation in the twenty-first century, nor indeed the twentieth, can

be anything other than an in-mixing of peoples and hence selves (Israel, with its demographic fears for its future as a Jewish state, is in full panicked confrontation with that reality as I speak). But because, the idea of self-sufficiency, in the world of nations, is a complete myth. This is just one of the very many ironies of Israel's original constitution as a nation-state. 'Paradoxical as it may sound,' Hannah Arendt wrote in her 1944 essay 'Zionism Re-considered', 'it was precisely because of this nationalist misconception of the inherent independence of a nation that the Zionists ended up making the Jewish national independence entirely dependent on the material interests of another nation.' Theodor Herzl, author of *Der Judenstaat*, the founder of political Zionism, 'did not realise,' she wrote, 'that the country he dreamt of did not exist, that there was no place on earth where a people could live like the organic national body he had in mind and that the real historical development of a nation does not take place inside the closed walls of a biological entity.' 'As for nationalism,' she remarked, 'it never was more evil or more fiercely defended than since it became apparent that this once great and revolutionary principle of the national organisation of peoples could no longer either guarantee true sovereignty of people within or establish a just relationship among different peoples beyond the national borders.'[13]

To recap then. No national 'right', as in organic and pre-given. No self-determination, as in self-sufficiency, of nations. To which we can add, no singular self-hood. Rights, as John Rawls has stressed, although without drawing the implications for his own theory, relies on a fully rational, monochromatic, conception of the person. I must know who I am when I claim them. But if the mind is not its own place? If my claim delves into the depths of my own history, trawling through my dreams and nightmares, to create its own law? The image we have of displaced persons tends to be cast in terms of endurance, survival, the fierce adherence of all human creatures to their own life. It bears no investigation of inner worlds. I suggest instead we see peoples on the move at least partly as sleep-walkers, trundling through each others' dark night.

Chapter 36

Lost and Found*

Doreen Baingana**

I am here, but I am not. Flying on a plane from Uganda to New York to Los Angeles doesn't really take you there. The United States of America. The desert of Los Angeles, cut across by long wide strips of gray asphalt that are too smooth to be real. Not a bump is felt as you cover distance; it's hard to tell you are even moving. As far as I know, roads have potholes and car rides are often treacherous. But here, they are flat and endless, matching the hard, high, indifferent rocks scattered with small dry shrubs like mean little favors. Los Angeles. I'm trying to put my feet firmly on the ground. I'm trying to be here.

I am in Los Angeles, not any other American city, because my cousin Kema lived here, she went back home a month after I arrived. I didn't know her before, but we immediately assumed affinity because of shared blood. Kema came to America in her late teens to study, and spent almost all her adult life here. But despite her Americanness, I could see home in her; she shared her family's sharp wit and rather mocking smile.

On my first day in L.A., Kema took me on a drive-by tour through Sunset Boulevard, the lush mansions of Beverly Hills, the endless, flashy Wiltshire

* This piece is adapted from a story in the book *Tropical Fish: Stories out of Entebbe* (Amherst: University of Massachusetts Press, 2005).

** **Doreen Baingana** is a writer from Uganda who lives both there and in the United States. Her short story collection, *Tropical Fish: Stories out of Entebbe*, won the Commonwealth Prize for First Book, Africa Region, in 2006, and is a finalist for the Hurston-Wright Prize for Debut Fiction, 2006. The book was published in 2005 by the University of Massachusetts Press after it won the Associated Writers and Writing Programs (AWP) Award in Short Fiction. It has been republished in South Africa. Baingana's stories have been nominated twice for the Caine Prize for African Writing, in 2004 and 2005, and won the Washington Independent Writers Fiction Prize, 2004. (She has also published essays in American journals, the *Guardian*, UK and Ugandan newspapers. She studied law at Makerere University, Uganda, and now teaches creative writing and works for Voice of America radio.)

Boulevard, and back to downtown L.A. to the cardboard tents, the scattered misery, trash and desperados of skid row. I was still jet-lagged and fatigued after almost two days of flight from Uganda, so all I absorbed was a surreal sequence of enormous, shiny images and grayish dirty despair rushing past the car window. Kema's voice-over alternated between admiration, envy, scorn and pity. I was stunned by the absurdly exaggerated opposites only a few miles from each other. More shaken than your typical tourist, I think, because I had nothing to compare such opulence with, however garish some of it appeared later. And, I thought I knew what real poverty looked like. Skid row? In my jet-lagged state, I thought I was in a nightmare back home because almost all the pitiful rejects were black like me. But we don't have skid row.

"See the Banyankore of here?" Kema warned. "This could happen to you too if you don't work hard." She switched to her American twang, "Wake up, honey, and smell the *black* coffee!" and laughed. She didn't really think someone like *me* could end up with a dirty cardboard box for a house; end up a heap of rubbish lying in the street, did she?

Kema did everything to help me settle in; talked to her boss, who got me my first job, and introduced me to her friends, who are all Africans. They live the southern Californian suburban life while saving money to build houses back home, educate their kids, make money, live well, be happy. What's so wrong with that? They are nice people, all shiny with cream and fatty food, and they welcome new Africans with open arms, those who are educated and ambitious, that is. In America, we're Africans abroad: generic, lumped together, black. Our voices are whiny and nasal too, but we can't erase the African lilt. Our children are American, though: noisy, demanding, insolent, confident, fat, American.

Every weekend there is a gathering at one house or another, and we talk about home. When we were there last, five years ago, ten, even twenty. But we aren't going back for good any time soon, oh no, who wants to live with the insecurity, the rule of army men and guns, the *magendo* – black market – a tough way of life. Here, we have grown soft and comfortable with steady salaries we can live on; why go back to desperately running around chasing deals, sweating in that dusty heat? Someone, another recent arrival, tries to protest. He says that was in Amin's time, during the economic war way back when. Now, now we have Mzee Museveni. A political debate erupts, in which we compare the different short-lived regimes, the deadly, musical-chair *coups*, rigged elections and corruption scandals.

"Obote I wasn't so bad, and it could have been even better if he had been given a chance during his second regime."

"Obote II? He was an alcoholic by then; he should never have come back!"

"No, moreover the Baganda hated him and they wanted a Muganda in power. Remember, *twagala* Lule/*oba tufa, tufe!*" Laughter rang out, which helped diffuse the rising anger.

"Daddy?" One of younger kids tugs at her father's sleeve. "What does that song mean?"

"See, Sharon? Didn't I want to teach you Luganda and you said 'It's weii-irrd.' " He imitates her accent, then laughs with the others while hugging her to him. "We had a president called Lule for a few months, and after he was removed, the Baganda protested. They took to the streets singing and shouting, 'We want Lule/if we're to die, we'll die!' "

The little girl continues staring up at her father, still puzzled. "But whyyyyy, Daddy?" Back home, no child would have dared interrupt adult conversation.

"Listen, darling, I'll explain it all later, okay? It's a long story."

"Darling"! I am shocked. Since when did Ugandan fathers call their daughters "darling"?

The debate shifts to whether Asians, as we call Indians, should have been allowed to return to Uganda after all these years. Amin expelled them in 'seventy-two. This is always a hot topic. "Let's be honest, Amin saved us from the Asians. You can call him a murderer, a cannibal – " [loud laughter] "What not, but he did that one good thing." The group laughs again, some in assent, some in refusal.

"But the Indians were Ugandans –"

"With British passports!" More laughter, grunts and head-shaking.

"Right or wrong, we suffered for it. Look what happened to our economy – it collapsed completely!"

"That was because all the Europeans and so on pulled out, stopped aid, trade. What country can survive with no foreign trade, no investment?"

"Yes, yes, blame it on someone else. It's easier that way." Laughter.

"But now they're back, these *Bayindi*!"

"Ah, but now they've learnt. They are more humble, careful."

"What careful? Their money does the talking. See how they bribe the ministers!"

"Are the ministers forced to take the money? And what Ugandan business-man doesn't bribe?"

"Then the *Bayindi* are very Ugandan!"

On and on go these debates about what really matters to us. We escape our American lives on the fringe and take center-stage again. At these moments, we're so far away, we might as well be at Sophie's Bar and Bakery in Wandegeya, sitting on wooden stools out in the open, eating roast meat and drinking Port Bell beer, swatting away the flies, washing away the day's sweat with sundowners. It feels that good.

"Daaaaad." The child's petulant cry swiftly brings us back. We are here in America, and we all need our reasons to stay, despite our vows not to die here, oh no! Alone in an apartment where your body may rot for days and no one will miss you? Here, where no one knows you even existed? Imagine ending life in a retirement home, where you have to *pay* someone to look after you, as if you have no children, no family? What a disgrace! We are going back home in two years; home is home. Five years maybe. No, for us, our kids have to get into college first – you know the schools at home. When I finish my house in the village; when I've set up my business; when I get the UN job I've been promised. If, when, if when, but in the meantime ... oh here's the food, let's eat.

We rally round the barbecued chicken, limp salads, meat stew and rice, *posho* made with semolina flour. It's the same food every time; not quite home food, but close enough. It's better than sandwiches or macaroni or some other fake food, and so we eat. The talk subsides to contented murmurs and grunts of appreciation. Afterwards, the women clear up, bustling up and down, their big hips swerving heavily with each move, as purposeful and confident as the huge swathes of bright-colored *kitenge* wrapped around them. What a warming sight to see. I don't help much; I prefer to watch. I imagine the single men canceling me off their lists, not to mention my hips aren't big enough.

My cousin, trying to help, makes a point of introducing me to the single men. Their dark coffee skin glows with health, they have on the right casual, loose-fitting jeans, sandals and brightly patterned African shirt, and have a college education, of course. I see fierce ambition rising like two horns from the top of their painfully neat haircuts. This agenda for success is not complete without a wife.

Kema pulls me over and warmly tells Bosco, Katende or Wilberforce, "This is Christine, my cousin, she's just arrived."

"Oooh, you're welcome." A moist limp handshake, a mere slipping in and out.

Him: "Christine who?"

Me: "Mugisha."

"Is it the Mugisha who was minister in Obote II?"

"No."

"Ohh ... which one?"

"We aren't known." Why am I being so rude? His smile stiffens, but he tries again.

"Where are you from?"

"Entebbe."

"Mugisha? Entebbe ... ?"

"We're from Ankole." I should say I am Rwandese or from the north, a Kakwa, and watch him disappear like the wind.

"Oh, I see ... so you must know the Mutembes, don't you? The ones of Mutembe Plastics?"

"No."

Mister Eligible-Social-Snob is fed up. His eyes rove around the room, thinking, "Next!" Luckily my cousin, who is as smooth as butter, eases him away. I should tell the next one, point blank: "I'm a nobody." The men need a point of reference, which may be what I am escaping from. And yet who, what am I apart from my sisters, my extended family, the schools I've been to: Gayaza, Makerere, my religion, my clan, my tribe? That's what I don't know.

But, at least I can drink and dance. What else do you do after eating, after covering all the usual topics of conversation, now that a few beers or whisky is swimming in your blood? You dance. The music is turned up, because the fast, syncopating, guitar-energized Congolese music is another way to go back home. It's a relief from battling the alien world outside that envelops us the minute we step outside our doors. We cluster together and dance to break away from the self or non-self we have to be at work, among foreigners, in the white world (even though they are blacks there). It's a difficult act, a tiring one. So why not let the wails of *lingala*, well-known oldies played again and again – Franco, Papa Wemba, Kanda Bongoman – why not let them take us back to that safe, *known* place. Sure, we left it willingly, and it wasn't heaven, though nostalgia and alienation seems to make it so.

We know the *dhombolo*, we love doing it together, churning our waists and hips, arms flung up in the air as if this will save us. But, I tire soon. Some of us ("*oba* who do they think they are," I imagine the others thinking) danced to more pop music, as we called it, than Congolese hits back home. Most of them were Black American hits actually, not white-*zungu*: Michael Jackson, Kool and the Gang, The Commodores. To be honest, my nostalgia now is largely borrowed, that's why it doesn't last long. The memories aren't mine. Perhaps I haven't been here long enough to feel African. I admit, I am not comfortable with the idea that these Ugandans, and Africans in general, are more *me* than anyone else.

After a month of weekends at these afternoon parties, I am sick of this game of going back home. I have just arrived; I want to be here, in Los Angeles, in America, whatever this means. To try and crack this new code if I can.

*   *   *

I learn about poetry readings in the *LA Weekly* and I wonder what that's all about. Perhaps I could make a friend or two. They are held at a coffee shop in Old Town, Pasadena, which also is close by my apartment, so why not? I decide to go one Wednesday night after working out at the gym. I have joined the army of those who insist we can and will reshape our bodies, who cares what God intended? Aerobics is fun, it's dancing really, the music is funky and fast, and small talk isn't too hard with naked women strolling casually around in the bathroom, their breasts drooping nonchalantly.

The energy after exercise makes me feel like a conqueror, as I drive to *LA Cafe*. It's a narrow, drab bare-brick room lined with old couches. A few metal tables and chairs in the center face a small podium. The room is shabby, smoky and dim, a comfortable hiding place to watch others, and to dream myself onto the stage. The room is full of shaggy-haired young people dressed like crazy people, all in black with chains, hooks and rings, or in long flowery shirts and what I come to learn are "ethnic" print blouses. They wear heavy black boots, ragged sandals or go bare foot. No one looks too clean, except me, of course. What do my clothes, my face say? That I work as a temp? I am African, or an immigrant, an alien, or simply black? All and none of the above. Then how should I say, I am me? But, I do like these people, this cult of carelessness, because there is no way they would know anything about me, or would be able to judge me, even if they cared to. And, I can never be who they are, so I don't even have to try. Nor do I want to be; there is nothing I need to be, here. Being lost is freeing.

The next Wednesday at the cafe, two girls come up to my table and ask if it's free. I nod, not wanting my accent to give me away, to lead to questions. I shrink into myself a little, but one of them insists on talking to me. She says her name is Light Feather and she is Native American. I hadn't asked. Her friend, Debbie, grunts. She is fat, with bulging cheeks and narrow, squashed-in eyes. She smells of something, old food maybe, I can't tell. Light Feather is just like her name, very small, thin and pale. One of her eyes is weak, unfocused, the cornea moves around unpredictably. Feather tells me everything about herself, her wild eye making the story stranger than it is. She was born in Nebraska, but her and her brother ran away to California to escape her parents, who belonged to a religious cult. I look at Debbie for confirmation. She shakes her head and turns the edges of her thin lips down. Why is this stranger telling me lies? Why is she even talking to me? I thought we are here for the poetry.

Light Feather can't stop talking; no wonder she has such a silent friend. She says too many people think she's white so she has to dye her blond hair brown. Debbie grunts. Light Feather asks where I am from, where I live, how I can afford to live in Pasadena, a new immigrant like me. She doesn't wait for my answers, but keeps saying she likes how I talk. "Your voice is like a song, do you know that? I'm sure you sing well, what black doesn't? Just like us Indians, you people are favored by the gods. That's why indigenous people suffer." Debbie grunts again, but remains expressionless. She seems to be half-asleep, and wheezes like a steam engine.

To stop Feather's stream of words, I ask, "Did you grow up on a reservation?"

This time Debbie interjects flatly, "She's not Indian."

I look at Feather. She flips back her long brown hair impatiently, and raises her high voice. "People are in denial here in America, you'll learn, you'll see. I accept my past; I know I'm Native." Debbie shrugs, rolls the little there is of her eyes and turns away. She isn't bothered enough to argue.

I say I'm leaving, but Feather insists I listen to her poems first. On stage, her thin voice strains even higher. She recites a poem about the long strong heritage of her people. The crowd is kind; we clap like we do for everyone else, and she blushes triumphantly. Her second poem has many animals in it, including a clever coyote, a strong eagle, a spirit bear. She does a little jig, making a circle, and ends with a loud whoop. The clapping is less enthusiastic. I feel pity for her, and clap longer than I mean to.

Back at the table, Feather, flushed from dancing, tells me I must write an African poem. Americans have no clue about Africa and native people in general, she says. It's our duty to set them straight. What do I know about Africans, I only became one after I left, I think but don't say. I am a Munyankore, but who here knows what that is, or cares? Feather preaches on in the dim light, long after the poetry reading is over. The constant refrain is her people, our people, native people, evil white people. Her weak eye seems to accuse me also, and yet I thought we were on the same side! Her good eye is kind, which is even more disorienting; two contradictory expressions on the same face. Everything Feather says is mingled with Debbie's smell and heavy passivity; she sits there like a log, like a big fat old dog. What is she thinking? I interrupt Feather abruptly, and, as if coming up for fresh air, ask Debbie if she writes poetry too. She shrugs and looks away. Thankfully, this silences Feather for a second, and I grab the chance to quickly say bye. Promising to come back, I escape.

Strange, strange, strange, is all that's passing through my head on the way home and as I lie in bed trying to sleep. My mind trails to the last poet, who exalted her menstrual cycle, calling it redder than a communist, and I burst out giggling, louder and louder, almost hysterical, alone in the dark. Thinking of Feather and Debbie slowly sobers me up. There are so many of us who are lost, so many.

That whole week I am unsettled inside. All my ways of thinking are re-arranging themselves in my head. What other people may be thinking about me recedes, as I grasp for ... for what? I decide to write a poem, to clarify things, to try, anyway. Not about home, no. Maybe something about the adventure of being lost and what I can find.

The next Wednesday I am at the cafe early. I sign up to read my poem before I change my mind. My palms are already sticky with sweat. On the small stage the stark light is terrifying. My piece of paper trembles to match my voice, but I read on, reminding myself: no one knows me here, no one real will ever know.

> ...
> have body, will travel
> through the maze of my unbelief
> to the stone wall of my yearning
> for more.

The applause could have been a little more lively, I think. I'm not even sure they heard what I said. The accent I can't escape. It is a desperate poem, but that's okay, I have done it. Light Feather likes it, and when I sit back down, she strokes my back reassuringly, smiling into my face. I've learnt to sit on her "good" side. She says, "Soon, you'll write about your people; the ancestors will speak through you. Your people need a voice, you know." I'm not so sure they don't have one, but in my euphoric state I agree. Later, we all go to smelly Debbie's house, also in Pasadena. We eat Big Macs, and then crunch granola down with ghastly red wine.

We keep meeting on Wednesdays at the cafe, and then on other days too. Light Feather has a softness, an innocent vulnerability I like to be around. She really believes I'm like her. I can imagine what Africans here would say if they were to meet us together: "Surely, Christine, if you want white friends, can't you pick better ones?" That's part of her attraction.

Feather walks people's dogs for a living, she says they speak to her. She lives in one small room and a tiny yard, what at home we would call a boys' quarter. She has five or six cats, I can't tell, they completely fill her wreck of a room. The cats are furry and huge, and slink or spread all over us like physical music. Their fur floats in streams of sunlight. We hike up the Altadena hills often, where we drink cheap wine, write and read poems, and shout them out to the smog of Los Angeles. Feather teaches me Pueblo chants and dances. "This is my people's land you know," she says. "All this," sweeping her arms wide, around.

"Mine too," I say. What the hell.

Chapter 37

Productive Anticipation

Irit Rogoff * *and Florian Schneider* #

"The subject is the boundary of a continuous movement between an inside and an outside ... If the subject cannot be reduced to an externalized citizenship, can it invest citizenship with force and life ?" (Negri to Deleuze)[1]

The visible modes of power, those invested in institutions of governance, bureaucracies, multinational corporations, international agencies, military-industrial complexes, media monopolies etc. are relatively easy to locate and characterize. But what of emergent configurations of power? Those not sustained by permanently constituted institutions, and therefore less easily discernible, are more difficult not just to locate and characterize, but also to imagine as being meaningful. What we are attempting is not just a shift away from institutionalized politics but also away from a principle of equation which is the heart of a representational mode of politics, a mode in which a set of realities is paralleled by institutional and other representations to which they are seemingly equal.

Instead of attempting an alternative mapping of forms of power just "coming into vision" we propose a notion of "productive anticipation". This

* **Irit Rogoff** is Professor of Visual Culture at Goldsmiths College and Director of AHRC 'Cross Cultural Contemporary Arts'. She publishes on conjunctions of critical theory, contemporary arts and contemporary politics. She is author most recently of *Terra Infirma – Geography's Visual Culture* (2001) and has recently curated 'De-Regulation *with the work of Kutlug Ataman*' (Antwerp, Herzylia, Berlin 2006/7) and 'Academy – Learning from the Museum' (Eindhoven, 2006).

Florian Schneider is a filmmaker, writer and research activist in the fields of new media, networking and open source technologies. He has organised the new media festivals *Makeworld* (2001), *Neuro* (2004) and *Borderlineacademy* (2005). His latest project is entitled *Dictionary of War*, which is a collaborative platform for creating 100 concepts on the issue of war, to be invented, arranged and presented by scientists, artists, theorists and activists.

constitutes a state which is both reflective and participatory but not one of indications and navigations, not one that tries to didactically point to where one might look and what one might see. This processual mode of observing and narrating a perception of the politics we are all mired in, this mode of political "becomings", is one that we feel exemplifies "contemporaneity" and is exemplary of a politics which is, as Rosi Braidotti might say, "transposed" from one modality to another.[2] It might also require us to produce and inhabit a series of fictions which serve as a location populated by new modes of politics, given that the so called realities around are not quite able to host, or allow legibility to what we are in search of. So in the first instance we need to see what might be out there, of how it is configured when it takes the form of so called "cultural" activity rather than so called "political" activity. Subsequently we might try our hand at seeing what kind of vocabulary these activities have generated in order to think through a coming politics.

Our inquiry focuses on the ways in which newly configured notions of "activism" and "participation" are providing alternative entry points and strategies of taking part; in politics, in culture, in life in general. To that end we are proposing a series of terms which do not offer an analysis of a given set of conditions, but rather they are "operational", describing an emergent operative mode of "being in the world". These terms include "access", "singularity", "collaboration", "activism" and "participation" and they work to anticipate an active modality and the inhabiting of a series of active positions in public life that cannot be captured by the existing of how we identify ourselves in the public sphere.

We are obviously aware that there is a proliferation of activisms at present – we understand their issues, we understand the relations between the groups and movements. But do we fully understand how this proliferation has changed our notion of access to the political? It is here, in the reflection regarding access that activism and participation become a complex continuum of modes providing a relation to access; to institutions, to world events, to one another. This leads us to ask what is "urgency" and how does it differ from "emergency", to an understanding that "emergency" is always a response to a set of immediate circumstances while "urgency" is a recognition of the systemic shift in relations between the constitutive elements of the world we live in. It is at this point that one can begin to chart relations between older groups such as "Amnesty International", "Greenpeace" and "Doctors without Borders" to more recent alter-globalization movements and many others. Equally this produces a frame to understand why professional groups such as doctors and architects, for example, have begun intervening in the political sphere from the perspective of what they specifically know and understand.

At the heart of our argument is an attempt to "look away" from the centres of power as defining both the questions that are being asked and the means we might have at our disposal to respond to these. Instead we want to focus our attention on the proliferation of "activist" and "participatory" manifestations around the globe. It is becoming clear that these are marking the desire of people to actually articulate their own questions and find ever more inventive modes of taking part in the processes that are determining their lives. Equally, that they are doing so in "minor gestures" that don't pretend a wholesale change but manifest an engagement and an involvement through series of minute transformations. It equally exemplifies the very significant shift between analysing long lines of developments and acting in the moment.

In addition we have become interested in the exceptionally manifest and performative quality of this new sensibility: The sheer numbers of people marching, demonstrating, writing statements, making their way to the World Social Forum, banding together on the internet, communicating ferociously, figuring out alternative ways of educating themselves for contemporary needs that are unfathomed by institutions. The new uses of cultural spaces such as art institutions, music festivals and international exhibitions as communicative forums – all these have clearly moved these activities away from the traditional model of "ideological protest" and towards an understanding that there are possibilities for insisting that "one is in the world" and "one is heard" without rushing to establish new institutional structures that will replace the old ones.

The blurred boundaries of what it is and what it means to be inside or outside and the resultant instability of the identities involved in making and remaking the world, have led us to shift our attention somewhat from new categories of identity such as global citizenship. Instead the very concept of "investment" moves centre stage making clear that it is not the inhabitation of power but the processes of intermingling subjectivities with it that is at stake. This "investment" does not imply the outlay, expenditure or the expansion of exiting structures. Instead it functions in an "anticipatory" mode, which means the translation of a general unease into a series of potentialities. Within this anticipatory mode, procedures are suspended, operating modes are speculative, issues are just on the cusp of articulation, analysis is not yet possible. In this mode the subject does not have a clear-cut position or a stable place from which to think its position and therefore acts in a speculative mode. The visible indicators of change are evolving in less formal and structured ways which are sometimes more difficult to discern since their manifestations are at times ephemeral and contingent. What concerns us here is the drive to appropriate the right to make changes, the right to transform the protocols by which subjects take part in the culture of politics both locally and globally. Equally it is to address questions of how people give themselves permission to voice positions when they have not been asked to do so, how they evolve new strategies for taking part in cultural and political events and processes, when these do not yet exist for eliciting their participation.

Instead of an analysis one has to produce a fiction in order to have a framework in which to operate, to grasp an idea of the strength and transformative power that it might have to offer. Political movements such as the so-called anti-globalization movement or even the notorious "movement of 1968", have never properly existed as tangible, experienceable or questionable expressions of power or counter-power. They came to life as a sort of "social fiction" that has produced new subjectivities and therefore has had tremendous performative effects in the world – "as an opening onto the possible" like Gilles Deleuze and Félix Guattari put it: "What counts amounted to a visionary phenomenon, as if a society suddenly perceived what was intolerable in itself and also saw the possibility of change."[3]

Contrary to proper functionality and epistemological facts, such social fiction does not only refer to its "constructedness" and very essence of being "made" or "made up" of something, as a concoction by mixing different desires as ingredients for a scheme that might offer new ways of living, working or learning together; it involves us in an imaginary project by considering things before they exist properly in time and by taking up developments that are not yet in place. Social fiction allows us to experiment with the possible and, at the same time, produce narrations that resonate in the present. It is anticipation in the most creative or productive sense and it needs to be discerned from reproductive anticipation as pure pre-emptiveness that works on the basis of a predictable and projected repetitivity.

From migration to new media, in the last instance the discourse of globalization is driven by imaginative powers which are capable of producing social fiction that shapes the present: the power to anticipate circumstances as if they were already given and hence they obtain their force to actualize what exists as a virtuality. This needs to be linked to the previous point. The ability of illegal bordercrossers to anticipate a world without borders constitutes their real threat to the current border regimes – because it questions the widely propagated idea of migration management – the paradigm of directing, filtering and selecting migratory fluxes in principle and not just on the basis of an individual case or by sheer numbers. Or, the capacity of peer-to-peer or filesharing networks to anticipate free and equal access to the sources of wealth in a knowledge economy which is the real basis of the superiority of peer-to-peer networking over traditional distribution systems.

Productive anticipation means playing with the unforseeable, unpredictable, uncalculable. The objective of any activity in this respect is what cannot be forecasted. In so far as it has nothing to do with dreaming about a better world or utopianism, it rejects the quasi-religious connotations of hope; its elementary openness, its experimental character puts forth a certain asynchronicity and strangeness while being entirely focused on the here and now. Productive anticipation marks precisely the unexplicable and unexploitable rest that makes the difference between networking and the "new economy", between wild and immanent forms of collaboration and the predictable, purpose-driven nature of co-operation, between freedom of movement on a global scale and narrow-minded notions of mobility that remain the privilege of a very few or are restricted to only certain aspects.

When addressed through "culture", the implication of this conceptual shift is that this is not a representational field in which the political developments of the material world are reflected. Not founded in analysis or in a set of material conditions, the ability to speculate and anticipate becomes central to its formation and its emergence. Culture then transforms from a set of mirroring effects through which you can read various material and systemic shifts, to the staging ground of irreconcilable paradoxes.

Thus for example the anti-globalization movement has produced an actual notion of the global, that which it seemingly opposes. As such it is producing a far more coherent concept of "global" which in turn gets taken up and worked through the major agencies of global management. It would seem that both a coherent category and its major points of concern, arrived at by an oppositional movement, have in fact become the lynch pins of the official discourse.

We do not see such paradoxes as the "failure" to arrive at an all encompassing insight or at an operational model except as precisely "anticipatory". Rather than creating conditions, dependencies and causalities such notions of speculative anticipation can be characterized by opening up spaces in which new forms of activities can take place even before they are actually grounded or rooted in a situation or context. In his speculation on the ferocity of the Chinese government's response to the protests in Tiananmen Square, Giorgio Agamben has commented:

> What was most striking about the demonstrations of the Chinese May was the relative absence of determinate contents in their demands (democracy and freedom are notions too generic and broadly defined to constitute the

real object of conflict, and the only concrete demand, the rehabilitation of Hu Yao-Bang, was immediately granted). This makes the violence of the State's reaction seem even more inexplicable ... The novelty of the coming politics is that it will no longer be a struggle between the state and the non-state (humanity), an insurmountable struggle between whatever singularity and the state organisation ... What the state cannot tolerate in any way, however, is that the singularities form a community without affirming an identity, that humans co-belong without any representable condition of belonging (even in the form of a simple presupposition).[4]

What Agamben is sketching out, even in the midst of a real crisis, is an anticipatory mode, a way of indicating a change in the rules without prescribing an alternative.

Thus productive anticipation is a mode of precipitating what is not explainable by the given context of a situation. It requires operating with a certain variability instead of reflectivity. Instead of drawing conclusions from events after they have taken place, a parallel reality is being set up in which the manifest is what we aspire to rather than what we already have and critically oppose. In a world where everything gets modified and modifiable, what are the ways in which culture becomes an investment of citizenship with life and force? How would we understand this notion of investment? Perhaps this investment signals the increasingly non-representational mode of culture? Culture then might be distanced from a creative mode in which representational forms for the existing and clearly discernible problems of the world are invented.

The terms offered below are an attempt at an alternative language through which to engage with contemporary urgencies. Instead of offering models of governance and social organization, they offer an attempt to signal other ways of characterizing the tasks before us and the ways in which we come together to deal with them. One of the most significant shifts of recent emergent politics is that points of entry into the political are shifting and ways of coming or gathering are becoming actual forms rather than simply a means to an end. As such these terms are poised between a notion of "multitude" politics suggested by Negri and the importance of rethinking public gatherings suggested by Bruno Latour.

Access

The dissemination of contemporary culture, operating through institutions such as funded museums, theatres, festivals etc., is under increasing pressure to be "accessible" since it is seen as having a purpose, and its purpose is to rehearse in another modality and with greater emphasis on subjectivity, conditions which exist in the world. Since the demise of the mid-twentieth-century model of culture as a source for contemplation and edification, an ever increasing pressure has set in to activate audiences and make them "aware". The discourses of "accessibility" propagated by both the state and the public institutions of culture are aimed at providing "points of entry" that forge an illusion of transparency and inclusion. Inadvertently they also espouse what is deemed as a necessary simplification on behalf of a notion of communicativeness. It is the role of culture, it would seem, to mediate between two levels of reality; objective and subjective and to put forward a model of translation. Like in any other model of translation, clarity and comprehension are its paramount values. The problem with these discourses of "accessibility", aside from the fact that they are deeply condescending, is that they produce a simplification of conditions that people actually experience as extremely complex and we would argue that instead of producing a simplified comprehension people might be searching for access to understanding that complexity which determines their lives.

And so instead we might posit an understanding of cultural practices viewed as inventing points of "access" to engaging urgent issues which are in the process of articulation. "Access" seems to us to be one of the most urgent drivers of contemporary culture. In contemporaneity it is a question of "access" – of how do we get to know things?, how do we get to take part in them?, how do we work out a position?, how do we intervene, not as a response to a demand to participate but as a way of taking over the means of producing the very questions that are circulating?

The state of "productive anticipation" we have broached encompasses the tension between the desire for "access" and the ability to actually inhabit the conditions and issues that shape our lives.

Direction (directed and undirected participation)

The question that dominates this understanding of participation is "what does it mean to take part in culture beyond the roles that culture allots us for this purpose?", beyond being viewers, listeners, visitors, beyond being voters, inmates and fillers of census forms ?

As these, we mostly encounter directed participation in which we are allotted both roles and protocols to follow. Even in the art world and even within those practices that have attempted to actually thematize participation as their subject, we find mostly instances of directed participation. Throughout the 1990s we saw many exhibitions that attempted to stage the viewer as an active participant in the life of the exhibition. Each one of these exhibitions, more or less successfully dealt with issues of the representation of the marginal and with strategies of participation within the larger map of culture. All put forward an alternative to that model of participation determined by the good intentions and democratic aspirations of curators and organizers. Running the gamut from Hans Ulrich Olbrist's project "Take Me I'm Yours" at London's Serpentine Gallery in 1996, to Christine Hill's far more complex "Thrift Shop" at Documenta X in 1997 – these exemplify the models of participation predicated on a predetermined strategy, its rules set out as if in a game, its audiences treated like mice in some scientific experiment in which they scuttle through mazes and pedal on carousels in order to prove some point.

What is so disappointing about such projects is not the effect of the projects themselves but the curatorial assumptions which sustain them – assumptions about processes of democratizing cultural institutions by giving audiences some mechanical task to carry out and involving the materials of everyday life: old clothes, chewed gum, newspapers, anonymous photographs, etc. In these choreographed games no attention is paid to the power bases of the institutions themselves, to the needs of the audiences, to the possibility that these visitors might have something of value and relevance to say, if only given the space and the possibility and the legitimacy to articulate it. Perhaps most irritating is the use of everyday materials galvanized to act out some fantasy of democracy in action. These materials are familiar and not highly valued and therefore presumably perceived as "popular"; in setting them up a priori as a set of alternative cultural materials not only is nothing new being introduced into the discursive realm of the exhibition but that very possibility of actually encountering either an unknown formulation or the unexpected subversive deployment of them, a Situationist "detournage" of familiar materials, is effectively blocked.

A conjunction of "access" and of "participation" in a contemporary vein would allow audiences and publics to set out the questions and to invent modes of participation, and would allow us to take part also at the level of the unconscious; gathering, muttering, nodding our heads, catching a glimpse from the corner of one's eye and adding all these together to give some mode of a collective and meaningful presence.

Singularities

To unpack "singularity" we are using Giorgio Agamben's argument in *The Coming Community* that asks how we can conceive of a human community that lays no claims to identity; of how a community can be formed of singularities that refuse any criteria of belonging; a community whose collective basis is neither the shared ideological principles nor the empathies of affinity and similarity. The potential that singularity holds out for the argument presented here is that it opens an alternative beyond dichotomies of "the individual" on the one hand and "the social" on the other. Instead "singularity" posits another model of individuals coming together in a collectivity which eludes a named identity and a familiar mode of operating.

> The coming community is whatever being ... The whatever in question here relates to singularity not in its indifference with respect to a common property (to a concept, for example; being red, being French, being Muslim) but only in its being such as it is. Singularity is thus freed from the false dilemma that obliges knowledge to choose between the ineffability of the individual and the intelligibility of the universal ... In this conception, such-and-such being is reclaimed from having this or that property, which identifies it as belonging to this or that set, to this or that class (the reds, the French, the Muslims) – and it is reclaimed not for another class nor for the simple generic absence of any belonging but for its being-such, for belonging itself. Thus being-such which remains constantly hidden in the condition of belonging and which is in no way a real predicate, comes to light itself: The singularity exposed as such is whatever you want, that is, lovable.

Thus Agamben has broached a "community without identity" devoid of belonging and driven by desire. Its unique contribution is that its boundaries are not closed through a form of negative differentiation with the other, but produces a completely different relationality.

> Whatever singularity has no identity, it is not determinate with respect to a concept, but neither is it simply indeterminate; rather it is determined only through its relation to an idea, that is, to the totality of its possibilities. Through this relation, as Kant said, singularity borders all possibility and thus receives its *omnimoda determinato* not from its participation in a determinate concept or some actual property (being red, Italian, Communist) but only by means of this bordering.[5]

The potential of "singularity" in relation to issues of "access" and of "participation" is that it proposes another relation between subjects, one of being. As J.-L. Nancy argues, this allows us a transition from a collective of "having (something) in common" to one of "being in common".[6] Thus "singularity" is another mode of relationality, another possibility of building community, not around a shared set of claims but rather around the sharing of momentary proximities and affiliations.

Collaboration and collectivities

Facing the challenges of digital technologies, global communications, and networking environments, as well as the inherent ignorance of traditional systems towards these, exciting new modes of "working together" have emerged. Collaboration has become one of the leading terms of a contemporary political sensibility that characterizes a new generation of practices in the fields of art, political activism, as well as software development.

In contrast to co-operation, collaboration is driven by complex realities rather than romantic notions of common grounds or commonality. It is an ambivalent process constituted by a set of paradoxical relationships between co-producers who affect one another.

Collaboration entails rhizomatic structures where knowledge is not arranged around a centre, but grows exuberantly and proliferates in unforeseeable ways. In contrast to co-operation, which always implies an organic model and a transcendent function, collaboration is a strictly immanent and wild praxis. Every collaborative activity begins and ends within the framework of the collaboration. It has no external goal and cannot be decreed; it is strict intransitivity, it takes place, so to speak, for its own sake.

Collaborations are voracious. Once they are set into motion they can rapidly beset and affect entire modes of production. "Free" or "open source" software development is probably the most prominent example for the transformative power of collaboration to "un-define" the relationships between authors and producers on one side and users and consumers on the other side. It imposes a paradigm that treats every user as a potential collaborator who could effectively join the development of the code regardless of their actual interests and capacities. Participation becomes virtual: It is enough that one could contribute a patch or file an issue, one does not necessarily have to do it in order to enjoy the dynamics, the efficacy and the essential openness of a collaboration.

In the last instance collaborations are driven by the desire to create difference and refuse the absolutistic power of organization. Collaboration entails overcoming scarcity and inequality and struggling for the freedom to produce. It carries an immense social potential, as it is a form of realization and experience of the unlimited creativity of a multiplicity of all productive practices.

Ownership

In the juridical sense ownership means exclusive possession or control of property. With the increasing digitization of knowledge and immaterial as well as material goods, exclusivity as the determinant aspect of ownership is more and more pressurized. The loss of, and cost-free "copyability" of, digital content and its distribution in networked environments poses the question of radically new models of ownership that do no longer operate on the basis of identity and leave the logics of inclusion and exclusion behind.

The emergence of open licensing models in the free and open source software movement, its expansion as "creative commons license" into the field of cultural production as well as non-legal forms of appropriation usually coined as "piracy" show the tremendous urgency of inventing, trying and evaluating a variety of concepts that facilitate multiplication and widest possible distribution regardless of their compatibility with the legal standards of Western civil law. Against the vision of digital rights management scenarios which are supposed to enable a system of control that operates in real time and is very likely to kill every aspect of further creativity, a notion of syndicated ownership is about to come into being which explicitly embraces asynchronicity, appropriation and further modification.

What Ravi Sundaram calls "pirated modernity"[7] has indeed become the blueprint of another globalization, one that opens up a notion of the global that runs through places:

> Local markets, neighbourhood music/video stores, grayware computer and audio-video assemblers, independent cable operators are usually part of the pirate network of distribution, which also 'bleeds' into other parts of the city. The commodities of the copy are multi-use, recombined/recycled and in near-constant circulation. In Delhi the media copy exists in a symbiotic relationship with all other commodities and industries: clothes, cosmetics, medicine, household goods, and also car and machine parts. As is evident, copy culture pits pirate modernity right into a global social conflict on definitions of property.[8]

The manifolded and unlimited variations which characterize pirate copy cultures and their imaginative strategies in launching ever new modes of redistribution may ironically lead back to an aspect that is constitutive for any kind of ownership: first of all ownership is a matter of imagination, an act of determining space and time, a rule of production. In order to own, one needs not only to construct oneself as a coherent and self-identical subjectivity, but one also has to make others believe in such a construction and be powerful enough to sustain it over a certain period of time and according to a certain territory. The more fluid and evasive contemporary configurations of the self and of ownership become the more unpromising these efforts seem. In order to mobilize imaginatory forces to hold up classical constructions of property in the realm of immaterial production and stretch the ideology of "possessive individualism" across the globe, conflicting concepts of ownership need to get not only systematically demonized and criminalized, but also effectively marginalized. In the last instance this would require a despotic homogenization of time and space on a global scale which makes the current discourse of globalization look just like a walk in the park.

These five terms may be taken as a basis for creative investigation and experimentation with a series of terminologies and methodologies that might be capable of examining the potential of what it could mean to "invest citizenship with force and life". What needs to be researched are processes of subjectivation and – like Deleuze suggests in his answer to Negri's question that opened up this text – "the extent to which they elude both established forms of knowledge and the dominant forms of power".

Culture which has first re-appeared in the debate on globalization under the banner of a "Cultural exception" cannot be characterized as an area that needs to be protected. Instead of lamenting about the "MacWorld", we have to believe in our powers to make world.

Chapter 38

Subjectivity in Times of Abundance of Choice

Renata Salecl*

Today's capitalist ideology is constantly encouraging individuals that everything in their lives is a matter of choice, that they are free to make out of themselves what they desire and that there are limitless ways to find enjoyment in life. A simple look at advertising on the streets shows that nowadays people are encouraged to choose their identity. One London university tries to attract new students with a slogan: "Become what you want to be"; a new music record is advertised with the saying, "I am who I am"; a travel company markets itself with a catchphrase "Life. Book now"; and even a bear company uses the logo "Be yourself!" We live in the world that seems to have less social prohibition in regard to how one is supposed to achieve happiness, where there seem to be endless possibilities to find fulfillment in life and where we are supposed to be some kind of self-creators. In this highly individualized society which gives priority to the individual's self-fulfillment over submission to the group causes, people however face an important anxiety provoking dilemma: "Who am I for myself?" This question is especially troubling in times when we are experiencing a change in the nature of social prohibitions and the push to perceive the idea of choice as the ultimate motto for today's times.

Historically, the idea of freedom of choice has been essentially linked to the democratization of political space. In the developed post-industrial world, however, choice became a theme that is now primarily linked to consumerism.

* **Renata Salecl** is Centennial Professor at the Department of Law at the London School of Economics. She is also Senior Researcher at the Institute of Criminology at the Faculty of Law in Ljubljana, Slovenia and also often teaches as a Visiting Professor at Cardozo School of Law in New York. She is currently working on a book, *Tyranny of Choice*, which analyses why late capitalist insistence on choice increases feelings of anxiety and guilt. The book also analyses how matters of choice apply to law and criminology.

In times when it often looks that people have less and less possibility to have an impact on social and political forces around them, ideology convinces them that they have all the power to create their private lives in the way they desire. Individuals, however, seem to be concerned with this abundance of choice and are often trying to limit the freedom and the possibility of choice. Some time ago, I remember reading an article in the *New York Times*[1] about the anxiety Americans experience when they need to choose their electricity provider. The article explained how the last twenty years were dominated by an ideology that people would be happier and better off if they were constantly shopping for the best deals. On the one hand we thus got a huge emergence of new products, manufacturers and providers to choose from, but on the other hand the idea of choice also became an end in itself. Some social scientists started to talk about the "tyranny of freedom" in today's world, since consumers are forced to make choice even on things they never envisioned they can have any power over (and did not even want to have) – an example here is the choice of the electricity provider. As the *New York Times* article claims, this choice has incited quite an anxiety on the side of the consumers. People are supposedly anxious for two reasons: first, it seems that no one seems to be in charge in society anymore; and, second, the freedom of choice actually does not give more power to con-sumers, but to corporations who are trying to sell their products. A person shopping around on the internet for the best price of a product, for example, gives corporations a chance to collect valuable data about a consumer's desires and spending habits. Anxiety provoking for people is therefore both that no one seems to be in control, and that someone (the corporations) is in charge in a hidden way.[2]

When people speak about anxiety today, they also invoke the idea that they are now asked to make choices in regard to their sexuality, marriage, childbear-ing that were not regarded as choices in the past. But the more choices there are, the more it can seem possible to achieve an ideal result in every case. This is the case not only for people who are continually changing their long-distance telephone service in hope that they will find the best deal, but also for those that are searching for their ideal love partner. That is why some claim that love is especially anxiety provoking today. When dominant ideology promotes that even love is a matter of choice, one gets the impression that one can either incite passions on the side of another (if one closely follows the step-by-step guide on how to "light his or her fire") or prevent falling out of love with someone (probably by using some other techniques on how to fuel the fire). People often perceive their love partner to be just another commodity they need to carefully select. Choosing a partner looks similar to buying a car: the person is supposed to check the qualities of the desired object, get professional advice, insure him or herself with a prenuptial agreement, search for repair-help in marriage counseling, replace old with new, or instead of bothering with "buying" the object just go for temporary leasing.

When people have the anxiety that no one is supposed to be in charge in society at large and that someone (for example, corporations) is already "choosing" in advance what they supposedly need, they question the status of what Lacanian psychoanalysis calls the Big Other – a symbolic order that we are born into and which consists not only of institutions, culture, but primarily of language that shapes our social sphere. It is Lacanian common sense that the Big Other does not exist, which means that the symbolic order we live in is not coherent, but rather marked by lacks, i.e., inconsistent. There has been wide literature to think through what this inconsistency means and one way to perceive the lack that marks the social has been to think of it in terms of various antagonisms that mark the social. In addition to stating that the Big Other does not exist, Lacan stressed the importance of people's belief that it does. That is why Lacan ominously concluded that although the Big Other does not exist, it nonetheless functions, i.e., people's belief in it is essential for their self-perception.[3]

The act of choosing is so traumatic precisely because there is no Big Other: making a choice is always a leap of faith where there are no guarantees. When we try to create self-binding mechanisms which will help us feel content with our choices and eventually help us to be less obsessed with choice, we are not doing anything but "choosing" a Big Other, i.e., inventing a symbolic structure which we presuppose will alleviate our anxiety in front of the abyss of choice. The problem, however, is that the very existence of the Big Other is always our "choice" – we create a fantasy of its consistency.

In recent years there has been growing debate whether something changed in our perception of the Big Other. Did the symbolic structure within late capitalism change? Or was the subject's belief in the Big Other altered when traditional authorities, which were often perceived as the embodiment of the Big Other (like state, church, nation, etc.), lost their power?

French psychoanalyst, Charles Melman, sees the change in subjects' perception of the Big Other as being related to the overwhelming assumption that the world is rationally organized.[4] This assumption is also behind the idea of rational choice. The domain of the Big Other seems to be overflowing with information which is supposed to help people make choices in their lives. However this expansion of information paradoxically increases people's dissatisfaction. Melman's pessimistic conclusion is that the perception of rational organization of the world sometimes brings people to the point of not leaving any space for alterity of the Other – or better a space where there is no Big Other at all.

Almost a decade ago, two other French psychoanalysts, Jacques Alain Miller and Eric Laurent, also speculated that there is no Big Other anymore in today's society and that today's obsession with various ethical comities attest to this change.[5] Scientific development opened many questions and there are no authorities on which one can rely for answers, which is why we create various temporary, ad hoc structures (like committees). The latter are supposed to help us in dealing with the inconsistency of the Big Other, but they, of course, always fail in providing the certainty we search for.

French philosopher, Dany-Robert Dufour, presents his own version of pessimistic view about the demise of our symbolic structures. Dufour departs from Freud's presupposition that each culture in its own way forms the subjects who then try to discern the always-specific footprints leading to their origin. For Dufour, this is "why one paints the Other, sings it, one gives it a form, a voice, stages it, gives it representations and even a super representation, including the form of irrepresentable."[6] The reference to the Other helps us when we try to figure out the meaning of our lives. This is why our history is always a history of the Other, or better figures of the Other. Dufour further points out that the subject is always subject of the Other, which in the past has taken many forms of some kind of big Subject – from Physis, God to King, the people, etc. Throughout history, the distance between the subject and this big Subject reduced itself. With modernity, however, there emerged plurality of the big Subjects, which is linked to the decline of the power of the church and the vast expanse of scientific progress.

In today's culture, the subject is permanently decentered, however; also the symbolic place around him or her is more and more anomic and diffused. Discussions on post-modernity have thus focused on the fact that there are no grand narratives anymore, that there are no strong authorities with whom the subject identifies, and that individualism seems to have been pushed to its limit, so that the subject more and more perceives him- or herself as a dynamic self-creator.

Does this trend of promoting understandings of self-creation contribute to the apparent rise in psychological problems that psychoanalysis is concerned about? What has happened with subjectivity in late capitalism? Why are people so concerned with the abundance of choice and why are feelings of anxiety and guilt so much on the rise? In the early seventies, Lacan made an observation that in a developed capitalistic system, the subject's relationship to the social field can be observed to form a particular discourse. In this "Discourse of Capitalism,"[7] the subject relates to the social field in such a way that he or she takes him- or herself as a master. The subject is not only perceived to be totally in charge of him- or herself, the subject also appears to have power to recuperate the loss of *jouissance*.[8] In late capitalism, the subject is thus perceived as an agent who has enormous power.

What does it mean that the subject is placed in the position of such an agent? First, it looks as if this subject is free from subjection to his history and genealogy and thus free from all signifying inscriptions. This seems to be the subject who is free to choose not only objects that supposedly bring him or her satisfaction, but even more the direction of his or her life, i.e., the subject chooses him or herself.

Capitalism more and more transforms the proletarian slave into a free consumer. But although the latter is perceived as being totally in charge or him- or herself and especially free to make numerous choices, one sees a paradoxical trend that this possibility of choice opens doors to an increase of anxiety.[9] One of the ways to deal with this anxiety becomes strong identification with some kind of new master – from gurus, religious leaders, political extremists to self-help authors.

The subject who seems to be liberated from the social constraints paradoxically appears powerless towards the figures of Time (Baudelaire): "Aging, dying, inscribing one self into the succession of the generations, all this became more and more difficult."[10] We can even say that aging, too, appears a matter of choice – it is up to every individual to "do" something against it, or better work on not showing the signs of aging, as well as try to follow many proposed suggestions on how to prevent death.

Some psychoanalysts are concluding that the "discourse of capitalism" does not leave space for love, especially not space for sublime courtly love. What we have instead is an increase of narcissistic illusion and a push towards sexuality that hopefully brings some lost *jouissance*. Jean-Pierre Lebrun concludes that today's subjects have problems determining how to situate themselves in regard to sexual difference. Sexual identification is linked to the way the subject places him- or herself after going through the process of castration, i.e. after the subject has been marked by language and has thus been marked by an essential lack. With the changes in the level of the castration complex there seems to be more of a turn towards androgyny and bisexuality. However, the main problem is that in "discourse of capitalism", sexuality becomes perceived in a narcissistic way: "Since sexuality is a matter of competitive rivalry and consummation, it does not concern anymore a choice of a stable object. It is primarily a matter of seduction."[11]

How does the ideology of choice and the push towards excessive *jouissance* affect personal relationships today? In the society determined by the idea of choice, matters of love and sexuality at first seem extremely liberating. What is better than envisioning a possibility to be free from social prohibitions when it comes to our sexual enjoyment; how wonderful it appears to finally stop bothering about what parents and society at large fashion as normal sexual relations; and how liberating it seems to change our sexual orientation or even physical appearance of sexual difference. It is more than obvious that such "freedom" does not bring satisfaction; on the contrary, it actually limits it.

In analyzing human desires, psychoanalysis has from the beginning linked desire with prohibition. For the subject to develop a desire for something, there have to be boundaries and objects of desire that are off limits. When the subject struggles with ever evolving dissatisfaction in regard to non-attainability of his or her object of desire, the solution is not to get rid of the limit in order to finally fuse with the object of desire, but to be able to somehow "cherish" the very limit and perceive the object of desire as worthy of our striving precisely because it is inaccessible.

It is not difficult to observe in contemporary media discussions and representations of sexuality that there are very few things that are prohibited (with the exception of child molestation, incest, and sexual abuse), while there is an overwhelming "push to enjoy." Sexual transgression is marketed as the ultimate form of enjoyment: the idea being that if one works on it, learns its tricks and then practices it relentlessly, there are no limits to the satisfaction a person can achieve. *Cosmopolitan* magazine thus encourages those who have not yet mastered new techniques of reaching ultimate joys to enroll in sex school. Simultaneously with this marketing of enjoyment, one reads in the popular media about the very impossibility to enjoy. John Gray, the famous author of *Men are from Mars, Women are from Venus* now writes about "Why my Grandmother seems to have more sex than I do."[12] His answer, of course, again turns into another form of advice: be more relaxed, follow these or that steps of arousing desire, etc.

When we look at how we deal with sexuality in this supposedly limitless society, it is easy to observe that limits did not actually disappear or that prohibitions still exist; however, the locus where they came from has changed. If, in the past, prohibitions have been transmitted with the help of social rituals (like initiation rituals in pre-modern society, and functioning of the paternal prohibitions in the traditional patriarchal society), today the subject sets his or her own limits. The contemporary subject is thus not only self-creator, but also his or her own "prohibitor." It is as if the subject constantly invents new forms of inner protections now that external social prohibitions are less and less opera-tive. In the last few years we have, for example, witnessed all kinds of new direc-tions: towards celibacy, inventions of new dating rules which play with the old idea of not making oneself too accessible to a potential love partner, as well as various new types of prohibitions and advice on how to master one's own body (from dieting, exercise, to self-healing).

When the subject deals with social prohibitions, he or she deals also with dissatisfaction. However, today, what we are observing is an increase in frustra-tion and not so much an escalation of dissatisfaction. Frustration is, in a special way, linked to a subject's problem with *jouissance*. Jean-Pierre Lebrun thinks that "when will to *jouissance* dominates the social field, brotherly solidarity of proletarians is replaced by competition and competitive rivalry. Which is where exacerbation of social hate emerges."[13] In contemporary racism, for example, the subject presupposes that the Other has access to some full *jouis-sance* which provokes frustration on the side of the subject. In personal rela-tionships, the problem is that the subject tries to get some excess enjoyment from the partner and after this attempt necessarily fails, the partner loses importance and becomes one of the objects one can easily reject. For the sub-ject who lacks stable identifications, has fluctuating choice of objects, instabil-ity in affective investments, and quickly passes to act, one way to try to find the lost *jouissance* is with the help of addictive substances. This may provide some insight into why there is an increase in addictive behavior today.

But are we to predict a rather bleak future? Instead of over-emphasizing the lack of prohibition in today's society, I would rather stress that the nature of prohibition has changed. On the one hand, the subject more and more searches for new forms of enjoyment and is thus under constant pressure to consume (which sadly often brings him or her to self-consumption – through excessive work, as well as dieting, exercise, etc.), but, on the other hand, the subject des-perately searches for new forms of social limits. Self-prohibition does open doors for new forms of despair. And with the lack of traditional authorities, the subject does not seem to be coming closer to "happiness." He or she rather des-perately searches for new authorities. A visit to any bookstore or a simple search on the internet shows us that the so-called self-help industry is one of the fastest growing businesses. Which is why it would be too quick to say that we live in society where the Big Other does not exist anymore or where subjects are more prone for psychosis. Dependence on advice culture shows that subjects still need recourse via the Big Other.

Chapter 39

Fashioning the Late Modern Body:

The Democratisation of Beauty

*Susie Orbach**

From Latvia to Fiji to Shanghai to Lagos to Medellin, beauty is no longer rationed, a category apart, bestowed on a few and honoured by the many. Indeed a feature of late capitalism has been the democratisation of beauty as an aspiration and an attainment for all women, a key feature in girls and women's desires. The desire to be beautiful has become so intensified in the last twenty years that beauty is experienced as almost a requirement of modernity, certainly an essential aspect of femininity. As the world gets smaller this democratisation of beauty is exported globally as aspiration. It offers an apparent entry point that girls and women use to establish identity and belonging.

Today we are poised between the post-industrial body – a physical body that is by and large no longer needed for the labour of producing goods as it was until the end of the twentieth century – and the soon-to-arrive precision engineered body with its individualised pharmaceuticals, replaced and resculpted body parts and the genetic screening and regenerative possibilities that will accompany twenty-first century corporeality. Into this space we have the late modern body which has found a purpose by becoming *a form of production itself.* This is particularly the case for girls and women. Their ability to make of their own bodies a facsimile of the visual images which flood the retinas and

* **Susie Orbach** is a psychoanalyst, author of ten books – four on the body – and numerous papers, co-founder of The Women's Therapy Centre, The Women's Therapy Centre Institute, Antidote, Psychotherapists and Counsellors for Social Responsibility. She is a consultant to the British National Health Service, Unilever, the World Bank, and is currently a visiting Professor at the London School of Economics and Political Science.

construct the internal pictures of femininity is an increasingly important part of their identity.

There is, of course, nothing new in girls and women taking on the project of self presentation. The marking of one's body is a fundamental aspect of all cultural belonging. From circumcision, to how facial hair is managed, to rings around the neck, the body has been sculpted to indicate from whence we come and to declare our membership of the group, nationality, class or station in life.

Uniforms predominate in every culture. Our clothes indicate and signal where we believe we belong or where we wish to be placed. Indeed in the massive migrations of the last century, entry into a new culture involves the taking on of the decorative tropes that allow one membership into the new cultural grouping. The development of the department store at the turn of the twentieth century was a crucial way in which immigrants to the United States could enter the host culture. The children of immigrants, in particular, seeking economic and social inclusion, learnt to dress in the ways of the new country. Buying in the department store, they could be confident that appropriate contemporary fashions were available at varying prices whether one was shopping in the bargain basement, on the modestly priced floors or on the more exclusive ones.[1] The department store had authority and purchases there assured them that their clothes would 'pass'. They purchased and wore their clothes as a sign of their membership in the new society. If their parents were aghast at the clothes they wore, this only served to emphasise how accurate had their reading been of how to become an American.

Today, the signology of clothes and of bodies has gone global. It is a rare non-western leader who is seen in local dress: the western suit is ubiquitous and the clothes in markets from Jakarta to Paris vary little. Of course, the non-western influence is evident but its visibility is mostly in the form of appropriation. The forms of material making, methods of dyeing, the designing and the colours and stylings from around the world influence what becomes global fashion. It looks like a complex interchange of cultural influence. But implicit in the interchange is the dominance of the western fashion makers who get their inspiration from the street and then gobble up the new influences to then return them to the market place where their economic muscle allows them to be disseminated and picked up in such a way that many 'local' forms of dresses become subtly undermined.

As modernity has gone global, McLuhan's statement that 'the medium is the message' has a particular salience.[2] The medium is the body. And the construction of the body takes place via a relationship with that pre-eminent medium of the contemporary world, visual culture which arrives via pixalated screens, from the tiny (telephones) to the large (TV screens), on billboards, in print and on film. Those mediums convey pictorially, often larger than life images – and certainly persistent and omnipresent images – which are constructing and reconstructing our relation to the body, to desire, to belonging. Hollywood's dream machine[3] created a visual language which has global reach and stirs up desire globally. Transporting those celluloid inspired dreams and operating as a medium in itself then, is the individual body: the bearer of the message of contemporary subjectivity and desire.

The bodies we live from are the outcome of our dialogue with the representation of bodies that we see around us. This is a lively but asymmetrical dialogue in which the individual attempts to construct a sense of her or his own physicality by reference to the images of beauty, of masculinity and femininity that press into their visual awareness. The digitalisation of culture has not increased our exposure to diverse images.[4] Although there are indeed more images around, paradoxically, there is a sense of conformity and uniformity in the images that insinuate themselves into our internal sense of what it means to look like a contemporary woman (or man). The use by advertisers and those in the style industries of less than a score of international models or faces of brands underscores this point. Girls and women all over the world, as an aspect of entering into and then belonging to global culture, count on being able to name not just the brands but the models who wear them. Branding by body and by product maker is a means of recognition and placement.[5] Wearing those brands and being able to identify them and understand what they are trying to convey about the sort of person who uses an Apple or wears Nike or listens to music through a Bose system is part of the meta-conversation of modernity. Ironic notes themselves become branded so that the sudden uptake of a downmarket brand (such as Primark today) becomes itself an attempt to play with fashion.

Identification with, purchase of, or longing for a particular brand portfolio is the hallmark of the new western citizenship. Consuming becomes a means by which civic engagement occurs and by which identity and the aspirational aspects of this 'branded' identity are signalled. What has perhaps remained unseen is the extent to which, in the new global economy, an individual woman's identity is bound up with the capacity to represent herself physically *as part of the brand called woman*. That womanhood itself requires a particular kind of body and this body is styled in a manner which is recognisably modern, recognisably thin and recognisably endowed with fashions' current contours.

The omnipresent images around her construct and determine her own relations to the body she feels at once impelled to desire and to have. Indeed she may not feel she has a body unless it mirrors those of the digitalised bodies in her visual field. Her desire is created in the context of how desire is represented – from the outside,[6] as something to be regarded upon, as something to possess and as a site for commentary and communication. For women today, the struggle for subjectivity is caught up with and entwines the struggle to have a body. I am not speaking here of some notion of an inviolable body. This is too idealist a notion in a world where crimes of violence from domestic and stranger rape, to physical assault, to clitorectomies infiltrate so many women's lives across the five continents. I am speaking rather of the ordinary difficulties women encounter in the attempt to constitute a secure corporeality in the face of a more taken-for-granted kind of violence with which she is presented daily through the concentration of the images she sees with their imperative and insistent limitations about her own possible physicality. This kind of violence, often unrecognised, is part of what women have to take on in their search for subjectivity.

This encounter with the world of images is something she unintentionally accedes to. It is akin to acquiring one's mother tongue. Visual language and sensitivity, like verbal language, occurs outside of conscious awareness. She is thus primed to make her own corporeality within the context of the image maker's dictates. She forges her sense of physical self, her place, her desires, her subjectivity via the engagement with what is available. She enters and involves herself with visual language. But in doing so she can't but help participating in a kind of violence to herself as she seeks to participate in the limited and limiting categories of physical subjectivity open to her and other women.

This is not mere masochism or 'false consciousness' but an inevitable consequence of engagement with the world as it is presented to her. Marx's aphorism that 'we enter a world not of our own making', has particular resonance for the struggle of women and their bodies today as they confront a visual world not of their own making. If we listen in to the young women of Fiji interviewed by Anne E. Becker from Harvard, 11.9 per cent of whom are now over the toilet bowl with bulimia, we discover that their attempt to reshape their bodies to conform to the bodies that they have seen on their televisions which screen western TV shows, is an expression of their desire to enter modernity. Fifteen years ago, there was a negligible amount of bulimia in Fiji, but three years after television was introduced to Fiji in 1995, teenage girls across the island were caught up in a dialogue with the propagation of images beamed at them. A desire was stimulated in them to enter the modern world and they saw the appropriation of a western body as essential to the success of that dream.[7]

The demise of the Fijian body and its replacement with a westernised ideal could not of course have happened without a concomitant economic penetration. Rapid cultural change is being led by the globalisation of markets and within that situation, individual girls and women across the globe enter into the construction of a body that will fit the requirements of modernity. What psychoanalysis helps us to understand is the way in which the outside – in this case the myriad of style images that are in the world – gets inside so that the having of a 'western' body is felt to be a personal desire of the individual. It is not so much a question of straightforward manipulation by canny advertisers and PR but how the individual comes to desire what is proposed and to reject what initially, they may find problematic. We all do this routinely. Fashion changes. Bodies, typography, furniture, lighting, clothing, hairstyles, the phrases we use and even the cuisines we once imbibed strike us now as quaint, ridiculous and dated. We may be initially unwelcoming to the new fashions – stripes with flowers, wide trousers rather than tight ones and we may feel dismay, even a certain revulsion about the look, as many did with the 'heroin chic'. But these new images pour out at us, all in the same vein. They fill our visual field. The tight trousers that were once so much a part of who we are come to feel shabby, or unrepresentative of who we feel ourselves to be or how we want to be seen. Instead of the trousers or the stripes with the flowers, or the skinny heroin chic model being unwelcome, we come to feel that it is *us in our own bodies and clothing and attitudes that are all wrong.*

Psychoanalysis (among other things) studies the process by which that which is not of one and furthermore is experienced as malign is transformed to become an internalised bad object relation, a part of one's self experience. How, psychoanalysis enquires, is that indigestibility (the what-has-been-done-to one) turned into an aspect of an individual's own desire and a propellant for their own sense of the individual? How is the 'assault' recast in a way that renders her not a victim but an actor in her own desires? And it sees that in her very embrace of the market's propositions is the means by which she overcomes the sense of being subjected. She becomes instead an active subject. The power of the images to offend or hurt is rendered less potent by the individual's re-alignment within herself of the desire to mirror and enact those images. It is she who is at fault for not matching up to them. The image is not discordant. It is her sightline that is faulty. It is she (or he) who is now energised to make them her own signature and to express herself through these new forms. She applies herself to the job of perfecting that image for herself and so makes it her own, not alien.

Any difficulties she has with capturing and expressing that image for herself become understood as a source of personal failure which can be worked on and perfected. If the body does not conform, it can be exercised, reshaped by food regimens or in the gym. If that is insufficient, then there is an industry of cosmetic surgeons and dentists who can resculpt faces, smiles, fat deposits and toe positioning (the latter important for many of the shoes now considered objects of desire). A recent operation in metropolitan China is the breaking of the thigh bone and the insertion of a 10cm rod of extra height. This procedure is done in order to create 'a level playing field' for the aspiring business folk of that region.[8] Similarly, under the hijab in Iran, 35,000 rhinoplasties are done annually in Teheran and the re-sculpting of the body is almost an expected course of events in certain Latin American countries where across classes this has become an aspiration and an expectation for women.[9] What is interesting to notice in Brazil is the new preponderance of breast augmentations. In Brazil we see the clash of two aesthetics: the conventional Brazilian admiration for a woman's bottom for which there were and continue to be many surgical enhancements, and the recent disneyification via Baywatch-type programmes of the Brazilian breast which is now perceived of as a site of modernity. This is a different order of business than the benign influence of cultural mixing. In changing her breasts the individual woman is announcing that she is part of modern femininity.

Throughout the world, girls and women grapple with the asymmetry of the images that are projected and their own attempt to find a place and a body that they can live from. That these images are powerful is in no doubt. Brands invest heavily in marketing. And their spending works. Where once religious iconography penetrated the consciousness of the people, brand iconography conveyed by particular kinds of bodies does that today. Because the market demands constant economic activity, we also become primed to change: to look out for, and to yearn for those images which will help us to situate ourselves with just the right, albeit, fleeting, identity markers. It is not just the Starbucks or the hotel chains with which the world traveller can reassure her- or himself of continuity and belonging. It is in a deeply personal manner through the appropriation of a body that is recognisable that a woman makes her way in the world.

Identity and bodies are formed with reference to our particular world. Desire is formed in dialogue with that world. It is relational. The global economy and visual culture make an impression on the individual and the individual makes a response and in doing so feels herself to be a part of late modernity. Secure she cannot be for her corporeality has become contingent rather than steady. What she has understood is that it needs to be at the ready to transform itself and her desire to do so and her enthusiasm for the project of transformation – or perhaps I should say the availability for transformation – becomes an aspect of self which she embraces and anticipates with a certain pleasure. It is an expression of her active involvement with the global conversation about femininity.

Endnotes

INTRODUCTION

1. But, see Berger and Huntingdon, 2002 for a discussion of the cultural dynamics of globalisation.

PART I CHAPTER 1

1. W. Benjamin, *Illuminations* (London: Fontana Press, 1992), p. 217.
2. Benjamin, ibid, p. 218.
3. B. Parry, "Bodily transactions: regulating a new space of flows in "bio-information"", in K. Verdery and C. Humphrey (eds), *Property in Question: Value Transformation in the Global Economy* (Oxford: Berg, 2004), pp. 29–33.
4. The literature on this subject is now voluminous, but helpful discussions include: M. Brown, *Who Owns Native Culture?* (Cambridge, MA: Harvard University Press, 2003); R. Coombe, *The Cultural Life of Intellectual Properties: Authorship, Appropriation, and the Law* (Durham, NC: Duke University Press, 1998); B. Ziff and P. Rao (eds), *Borrowed Power. Essays on Cultural Appropriation* (New Brunswick: Rutgers University Press, 1997).
5. S. Harrison, 'From prestige goods to legacies: property and the objectification of culture in Melanesia', *Comparative Studies in Society and History* 42 (2000), 663–4.
6. Harrison, ibid, pp. 666–8.
7. Harrison, ibid, pp. 673–6.
8. International Labour Organisation, Convention 169, "Concerning Indigenous and Tribal Peoples in Independent Countries", 27th June, 1989, art. 13(1).
9. T. Cowen, *Creative Destruction: How Globalization is Changing the World's Cultures* (Princeton: Princeton University Press, 2002), pp. 6–32.
10. Cowen, ibid, pp. 49–55.
11. Cowen, ibid, pp. 59–66.
12. See J. Urry, *Sociology Beyond Societies: Mobilities for the Twenty-First Century* (London: Routledge, 2000).

13. M. Brown, 'Heritage trouble: recent work on the protection of intangible cultural property', *International Journal of Cultural Property* 12 (2005), 47–9.
14. See Coombe, ibid.
15. D. Harvey, 'The art of rent: globalization, monopoly and the commodification of culture', *Socialist Register* (2002), 93–110.
16. Benjamin, ibid, p. 234.

CHAPTER 3

1. David Held, *Global Covenant: The Social Democratic Alternative to the Washington Consensus* (Cambridge: Polity, 2004), p. 178.
2. Hannah Arendt, *The Origins of Totalitarianism* (New York: Harcourt Brace Jovanovitch, 1973), p. 297.
3. Ibid, p. 294.
4. Held, *Global Covenant*, p. 173.
5. Arendt, *The Origins of Totalitarianism*, p. 302.
6. Etienne Balibar, *We, the People of Europe? Reflections on Transnational Citizenship* (Princeton: Princeton University Press, 2004), p. 122.
7. Michel Foucault, "*Society Must Be Defended*", *Lectures at the Collège de France 1975–1976* (New York: Picador, 2003), p. 256.
8. Balibar, *We, the People of Europe*, pp. 126–7.
9. Held, *Global Covenant*, p. 162.
10. Ibid, p. 172.
11. William Edward Burghart Du Bois, *Darkwater* (New York: Harcourt, Brace and Howe, 1920), p. 131.
12. R. Rorty, *Philosophy and the Mirror of Nature* (Princeton: Princeton University Press, 1979), p. 163.
13. Immanuel Kant, *Political Writings* (Cambridge: Cambridge University Press, 1991), p. 55.
14. Linda Bosniak, *The Citizen and the Alien* (Princeton: Princeton University Press, 2006), p. 140.
15. Habermas, this volume.
16. Amartya Sen, *Identity and Violence: The Illusion of Destiny* (London: Penguin, 2006), p. 184.
17. Adrienne Rich, *An Atlas of the Difficult World* (New York: W.W. Norton & Co., 1991), p. 44.
18. Walter Benjamin, *Illuminations* (New York: Schocken Books, 1968), p. 258.
19. Incident no: 36. AR 15–6 Investigation of the Abu Ghraib Detention Facility and Military Intelligence Brigade (U) MG George R. Fay Investigating Officer, p. 124.
20. http://riverbendblog.blogspot.com. Friday, 30th April, 2004.

21. Hannah Arendt, *The Human Condition* (Chicago: University of Chicago Press, 1999), pp. 182–5.

22. David Held, et al., *Global Transformations* (Stanford: Stanford University Press, 1999), p. 445.

23. Ian McEwan, *Saturday* (New York: Doubleday, 2005), p. 185.

CHAPTER 4

1. I have tried to have a go at that issue in "How Does Culture Matter?", in Vijayendra Rao and Michael Walton (eds), *Culture and Public Action* (Stanford, CA: Stanford University Press, 2004).

2. See Joel Mokyr's balanced assessment of this difficult issue in *Why Ireland Starved: A Quantitative and Analytical History of the Irish Economy, 1800–1850* (London, Allen & Unwin, 1983), pp. 291–2. See also Mokyr's conclusion that 'Ireland was considered by Britain as an alien and even hostile nation' (p. 291).

3. See Cecil Woodham-Smith, *The Great Hunger: Ireland, 1845–9* (London: Hamish Hamilton, 1962), p. 76.

4. See Andrew Roberts, *Eminent Churchillians* (London: Weidenfeld & Nicholson, 1994), p. 213.

5. Lawrence E. Harrison and Samuel P. Huntington (eds), *Culture Matters: How Values Shape Human Progress* (New York: Basic Books, 2000), p. xiii.

6. On this, see Noel E. McGinn, Donald R. Snodgrass, Yung Bong Kim, Shin-Bok Kim and Quee-Young Kim, *Education and Development in Korea* (Cambridge, MA: Council on East Asian Studies, Harvard University, 1980).

7. William K. Cummings, *Education and Equality in Japan* (Princeton, NJ: Princeton University Press, 1980), p. 17.

8. See Herbert Passin, *Society and Education in Japan* (New York: Teachers College Press, Columbia University, 1965), pp. 209–11; also Cummings, *Education and Equality in Japan*, p. 17.

9. Quoted in Shumpei Kumon and Henry Rosovky, *The Political Economy of Japan: Cultural and Social Dynamics* (Stanford, CA: Stanford University Press, 1992), p. 330.

10. See Carol Gluck, *Japan's Modern Myths: Ideology in the Late Meiji Period* (Princeton, NJ: Princeton University Press, 1985).

11. The inclusion of cultural freedom in the list of concerns of 'human development' in the United Nations' *Human Development Report 2004* (New York: UNDP, 2004) is a substantial enrichment of the coverage of human development analysis.

12. See 'Other People', published in the *Proceedings of the British Academy* (2002), and also as 'Other People – Beyond Identity', *The New Republic*, 18th December (2000).

CHAPTER 5

1. U. Beck, *The Cosmopolitan Vision* (Cambridge: Polity Press, 2006).
2. S. Huntington, *The Clash of Civilizations and the Remaking of World Order* (New York: Simon & Schuster, 1996).
3. F. Fukuyama, 'The End of History', *National Interest* 16 (1989), 3–18. See also F. Fukuyama, *The End of History and the Last Man* (London: Hamish Hamilton, 1992).
4. R. Koselleck, *Futures Past* (Cambridge: MIT Press, 1985), p. 231.

CHAPTER 6

1. F. Jellinek, *Die Krise Des Bürgers* (Zürich: Europa, 1935).
2. K. Loewenstein, 'Militant Democracy and Fundamental Rights', *American Political Science Review* 31 (1937); see also his *Verfassungslehre*, 3rd edition (1975), p. 348 ff.
3. On the problematic issue of civil disobedience see my two essays in J. Habermas, *Die Neue Unübersichtlichkeit* (Frankfurt/M. 1985), pp. 79–117.
4. R. Forst, 'Der schmale Grat zwischen Ablehnung und Akzeptanz', *Frankfurter Rundschau* 28th December (2001).
5. J. Rawls, *Political Liberalism* (New York: Columbia University Press, 1993), p. 58 ff.
6. See the list offered by D. Grimm in the *Frankfurter Allgemeine Zeitung* 21st June (2002), p. 49: 'Can a Sikh riding a motorcycle be excused from obeying the general law to wear a helmet on grounds of his religious duty to wear a turban? Must a Jewish prisoner be offered kosher food? Does a Muslim employee have the right to briefly interrupt his work time in order to pray? Can an employee be fired because he did not appear for work on the High holy days? Does an employee dismissed for this reason forfeit his entitlement to unemployment benefits? Must Jewish entrepreneurs be permitted to open their businesses on Sundays simply because for religious reasons they had to keep them shut on Saturday? Does a Muslim pupil have the right to be exempted from PE classes because she is not allowed to show herself to other pupils wearing sports clothes? May Muslim pupils wear headscarves in class? What is the case if the woman concerned is a teacher at a government-owned school? Should the law be different for nuns than it is for a Muslim teacher? ... Must muezzins be allowed to broadcast their call to prayer by loudspeaker in German cities just as churches are allowed to ring their bells? Must foreigners be allowed to ritually slaughter animals although it contravenes the local animal protection regulations? ... Must Mormons be permitted to practice polygamy here because it is allowed them in their country of origin?'
7. On the unity of political culture in the diversity of sub-cultures, see J. Habermas, *The Inclusion of the Other* (Cambridge, MA: MIT Press, 1998), p. 117 ff.
8. On this distinction, see N. Fraser, "From Redistribution to Recognition?", in C. Willett (ed.), *Theorizing Multiculturalism* (Oxford: Blackwell, 1998), pp. 19–49.

9. A. Honneth, *Das Andere der Gerechtigkeit* (Frankfurt/Main: Suhrkamp, 2000) focuses specifically on these pathologies of refused recognition.

10. C. Taylor, *Multiculturalism and 'The Politics of Recognition'*, with Commentary by A. Gutmann (ed.), S.C. Rockefeller, M. Walzer and S. Wolf (Princeton: Princeton University Press, 1992). See in the German edition my critique of the communitarian conception of cultural rights as collective rights (pp. 117–46).

11. On the concept of such 'encompassing groups', see A. Margalit and J. Raz, "National Self-Determination", in W. Kymlicka (ed.), *The Rights of Minority Cultures* (Oxford: Oxford University Press, 1995), pp. 79–92, esp. 81 ff.

12. The more comprehensive the cultural life form is, the stronger its cognitive content, the more it resembles a way of life structured by religious worldviews: 'The inescapable problem is that cultures have propositional content. It is an inevitable aspect of any culture that it will include ideas to the effect that some beliefs are true and some are false, and that some things are right and others wrong'. T.B. Barry, *Culture and Equality* (Cambridge, UK: Polity Press, 2001), p. 270.

PART II   CHAPTER 7

1. John Tomlinson, *Globalization and Culture* (Cambridge: Polity, 1999).
2. See Ben Agger, 'Introduction', *Fast Capitalism* 1(1) (2005). Retrieved from http://www.fastcapitalism.com/1_1/agger.html.
3. Will Hutton and Anthony Giddens (eds), *On the Edge: Living with Global Capitalism* (London: Jonathan Cape, 2000).
4. Manuel Castells, "Information Technology and Global Capitalism", in Hutton and Giddens (eds), *On the Edge*, pp. 52–74.
5. Edward Thompson, "Time, Work-Discipline and Industrial Capitalism", in *Customs in Common* (London: The Merlin Press, 1991), pp. 352–403; p. 358.
6. Thompson, ibid, p. 359.
7. See Zygmunt Bauman, *Liquid Modernity* (Cambridge: Polity, 2000); Zygmunt Bauman, *Liquid Life* (Cambridge: Polity, 2005).
8. Teresa Brennan, *Globalization and its Terrors* (London: Routledge, 2003), p. 133.
9. Hubert Dreyfus, *On the Internet* (London: Routledge, 2001).

CHAPTER 8

1. The examples are drawn from a series of studies:

   1. Study of northern amateur online pornography traders, mid-1990s. See D. R. Slater, 'Trading sexpics on IRC: embodiment and authenticity on the internet', *Body and Society* 4 (4) (1998), 91–117; D. R. Slater, "Consumption without scarcity: exchange and normativity in an internet setting", in P. Jackson,

M. Lowe, D. Miller and F. Mort (eds), *Commercial Cultures: Economies, Practices, Spaces* (London: Berg, 2000), pp. 123–42; D. R. Slater, 'Making things real: ethics and order on the Internet', *Theory, Culture and Society* 19 (5/6: Special issue: Sociality/Materiality) (2002), 227–45.

2. Ethnography of the internet in Trinidad, with Daniel Miller, 1998–2000. See D. Miller and D. Slater, *The Internet: An Ethnographic Approach* (London: Berg, 2000).

3. *Evaluation of Kothmale Community Radio and Internet Centre*, with Jo Tacchi and Peter Lewis, 2002. Funded by UK Department for International Development (DFID), in cooperation with UNESCO.

4. ICTs for Poverty Reduction (ictPR), UNESCO programme in India, Bangladesh, Sri Lanka, Nepal, 2002–4. See D. Slater and J. Tacchi, *Research: ICT Innovations for Poverty Reduction* (New Delhi: UNESCO, 2004). http://eprints.qut.edu.au/archive/00004398/01/4398.pdf.

5. Information Societies, funded by DFID, 2003–5: Comparative ethnographies of ICTs and poverty reduction in Ghana, South Africa, India, Jamaica. Lead researchers: Don Slater, Daniel Miller, Andrew Skuse, Jo Tacchi. Ghana research discussed in this paper was conducted with Janet Kwami and Jenna Burrell.

2. Miller and Slater (2000).

3. K. A. Appiah, *Cosmopolitanism: Ethics in a World of Strangers* (London: Allen Lane, 2006), p. 92.

4. M. Castells (ed.), *The Network Society: A Cross-cultural Perspective* (London: Edward Elgar, 2005), pp. 3–15.

5. C. Geertz, *The Interpretation of Cultures* (New York: Basic Books, 1973).

6. See D. Slater and J. Kwami, 'Embeddedness and escape: Internet and mobile use as poverty reduction strategies in Ghana', Information Society Research Group Working Paper 4, University of Adelaide (2005); cf. H. Horst and D. Miller, *The Cell Phone: An Anthropology of Communication* (Oxford: Berg, 2006).

7. B. Latour, *Reassembling the Social: An Introduction to Actor-Network Theory* (Oxford: Oxford University Press, 2005).

CHAPTER 9

1. Douglas Kellner, *Media Spectacle* (London and New York: Routledge, 2003); see also footnote 6 of http://www.utpjournals.com/product/cras/321/Villmoare-Stillman.html.

2. See the full text of the interview at http://www.smirkingchimp.com/article.php?sid=9194.

3. See http://www.cjrdaily.org/the_water_cooler/john_carroll_on_winning_ pulitz.php.

4. See http://www.thenation.com/doc/20000626/leonard/5.

5. See http://www.washingtonmonthly.com/features/2004/0407.turner.html.
6. http://www.cnn.com/2005/SHOWBIZ/TV/06/01/turner.25th.cnn.
7. See http://carlisle-www.army.mil/usawc/Parameters/97summer/peters.htm.
8. Danny Schechter, "A Blow to the City", in *Media Wars: News at a Time of Terror* (New York & London: Roman and Littlefield); and in *Urban Ecology* magazine.
9. James B. Goodno, 'New York, 9/11: An Attack on Urban Culture?' *Urban Ecology*, Winter (2001–2), pp. 16–18.

CHAPTER 11

1. See Sanjay Sharma and Ashwani Sharma, 'So far so good, so far so good ... *La Haine* and the poetics of the everyday', *Theory Culture and Society*, 17(3) (2000), 103–16, 105.
2. http://www.adfed.co.uk/htmlversion/futureprojects.html.
3. http://www.richmix.org.uk.
4. Sharma and Sharma, op. cit., p. 103.
5. Martin Heidegger, "The Pathway", in *Political Writings* (New York: Continuum, 1949/2003), p. 78.
6. Martin Heidegger, "Discourse on Thinking", in *Political Writings* (1955/2003), p. 89.
7. Ibid, p. 90.
8. The political activism of Heidegger as Nazi philosopher has been subject to much attention. Gossip and rumour abound regarding his relation to national socialism and the status of his 1933–4 period as Nazi Rector of Freiburg University. For a recent commentary on this see Philippe Lacoue-Labarthe, *Heidegger, Art and Politics* (Oxford: Basil Blackwell, 1990).
9. Heidegger, "Discourse on Thinking", op. cit. (1955/2003), pp. 91–2.
10. http://www.asiandubfoundation.com/adf_home_fs.htm.
11. A film by Dan Ross and David Barison which deals with Heidegger's 1942 lecture series on Holderin, with commentary from Bernard Stigler, Jean-Luc Nancy and Philippe Lacoue-Labarthe.
12. Heidegger, "The Question Concerning Technology", in *Political Writings* (1949/2003), p. 297.
13. Thanks are due to Sonja Grussendorf, Brianne Selman, Kevin Young and Tara Blake Wilson for help with keeping this piece in order.

PART III CHAPTER 12

1. S. Rushdie, *Satanic Verses* (New York: Viking, 1988). Rushdie's book caused offence to many Muslims and resulted in the book being publicly burned in Bradford and other cities. However, the controversy took a further turn with the issue of *fatwa*

against Rushdie by Ayatollah Khomeini. The *fatwa* or judgement issued a death sentence against Rushdie and forced him into hiding. Khomeini's intervention divided many Muslims.

2. The Danish newspaper published a series of cartoons including a depiction of the Prophet as a terrorist, on 30th September, 2005. The subsequent controversy became global in February 2006 with riots and deaths in many Muslim countries.

3. *Bezhti* (*Dishonour*), by the Sikh playwright Gupreet Kaur Bhatti, was forced to close its run at the Birmingham Repertory Theatre after violent protests and threats by radical Sikhs.

4. B. Parekh, *Rethinking Multiculturalism* (Basingstoke: Palgrave, 2001), pp. 295–335.

5. The contemporary Western fear of Islam closely echoes the seventeenth- and eighteenth-century fear of Roman Catholics in Britain and of Protestants in France.

6. See A. MacIntyre, *Whose Justice? Which Rationality?* (London: Duckworth, 1988).

7. T. Modood, *Multiculturalism (Themes for the Twenty-First Century)* (Cambridge: Polity Press, forthcoming).

8. R. Dawkins, *The God Delusion* (London: Bantam Press, 2006).

9. J. Rawls, *A Theory of Justice* (Oxford: Oxford University Press, 1972).

10. R. Dworkin, *Sovereign Virtue* (Cambridge MA: Harvard University Press, 2000).

11. Underlying this simple argument is the complex problem of stability that preoccupied Rawls in his later work *Political Liberalism* (New York: Columbia University Press, 1993).

CHAPTER 13

1. See Kok-Chor Tan, "The Rights of Peoples", in *Toleration, Diversity and Global Justice* (Penn State Press, 2000), pp. 103–28.

2. For example, Will Kymlicka, *Liberalism, Community, and Culture* (Oxford: Oxford University Press, 1989); and Joseph Raz, "Multiculturalism: A Liberal Perspective", in *Ethics in the Public Domain* (Oxford: Oxford University Press, 1995), pp. 155–76.

3. Kymlicka, *Liberalism, Community and Culture*, pp. 196–200; and *Multicultural Citizenship: a Liberal Theory of Minority Rights* (Oxford: Oxford University Press, 1995), Chapter 8; and Raz, pp. 183–7.

4. Kymlicka, *Liberalism, Community and Culture*, pp. 169–71.

5. Kymlicka, *Multicultural Citizenship*, pp. 94–5.

6. Charles Taylor, "The Politics of Recognition", in Amy Gutmann (ed.), *Multiculturalism* (Princeton: Princeton University Press, 1994), pp. 72–3.

7. See also Michele M. Moody-Adams, *Fieldwork in Familiar Places* (Cambridge, MA: Harvard University Press, 1997), p. 193.

8. David Miller, *On Nationality* (Oxford: Oxford University. Press, 1995), p. 127, my emphasis.

9. Bhikhu Parekh, "British Citizenship", in Geoff Andrews (ed.), *Citizenship* (London: Lawrence and Wishart, 1991), pp. 183–204, pp. 194–5, my stress.

10. Frank Cunningham, *The Real World of Democracy Revisited* (Atlantic Highlands, NJ: Humanities Press, 1994), pp. 103–5, p. 108.

11. Miller, pp. 127–8.

12. For the kinds of social policies enforced in the name of Asian Values, see Diane K. Mauzy, 'Singapore in 1994', *Asian Survey* Vol XXXV/2 (1995), 179–85. For a historical and evaluative survey of the Asian Values discourse, see Peter R. Moody Jr, 'Asian Values', *Journal of International Affairs* 50/1 (1996), 166–92.

13. As Lee Kuan Yew says, 'The more communitarian values and practices of the East Asians – the Japanese, Koreans, Taiwanese, Hong Kongers, and the Singaporeans – have proved to be clear assets in the catching up process ... The values that East Asian cultures uphold, such as the primacy of group interests over individual interests, support the total group effort necessary to develop rapidly'. Quoted in Samuel P. Huntington, *The Clash of Civilization and the Remaking of World Order* (New York: Simon & Schuster, 1996), p. 108.

14. Bilahari Kim Hee Kausikan, 'An East Asian Approach to Human Rights', *Buffalo Journal of International Law* 2 (1995–96), 263–83, 277. Also Kishore Mahbubani, "The West and the Rest", in *Can Asians Think?* (Singapore: Times Books International, 1997).

15. Kausikan, p. 277.

16. C. B. MacPherson, *The Political Theory of Possessive Individualism: Hobbes to Locke* (Oxford: Oxford University Press, 1964).

17. For instance, Lee Kuan Yew laments that in a liberal society, '[t]he expansion of the right of the individual to behave or misbehave as he pleases has come at the expense of orderly society'. Quoted in Fareed Zakaria, 'Culture is Destiny: A Conversation with Lee Kuan Yew', *Foreign Affairs* 73/2 (1994), 111.

18. For more discussion on how communitarians have mischaracterized liberalism as an asocial doctrine, see Kymlicka, *Liberalism, Community, and Culture*, Chapters 4 and 5. See also my *Toleration, Diversity, and Global Justice*, Chapter 3.

19. Julia Ching, "Human Rights: A Valid Chinese Concept?", in Wm Theodore de Bary and Tu Weiming (eds), *Confucianism and Human Rights* (New York: Columbia University Press, 1997), pp. 67–82, pp. 73–4.

20. See the remarks of the President of Taiwan, Lee Teng-hui, in 'Chinese Culture and Political Renewal', *Journal of Democracy* 6/4 (1995), 4–8, 8.

21. James Gomez, book rev. of *To Catch a Tartar* by Francis Seow, *Human Rights Quarterly* 18 (1996), 507–10, 509.

22. Gomez, p. 509.

CHAPTER 14

1. Samuel P. Huntington, *The Clash of Civilizations and the Remaking of World Order* (New York: Simon and Schuster, 1996).

2. The German concept of *Bildung* has no exact English equivalent. It is a process of the formation or cultivation of a moral personality according to an ideal image (*Bild*). I have discussed this concept at length in *Spectral Nationality: Passages of Freedom from Kant to Postcolonial Literatures of Liberation* (Columbia University Press, 2003), pp. 38–48.

3. Huntington, *The Clash of Civilizations*, p. 82.

4. John Locke, *Two Treatises of Government*, Peter Laslett (ed.), 2nd edn (Cambridge: Cambridge University Press, 1988), p. 283.

5. Ibid, p. 357. The state and civil society are synonymous here. The distinction is only sharply made by Hegel who draws on the writings of the Scottish Enlightenment.

6. For an extended historical study, see John Marshall, *John Locke, Toleration and Early Enlightenment Culture: Religious Intolerance and Arguments for Religious Toleration* (Cambridge: Cambridge University Press, 2006). For an incisive critique of the discourse of tolerance in the current conjuncture, see Wendy Brown, *Regulating Aversion: Tolerance in the Age of Identity and Empire* (Princeton: Princeton University Press, 2006).

7. John Locke, *Epistola de Tolerantia. A Letter on Toleration*, Raymond Klibansky and J. W. Gough (eds) (Oxford: Clarendon Press, 1968), pp. 65, 67.

8. John Stuart Mill, *On Liberty*, in *On Liberty in Focus*, John Gray and G. W. Smith (eds) (London: Routledge, 1991), p. 68.

9. Ibid, pp. 78–9.

10. Ibid, p. 86.

11. Alexis de Tocqueville, *Democracy in America*, trans. Harvey C. Mansfield and Delba Winthrop (Chicago: University of Chicago Press, 2000), Vol. 1, Part 2, Chapter 9, p. 280.

12. Jehangir S. Pocha, "Beijing Eyes Biotech Business: Scientists are Returning to China After Working in the United States", *San Francisco Chronicle*, 16th September (2006), C1.

13. Ronna Kelly, "Delegates from China to Visit U.C. Berkeley for New Innovation and Intellectual Property Rights Program", 10th October, 2006. http://www.berkeley.edu/news/media/releases/2006/10/10_ip.shtml, accessed on 10th October, 2006.

14. Mill, *On Liberty*, p. 87.

15. See Tu Wei-ming, "Cultural China: The Periphery as the Center", in Tu Wei-Ming (ed.), *Tree. The Changing Meaning of Being Chinese Today* (Palo Alto: Stanford University Press, 1994), p. 8.

16. See Wang Gungwu, "The Culture of Chinese Merchants", in Wang, *China and the Chinese Overseas* (Singapore: Times Academic Press, 1991), pp. 181–97.

17. It is an open secret that the former Prime Minister of Singapore, Lee Kuan Yew, one of the key champions of Asian values, was an Anglophile.

18. On the contemporary use of Overseas Chinese Voluntary Associations to create and maintain transnational business networks, see Hong Liu, 'Old Linkages, New Networks: The Globalization of Overseas Chinese Voluntary Associations and its Implications', *China Quarterly* no. 155 (September 1998), 582–609.

19. See Wang Gungwu, 'Greater China and the Chinese Overseas', *China Quarterly*, no. 136 (December 1993), 930–1.

20. See *Dangerous Meditation: China's Campaign Against Falungong*, Human Rights Watch, January 2002. http://hrw.org/reports/2002/china.

21. See Kenneth Dean, *Lord of the Three in One: The Spread of a Cult in Southeast China* (Princeton: Princeton University Press, 1998), pp. 284–5.

22. My discussion draws on and summarizes Liao Ping-hui's fascinating unpublished manuscript, "The Temple of Boom and the Tao of Creolized Second Harmony", paper delivered at The Creolization of Theory conference, UCLA, May 5–6, 2006. The website of the U.S. branch of *Heqidao* located in San Jose is http://www.hochi.org/index_us.htm. The website of the Taiwan center is http://www.hochi.org.tw.

23. Liao, "The Temple of Boom", p. 11.

24. Ibid, p. 12.

25. Unlike the U.S. government, Mill warned his readers about conflating the doctrine of free trade with the principle of individual liberty. See *On Liberty*, p. 109.

CHAPTER 15

1. D. Held, 'Law of States, Law of Peoples,' *Legal Theory* 8:1 (2002), 1–44.

2. For an extended version of the discussion of national identity versus cosmopolitan identity, including a detailed analysis of the relationship between nationalism and cosmopolitanism, see M. Guibernau, *The Identity of Nations* (Cambridge: Polity Press, 1999), Chapter 7.

3. *Collins Concise English Dictionary*, 3rd edn (1993), p. 297.

4. P. Norris, 'Global governance and cosmopolitan citizens', in D. Held and A. McGrew, *The Global Transformations Reader*, pp. 287–97, p. 294.

5. J. Tomlinson, *Globalisation and Culture* (Cambridge: Polity Press, 1999).

CHAPTER 16

1. See D. Held, 'Law of States, Law of Peoples', *Legal Theory* 8:1 (2002), 1–44, from which I have adapted the following four paragraphs.

2. Ibid. For an elaboration of these principles also see Appendix of D. Held, *Global Covenant* (Cambridge: Polity Press, 2004).

3. See T. McCarthy, *Ideals and Illusions* (Cambridge, MA: MIT Press, 1991), pp. 181–99.

4. Cf. J. Rawls, 'Justice as fairness: political not metaphysical', *Philosophy of Public Affairs* 14:3 (1985), 254 ff.

5. Cf. B. Barry, "International Society from a Cosmopolitan Perspective", in D. Mapel and T. Nardin (eds), *International Society* (Princeton, NJ: Princeton University Press, 1998); and D. Miller, "The Limits of Cosmopolitan Justice", in Mapel and Nardin, ibid.

6. Cf. J. Tully, *Strange Multiplicity* (Cambridge: Cambridge University Press, 1995).

7. See J. Habermas, *Between Facts and Norms* (Cambridge: Polity Press, 1996); and T. McCarthy, 'On reconciling cosmopolitan unity and national diversity', *Public Culture* II (1999), 175–208.

8. See A. Kuper, 'Rawlsian global justice', *Political Theory* 28 (2000), 640–74, esp. 649 f.

9. K. Tan, 'Liberal toleration in the law of peoples', *Ethics* 108 (1998), 276–95, esp. 283.

10. B. Ackerman, 'Political Liberalism', *Journal of Political Philosophy* 91 (1994), 382–3.

11. See A. Sen, 'Humanity and Citizenship', in J. Cohen (ed.), *For Love of Country* (Boston: Beacon, 1996).

12. See F. Halliday, *Islam and the Myth of Confrontation* (London: I. B. Tauris, 1996).

PART IV CHAPTER 17

1. Joseph S. Nye, Jr, *Bound to Lead: The Changing Nature of American Power* (New York: Basic Books, 1990).

2. See Peter Katzenstein and Robert Keohane (eds), *Anti-Americanisms in World Politics* (Ithaca: Cornell University Press, 2006), and Julia Sweig, *Friendly Fire: Losing Friends and Making Enemies in the Anti-American Century* (New York: Public Affairs Press, 2006).

3. Hubert Vedrine with Dominique Moisi, *France in An Age of Globalization* (Washington: Brookings, 2001), p. 3.

4. Anthony Giddens, *Runaway World: How Globalization is Reshaping Our Lives* (New York: Routledge, 2000), p. 22.

5. Kishore Mahbubani, "The Rest of the West?" Text of RSA/BBC World Lectures, London, 1st June, 2000 (at http://www.bbc.co.uk/worldservice/people/features/world_lectures/mahbub_lect.shtml), p. 26.

6. Neal M. Rosendorf, "Social and Cultural Globalization: Concepts, History, and America's Role", in Joseph S. Nye and John D. Donahue (eds), *Governance in a Globalizing World* (Washington, D.C.: Brookings Institution Press, 2000), p. 133, fn. 51.

7. Frederick Schauer, "The Politics and Incentives of Legal Transplantation". in Nye and Donahue (eds), cited.

8. Walter LaFeber, *Michael Jordan and the New Global Capitalism* (New York: Norton), p. 110.

9. Ronald Burt, *Structural Holes: The Social Structure of Competition* (Cambridge, MA: Harvard Univ. Press, 1992), Chapter 1.

10. Tony Saich, "Globalization, Governance, and the Authoritarian State: China", in Nye and Donahue (eds), cited, p. 224.

11. Bill Joy et al., 'Why the Future Doesn't Need Us', *Wired*, April (2000).

12. See *Daedalus*, special issue on 'Multiple Modernities', Winter (2000). See also John Tomlinson, *Globalization and Culture* (Chicago: University of Chicago Press, 1999).

13. Alex Inkeles, *One World Emerging? Convergence and Divergence in Industrial Societies* (Boulder: Westview, 1998), pp. xiv–xv.

14. Sharon Moshavi, "Japan's Teens Take Trip to US Hip-Hop", *Boston Globe*, 29th October (2000), p. A18.

15. Mario Vargas Llosa, "The Culture of Liberty", *Foreign Policy* January–February (2001), available at http://www.foreignpolicy.com/issue_janfeb_2001/vargasllosa.html.

16. Giddens, cited, p. 31.

17. Dan Barry, "Gaelic Comes Back on Ireland's Byways and Airwaves", *New York Times*, 25th July (2000), p. A6.

CHAPTER 18

1. See Anne-Marie Slaughter, "Hubris and Hypocrisy: America Is Failing to Honor Its Own Codes", *International Herald Tribune*, 22nd May (2004).

2. "No Global Warming Alarm in the U.S., China: America's Image Slips, but Allies Share U.S. Concerns over Iran, Hamas", Pew Global Attitudes Project, 13th June (2006). Available at www.pewglobal.org.

3. Theo Sommer, "Presentation to Bucerius Summer Program for Young Leaders", August, 2004, Hamburg.

4. George W. Bush, Address to Congress, 20th September, 2001, Washington D.C.

5. "The National Security Strategy of the United States of America", March, 2006. Available at http://www.whitehouse.gov/nsc/nss/2006.

6. "No Global Warming Alarm in the U.S., China: America's Image Slips, but Allies Share U.S. Concerns over Iran, Hamas", Pew Global Attitudes Project, 13th June, 2006. Available at www.pewglobal.org.

7. Ibid.

8. Reverend Forrest Church, "From Nationalism to Patriotism: Reclaiming the American Creed", in *Spiritual Perspectives on America's Role as a Superpower* (Skylight Paths: Woodstock, 2003).

9. Reverend Forrest Church, "We Need More Patriots in the Struggle Against Nationalism", *UU World* January/February (2003). Available at http://www. uuworld.org/2003/01/commentary.html.

10. G. K. Chesterton, *What I Saw in America* (1922).
11. "Ode", Sung in the town hall, Concord, New Hampshire, 4th July, 1857. Available at http://www.potw.org/archive/potw369.html.
12. Dr Martin Luther King Junior, "I Have a Dream" speech, delivered 28th August, 1963, Washington, D.C. Available at http://www.mtholyoke.edu/acad/intrel/speech/dream.htm.
13. John Winthrop, "A Citty upon a Hill: A Modell of Christian Charitie", 1630. Available at http://vassun.vassar.edu/~juweisen/382/winthrop.html.
14. Thomas Carothers, "The Backlash against Democracy Promotion", *Foreign Affairs* March/April (2006), 55.
15. Golnaz Esfandiari, "Political Activists Steer Clear of Possible U.S. Funding," RadioFreeEurope, Prague, 4th April, 2006. Available at http://www.rferl.org/featuresarticle/2006/04/d610e8e6–5549–4ea5–8922–0cd07b44d799.html.
16. Condoleezza Rice, Speech at Southern Baptist Convention Annual Meeting, 14th June, 2006, Greensboro, North Carolina. Available at http://www.state.gov/secretary/rm/2006/67896.htm.

CHAPTER 19

1. Mark Rice-Oxley, "In 2,000 Years, Will the World Remember Disney or Plato?", *Christian Science Monitor* 15th January (2004).
2. " 'Star Wars' Film Legend George Lucas Wants More Worldly Hollywood", Brietbart.com. 23rd March, 2006. Online. http://www.breitbart.com/news/2006/03/23/060323083516.2phtlue4.html. Accessed 10th August, 2006.
3. See, for instance, Scott R. Olson, *Hollywood Planet: Global Media and the Competitive Advantage of Narrative Transparency* (Mahwah: Lawrence Erlbaum, 1999).
4. John Meisel, "Escaping Extinction: Cultural Defense of an Undefended Border", in D. Flaherty and W. McKercher (eds), *Southern Exposure: Canadian Perspectives on the United States* (Toronto: McGraw-Hill Ryerson, 1986).
5. Thomas H. Guback, *The International Film Industry: Western Europe and America Since 1945* (Bloomington: Indiana University Press, 1969); Kristin Thompson, *Exporting Entertainment: America in the World Film Market, 1907–1934* (London: British Film Institute, 1986); Jens Ulff-Møller, *Hollywood Film Wars with France: Film-Trade Diplomacy and the Emergence of the French Quota Policy* (Rochester, NY: University of Rochester Press, 2001).
6. From the MPAA's website at http://www.mpaa.org/inter_landing.asp.
7. Quoted in Toby Miller et al., *Global Hollywood* (London: British Film Institute, 2001).
8. Allen J. Scott, "Hollywood in the Era of Globalization", YaleGlobal Online, 29th November, 2002. Online. http://yaleglobal.yale.edu/display.article?id=479. Accessed 1st August, 2006.

9. For instance, see Christina Klein, "The Asia Factor in Global Hollywood: Breaking Down the Notion of a Distinctly American Cinema", YaleGlobal Online, 25th March, 2003. Online. http://yaleglobal.yale.edu/display.article?id=1242. Accessed 1st August, 2006.

CHAPTER 20

1. Samuel P. Huntington, *Who Are We? The Challenges To America's National Identity* (New York: Simon and Shuster, 2004), esp. Chapter 7.
2. Michael J. Weiss, *The Clustered World: How We Live, What We Buy, and What It All Means About Who We Are* (London: Little Brown, 2000).
3. The Pew Global Attitudes Project: "A 16-Nation Pew Global Attitudes Survey", June, 2005. www.pewglobal.org.
4. This phrase is Benjamin Barber's. See Jeff Fleischer "Operation Hollywood: How the Pentagon bullies movie producers into showing the U.S. Military in the best possible light", *Mother Jones*, 20th September (2004).
5. This is a phrase of Susan Buck Morss, see her *Thinking Past Terror* (London: Verso, 2004).
6. Freud, "Disillusionment In Times of War", in *The Standard Edition*, Volume IV, 1914–1916, in Edward Bernays, *Propaganda* (New York: Liveright, 1928); Peter Davidson (ed.), *Orwell And Politics* (London: Penguin, 2001).
7. Robert N. Proctor, *Cancer Wars* (New York: Basic Books, 1996); Londa Schiebinger, *Plants And Empire* (Harvard, Cambridge, 2004).
8. Catherine Philip, "Marine sings about shooting child dead", *The Times* 15th June (2006).
9. Reporters Without Borders, 29th August, 2005.
10. James Yee, *For God And Country: Faith And Patriotism Under Fire* (New York: Public Affairs Press, 2005).
11. Janis Karpinski with Steven Strasser, *One Woman's Army* (New York: Hyperion, 2005), p. 219.
12. President Bush's recent acknowledgment at the 2006 convention of the NAACP should be understood in this light.
13. Richard Norton-Taylor and Jamie Wilson, "US army in Iraq institutionally racist, claims British officer", *Guardian*, 12th January (2006).
14. Karen Gilchrist, "Soldier rapper tells his tale of Iraq", BBC news website, 22nd March (2006). http://news.bbc.co.uk/2/hi/americas/4828816.stm. See also: Scott Johnson and Eve Conant "Soldier Rap, The Pulse of War", *Newsweek*, 13th June (2006).
15. Frank Main, "Gangs claim their turf in Iraq", *Chicago Sun-Times*, 1st May (2006).
16. Whitney Joiner, "THE ARMY BE THUGGING IT". http://www.salon.com/mwt/feature/2003/10/17/army/print.html.

CHAPTER 21

1. Pew Global Attitudes Project reports: "America's Image Further Erodes, Europeans Want Weaker Ties", 18th March (2003), http://pewglobal.org/reports/pdf/175.pdf; "A Year After Iraq War Mistrust of America in Europe Ever Higher, Muslim Anger Persists", 16th March (2004), http://pewglobal.org/reports/pdf/206.pdf;: "U.S. Image Up Slightly, But Still Negative", 23rd June (2005), http://pewglobal.org/reports/pdf/247.pdf; "America's Image Slips, But Allies Share U.S. Concerns Over Iran, Hamas", 13th June (2006), http://pewglobal.org/reports/pdf/252.pdf.
2. See for example *The Economist*, 'The view from abroad', Special Report on Anti-Americanism, 17th February (2005); 'Still not loved. Now not envied', 23rd June (2005).
3. Thierry Meyssan, *11 Septembre 2001: L'effroyable Imposture* (Editions Carnot, 2002).
4. John Micklethwait and Adrian Wooldridge, *The Right Nation: Why America is Different* (London: Allen Lane, 2004).

PART V: CHAPTER 22

1. Thomas L. Friedman, *The World is Flat: A Brief History of The Twenty-First Century* (New York: Farrar, Straus and Giroux, 2005).
2. Thomas L. Friedman, *The Lexus and the Olive Tree: Understanding Globalization* (New York: Farrar, Straus and Giroux, 1999).
3. For a fuller discussion of these conflicts see Amy Chua's *World on Fire*, 2003. Amy Chua, *World on Fire: How Exporting Free Market Democracy Breeds Ethnic Hatred and Global Instability* (New York: Doubleday, a Division of Random House Inc., 2003).
4. Evelyn Howell, *Mizh: A Monograph on Government's Relations with the Mashud Tribe* (Karachi: Oxford University Press, 1999; original 1931).
5. Akbar S. Ahmed, *Resistance and Control in Pakistan* (London: Routledge, 2004. Revised edition. Originally published in 1991).
6. Madeleine Albright, *Madam Secretary: A Memoir* (New York: Hyperion, 2003), p. 469.
7. N. Schmidle, 'Migration Season: The Taliban and Their Expanding Influence in Pakistan', *ICWA Letters*, NES-4 Pakistan (2006).
8. Christina Lamb, *The Sewing Circles of Herat: A Personal Voyage Through Afghanistan* (London and New York: Harper Collins, 2002).

CHAPTER 23

1. A much more extended treatment of this topic will be found in my book, *Re-Enchanting Modernity: Sovereignty, Ritual Economy, and Indigenous Civil Order in Coastal China* (in-progress).

2. J.K. Gibson-Graham, *The End of Capitalism (as we knew it): A Feminist Critique of Political Economy* (London: Blackwell, 1996).

3. For an argument that differential rates of capitalist development in the world can be traced to cultural traditions of entrepreneurship and commercial activity, see the collection edited by Harrison and Huntington. Lawrence E. Harrison and Samuel P. Huntington (eds), *Culture Matters: How Values Shape Human Progress* (New York: Basic Books, 2001). For a more detailed exposition of my views on hybrid economy and the importance of ritual expenditures in rural coastal China, inspired by Georges Bataille's theory, see 'Putting Global Capitalism in its Place: Economic Hybridity, Bataille, and Ritual Expenditure', *Current Anthropology* vol. 41, no. 4 (2000).

4. Karl Marx, *The Grundisse: Introduction to the Critique of Political Economy*. Martin Nicholaus, trans. (Middlesex, England: Penguin Books, 1973). Studies in political economy and economic history inspired by Karl Polanyi and Fernand Braudel have been much more attentive to the presence and impact of pre-capitalist forms in capitalism. See Fernand Braudel, *Civilization and Capitalism: 15th–18th Century*, Vols 1–3 (Berkeley: University of California Press, 1992); Karl Polanyi, *The Great Transformation* (New York: Rinehart, 1944); Karl Polanyi, "The Economy as Instituted Process", in Karl Polanyi and Conrad Arensberg (eds), *Trade and Market in Early Empires* (Glencoe, IL: The Free Press, 1957).

5. See Janet Abu-Lughod, *Before European Hegemony: the World System* A.D. 1250–1350 (Oxford: Oxford University Press, 1989); Andre Gunder Frank, *ReOrient: Global Economy in the Asian Age* (Berkeley: University of California Press, 1998); R. Bin Wong, *China Transformed: Historical Change and the Limits of European Experience* (Ithaca: Cornell University Press, 1997); Kenneth Pomeranz, *The Great Divergence: China, Europe, and the Making of the Modern World Economy* (Princeton: Princeton University Press, 2000).

6. Hill Gates, *China's Motor: A Thousand Years of Petty Capitalism* (Ithaca: Cornell University Press, 1996).

7. Max Weber, *The Protestant Ethic and the Spirit of Capitalism*. Talcot Parsons, trans. (New York: Charles Scribner's Sons, 1958).

8. Gordon S. Redding, *The Spirit of Chinese Capitalism* (Berlin: Walter DeGruyter, 1990).

9. Timothy Brook, *The Confusions of Pleasure: Commerce and Culture in Ming China* (Berkeley: University of California Press, 1998); Mayfair Yang, "Agrarian Sovereignty vs. Coastal Economy: the Puzzle of the Wenzhou Model", unpublished paper presented at Center for Chinese Studies, University of California, Berkeley, and UCLA.

10. Zhichen Zhang, "The Wenzhou Model," *Wenzhou City Gazeteer* vol. 2 (1998), Chapter 26, p. 1032.

11. See my discussion of the history of radical state secularism in twentieth-century China, and the effects of the introduction of the Western categories of "religion" and "superstition", which produced perhaps the largest-scale destruction of

religious life and properties in the modern world. See Mayfair Yang, "Introduction", in Mayfair Yang (ed.), *Chinese Religiosities: Afflictions of Modernity and State Formation* (University of California Press, forthcoming).

12. See Mayfair Yang, 'Spatial Struggles: State Disenchantment and Popular Re-appropriation of Space in Rural Southeast China', *Journal of Asian Studies* August (2004).

13. The Book of Changes (*Yi Jing*) is a Western Zhou (1027–771 BCE) divination text that has been consulted down to the present day for glimpses into the future. Expressing ancient Chinese philosophy and thought on living in harmony with natural forces and balancing between yin and yang forces, calculations on the future are based on reading "hexagrams", made up of six lines, broken or solid, stacked on top of each other.

14. Indeed, where Chinese popular religion has been supported by economic prosperity, it has not shied away from making use of new technologies to promote itself. See my discussion of the Taiwan cult and pilgrimage of the maritime goddess Mazu and its deployment of satellite television. See Mayfair Yang, 'Goddess across the Taiwan Straits: Matrifocal Ritual Space, Nation-State, and Satellite Television Footprints', *Public Culture* May (2004).

15. Of course, even Western capitalism is embedded in social institutions, although these institutions tend to be modern ones that capitalism itself created to facilitate its own movements, such as occupational associations and interest groups.

16. As French philosopher and theorist of religion Georges Bataille has noted, in the history of the West, Christianity also encouraged great ritual expenditures, from giant medieval cathedrals to religious festivals and charities, but the Protestant Reformation cut down a great deal on this "waste". See Georges Bataille, *The Accursed Share: An Essay on General Economy,* Vol. 1: Consumption, Robert Hurley, trans. (New York: Zone Books, 1989).

CHAPTER 24

1. John Stuart Mill, "On Liberty", in John M. Robson (ed.), *Essays on Politics and Society*, vol.18 of the *Collected Works of John Stuart Mill* (Toronto: University of Toronto Press, 1977), p. 270.

2. Quoted in Larry Strelitz, 'Where the Global Meets the Local: Media Studies and the Myth of Cultural Homogenization', *Transnational Broadcasting Studies* no. 6, Spring/Summer (2001). http://tbsjournal.com/Archives/Spring01/strelitz.html.

3. Ien Ang, *Watching "Dallas": Soap Opera and the Melodramatic Imagination* (London: Methuen, 1985); Tamar Liebes and Elihu Katz, *The Export of Meaning: Cross-cultural Readings of Dallas* (New York: Oxford University Press, 1996); Rob Nixon, *Homelands, Harlem and Hollywood: South African Culture and the World Beyond* (New York: Routledge, 1994); L. Strelitz, "Where the Global Meets the Local".

4. See J.D. Straubhaar, 'Beyond Media Imperialism: Asymmetrical Interdependence and Cultural Proximity', *Critical Studies on Mass Communications* 8 (1991), p. 394.

5. The quotes from the Zulu student Sipho are from Larry Strelitz, *Where the Global Meets the Local: South African Youth and Their Experience of the Global Media* (PhD Thesis, Rhodes University, 2003), pp. 137–41.

6. Salman Rushdie, *Imaginary Homelands: Essays and Criticism, 1981–1991* (London: Granta Books, 1991) p. 394.

CHAPTER 25

1. Ian Hacking, "Making up people", in *Historical Ontology* (Cambridge, MA: Harvard University Press, 2002 [1986]).

2. There is a vast body of literature in anthropology on the viability of the culture-concept, which critiques older essentialising tendencies inherent in understanding culture as a whole on the one hand and on the other, as a common shorthand that explains less than it glosses over. See Lila Abu-Lughod, "Writing against culture", in R. Fox (ed.), *Recapturing Anthropology: Working in the Present* (Santa Fe: School of American Research Press, 1991). Compare Terence Turner, 'Anthropology and multiculturalism: what is anthropology that multilculturalism should be aware of', *Cultural Anthropology* 8 (4), 411–29.

3. Michel Foucault, "Governmentality", in G. Burchell, C. Gordon and P. Miller (eds), *The Foucault Effect: Studies in Governmentality* (Hemel Hempstead: Harvester Wheatsheaf, 1991); Dipesh Chakrabarty, *Habitations of Modernity: Essays in the Wake of Subaltern Studies* (Chicago: Chicago University Press, 2003); Partha Chatterjee, *The Politics of the Governed: Reflections on the Popular Politics of Most of the World* (New York: Columbia University Press, 2004).

4. K. S. Singh, *People of India*. Various volumes (Delhi: Oxford University Press, Anthropological Survey of India, 2002).

5. For example, Arjun Appadurai, "Numbers in the colonial imagination", in C. A. Breckenridge and P. van der Veer (eds), *Orientalism and the Postcolonial Predicament* (Philadelphia: University of Pennsylvania Press, 1993); Bernard Cohn, "The census, social structure and objectification in South Asia", in *An Anthropologist Amongst Historians and Other Essays* (Delhi: Oxford University Press, 1987); Nicholas B. Dirks, *Castes of Mind: Colonialism and the Making of Modern India* (New Jersey: Princeton University Press, 2001).

6. The Constituent Assembly was responsible for writing the Constitution for independent India and was headed by the eminent leader of the depressed classes and jurist, B. R. Ambedkar. India became independent in 1947 and the Constitution was adopted in 1950 when it became a Republic.

7. Nandini Sundar, 'Caste as a census category: implications for sociology', *Current Sociology* 48 (3), 111–26; p. 122.

8. See Susan Bayly, *Caste, Society and Politics in India from the Eighteenth Century to the Modern Age* (Cambridge: Cambridge University Press, 1999); Andre Beteille, 'The idea of indigenous people', *Current Anthropology* 39 (2), 187–91; Stuart Corbridge, 'Competing inequalities: the scheduled tribes and the reservation system in India's Jharkhand', *The Journal of Asian Studies* 59 (1), 62–85; L. Rudolph and S. Rudolph, "Living with multiculturalism: universalism and particularism in an Indian historical context", in R. Shweder et al. (eds), *Engaging Cultural Differences: The Multicultural Challenge in Liberal Democracies* (New York: Russell Sage Foundation, 2002), pp. 43–62.

9. M. Galanter, *Competing Equalities: Law and Backward Classes in India* (Delhi: Oxford University Press, 1984).

10. Jagdish Bhagwati, *In Defence of Globalisation* (Oxford: Oxford University Press, 2004).

11. Jan Breman and Arvind N. Das, *Down and Out: Labouring Under Global Capitalism* (Delhi: Oxford University Press, 2000); Vinay Gidwani and K. Sivaramakrishnan, 'Circular migration and the spaces of cultural assertion', *Annals of the Association of American Geographers* 93 (1), 186–213; Barbara Harriss-White (ed.), *Globalisation and Insecurity: Political, Economic and Physical Challenges* (London: Palgrave, 2004); Kriti Kapila and Akhil Gupta (eds), *Globalisation at Work: Making a Living in Contemporary India* (Durham: Duke University Press, forthcoming).

12. Kriti Kapila, 'The measure of a tribe: the cultural politics of constitutional reclassification in north India', *Journal of the Royal Anthropological Institute* (forthcoming); Beppe Karlsson, 'Anthropology and the indigenous slot: claims to and debates about indigenous peoples' status in India', *Critique of Anthropology* 23 (4) (2003), 403–23.

13. For example, V. Xaxa, 'Tribes as indigenous people of India', *Economic and Political Weekly* (1999), pp. 3389–595.

14. Anulabha Basu, Partha Majumder et al., 'Ethnic India: A genomic view with special reference to peopling and structures', *Genomic Research* 13 (2003), 2277–90; Partha Majumder, 'People of India: biological diversities and affinities', *Evolutionary Anthropology* 6 (3) (1998), 100–10.

15. The instrumental use of the science of archaeology by Hindu nationalist leaders and ideologues in the debate surrounding the original status of the Babri Masjid in Ayodhya as the birthplace of Lord Ram comes immediately to mind (see Sarvepalli Gopal (ed.), *Anatomy of a Confrontation: The Babri Masjid* (New Delhi: Viking, 1991).

16. Paul Rabinow, *French DNA: Trouble in Purgatory* (Chicago: University of Chicago Press, 1999).

CHAPTER 27

1. F. Halliday, 'Terrorism and Delusion', *Open Democracy* 12th April (2006), www.openDemocracy.net.

2. M. Engström, 'The Fear Haunting Europe', *Open Democracy* 26th May (2006), www.openDemocracy.net.

3. The distinction between low intensity democracy and a more open-ended and participatory democracy emerged in the early 1990s in area studies of the non-European world. In the early years of this century it began to be applied to the study of the restricted and elite character of representative democracies in Europe and North America and to the narrow definition of democracy in policies of global democratization in international law. See, respectively: B.J. Gills, J. Rocamora and R. Wilson, 'Low Intensity Democracy', in Gills et al. (eds), *Low Intensity Democracy: Political Power in the New World Order* (London: Pluto, 1993), pp.1–21; B. de Sousa Santos, *The World Social Forum: A User's Manual* (2003), pp. 104–15 and http://www.ces.us.pt/bss/documentos/fsm_eng.pdf; and S. Marks, *The Riddle of All Constitutions: International law, democracy and critique of ideology* (Oxford: Oxford University Press, 2000).

4. J. Tully, "Wittgenstein and Political Philosophy: Understanding practices of critical reflection", in C. Heyes (ed.), *The Grammar of Politics: Wittgenstein and Political Philosophy* (Ithaca: Cornell University Press, 2003), pp. 17–41.

5. A. Weiner, *The Invisible Constitution: Making meanings accountable for democratic politics* (forthcoming).

6. This section is a brief summary of the central section of the article from which this chapter is drawn: 'A New Kind of Europe? Democratic Integration in the European Union', *CRISPP* Fall (2006).

7. Paul Gilroy, *After Empire: Melancholia or convivial culture?* (London: Routledge, 2004).

8. Peter Swan, "American Empire or Empires? Alternative Juridifications of the New World Order", in A. Bartholomew (ed.), *Empire's Law: The American Imperial Project and the war to remake the world* (London: Pluto, 2006), pp. 137–60.

9. J.C. Scott, *Seeing Like a State: How Certain Schemes to Improve the Human Condition have Failed* (New Haven: Yale University Press, 1998).

10. N. Quastel, *Contract, Sustainability and the Ecology of Exchange* (LLM Dissertation, Faculty of Law, University of Victoria, 2006).

11. P. Mair, 'Popular Democracy and the European Union Polity', *European Governance Papers*, C-0503 (2005), www.connnexx-network.org/eruogov/pdf/egp-connex-c-0503.pdf.

12. M. Castells, *The Information Age: Economy, Society and Culture*, 3 Vols (Oxford: Blackwell, 1998).

13. R. Bellamy and A. Warleigh "Introduction: The Puzzle of EU Citizenship", in Bellamy and Warleigh (eds), *Citizenship and Governance in the European Union* (London: Routledge, 2001), pp. 3–18.

14. See B. Latour, *Reassembling the Social: An introduction to actor-network theory* (Oxford: Oxford University Press, 2005); J. Law and J. Hassard (eds), *Actor Network Theory and After* (Oxford: Blackwell, 1999); N. Quastel, *Contract, Sustainability*

and the Ecology of Exchange (LLM Dissertation, Faculty of Law, University of Victoria, 2006).

15. J. von Bernstorff, 'Democratic Global Internet Regulation? Governance Networks, International Law and the Shadow of Hegemony', *European Law Journal* 9(4) (2003), 511–26.

16. N. Walker, "Making a World of Difference? Habermas, Cosmopolitanism and the Constitutionalization of International Law", in O.P. Shabani (ed.), *Multiculturalism and the Law: Critical Debates* (Cardiff: University of Wales Press, 2007); A. Weiner, 'The Dual Quality of Norms: Stability and Flexibility', *CRISPP* (forthcoming); J. Tully, "Exclusion and Assimilation: Two forms of domination in relation to freedom", in M. Williams and S. Macedo (eds), *Political Exclusion and Domination* (New York: New York University Press, 2005), pp. 191–230, 250–8; J. Tully, 'Communication and Imperialism', *100 Days of Theory, CTheory,* www.ctheory.net/articles.aspx?id =508.

17. For the deep problems in conceptualizing this relationship between the people and the European Union I am indebted to Christodoulidis 2003, Lindahl 2003, 2007.

PART VI CHAPTER 28

1. Thomas L. Friedman, "Big ideas and no boundaries", *New York Times,* 6th October (2006). Available at http://select.nytimes.com/2006/10/06/opinion/06friedman.html. For an extended account of Friedman's view that globalization is enabling a transformation in the way that people connect, collaborate and compete, see his book, *The World is Flat: A Brief History of the Twenty-First Century,* updated and expanded edition (New York: Farrar, Straus and Giroux, 2006).

2. See Anne-Marie Slaughter, *A New World Order* (Princeton, New Jersey: Princeton University Press, 2004).

3. Gro Harlem Brundtland, "Public health challenges in a globalizing world", *European Journal of Public Health* 15, no. 1 (2005), 3–5, at p. 3. See also Richard L. Harris and Melinda Seid (eds), *Globalization and Health,* International Studies in Sociology and Social Anthropology, 95 (Leiden, The Netherlands: Brill, 2004); and Kelley Lee (ed.), *Health Impacts of Globalization: Towards Global Governance* (London: Palgrave Macmillan, 2003).

4. See, for example, the recent essay by IBM CEO Samuel Palmisano on "The globally integrated enterprise", *Foreign Affairs* 85, May/June (2006), 127–36.

5. A good introduction is Michael Reich (ed.), *Public-Private Partnerships for Public Health* (Cambridge, MA: Harvard Center for Population and Development Studies, 2002).

6. Michael R. Reich, 'Public-private partnerships for public health', *Nature Medicine* 6, June (2000), 617–20, at page 618. PPPs take a number of structural forms, ranging from simple affiliation through formal joint ventures, with different implications for

approaches to governance, planning, resources, operations and evaluation; see Bill & Melinda Gates Foundation, "Developing *successful* global health alliances", Seattle, Washington, April 2002, available at http://www.gatesfoundation.org/nr/ Downloads/ globalhealth/GlobalHealthAlliances.pdf.

7. William H. Foege, "Blurring the lines: public and private partnerships addressing global health", in Michael A. Santorro and Thomas M. Gorrie, *Ethics and the Pharmaceutical Industry* (Cambridge: Cambridge University Press, 2005), pp. 386–92, at p. 392.

8. Raymond V. Gilmartin, "A new role for corporate America: partners in global health and development", in William H. Foege et al. (eds), *Global Health Leadership and Management* (San Francisco, California: Jossey-Bass, 2005), pp. 9–24, at p. 23. See also Jane Nelson and Dave Prescott, *Business and the Millennium Development Goals: A Framework for Action* (London, England: International Business Leaders Forum, 2003).

9. Linda Distlerath and Guy MacDonald, 'The African Comprehensive HIV/AIDS Partnerships – A new role for multinational corporations in global health policy,' *Yale Journal of Health Policy, Law and Ethics* IV:1 (2004), 147–55; Merck & Co., Inc., *Committed to Making a Difference: Corporate Responsibility 2004–2005 Report* (Whitehouse Station, New Jersey: Merck & Co., Inc., 2005), at p. 6, available at http://www.merck.com/cr/docs/Merck_Corporate_Responsibility_Report_2005.pdf; and David L. Finegold, "Merck: Staying the course", in David L. Finegold et al. (eds), *Bioindustry Ethics* (Amsterdam, The Netherlands: Elsevier Academic Press, 2005), pp. 19–53. For perspective on this view of corporate social responsibility (CSR), see Sheila M.J. Bonini, Lenny T. Mendonca and Jeremy M. Oppenheim, 'When social issues become strategic', *McKinsey Quarterly* Number 2 (2006), 20–32; Ian Davis, 'What *is* the business of business?', *McKinsey Quarterly* Number 3 (2005), 105–13; Commission on the Private Sector & Development, *Unleashing Entrepreneurship Making Business Work for the Poor*, Report to the Secretary-General of the United Nations (New York: United Nations Development Programme, 2004), esp. pp. 34–6; and Ira A. Jackson and Jane Nelson, *Profits with Principles: Seven Strategies for Delivering Value with Values* (New York: Currency/Doubleday, 2004). For a more critical stance toward CSR, see Marina Prieto-Carrón et al., 'Critical perspectives on CSR and development: what we know, what we don't know, and what we need to know', *International Affairs* 82, September (2006), 977–87.

10. See, for example, International Federation of Pharmaceutical Manufacturers and Associations (IFPMA), *Partnerships to Build Healthier Societies in the Developing World*, Geneva, May 2007, available at http://www.ifpma.org/documents/NR7345/ %20-%20Building%20Healthier%202007.pdf.

11. For further information on Merck's experience in public health initiatives in the developing world, go to: http://www.merck.com/cr/enabling_access/developing_world/.

12. A compendium of articles on the MECTIZAN Donation Program was published in the March 2004 issue of *Tropical Medicine and International Health* (Volume 9,

Issue 3, pp. A1–A56), also available at: http://www.mectizan.org/impact.asp. See also Jeffrey L. Sturchio and Brenda Colatrella, "Successful public private partnerships in global health: lessons from the MECTIZAN Donation Program," in Brigitte Granville (ed.), *The Economics of Essential Medicines* (London: Royal Institute of International Affairs, 2002), pp. 255–74; and P. Roy Vagelos and Louis Galambos, *Medicine, Science and Merck* (Cambridge: Cambridge University Press, 2004), pp. 246–54.

13. African Comprehensive HIV/AIDS Partnerships, *ACHAP Annual Report 2006* (Gaborone, Botswana: ACHAP, 2007); Bill & Melinda Gates Foundation, "Working with Botswana to confront its devastating AIDS crisis", June 2006, available at www.gatesfoundation.org/whatwerelearning; Ilavenil Ramiah and Michael R. Reich, 'Public-private partnerships and antiretroviral drugs for HIV/AIDS: lesson from Botswana', *Health Affairs* 24, March/April (2005): 545–51; Ramiah and Reich, 'Building effective public-private partnerships: experiences and lessons from the African Comprehensive HIV/AIDS Partnerships (ACHAP)', *Social Science & Medicine* 63 (2006), 397–408; and Patricia A. Watson (ed.), *The Front Line in the War Against HIV/AIDS in Botswana: Case Studies from the African Comprehensive HIV/AIDS Partnership* (Gaborone, Botswana: ACHAP, 2004). See also www.achap.org.

14. Kofi Annan, "The Global Challenges of AIDS", Diana, Princess of Wales Memorial Lecture, London, England, 25th June, 1999, available at www.un.org in Press Release SG/SM/7045.

CHAPTER 29

1. See http://www.legalserviceindia.com/articles/ppch.htm.
2. Marcia Angell, *The Truth About the Drug Companies* (New York: Random House, 2004).

CHAPTER 30

1. D. Harvey, *The New Imperialism* (Oxford: OUP, 2005).
2. N. Thrift, *Knowing Capitalism* (London: Sage, 2005), p. 3.
3. This work led in part to my study of the BBC in its political and industrial milieu, *Uncertain Vision: Birt, Dyke and the Reinvention of the BBC* (London: Vintage, 2005).
4. M. Castells, *The Rise of the Network Society* (Oxford: Blackwell, 1996).
5. J. L. Austin, *How To Do Things With Words* (Oxford: Clarendon, 1962).
6. P. Osborne, *The Politics of Time* (London: Verso, 1995), p. ix.
7. D. Mackenzie, 'Physics and finance: S-terms and modern finance as a topic for science studies', *Science, Technology and Human Values* 26, 2 (2001), 115–44, p. 128.
8. Thrift (2005), p. 4.

9. D. Slater, "Capturing markets from the economists", in P. Du Gay and M. Pryke (eds), *Cultural Economy* (London: Sage, 2002), pp. 246–8.

10. M. Callon (ed.), *The Laws of the Markets* (Oxford: Blackwell, 1998), p. 29.

11. A. Barry and D. Slater, "Introduction: The technological economy", in A. Barry and D. Slater (eds), *The Technological Economy* (London: Routledge, 2005), p. 13.

12. D. Miller, 'Turning Callon the right way up', *Economy and Society* (special issue on *The Technological Economy*), 31, 2 (2002).

13. Barry and Slater (2005).

14. M. Callon, 'The economy of qualities', *Economy and Society* (special issue on *The Technological Economy*), 31, 2 (2002), p. 196.

15. H. Miyazaki, 'The temporalities of the market', *American Anthropologist*, 105, 2 (2003), 255–65, 259, 261.

16. B. Maurer, 'Repressed futures: Financial derivatives' theological unconscious', *Economy and Society*, 31, 1 (2002), 29–30.

17. Mackenzie (2001), p. 133, p. 138.

18. See G. Born, *Uncertain Futures: Public Service Television and the Transition to Digital – A Comparative Analysis of the Digital Television Strategies of the BBC and Channel Four. Media@LSE* Working Papers no. 3 (2003a) (online at: http://www.lse.ac.uk/collections/media@lse/mediaWorkingPapers/ewpNumber3.htm); G. Born, 'Strategy, positioning and projection in digital television: Channel Four and the commercialisation of public service broadcasting in the UK', *Media, Culture and Society*, 25, 6 (2003b).

19. Callon (2002).

20. G. Born, *Uncertain Vision*, Chapter 7.

21. D. Slater, 'From calculation to alienation: Disentangling economic abstractions', in A. Barry and D. Slater (eds), *The Technological Economy* (London: Routledge, 2005), p. 63.

22. I take this to be the message of Callon (2002).

23. T. Mitchell, *Rule of Experts* (Berkeley, Ca. and London: University of California Press, 2002), p. 303.

CHAPTER 31

1. Suzanne Berger, *How We Compete: What Companies Around the World are Doing to Make It in Today's Global Economy* (New York: Currency Doubleday, 2006).

2. Shoshana Zuboff and James Maxmin, *The Support Economy: Why Corporations are failing Individuals and the Next Episode of Capitalism* (London: Penguin Books, 2002).

3. Ronald Inglehart, *Modernisation and Postmodernisation: Cultural, Economic and Political Change in 43 Societies* (Princeton: Princeton University Press, 1997). Cited by Zuboff and Maxmin, op.cit. p. 96.

4. For a discussion of definitions of the Knowledge Economy, see the *Ideopolis Report* (London: The Work Foundation, 2006).
5. David A. King, 'The Scientific Impact of Nations', *Nature* 430 (2004), 311–16.
6. See The Work Foundation *Knowledge Economy Paper No.1*, July 2006, available at theworkfoundation.com.
7. Geoffrey Garrett, *The Three Worlds of Globalisation: Market Integration, Economic Growth and the Distribution of Income in High, Middle and Low-Income Countries*, UCLA Working Paper, February 2004.

CHAPTER 32

1. See Martin Wolf, 'What liberal globalization means', in *Why Globalization Works* (New Haven: Yale Nota Bene, 2005).
2. *Finance for Growth: Policy Choices in a Volatile World* (Washington DC: World Bank, 2001).
3. Kose, Prasad, Rogoff and Wei (eds), *Financial Globalization: A Reappraisal* (Washington DC: International Monetary Fund, June 2006).
4. See Joseph Stiglitz, *The Roaring Nineties: Seeds of Destruction* (London: Allen Lane, 2003) for a lively description of the period.
5. 'Financial Crises and the Reform of the International Financial System'. National Bureau of Economic Research Working Paper 9297, 2002.
6. For longer description please see 'Financial Reform in China', K. C. Wu Memorial Lecture, Howard Davies, September 2005 (www.lse.ac.uk).
7. 'Review of the Role and Effectiveness of non-executive directors', Derek Higgs, Department of Trade and Industry, 2003.
8. William O. Douglas, 1938: 'these financial termites are those who practice the art of predatory or high finance', in Charles Geist, *Wall Street: a History* (OUP, 1997), p. 248; originally from Vincent Carosso, *Investment Banking in America: A History* (Cambridge: Harvard University Press, 1970), p. 385.
9. John Kenneth Galbraith, *The Essential Galbraith* (New York: Houghton Mifflin, 2001).

PART VII: CHAPTER 33

1. Jacques Attali, *La Voie Humaine: Pour une nouvelle social-démocratie* (Paris: Fayard, 2004).
2. Joseph Brodsky, *On Grief and Reason* (New York: Farrar, Straus and Ciroux, 1995), pp. 107–8.
3. Andrzej Stasiuk, *Tekturowy samolot* (Warsaw: Wydawnictwo Czarne, 2000), p. 59.
4. Sławomir Mrożek, *Male Listy* (Warsaw: Noir sur Blanc, 2002), p. 123.

5. 'Blaise Pascal' (trans. A.J. Krailsheimer), in Peter Kreeft (ed.), *Christianity for Modern Pagans: Pascal's Pensées* (London: Penguin, 1966).

CHAPTER 34

1. Richard Sennett, *The Fall of Public Man* (London: Faber, 1986); Nikolas Rose, *Governing the Soul*, 2nd edn (London: Free Association Books, 1999).
2. Sigmund Freud, "Civilisation and its Discontents", *Standard Edition of the Complete Psychological Works of Sigmund Freud*, Vol. 21 (London: Hogarth Press, 1961); Melanie Klein, *Love, Guilt and Reparation* (London: Hogarth, 1975); Michael Balint, *The Basic Fault* (London: Tavistock, 1968).
3. Jacques Lacan, 'La Relation d'Objet' (1956–7), in J.-A. Miller (ed.) (Paris: Seuil, 1992).
4. Slavoj Žižek, *The Ticklish Subject* (London: Verso, 1999).
5. Anthony Giddens, *The Consequences of Modernity* (Oxford: Polity, 1991).
6. Nikolas Rose, *Inventing Our Selves* (Cambridge University Press, 1996).
7. Nikolas Rose, ibid; see also Michel Foucault, *Discipline and Punish: The Birth of the Prison* (Harmondsworth: Penguin, 1979).
8. Anthony Bateman and Peter Fonagy, *Psychotherapy for Borderline Personality Disorder* (Oxford University Press, 2004).
9. See John Grey, *Men are from Mars, Women are from Venus: a practical guide for improving communication and getting what you want in your relationships* (New York: Harper Perennial, 1994).

CHAPTER 35

1. Chris McGreal, "Gaza's settlers dig in their heels", *Guardian*, 4th February (2004).
2. Daniel Ben Simon, "Monsieur, this is not the true France", *Ha'aretz*, 26th December (2003).
3. David Grossman, 'Two Years of Intifada', *Death as a Way of Life – Dispatches from Jerusalem*, trans. Haim Watzman (Bloomsbury, 2003), p. 177.
4. Varda Shiffer speaking at the second meeting of the Jewish Forum for Justice and Human Rights, London, 9th February, 2004.
5. In the week of this lecture, I read in *Ha'aretz* a feature on the settlers of Gush Katif in Gaza, which includes the following comment from Laurence Baziz, a former Parisian who has lived in the settlement for 18 years: 'They [the settlers] are very attracted by the soul, the ideological theme [...] There is a rise of Islamic influence in France. The French themselves don't like outsiders; there are a great many French people who feel the takeover of Islam. I illuminate that point.' *Ha'aretz*, 20th February (2004).

6. Sigmund Freud, 'The Neuro-Psychoses of Defence', 1894, *The Standard Edition of the Complete Psychological Works* 3 (Hogarth).
7. Freud, 'Screen Memories', 1899, *Standard Edition* 3.
8. Tom Segev discusses the extent to which later Arab attacks were seen as pogroms in his *One Palestine Complete – Jews and Arabs under the British Mandate* (Abacus, 2000), pp. 137–8, pp. 180–1, pp. 324–5.
9. According to Daud Abdullah of the Palestinian Return Centre, 2 per cent of Israelis live on refugee land, 62 per cent of all refugees came from rural areas in mandate Palestine, most of which villages are still vacant; over 75 per cent of Israelis live in 15 per cent of Israel's areas, letter to *Guardian*, 9th January (2004).
10. Chaim Weizmann, 'Awaiting the Shaw Report', Paper 116, *Letters and Papers* 1, p. 591.
11. Yeshayahu Leibowitz, "Right, Law and Reality", 1976, in Eliezer Goldman (ed.), *Judaism, Human Values and the Jewish State* (Harvard, 1992), pp. 230–1.
12. Bikhu Parekh, "Love is ... desireable but it's by no means a right", *Times Higher Educational Supplement*, 6th February (2004), and "Finding a Proper Place for Human Rights", in Kate Tunstall (ed.), *Displacement, Asylum, Migration*, 2004 Amnesty Lectures (Oxford University Press, 2006).
13. Hannah Arendt, "Zionism Reconsidered", in Ron Feldman (ed.), 1944, *The Jewish State Fifty Years After – Where Have Herzl's Politics Led?*, 1946, *The Jew as Pariah* (Grove Press, 1978), p. 156, p. 172, p. 141.

CHAPTER 37

1. " 'Control and Becoming', Gilles Deleuze in conversation with Antonio Negri", *Futur Anterieur* 1, Paris 1990.
2. Rosi Braidotti, *Transpositions – On Nomadic Ethics* (Cambridge: Polity, 2006).
3. Gilles Deleuze, "May '68 Didn't Happen", in *Two Regimes of Madness* (Cambridge: MIT Press, 2006).
4. Giorgio Agamben, "Tiananmen", in *The Coming Community* (Minneapolis: University of Minnesota Press, 1993), pp. 85–7.
5. Agamben, *Coming Community*, "Outside", p. 67.
6. Jean-Luc Nancy, *Being Singular Plural* (Stanford: Stanford University Press, 2000).
7. Ravi Sundaram, *Recycling modernity: Pirate electronic cultures in India, Sarai Reader 01: The Public Domain* 12 (Delhi, 2001), p. 95.
8. Ravi Sundaram, "Uncanny networks: Pirate Urban and the New Globalisation", in *Economic and Political Weekly*, 3rd January (2004).

CHAPTER 38

1. *New York Times*, 27th August (2000).
2. More on this in Renata Salecl, *On Anxiety* (London: Routledge, 2004).
3. See Jacques Lacan, *The Four Fundamental Concepts of Psycho-Analysis*, Jaques-Alain Miller (ed.), trans. Alan Sheridan (New York: W.W. Norton & Co., 1981).
4. See Charles Melman, *L'Homme sans gravité: Jouir à tout prix (Entretiens avec Jean-Pierre Lebrun)* (Paris: Denoël, 2002).
5. Jacques-Alain Miller and Eric Laurent, 'The Other Who Does not Exist and His Ethical Committees', in *Almanac of Psychoanalysis* 1 (1998), pp. 15–35.
6. Dany-Robert Dufour, *L'art de réeduire les têtes: Sur la nouvelle servitude de l'homme libéré à l'ère du capitalisme total* (Paris: Denoël, 2003).
7. Jacques Lacan developed this theory in his lecture at the University in Milan on 12th May, 1972. The original text is unpublished. In his seminar "L'Envers de la psychanalyse" delivered in the years 1969/70, Lacan already touches on some of these ideas, but does not use yet the term "discourse of capitalism". See Jacques Lacan, *L'Envers de la psychanalyse, Le Seminaire, livre XVII, 1969–70*, Jacques Alain Miller (ed.) (Paris: Seuil, 1993).
8. Lacanian psychoanalysis keeps this term *jouissance* in French, since the English word enjoyment does not connote the painfulness of pleasure.
9. A number of social scientists and psychologists have been lately analyzing the anxieties that too much choice brought to consumers. See, especially, Barry Schwartz, *The Paradox of Choice: Why More is Less* (New York: Ecco, 2004). For an astute analysis of how late capitalism affected peoples' private lives, see, Arlie Russell Hochschild, *The Commercialization of Intimate Life: Notes from Home and Work* (Los Angeles: University of California Press, 2003). See also Richard Sennett, *The Corrosion of Character: The Personal Consequences of Work in New Capitalism* (New York: Norton, 2000); and Edward C. Rosenthal, *The Era of Choice: The Ability to Choose and Its Transformation of Contemporary Life* (Cambridge, MA: MIT Press, 2005).
10. Jean-Pierre Lebrun, *Un monde sans limite: Essai pour une clinique psychanalytique du social* (Ramonville Saint-Agne: Èrès, 2001), p. 250.
11. Ibid, p. 251.
12. This theme was discussed on John Gray's web site. See http://www.marsvenus.com.
13. Lebrun, p. 250.

CHAPTER 39

1. E. Ewan and S. Ewan, *Channels of Desire* (McGraw Hill: New York, 1982); S. Orbach, *Hunger Strike* (London: Faber & Faber (now Karnac Books), 1986).
2. See Marshall McLuhan, *Understanding Media: The Extensions of Man* (London: Routledge, 2001).

3. Itself created by immigrants to the United States who constructed a view of the ideal family, gangster, fighter for justice and so on as well as of love, romance, hope and the tragic.

4. Even if in fact we see more different and varied images today than ever before, this is overridden by the impact of repetitious images of a very few faces and body types.

5. By an early age children in the west can identify many brands visually. It is part of the catechism of their life.

6. John Berger was to make this compelling point in *Ways of Seeing* when talking of the bourgeois woman's relation to self. I extend his idea. As we have seen the democratisation of beauty so we have seen the democratisation of this externalisation of self-regard. See J. Berger, *Ways of Seeing* (London: BBC & Penguin, 1972); also S. Orbach, *Fat is a Feminist Issue* (London: Paddington Press, 1978).

7. A. E. Becker, 'Television, disordered eating and young women in Fiji: negotiating body image and identity during rapid social change', *Cult Med Psychiatry*, 28 (2003), 533–59.

8. *Time Asia*, 17th December (2001).

9. With long-term payment plans for the working class women so they can afford the procedures.

Index

Permissions

The cover image is of the sculpture "Mobility", by Yinka Shonibare, MBE, 2005 (installation on view at James Cohan Gallery, New York); photograph courtesy of Stephen Friedman Gallery (London) and James Cohan Gallery (New York).